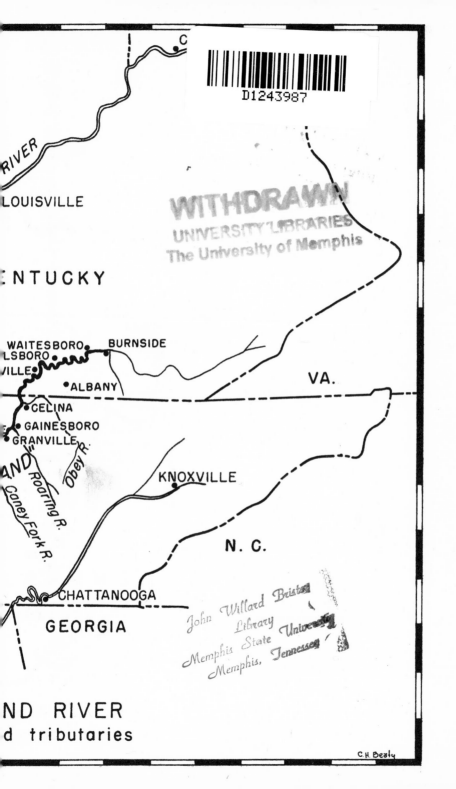

RIVER

LOUISVILLE

ENTUCKY

WAITESBORO
LSBORO
VILLE
ALBANY
CELINA
GAINESBORO
GRANVILLE
BURNSIDE

VA.

Obey R.

Roaring R.

Coney Fork R.

AND

KNOXVILLE

N. C.

CHATTANOOGA

GEORGIA

ND RIVER
d tributaries

C.H. Bealy

Emmons H. Woolwine

"I love rivers; they do more than bear merchandise. Ideas float along their surface.
Rivers like clarions sing to the ocean of the
beauty of the earth, the fertility of the plains,
and the splendor of the cities."

VICTOR HUGO

STEAMBOATIN'
ON THE
CUMBERLAND

by BYRD DOUGLAS

Published by
Tennessee Book Company
Nashville

TYPOGRAPHY, PRINTING, AND BINDING
IN THE U. S. A. BY KINGSPORT PRESS, INC.
KINGSPORT, TENNESSEE

to my wife
MARY STAHLMAN DOUGLAS

Cumberland
Falls

From the powerful forces in the falls of the Cumberland
to the placid waters below Nashville the Cumberland is
truly a beautiful river.

Fox
Bluff

Contents

List of Maps and Illustrations

MAPS

ILLUSTRATIONS

* Furnished by Steamboat Photo Co., Sewickley, Pa.
** Furnished by Marine Photo Co., St. Louis, Mo.
*** Furnished by U. S. Engineers, Nashville, Tenn.

Prologue

American Indians in crude dugouts or aboard improvised rafts were the first to navigate the Cumberland River. They wandered over the fertile lowlands, the deep forests and the high bluffs along the river's winding, twisting and tortuous course. The Shawnees, related to the Algonquins of the North, famed for their musical language, fine canoes and hunting prowess, settled around old French Lick, later known as Sulphur Dell, in the heart of present Nashville. From the southeast and across the Appalachians, came the wiry, warlike Cherokees. The Creeks, a very brave and haughty people, moved up from the South and the Chickasaws, kinsmen of the Muskhogeans, living along the bluffs of the Mississippi to the West, from time to time ventured across the Tennessee into the lower Cumberland Valley and along the Western Highland Rim.

From whence any of these people originally came and how long they had roamed the Cumberland Territory is debatable, but they opened up trails, established small settlements and hunted big game along the river and fished its waters for many, many years before the first white man arrived. The Cumberland River Basin was one of the finest game preserves on the North American continent. Buffalo, deer and bear roamed the virgin forests and unmolested quenched their thirst in the placid streams. The now extinct carrier pigeon and wild turkey were found in great droves throughout the region. In the deep pockets of the Cumberland were every variety of fish. Favorite herbs and wild roots were gathered with ease. There were flint for the arrowheads, skins and furs for clothing and trading, clay for pottery, and a climate particularly satisfactory for health and the curing of meat.

The Cumberland, with its navigable course of 516 miles, flowing east to west, draining 17,750 square miles of land, or nearly one-half of the present State of Tennessee, emptying into the Ohio, and accessible to the Tennessee and Mississippi, afforded a water highway of matchless beauty and gave an unlimited sphere of action to traveler, trader and warrior. It was this great stream and its major tributaries that held the chief fascination for both man and beast, and became the great benefactor of both. The first white man recorded on the Cumberland was Martin Chartier, a Frenchman and a deserter from LaSalle's forces. He married a Shawnee and journeyed with this tribe south, reaching the Shawnee settlement at the old French Lick now known as Nashville. Chartier lived three years on the Cumberland and as early as 1692, went up the Cumberland to a point below Cumberland Falls, and thence overland through Cumberland Gap into Virginia. He later settled with his son, Peter, at French Lick, where they were known as "white Indians."

In 1714, another Frenchman, Jean du Charleville, was using the Cumberland River and trading with the Indians along its banks near the French Lick. He was attacked by the Chickasaws, who killed him and many of the Shawnee Indians.

The first map of the Cumberland, then known as the "Chaouanon," (French for Shawnee) was that of Jolliet, made in 1674. This was followed in 1684 by Franquelin's map, which designated the Cumberland as the Skipakicipi. Dr. John Mitchell, an early explorer, issued his map in 1755. He was assisted by Dr. Thomas Walker who had already penetrated Cumberland Gap in 1750 and gave the name of the Duke of Cumberland to the mountains and the river. Mitchell was the first to include the name of Cumberland on a map. James Adair, on his map of Tennessee once more referred to the name "Old Shaunanon River," but after that the name Cumberland was always used.

After the close of the Cherokee War in 1760, Richard Henderson of North Carolina, one of the first great American land speculators, sent Daniel Boone into the Cumberland Territory to locate desirable sites for settlements. In 1761, the first big company of speculators and adventurers appeared. Elisha Walden, Henry Scaggs, William Blevins and Charles Fox headed a company of two hundred that came through Cumberland Gap and explored the upper reaches of the Cumberland River. Henry Scaggs in 1765 became the first white man to navigate the Cumberland River from its upper reaches down to French Lick. This was a notable and outstanding event and ranks with Chartier's earlier feat of going up the river over the same route.

In 1766–67, several parties of long hunters, led by James Smith of Pennsylvania, Kasper Mansker, for whom Mansker Creek is named, Isaac Bledsoe, for whom Bledsoe Creek is named, and Uriah Stone, for whom Stone's River is named, explored the Cumberland River Basin. At the French Lick they met Timothy Demonbreun, a Frenchman from Illinois, who for many years lived in a cave near the mouth of Mill Creek on the Cumberland. Demonbreun ascended the Cumberland many times in a large boat with six or eight hired hands and hunted for many years in the region about Nashville. He told his friend Henry Rutledge at a later date that he found hunting so good upon arrival that he soon loaded a boat with hides and tallow and set out for New Orleans. Demonbreun served under George Rogers Clark, the noted explorer, and also General LaFayette. He had the pleasure of greeting LaFayette on his memorable visit to Nashville in 1825.

Jacob Sandusky, a Pole, hunted on the Cumberland around 1774 and took a cargo of skins and tallow down the Cumberland to the Ohio, and thence down the Mississippi to New Orleans. He is generally credited as the first white man to make such a hazardous voyage.

Prior to Sandusky's remarkable trip, Joseph Hollingshead in 1768–69 had been employed by a trading house in Philadelphia to come to the Cumberland Territory and supervise the killing of game and the packing of meat in casks for the New Orleans market and for the garrison at Fort Chartres in what is now Illinois. Hollingshead operated three hundred miles up the Cumberland above its mouth and even farther up the Tennessee. He employed twenty large pirogues in his activities, which marked the beginning of commercial transportation on the Cumberland.

About this same time, Thomas Hutchins, a Lieutenant and Engineer in the British Army stationed at Fort Chartres was ordered to survey the Cumberland and Tennessee Rivers. He did so after endless difficulties and thereby left a remarkably accurate description of the Cumberland River from its mouth to Stone's River above Nashville.

The next great event in the history of transportation on the Cumberland was the voyage of John Donelson in his scow, the *Adventure*. This epochal trip involved a problem of transportation of huge proportions for that day and time. On December 22, 1779, Donelson left Fort Patrick Henry on the Holston River where Kingsport now stands, and headed a flotilla of thirty boats carrying about one hundred and fifty settlers, their wives and children, slaves and household goods, down the Tennessee, up the Ohio and the Cumberland, arriving at the present site of Nashville on April 24, 1780. There, by prearrangement, he met his friend, James Robertson and his party of two hundred and fifty. The true meaning of Donelson's voyage as a landmark in the history of Tennessee and particularly in the history of the Cumberland, can hardly be overemphasized. He blazed the path for the first flat boats, barges and keel boats that soon appeared on the Cumberland in abundance.

From the arrival of Donelson in 1780, barge and keel boat transportation on the Cumberland became the largest enterprise in the city. John Coffee, George Poyzer, Christopher Stump and Messrs. Rappier, Turner, Spriggs and others were operating many such boats between Nashville and New Orleans. Regular commercial transportation was an accomplished fact on the Cumberland. Tobacco, corn, indigo, hogs, horses, flour and cotton were the principal items hauled from Nashville and Clarksville down the river.

The *General Jackson* was a very large barge, and one of the best known. Another unusually large barge was operated by Richard Rappier & Company and had an advertised capacity of ninety tons. It took about five months to make the trip from Nashville to New Orleans and return. A trip made down the river to the latter city in less than sixty days was a real achievement.

Nashville had rapidly developed as a leading business and industrial town on the rim of the Southeastern Territory. By 1819 the Cumberland was fully prepared to make its bid as one of the leading rivers and anxiously awaited the arrival of the greatest invention of the age—the two stacked, swashbuckling, colossal, elegant and majestic steamboat.

CHAPTER ONE

A Prophecy and a Beginning

Period 1819–1830

Zadok Cramer, author and publisher of the famous "Pittsburgh Navigator and Almanac" was not only an authority but a prophet on matters connected with the rivers of America. In describing the towns and villages located on the Western Rivers in the Almanac of 1814, he had this to say about Nashville and the possibilities of steam navigation on the Cumberland—

"Nashville is handsomely situated on the south side of the river, about 190 miles by water and 140 by land from its mouth; 200 from Lexington, and 180 west of Knoxville. The town stands on a high cliff of rocks, 200 feet above the level of the river and commands a fine view of a picturesque country around it. Nashville is in Mero District, Davidson County, and is the seat of government for the state of Tennessee and is in a flourishing state of improvement. It has a respectable banking company; a cotton manufactory by Mr. George Poyzer, and Mr. Stump and his family have a ropewalk, a powder mill,—and a cotton gin,—all in handsome operation. Wm. Carroll & Co. in connection with Mr. Cowan of Pittsburgh, have a nail manufactory and an extensive ironmongery store. And the citizens generally are turning their attention to the establishment of such manufacturers as will tend to render them independent and happy, in spite of wars, and the impudence, wickedness

1

and aggressions of foreign nations, either of the English, French, Tartars, Mongols or any other partly-colored race upon the earth.

"Nashville contains about 200 houses, some of which are large, elegant buildings of brick; it has an academy, two churches, a court-house, jail, etc. The town is said to take its name from General Francis Nash who fell at the battle of Germantown October 4, 1777.

"There is a line of barges constantly running from Nashville to New Orleans, loaded down with the rich products of Tennessee and up with sugar, coffee, rice, hides, liquors, dry goods, etc., conducted principally by Mr. Spriggs, a very active and industrious trader, and from long habit, among the most expert conductors of a barge, of any person on the river. These add facility to trade and commerce, and give employment to a number of active hardy men. *Boats conducted by the steam principle would most probably be more advantageous and save an immense manual labor. The day is not far distant I hope, when the citizens of Nashville, will see a steam boat winding her course up the Cumberland, in all the majesty and nobleness of her internal and secreted power, without the assistance of poles, oars or sails. It wants nothing to do this but the spirit of beginning."*

At the time Cramer published this statement, steamboats were already appearing frequently on the Ohio and Mississippi Rivers. Three years had elapsed since the *New Orleans* had been launched in Pittsburgh by Nicholas J. Roosevelt, who had superintended the work and was backed financially by Chancellor R. R. Livingston and Robert Fulton of New York. The *New Orleans* was the first steamboat on the Western Rivers and the first to make a successful trip from Pittsburgh to New Orleans.

The story of the perilous trip made by this famous boat down the Ohio and Mississippi, during the earthquake of 1811–12, forms one of the most interesting chapters in the history of transportation. It is amazing that any steamboat, much less the first one, could have navigated the Mississippi during such an upheaval, which was probably the worst ever recorded in the United States. Some idea of its violence may be gained from the fact that Reelfoot Lake in West Tennessee was created by it in less than twenty-four hours, and the course of the Mississippi for a distance of two hundred miles was altered beyond recognition at many points.

The successful trip of the *New Orleans* was indeed a landmark in the history of transportation. Shortly, vast resources were to be developed through the medium of the steamboat. The indomitable Roosevelt had dispelled the doubts of those who had boasted that a steamboat would never stem the swift currents of the Western Rivers. Twice during the historic trip of the *New Orleans,* once at Louisville and again at Vicksburg, Roosevelt, to the amazement of the skeptics, had turned the boat against the current and landed with perfect safety. Thereafter it was acknowledged that the steamboat had mastered the rivers. The steamboat had arrived as an American Institution.

Shortly after the *New Orleans* was built, other steamboats were launched in and around Pittsburgh. First, the *Comet,* built at Brownsville, Pennsylvania, in 1813, made a trip from New Orleans to Louisville in 1814. Then came the *Vesuvius,* built at Pittsburgh in 1814 which made a trip from that point to New Orleans. The *Enterprise,* which was the fourth steamboat, was also built at Brownsville in 1814, and went from Louisville to New Orleans and back. When the *Washington* built at Wheeling in 1814 made a trip from Louisville to New Orleans and back in twenty-one days, most of the skepticism against steamboats had vanished. Steamboats were soon to revolutionize not merely transportation on the Western Rivers, but the whole trend of the social and economic life of America, particularly that section commonly referred to as the Western Country.

In keeping with the prophecy and advice of Zadok Cramer, the first steamboat was soon to ply the Cumberland. She was appropriately named the *General Jackson* for

Tennessee's distinguished son, General Andrew Jackson, who had won the Battle of New Orleans.

The name or ownership of the first steamboat to ply the Cumberland has never been questioned, but there has been much confusion among historians regarding the exact date of its arrival in Nashville. There is no reason for this in view of the available records. Before mentioning these, however, let us turn our attention to the sequence of events leading up to the first steamboat to ply the Cumberland.

Nashvillians had heard about the successful operation of steamboats on the Ohio and Mississippi almost as soon as it was an accomplished fact. Roosevelt's accomplishment with the *New Orleans* was a matter of comment in every newspaper, especially those published along the Ohio and Mississippi. It ranked side by side with the publicity given the great earthquake of the same year which has already been mentioned. In addition, barge and keelboat pilots, upon returning to Nashville from New Orleans and other points, had every opportunity to observe the early steamboats and give an eye witness account of their successful operation.

An announcement was made in the Nashville Whig of April 16, 1816, calling attention to a public meeting to be held at the Court House on May 1st, instant, for the purpose of organizing a steamboat company at Nashville to build one or more steamboats. At this meeting, first of its kind in the town, Thomas Claiborne was Chairman and Alfred Balch, Secretary. Claiborne and Balch were well known citizens of Nashville. Claiborne took an active part in political affairs, serving from 1817 to 1819 as a Congressman. Later he was director of the Bank in Nashville, and in 1825 served as Chairman of the Public Meeting to arrange for the reception of General LaFayette in Nashville. Proper resolutions were adopted which stated "That the meeting was deeply impressed both by the necessity and advantages of building one or more steamboats to run between Nashville and New Orleans and Nashville and Pittsburgh," and that a "Committee of five persons—to wit, Jenkins Whiteside, Wilkins Tannehill, General William Carroll, Major Christopher Stump and

Captain Alpha Kingsley—hold a correspondence with such companies or persons as they may deem proper to ascertain the cost of one or more steamboats to be built at Nashville," and "that the said committee draw up articles of association for the purposes aforesaid, to be submitted to the consideration of a public meeting to be held at court house in Nashville on Saturday preceding the third Monday in May, instant."

It is significant that the organization of such a company attracted the attention of such able men as those mentioned above. General William Carroll needs no introduction to students of Tennessee history. He was second in command to Jackson at the Battle of New Orleans, one of the best governors the State ever produced, a splendid business man, trader and civic minded citizen who sponsored the first real system of internal improvements in Tennessee. Jenkins Whitesides was a pioneer of Nashville, a financier and banker of note, whose influence extended to many walks of life. Wilkins Tannehill was Mayor of Nashville in 1825–26 and for years served as an Alderman. Major Stump and Captain Kingsley were not only pioneers in the development of Nashville, but were identified with the river and its barge and keelboat business. Stump was a prosperous hardware and leather goods merchant in addition to his other business connections. Kingsley as early as 1818 was engaged in a profitable coffee, salt and sugar business. Both of these men had fought for the protection of their country.

What transpired at the followup meeting scheduled for the "Saturday preceding the third Monday in May," or whether it ever took place is not a matter of record, at least in the newspapers.

The Nashville Whig of May 7, 1816 stated—"Steamboat companies are already formed, or forming, in every section west of the Alleghanies. In less than one year, at least a dozen steamboats have been put in successful operation or are now ready to run. The spirit of Tennessee is up and we hope in a few months to see the banks of the Cumberland lined with these powerful and useful engines." Notwith-

standing this stirring article, it appears that no action was
taken by the proposed company and steamboat traffic on
the Cumberland was not to come as soon as hoped for.

The next record of any steamboat activity at Nashville
appears in an article from the Nashville Whig of Saturday,
March 28, 1818, which is as follows:

"The steamboat *General Jackson* is owned by General
Carroll and Mr. Whiting of this place, and is thus handsomely noticed in the Louisville (Kentucky) Herald of the
18th instant:

'We are gratified in announcing the arrival at this
place on last Sunday of the Steamboat *General Jackson*,
Captain B. Hoskins, 6 days out of Pittsburgh, bound for
New Orleans. Were we to judge from outward appearance we should pronounce her one of the first boats on
the Ohio River. She is intended as a regular trader between Nashville and New Orleans. She left Shipping-
port yesterday with full freight of flour, whiskey, etc.
General DeLaage and Lady, Mrs. Savage, Messrs.
Thos. G. Prentiss, Dr. Peters, Dr. Croghan, James Bris-
bane and J. M. McClanahan, passengers.' "

From this record, we know that the *General Jackson* was
in Louisville on March 15, 1818, and she was owned by Carroll and Mr. Whiting, who is not identified further. There
was a Mr. A. Whiting of Nashville engaged in the prosperous hardware business in 1825 on the north side of the Public Square. This may or may not be the Whiting referred to.

E. W. Gould, in his "Fifty Years on the Mississippi," states
that the *General Jackson* arrived in New Orleans on its
maiden trip on April 1, 1818. That seems probable, for it
would allow fifteen days for the trip, which was well within
the running time of average packets. The next we hear of
the *General Jackson* is this squib from The Nashville Whig
of June 13, 1818—"New Orleans, May 29. Str. *General
Jackson* arrived at New Orleans from Cross Creek on the
Cumberland." Cross Creek is about ninety-five miles below
Nashville. We know from this article that the *General Jack-*

son after her first visit to New Orleans in April tried to come to Nashville but could not make it—probably on account of shallow water—and stopped at Cross Creek on the lower river. If the *General Jackson* made any other attempts to get to Nashville in 1818, they were not reported.

On the other hand it is definitely established that the *General Jackson* arrived in Nashville for the first time on March 11, 1819, which was on a Thursday and that an account of the event was carried in the Nashville Whig and Tennessee Advertiser in its Edition of March 13, 1819, which is verbatim as follows:

> "The steamboat *General Jackson,* Captain Smith, arrived at this place, on Thursday last, from New Orleans, having run from that place to Harpeth Island (20 miles below this place) in 21 days, 6 hours. She remained there several days waiting the rise of the water and had nearly unloaded when the river on Wednesday night took a rise.
>
> "A sight so novel at this place, has attracted large crowds of spectators."

This news item was copied by The National Intelligencer in Washington in its edition of April 8, 1819. For some inexplicable reason the fact that it first appeared in The Nashville Whig and Tennessee Advertiser has been overlooked.

Another news item appearing in the same newspaper on Saturday, May 1st, 1819, is enlightening and is as follows:

> "We learn that the steamboat *General Jackson,* Captain Young, left New Orleans on the 5th of April and arrived at mouth of Cumberland on the morning of the 20th— performing the trip in 15 days, making known deduction for time lost in getting wood, etc.
>
> "It is believed that this is the quickest passage ever made by any boat—Whilst on her passage the *Jackson* passed a number of Steam Boats and we understand fairly beat the fast running boat *Tamerlane.*
>
> "This fine boat has given us but 'one' visit since she has been in action and it is not because she is displeased with

Nashville; but it is because we have done nothing to remove the small obstructions in the navigation of our rivers. It is hoped the next Legislature of Tennessee, will make a law, with provisions and requisitions permitting steamboats to pass to Nashville, at all seasons of the year."

These articles should end any debate concerning the ownership of the *General Jackson,* its first visit to Nashville, its captains and first year of activity.

The *General Jackson* was built at Pittsburgh; her keel laid in the summer or early fall of 1817, she must have gone off the ways in early 1818. Her cost was $16,000.00. She was 150 tons burden and Gould says she was the twenty-second boat to ply the Mississippi. In 1819, in addition to her maiden trip to Nashville, she made four trips between New Orleans and the mouth of the Cumberland, three of which averaged better than fifteen days. Her second trip to Nashville was delayed and did not occur until April 13, 1821. She was then in command of Captain T. T. Minor. It may be presumed from this delay that the *General Jackson* was of heavy draft which made it extremely difficult to pass over the shoals at Harpeth Island except on a good "tide." Her agents in Nashville were Young, Green & Company, in 1819–20, and Thomas Yeatman in 1820–21. Shortly after her second arrival in Nashville she was sold by her owners to Messrs. Fletcher, Marr & Young of Nashville for the tidy sum of $33,000.00, and on May 30, 1821, she sank at Harpeth Shoals. She was raised, and while in a bad state of repair, was sold at public auction on September 12th of that same year for a nominal sum.

One witness, writing fifteen years after the event, describes the first arrival of the *General Jackson* thusly—"The whole population, men, women, and children, collected on the bank of the river and loud cheers rent the air. As long as she remained in port, she was the object of curiosity to thousands who came from far and near to behold this wonder of the waters."

The Nashville Gazette, on June 9, 1819, editorialized the *General Jackson* as follows:

"The *General Jackson* arrived at Eddyville from New Orleans, making the trip in 14 days from port to port. Her cargo will be barged from Eddyville to this place, the depth of the river not being sufficient at this season to suffer the boat herself to come up. To the inhabitants of a country so fertile and so extensive as borders the Cumberland River, what a prospect of realizing wealth is confirmed by the last two trips of this fine vessel. Its great distance from market, which many well informed men viewed as an obstacle so great as not to be surmounted, is demonstrated by the trips of the steamboat *General Jackson* to be a mere trifle, as twenty-odd days is sufficient to waft the produce of the country to New Orleans and return the proceeds to the exporter."

The arrival of the *General Jackson* and other steamboats soon elevated Nashville from an outpost town to a top ranking position in the South. Knoxville, which had been the larger center of trade in Tennessee, quickly yielded her "place in the sun," because the famous Muscle Shoals in the vicinity of Florence, Alabama, cut traffic on the Tennessee River into two parts. Boats which would have been very glad to enter the Tennessee trade up to flourishing Knoxville, also had to traverse the famous sucks in the river in and about what is now known as Chattanooga. Muscle Shoals, in early days, was an insurmountable barrier to complete traffic on the Tennessee, despite all the machinations of men.

By a queer prank of nature, the Cumberland was also afflicted with a great hazard, known as Harpeth Shoals. This piece of shoal water was thirty-eight miles below Nashville and extended over a distance of about five miles. It more nearly disrupted steamboat business than all other natural impediments along the 516-mile navigable course of the Cumberland. One old-timer said that every gravel in the Shoals stood for a "cuss" word. Captains, pilots, mates, engineers, firemen, cooks, roustabouts and even male passengers united to pull, shove, grunt and groan boats through this insidious barrier to river traffic. Many splendid packets were sunk in the narrows of Harpeth Shoals. Others were irreparably damaged and quite a few caught fire while "puffing" and "blowing" through the shallow water.

Despite its many hazards, Harpeth Shoals, however, unlike Muscle Shoals, was seldom impassable for any length of time. With only three feet of water passing through the narrows smaller steamboats could "hog" through. This antiquated method of moving a boat is explained in the glossary. Also, larger packets frequently transferred their cargo to small barges called "lighters," and in this way got over the Shoals. Some of the largest packets coming up the river would stop below the narrows, where smaller steamboats or lighters would then take the passengers and cargo the remaining distance to Nashville. If the river remained unnavigable, smaller boats and lighters would return with passengers and freight bound for such points as New Orleans, Louisville, Cincinnati and Pittsburgh. The redeeming feature of this trying situation, if there was one, came about because of the close proximity of Nashville to the Shoals. Knoxville on the Tennessee held no such position in regard to Muscle Shoals. Besides, they were very long and much more dangerous than Harpeth Shoals. Consequently, cargo from boats delayed below Muscle Shoals could not be transferred to Knoxville. For this reason, the Cumberland became the dominant river-borne transportation facility in Tennessee, and Nashville, became the chief distribution point for commerce from the mid-west and west moving to the southeastern states.

Harpeth Shoals remained a nemesis until 1904, when Lock A at Fox's Bluff was opened. Prior to that time it had received more attention from engineers than any other spot on the Cumberland. Dikes and wing dams cluttered its ancient course. Many plans were advanced to overcome Harpeth Shoals. Some seemed sound in theory, but did not work in practice. The Cumberland would reach one of its high tides, wash away pilings, dirt and stone embankments, dams and everything else except the familiar gravel bars, sand bars and other obstacles.

Steamboat men for years complained about this obstacle in the river, but most of them at a very early date accepted Harpeth Shoals as a cross to carry. Only in one respect did the Shoals prove beneficial. When the War Between the States broke out, they prevented many a Federal gunboat and river convoy from reaching Nashville. Man-created forts, such as Donelson, succumbed to shot and shell, but Harpeth Shoals remained defiant. Buell, Rosecrans, Thomas, and particularly Sherman, spent many sleepless nights worrying about men and supplies coming by river to Nashville. Their worries were justified. Harpeth Shoals frequently cut the Federal supply lines better even than Forrest's Cavalry.

It was significant that Carroll named the first steamboat on the Cumberland for his distinguished friend, General Andrew Jackson. Jackson lived very near the river at the Hermitage and in addition to his varied political career was a trader, business man and plantation owner. He early used the river and recognized its benefits. Another good friend, General John Coffee, who lived at nearby Haysborough, had established a trading post and general merchandise store and was the owner of several barges and keelboats, two of which, the *Adventure* and *Resolution* as early as 1803, were in the New Orleans trade. He also owned a store in Nashville.

Jackson's plantation bordered on the river and the Lebanon Turnpike. He received supplies from time to time by barge or keelboat which came up the river from Nashville. In later days, steamboats delivered supplies for the Hermitage at the landing near the mouth of Stone's River. Jackson's Landing, or Hermitage Landing, was a thriving place. Much of the household furniture and effects at the Hermitage were brought there by boats from larger cities such as New Orleans.

Jackson was the first President to use a river steamboat for an inaugural voyage. He left Nashville on January 18, 1829, on board the *Fairy*, a nice but comparatively small packet of eighty registered tons, built at Cincinnati in 1827. He arrived at Louisville on January 22, 1829 and left there on board the *Pennsylvania*, a more palatial packet built in Pittsburgh in 1823. The National Banner and Nashville Whig of January 30, 1829 carried the following dispatch from Louisville dated January 24th:

"General Jackson arrived at this place Thursday (January 22nd) and departed about twelve noon Friday for Washington. He was accompanied by Judge Overton, Major W. B. Lewis, Major Lee, Captain A. J. Donelson, Andrew Jackson, Jr., Mrs. Lewis, Mrs. Donelson and other ladies. The General was received and entertained in a plain and hospitable manner at Mr. Perkins' Union Hall, where apartments had been provided for him. During his stay he was visited by a large proportion of our citizens. National salutes were fired on his landing and at sunrise Friday morning immediately preceding his departure for Cincinnati in the steamboat *Pennsylvania*, which had been dispatched from Pittsburgh to receive him at this place."

After an easy trip up to Cincinnati, where the *Pennsylvania* was accompanied by the steamboat *Robert Fulton*, with a large band and crowd aboard, he proceeded to Wheeling and thence to Pittsburgh, where he arrived and took lodgings at the Mansion House Hotel. The National Intelligencer in Washington on Thursday, February 12th, announced that General Jackson had arrived in the Capital at 10:00 A.M. on February 11th, but due to lack of information concerning the exact time, he was met by only a comparatively few friends. As soon as knowledge of his arrival spread, salutes were fired.

Due to the fact that Mrs. Jackson had died at the Hermitage less than a month before General Jackson left on his inaugural trip, his reception en route to Washington was considerably restrained.

While the *General Jackson* was the first steamboat to reach Nashville and is entitled to extended treatment for that reason, there were other boats of nearly equal fame which shortly plied the Cumberland and which should be noticed.

The *Rifleman* was the second steamboat to reach Nashville, coming up to the wharf on Thursday, February 10, 1820, under command of Captain Sterling M. Barner, one of the best pilots of the early days. The Nashville Whig of February 16, 1820, noticing this achievement, had the following to say:

> "The steamboat *Rifleman*, Captain Barner, arrived here on Thursday, last, and having received as much freight as was desired she moved off on Monday morning in handsome order, at the rate of about twelve miles an hour —several passengers aboard."

The *Rifleman* was built at Louisville in 1818 and was a larger boat than the *General Jackson,* being 231 gross tons burden. Her owners were James and Robert Woods, outstanding bankers of Nashville, and closely identified with the financial affairs of the entire State. For a number of years they operated with the Yeatman family, also wealthy and prosperous, the institution known as Yeatman, Woods & Company, located on College Street (now Third Avenue and Union Street) in Nashville. One historian records that this firm "was very solvent," which is putting it mildly. The Woods and Yeatmans were also jointly interested in the operation of the blast furnaces and rolling mills near Dover and Bear Springs on the Cumberland below Nashville, and had a financial interest in many other businesses in Nashville, all of which tied into the steamboat business. Thomas Yeatman was early identified with the river and was an excellent master and pilot.

In later years, the *Rifleman* was captained by Thomas Gilbert who became a famed pilot. His first great feat with the *Rifleman* was a trip from New Orleans to Nashville, which according to the Nashville Whig of April 17, 1822, was made in twelve days. She was burned at Mobile, the exact date unknown.

The third steamboat to reach Nashville was the ill-fated *General Robertson*, named for the founder of Nashville and owned by the Nashville Steamboat Company. She was built in 1819 at Newport, Kentucky, and was 238 gross tons. She arrived at the city wharf on December 12, 1820, under command of Captain Joseph Smith. He had also had a turn at the wheel of the *General Jackson*. Ephriam Foster and Moses Norvel, leading citizens of the time, were connected with the company that owned this boat.

The first visit of the *General Robertson* was made without any difficulty, but on her second trip on April 16, 1821 she was nearly torn asunder by a boiler explosion eight miles below Eddyville. Five passengers were killed and two more were never heard from. This was the first great calamity on the Cumberland and shocked the whole river valley. Despite this disaster, the *General Robertson* hobbled up to Nashville with her cargo and left on April 22nd for New Orleans with another heavy cargo of freight.

The fourth boat to port at Nashville was the *Cumberland* which arrived during the week of April 9, 1821, under command of Captain Crawford. She was a familiar sight on the river for years. In 1821, Captain Barner became her master.

The fifth boat was the *General Greene,* said by the Nashville Whig to have been owned by a steamboat company at Columbia, Tennessee. She arrived under command of Captain T. T. Minor on February 20, 1822. The sixth boat was the *Nashville,* first of many steamboats by that name which were destined to add fame to the City whose name she bore. She was owned by J. and R. Woods, and Captain Tom Yeatman, who was her master when she arrived in Nashville on the usual June rise of the river—1822—exact date uncertain. She was 200 tons, built at Cincinnati and ran for four years before being snagged above New Orleans in 1826. John Hall, to be mentioned later in connection with the steamboat *Mechanic,* and the intrepid Thomas Bellsnyder also were in command of this money-maker at one time or another. The seventh boat to make Nashville was the *Penn-*

sylvania, which arrived on December 16, 1822, under Captain Hart. She was 100 tons and a new boat just launched at Pittsburgh.

Others might be listed in order, but it is sufficient to say that with the year 1823, the infant days of steamboatin' on the Cumberland had passed.

Each year thereafter, several steamboats made their maiden trips up the river and finding business good, came back periodically for more. Many were owned by Nashville interests. Many more came from the upper reaches of the Ohio, which at a very early date became the center of steamboat business.

In the Appendix the names of all boats plying the river during this and succeeding periods will be found and, whenever known their captains and dates of launching given. From time to time certain of the more important packets, their licensed officers and owners, will be mentioned in the context.

During this period there were three *Nashvilles*, two *Cumberlands* and an *Andrew Jackson*. Also there were the *Rambler* a very popular packet owned by Johnson and Rayburn and captained by Frank Stratton; the *General Coffee* owned by J. and M. Norvel. J. Norvel was one of the publishers of the Nashville Whig. Another fine boat was the first *Tally-ho* owned by Nichol and Hill, under Captain Jacob Hunter. She was considered one of the fastest boats on the river. The first *Red Rover* owned by James Woods and Company under Captain Joseph Miller was the forerunner of several boats by this name and on one of them Captain Merritt S. Pilcher gained renown. The *Lady Washington,* trim and elegant, was owned by Doyle and Eastland and was for years commanded by Captain Athy. The *Pacific,* another excellent packet was owned by Wood and Crutcher and captained by James Wood. These are but a few of the many old boats that "broke the ice" and paved the way for further development.

Other pioneers in the steamboat business on the Cumberland were Colonel A. W. Johnson, Jesse and Baily Johnson,

C. A. Crutcher, C. M. Bradford, George Stacker and Samuel Seay, all of whom either owned boats or acted as agents for them.

It is true that the life of the early steamboat captain or pilot was far removed from that of the drawing room or parlor while he was on duty, yet it was not such a life as was frowned upon by the so-called "first citizens." Many of the captains either owned their boats outright or had an interest in them. This was not generally true of the pilots, who were nevertheless well paid and gained their prominence by daring adventures. Steamboat business in Nashville, as observed, was backed by representative citizens, amply able to finance it during its infancy. This is a matter of great significance and added to its continued growth and prosperity.

This period should be recognized as an overlapping period between the old style manual boats, such as flat boats, keelboats and barges, and the steamboats. This method of transportation did not leave the river all in one year, but continued during the entire period. For example, the Nashville Gazette, of June 27, 1819, announced the arrival of the keelboat *Shakespeare* from New Orleans in sixty-seven days, under command of Captain Butts, with groceries for Thomas Hill. Apparently, this was a record-breaking trip and was given considerable newspaper publicity. Other keelboats mentioned by the Gazette during June 1819 were the *Perseverance* under command of Captain Evans, which took eighty days for the same trip, with a load of groceries to S. Cantrell & Company, J. and R. Woods and J. T. Elliston. The *Adventurer* under Captain Swany, bound upriver from Cairo Landing above Nashville, loaded with groceries and salt for Messrs. Bledsoe and Morgan also arrived in June of the same year.

The keelboat *Jackson,* mentioned in the Introduction, was also making regular trips to New Orleans in 1819. Other keelboats were the *Royal George* under Captain Clark, plying between Nashville and Pittsburgh; the *Dolphin* owned by James Stewart; the *Grampus, Fearnaught,* and the *Cham-*

pion under Captain Dickinson, between Nashville and New Orleans; the *Seahorse* under Captain Wolf, arriving from Pittsburgh with copper to I. and J. W. Sitler; the *Mary Ann* under Captain Fox from New Orleans; the *General Pike* under Captain Travis from points on the Ohio, and the *Hotspur* under command of Captain Boyd from Pittsburgh and Cincinnati. It is regretted that old newspapers do not give the full names of many of the early keelboat operators. This explains their absence here.

Some old barges and keelboats still remained on the river at the close of the period. In later days, steamboats towed them from one point to another. Their owners and operators were stout-hearted and vigorous. History has not singled out any particular celebrity on the Cumberland to match the outstanding rascal, Mike Fink, of Ohio and Mississippi River fame. Fink and his prototypes on the Western Rivers in the early transition days from keelboats to steamboats were about as rough and tough as men could be and still call themselves civilized. Such men, however, were not the rule but the exception. Most of the old type river men operated their barges and keelboats with an eye for business. They were fearless and courageous, but with it all, kind and obliging. It was the "Unwritten Law" to help a fellow boatman when in trouble. They were disseminators of the news to the ever watchful settlers along the rivers.

In the final years of their existence, most of the keelboats and barges were very large, averaging fifty or sixty and often eighty tons capacity. History should be kind and generous to the operators of these vessels, which were the forerunners of the packet boats. They served a purpose and performed a great service, and their exploits will ever remain one of the finest chapters in early river history. As we look back, it is almost beyond belief that men floated a keelboat some 1,200 miles down the river to New Orleans, and pushed it back again. Many boats were sold for lumber, and the owners and crews came back over land rather than stem the swift Mississippi. James Stewart and James Gordon, who pushed the first barge from New Orleans to Nashville in

1806, with sugar and coffee and other groceries; Messrs. Stump, Rapier and Turner, who closely followed, with barge after barge, and Richard H. Barry, who is said to have made a trip in 1803 down to New Orleans in sixty days with a heavily laden barge, should be admired for their courage and spirit of adventure.

Barge and keelboat operators also assisted the steamboat business in a very practical way. When steamboats began to operate, pilots and deck hands were drawn from operators of the old type boats. This was natural since they knew every foot of the river.

With the close of this period seventy-nine different steamboats had plied the Cumberland. Many of them were the largest and most commodious on the Western Rivers. They followed the cargo and not necessarily any beaten path. If a Captain ascertained there was a good cargo at a given point on the Ohio, the Mississippi or the Cumberland, the boat would go to these points.

By 1821 definite calls or landings had already been established between the mouth of the Ohio and Nashville. These were listed as—America, Illinois; Belgrade, Illinois; Paducah, Kentucky; Smithland, Kentucky; Eddyville, Kentucky; Canton, Kentucky; Dover; Palmyra; Red River; Harpeth River; and Nashville.

On April 17, 1822, the *Rifleman* under command of Captain Thomas Gilbert made a trip in twelve days from Nashville to New Orleans. Three years later, this time had been cut by three full days. On April 22, 1825, according to the Nashville Whig, the *William Penn* under command of Captain Barner, had arrived up river from New Orleans in eight days, twenty hours, and had lost twenty-one hours en route. This was the shortest time as of that date. It was these record-breaking runs which inevitably led to useless accidents and public criticism, much of which was deserved. Most of the major accidents took place on the Ohio and Mississippi, which, because of broader channels, were better suited to racing and other daring exploits.

On April 1, 1826, the *Paul Jones*, a new boat, made the

trip from New Orleans to Nashville in eight days, twenty-one hours, with 150 tons of cargo, twenty cabin and forty-five deck passengers. The cabin passengers paid $40.00 from New Orleans to Nashville, and the freight was transported at an average of $1.50 per one hundred pounds. The passage from Nashville to New Orleans for cabin passengers was $30.00, and the freight 62½ cents to seventy-five cents per one hundred pounds.

Most of the cargo brought up river to Nashville by the early steamboats consisted of sugar, molasses, coffee, whiskey, ironware, plows, furs, clothing, rice, broadcloth, china, cutlery, and various other merchandise of practically every description. The cargo leaving Nashville was mostly hides, meat, cotton and tobacco. By 1829, ten years after the *General Jackson* arrived in Nashville, the National Banner and Nashville Whig of February 6, 1829, reported that the new steamer *Nashville* left the mouth of the Cumberland bound down stream with 1,467 bales of cotton and 160 tons of tobacco, and wanted 200 more bales of cotton to complete her cargo. Just how this boat handled that amount of cargo is difficult to understand. Figuring 1,467 bales of cotton at 500 pounds, and 2,000 pounds to the ton, would amount to 416 tons, which, added to the other cargo, would make her total cargo 600 tons. She must have been "flattened out" and had very little freeboard.

As early as July 2, 1825, the Nashville Whig reported that nine steamboats, to wit, the *Andrew Jackson, President, Nashville, Eclipse, Lafayette, Natchez, Courier, Belle Creole* and the *Emerald* carried out a total of 15,037 bales of cotton in the previous season from Nashville, the *Andrew Jackson* leading with 4,336 bales. If each of these bales was valued at $50.00, which would mean a market price of 10 cents per pound, the total value would amount to $216,800.00. This figure is undoubtedly an irreducible minimum, as keelboats, barges and other steamboats probably took out as much, if not more, than the eight steamboats listed above. One authority has placed the value of cotton exported from Nashville in 1825 at $1,000,000.00.

Although cotton and tobacco were the chief commodities shipped by river out of Nashville, iron and its kindred products were close seconds. The Western Highland Rim of Tennessee and Kentucky was early recognized as one of the finest iron ore belts in the western country. It was destined to add great prestige to Tennessee as an industrial state. If it had not been for the Cumberland River, which served as the only medium of transportation, this essential product, which played such an important part in the development of our country, could not have reached the market.

The first blast furnace erected for the manufacture of iron in Tennessee was built in the area around Cumberland Furnace in the northern part of Dickson County above the present township of Charlotte, and a few miles from the Cumberland River. It has been said that General James Robertson, founder of Nashville, started operations at this point as early as 1792 or 1793. A good quality of iron was made in quantity at this furnace in 1797. It was at this location or very nearby that Montgomery Bell gained his reputation as one of the foremost iron masters south of the Ohio. He manufactured cannon balls for General Jackson at the Battle of New Orleans, and shipped them down the river by boat. As time progressed Highland Rim iron was recognized as especially adaptable for the manufacture of steam boiler plates, being preferred by steamboat operators over that produced along the Ohio River. During these early days, the small forges manufactured a great many iron boiling kettles which became famous on the Western Rivers.

By 1802, a small blast furnace was in operation on Yellow Creek, in Montgomery County, and in 1828 the Carlisle furnace was erected near Dover on Bear Creek. In 1830, or early 1831, there were no less than six blast furnaces in operation in the Highland Rim of Western Tennessee, and practically all of their output was transported by steamboat to market. Near the close of this period, the number of blast furnaces had grown to a total of twenty-seven, producing approximately 28,000 tons of iron annually.

Most of the early furnaces were very crude, being made

of stone, and used charcoal as fuel. They had a capacity of from three to six tons of pig iron at a blast. The first pig iron in Tennessee was manufactured in 1830 in Stewart County near Dover, at the Cumberland Iron Works, and the first cargo was shipped to Pittsburgh in 1831. Of course it went by steamboat. Many of the early furnaces had bloomeries and refining forges.

In addition to James Robertson and Montgomery Bell, both of whom need no introduction to Tennesseans, there were others by the end of this period vitally interested in the early development of the iron industry. James and Robert Woods, and J. and R. Yeatman, A. W. VanLeer, R. Baxter, John Sullivan, A. Ewing and J. Hicks, all of Nashville, eagerly seized the opportunity to cast their lot with the new industry.

Daniel Hillman, Sr., from New Jersey, had arrived in Western Kentucky near the Cumberland River in 1822 and was already teaching his three young sons, Daniel, Jr., George W., and C. E. Hillman, the tricks of iron making. In a relatively short time Hillman iron from Trigg and Lyon Counties, Kentucky, was to be shipped out by steamboat on the Cumberland to industrial centers on the Ohio and Mississippi, there to gain recognition as the best boiler plate iron in the country.

When all of these pioneers perfected their plans, the success of the early iron industry was not only assured, but for nearly sixty years ranked as one of the most important and lucrative enterprises in our State. Its importance to transportation on the Cumberland cannot be overemphasized.

There still remained a great river trade reservoir above Nashville which had not been tapped. The Cumberland River, let us not forget, was navigable above Nashville approximately 325 miles (modern survey), and while this area was not thickly populated, there were various towns and villages that were longing and waiting for the arrival of steamboats. But the discussion of this interesting development belongs to the next succeeding chapter.

No exact figures can be given on the amount of cargo

handled annually during this period by the steamboats operating between Nashville and other points on the Western Rivers. Some idea, however, may be obtained by simple arithmetic. As stated, seventy-nine steamboats came up the Cumberland during this entire period. The majority of these came on the river after 1825. At the close of 1830, there were thirty of these boats plying the rivers between Nashville and New Orleans, and Nashville and points on the Ohio. They had increased their normal cargo capacity to 250 tons and when "flattened out" often carried 300 to 350 tons. The seasonal operations lasted about seven months and each of these packets made at least two trips per month. Assuming that a minimum cargo upstream was 150 tons, and 250 tons downstream, each of these thirty packets in the season would transport 2,100 tons of freight (14 trips times 150 tons) up to Nashville, and (14 trips times 250 tons) 3,500 tons of freight from Nashville, or a total of 5,600 tons of freight both ways. The total freight for all thirty packets would amount to 168,000 tons. On a present day basis, this would be 4,200 railroad box cars of forty tons each. These figures probably do an injustice to the packets of this era, many of which are known to have carried much greater tonnage and made more than two trips per month up the river to Nashville.

Steamboating in 1830 was "big" business, we may rest assured. Many cities to the south and southeast of Nashville had no means of steamboat transportation and depended upon Nashville as the nearest city connected with the rest of the inland waterways leading to the great industrial markets on the Ohio and the Mississippi. Merchants from the cities south of Nashville still had to rely on wagons and other vehicles to haul their goods over-land.

Robert, in his book "Nashville and Her Trade" published in 1870 states that in 1804 the population of Nashville was 400, and by 1810 had grown to a sizeable town of 1,100. Eastin Morris, a much earlier writer, in his "Tennessee Gazateer or Topographical Dictionary" published in 1834, stated that the population had grown from 3,463 in 1823 to 5,566 in 1830. This thriving metropolis as early as May, 1797, had entertained among others such outstanding celebrities as the three sons of the Duke of Orleans, the eldest of whom became Louis Philippe, King of France. Thomas Bailey, famed astronomer and first President of the Royal Astronomical Society of London, had also enjoyed the hospitality of the city in the same year. In June, 1819, President James Monroe, accompanied by Major General E. P. Gaines of Revolutionary fame, arrived for a visit with General Jackson, and on May 4, 1825, the distinguished guest of the Nation, General LaFayette, arrived in Nashville on board the steamboat *Mechanic* to spend several days and to be dined and feted.

Before his arrival at Nashville, General LaFayette had reached Smithland aboard the *Natchez,* one of the larger Mississippi packets. He had just previously made a short visit to St. Louis, Missouri, and Kaskaskia, Illinois. At Smithland he was transferred to the smaller *Mechanic*, a light-draft packet more suitable to the Cumberland. He was accompanied up the river by a distinguished group of citizens, including General William Carroll of Tennessee.

In Nashville he was met by General Jackson, his good friend Timothy Demonbreun and hundreds of officers and veterans of the Revolutionary War. A civic arch on Market Street (now Second Avenue, North) near the entrance to the public square had been erected for the occasion. During his two days visit to Nashville, LaFayette resided at the Dr. McNairy home, situated on the northwest corner of Summer (now Fifth Avenue, North) and Church Street. He visited the famous Female Academy and the Nashville Inn, ran up to the Hermitage on the *Mechanic* for an afternoon call on General Jackson; reviewed the troops on South Field (the old Commons), extending from Spruce Street (now Eighth Avenue, South) to a point near the river; made an official call on Governor Carroll; attended a reception at Cumberland College, the forerunner of the University of

Nashville, and topped off the festivities by attending a special ceremony and grand ball held in his honor by the Grand Lodge of Masons.

No other visitor in the early life of Nashville received a warmer reception than the famous soldier of France who so willingly fought for American Independence. General LaFayette left Nashville on board the *Mechanic* on May 6 and on his journey down the Cumberland stopped at Clarksville where he received a brief but splendid ovation and then proceeded to Smithland and Shawneetown, Illinois.

His trip on the *Mechanic* had thus far been a gala one. But on Sunday, May 8, near midnight, the *Mechanic* in command of Captain James (?) Hall, as it ascended the Ohio, about 125 miles below Louisville near Deer Creek on the Kentucky side of the river, struck a snag and sank within a very short time. The grave danger was immediately discovered and LaFayette and others on board were hastily aroused and put ashore. The next day the General and other members of his party were placed aboard the *Paragon* and taken to Louisville where the distinguished visitor was given a hearty welcome. It is well worth noting that LaFayette, who was then nearing seventy years of age, bore the shipwreck without criticism, or apparent physical disability. At a later date he wrote a letter graciously exonerating Captain Hall. When the news of the tragic accident reached Nashville some days later there was general rejoicing that the unfortunate event had not resulted in fatal consequences. The *Mechanic* had been a frequent visitor to the city and a favorite packet.

The first bridge across the Cumberland River was erected at Nashville. It was completed on July 1, 1823, by Messrs. Stacker and Johnson of Pittsburgh, at a cost of $75,000.00. It was located slightly to the north of the present Woodland Street Bridge and was a toll bridge, built by the old Nashville Bridge Company, organized on August 19, 1819. It was covered and had massive rock pillars for support. This bridge remained until the new suspension bridge was built shortly after 1850 under the direction of A. Heiman, architect, and M. D. Field, contractor. While it is getting ahead of the story somewhat, for the sake of continuity, it should be stated that this latter bridge was the one destroyed shortly before the capture of Nashville in 1862. The Federal Government replaced it in 1863. This bridge lasted until the present Woodland Street Bridge was completed on April 20, 1886, at a cost of $343,525.00. Flanery & Holmes, of Indianapolis, Indiana, were the architects and the Louisville Bridge and Iron Company the contractors. The rock for the piers for this last bridge came from the George Washington quarry on the Lebanon Pike, and were hauled down the river by steamboat.

The steamboat wharf at Nashville was built and graded in October 1828. Its location was very near the present wharf at the foot of Broad Street. It was much longer, however, extending roughly from the present Sparkman Street Bridge north to a point well below the present reproduction of Fort Nashborough. There was a smaller upper wharf below the present City Hospital.

Although Nashville was the largest, it was by no means the only thriving town along the Cumberland.

Situated at the mouth of the Cumberland as it enters the Ohio was Smith Town, later called Smithland. From the arrival of the first steamboat this village took on an air of prosperity and during the next thirty years became a town of some 3,000 residents, most of whom derived their livelihood from the river and its traffic. Most packets stopped at Smithland to discharge and receive passengers and freight whether they turned up the Cumberland or not. The village was a haven for river men of all types and a focal point for river news and gossip. During the War Between the States Smithland was a rendezvous for Federal gunboats and transports. It took on the aspect of a boom town. It was only after the war that Smithland gradually lost its prestige. When the packets left the river many years later, Smithland was bereft and never recovered.

Forty-two miles above Smithland was Kuttawa, one of the more prosperous river towns of Lyon County, Kentucky, situated in one of the best iron-producing sections of the Western Highland Rim. A picturesque town likewise noted for its mineral springs, Kuttawa made an early and serious bid for river supremacy. It was here that William Kelly around 1850 invented the famous air-boiling process for making steel which was later referred to as the Bessemer process. For nearly fifty years Kuttawa was a favorite steamboat town and many packets left its busy landing loaded flat with iron.

Eddyville, located on a beautiful bluff a mile above Kuttawa, was the seat of Lyon County and early became one of the busiest towns on the lower Cumberland. Not far distant from Eddyville were some of the largest iron furnaces in Kentucky. It was destined to far surpass Kuttawa and other Kentucky river towns as a shipping point for iron and rolling mill products. Around 1840 Eddyville had made good its boast as the recognized center of the iron industry on the lower river, and its wharf was teeming with packets from Pittsburgh, Cincinnati, Louisville, New Orleans and Nashville, all eagerly awaiting their turn to take on their lucrative cargo. It also had the distinction of being a transfer point for freight from large packets which frequently on account of low water could not run up to Nashville.

During the War Between the States Eddyville, like Smithland, became a large supply base for the Federal Government. It served as an ideal spot for making up convoys bound for Nashville.

Canton, sixty-two miles above Smithland, over in Trigg County, Kentucky, was another prosperous river town. Large shipments of iron and tobacco left this village by steamboats. It was at Canton on October 18, 1861 that Nathan Bedford Forrest, then a Lt. Colonel of Cavalry in the Confederate Army, had a skirmish with the Federal gunboat *Conestoga* as she ran up the Cumberland to seize supplies and if possible reconnoitre the fortifications at Fort Donelson. This engagement marked the opening of warfare on the Cumberland in the War Between the States.

Dover, Cumberland City, Palmyra and Clarksville, farther up the river toward Nashville and located within forty miles of one another, gave every promise of sustained growth and development, thanks to their close proximity to the iron and dark-fired tobacco sections of Tennessee.

Dover, the county seat of Stewart County, was laid out in 1805–6. There was a settlement near Dover in 1795. At one time Stewart County, which has the peculiar distinction of being named for an "energetic and prosperous farmer," Duncan Stewart, rather than for some renowned military hero, included the entire area from the Cumberland to the Tennessee River south to Alabama. Dover was incorporated in 1836 by an act which designated it as Monroe for the fifth president, but the English name was retained. From 1835 through 1860, Dover prospered. Hardly a steamboat passed without stopping at its fine landing. With the attack on nearby Fort Donelson in 1862, the town was practically wiped off the map. Only four houses remained standing and all of the iron furnaces in the county were destroyed. After the War Between the States, Dover made an effort to regain its leadership in this industry. When the railroads bisected the lower river, however, and took this heavy cargo from the packets, it could never regain its former position.

Cumberland City and Palmyra were prominent towns on the Cumberland during the boom days of the iron business. Palmyra gained early recognition as the first Port of Entry in the West. French settlers are said to have been in the vicinity of Palmyra as early as 1777. Like Dover, it was reduced to ashes during the War Between the States and never regained its former industrial prominence.

Clarksville, second town to be established in what is now known as Middle Tennessee, was named for George Rogers Clark, the famous Northwest explorer. It was settled on April 12, 1780 by Moses Renfroe and his company who left Colonel John Donelson's expedition en route to Nashville. At that time the area now known as Montgomery County, of which Clarksville was the county seat, was on the rim of western civilization and for this reason pioneer settlers were subject to frequent attacks by Indians. Long hunters, including such men as Boone and Mansker, had already followed the trails in the lower Cumberland basin and marvelled at its beauty. Renfroe was struck by the hills about the present site of Clarksville, the large crystal clear spring near by and the river, which he later named Red River, flowing into the Cumberland. Indians or no Indians, he decided to settle on the spot, a decision which soon proved to be catasthropic, for within a few months his party was massacred.

In 1794, ten years after Clarksville was incorporated, Colonel Isaac Titsworth, his brother John, and their families and negro servants came from North Carolina to the Cumberland country, intending to settle on Red River. They encamped at the mouth of Sulphur Creek and there were attacked and killed by Indians. It is said only one person, a negro woman, escaped.

About 1790 Colonel Valentine Sevier, brother of Governor John Sevier, and his four sons, moved to the mouth of Red River to establish a station. Three of Colonel Sevier's sons were killed while attempting to go to the relief of distressed families on the Cumberland.

John Dier, Benjamin Lindsey, John Montgomery, for whom Montgomery County was named, and Major Evan Shelby, brother of Isaac Shelby, were prominent first settlers of Clarksville who were victims of Indian attacks in 1793 and 1794.

From an industrial standpoint, Clarksville gave every promise of rapid growth and development. Several factors contributed to the importance of Clarksville from the standpoint of river commerce. When the river was at a low stage, large packets could reach Clarksville when they would not get to Nashville, thanks to Harpeth Shoals which were between the two towns. For this reason alone, Clarksville built up a good river business, which during early days for two or three months each year often equalled that of Nashville.

But Clarksville was a good river town regardless of the blessings brought about because of its location below Harpeth Shoals. It was in a rich agricultural section, close to the iron industry in Tennessee and served an extensive trade area in its own right. It early took the lead in the dark-fired tobacco industry; in fact, a tobacco inspection was established there in 1788. Politically and commercially, it soon became a city of importance second only to Nashville on the river.

Red River, which empties into the Cumberland a little way below Clarksville, is navigable for a short distance. It is the only navigable tributary of the Cumberland which enters it from the north. In old days, top-water or light draft boats and barges plied this tributary of the Cumberland for a distance of twenty-five miles up to Port Royal, which in the early days was a thriving settlement. Dunbar's Cave, a landing six miles up this river, was an active landing, and there were several more. Providence, across Red River from Clarksville and on the same side of the Cumberland, received its share of river commerce. Prior to the War Between the States, this small hamlet vied with Clarksville as a shipping point for tobacco. Large shipments of hogs and cattle, considerable iron and foundry products, grain, fresh meat and barter also found their way to market from this landing, and from others further up the Red River to Port Royal. Before steamboats, barges and flat boats in large numbers left Red River for New Orleans and established a good trade. One of the earliest steamboat calls on the Cumberland was "Red River," which designated the landing for both Providence and Clarksville. Steamboats on good tides plied the Red River until the turn of the century.

Ashland City, situated about thirty-three miles below Nashville and near the head of Harpeth Shoals, was not known by that name during this period. It became the seat of Cheatham County when it was established in 1856. There was a landing on the river long before the town was erected. One historian says that Robert and Braxton Lee settled on the site of Ashland City in 1796.

Nearby Sycamore Mills was first settled by Benjamin Darrow in 1790. Betystown, probably first named Betts' Town, at the foot of Harpeth Shoals, was a small place in the early steamboat days, but for its size had a large packet business, especially for iron. Ashland City and Betystown also thrived as a result of the "lighter" business and transfer of freight made necessary by Harpeth Shoals. In later years, Ashland City built up an excellent tobacco and general merchandise business for the packets.

Steamboats on the Cumberland with unexpected suddenness had revolutionized transportation, captured the fancy of a grateful public and touched off an era of progress which exceeded the expectations of their most ardent supporters. They had brought untold wealth and happiness to the sturdy pioneers of Tennessee and Kentucky during this period.

CHAPTER TWO

From Smithland to Point Isabel in Fourteen Years

Period 1830–1840

Steamboats, during this period of unparalleled growth and development, remained the dominant factor in continued national progress. Both the larger and the smaller rivers were cluttered with the faithful and ever increasing packets, seeking an opportunity, not only to carry passengers and cargoes over familiar traffic routes but also to find new frontiers.

It was distinctly a period of adventure. Steamboat owners, captains and pilots, noted for their daring and courage, quickly grasped the opportunity to exploit this roving spirit of the times. Every season new frontiers were opened up, new speed records established and bigger and better packets built. Despite accidents and other difficulties, many of which were unnecessary, a grateful people patronized the packets as never before. A great nation was coming into its own and the steamboats were making a monumental contribution to that achievement. It takes but a fleeting glance at events during this interesting period to see what this contribution really amounted to.

In the short span of twenty-five years since Roosevelt had made his historic trip from Pittsburgh to New Orleans with the good boat *New Orleans,* the river packets had not only grown in size and speed, but had nudged their way up

31

practically every navigable river in the United States. The famous *New Orleans* was a spunky craft, only 116 feet long, driven by one engine and a stern wheel. The Ohio and Mississippi and many of their larger tributaries were now alive with majestic packets driven by twin engines and side wheels. Many had an overall length of 200 feet and registered tonnage of over 600 gross tons. Some ran on regular schedule based on an operational speed of eight miles per hour. They had, as one reporter put it, "devoured speed and conquered cargo." Due to the new invention of the low pressure type boilers, they were also much safer, except when a daring captain, intent on breaking a record, weighted down the safety valves and thereby took the lives of all on board in his own hands. Unfortunately, such exploits during this decade were all too frequent, resulting in loss of life and property.

A large number of Ohio and Mississippi packets were making trips up the Cumberland. Many were so big that they found it difficult to maneuver the bends and narrow channels. Not to be outdone, the steamboat men in Nashville themselves began to build very large packets. From 1830 to 1840 the Cumberland had an unprecedented number of fine steamboats which were owned and operated by Nashvillians or other Tennesseans and Kentuckians. Among these were the luxurious *John Randolph, Ellen Kirkman, T. Yeatman, Nashville, Memphis* (launched in 1831 and the first steamboat built in Nashville), *Rambler, Tobacco Plant, Lady Jackson, Dover, Harry Hill, Smithland, Burkesville* (launched at Burkesville, Kentucky, in 1834 and the first steamboat built on the upper Cumberland), *Tennessean, Jefferson, Water Witch, Passenger, Clarksville, Red Rover* and many others.

It is difficult if not impossible to pick the outstanding packets from such a list. From the publicity and other data found in old records and newspapers of the time, perhaps the finest of the number were the *John Randolph*, the *Ellen Kirkman*, the *Nashville*, the *Clarksville* and the *Red Rover*. The *John Randolph*, according to the records, was 190 feet long with a beam of 30 feet and a draft of 10 feet, 6 inches.

She had registered tonnage of 549 tons and was owned by Joseph Miller, her captain, John Robinson, and William T. Yeatman, Joseph G. Dally and John Stacker. The *John Randolph* is not to be confused with the (John) *Randolph* which was built in 1833 and was an earlier palatial packet that burned at the Nashville wharf on March 16, 1836 with a loss of three lives and a cargo which included a large amount of furniture and the famous French wallpaper for General Jackson's "Hermitage." The total loss of the cargo and boat was estimated at $200,000.00.

The *Ellen Kirkman* named for a wealthy and influential lady of Nashville, had a registered tonnage of 602 tons and was owned by Anthony M. Johnson, John K. Rayburn, Thomas K. Price, James Johnson, the three Yeatmans and Sterling M. Barner, who was her captain. Barner was one of the best pilots of this era. The *Ellen Kirkman* was one of the best known packets of that day, and was conceded to be one of the most beautiful yet serviceable of all the boats on the river.

The *Nashville,* of less tonnage, was one of the trimmest and most beautiful of all the Nashville-owned packets. She was owned by Ed D. Hicks, Robert Baxter, A. W. Van Leer and her captain, Amon L. Davis. She plied regularly between Nashville and New Orleans.

The *Clarksville,* which was the first of a number of boats of this name, had been built by her captain, Joseph Erwin, J. Anderson and Captain John B. Eastland of New Orleans. She measured 182 feet long and had a twenty-seven foot beam. She had a registered tonnage of 350 tons. General Jackson made his last visit to New Orleans in January, 1840, on this famous packet. Shortly after this trip, the career of the *Clarksville* was suddenly ended. In the summer of 1841 she struck a snag on her way up from New Orleans near Point Chicot, Arkansas, and sank immediately.

The *Red Rover,* the third boat of that name, had a registered tonnage of 381 tons and was built in 1840. She was a magnificent boat and plied the Ohio, Mississippi and Cumberland. M. S. Pilcher was captain of all three of these boats. He broke in on the *Talma* and also was a pilot. I have heard the first *Red Rover,* built in 1828, made a trip up the Big Hatchie to the vicinity of Brownsville. Captain Pilcher was one of the most beloved and respected members of the steamboat fraternity in Nashville for many years and his boats were always well patronized.

During this decade there were 131 steamboats added to the list of the seventy-nine boats that had previously plied the Cumberland. Of the seventy-nine boats which had appeared on the river prior to 1830, old newspapers and other records prove that thirty-three continued to operate on the Cumberland during this decade. Therefore a total of more than 164 steamboats engaged in traffic on the Cumberland at one time or another between 1830 and 1840. It is difficult to determine the number of boats registered in the Cumberland River trade during any given year, but the best records available show that in 1830 the number was twenty-one and this gradually increased until there were forty-five in 1840. In 1838–39 old newspapers establish there were forty-three boats that made fairly regular trips up the river to Nashville. This should give some idea of the growth of traffic on the Cumberland and the service which it was rendering to the people of Tennessee and Kentucky.

The outstanding feature of this particular period, insofar as the Cumberland was concerned was the opening of traffic on the river above Nashville to Point Isabel, now known as Burnside, Kentucky, a distance of 325 miles. This was a feat which relatively speaking equalled that of the *Zebulon M. Pike,* the first steamboat to ascend the Mississippi above the mouth of the Ohio, on August 2, 1817, or that of the *Independence* which ascended the Missouri for a distance of 200 miles in May, 1819, or even the *Virginia,* the first steamboat to ascend the Mississippi to Fort Snelling, below Minneapolis, in 1823. To those unfamiliar with the natural resources of the upper Cumberland, and the hazards involved this comparison may seem fantastic, but as the facts are developed this may not be the case. This section of the river from the very beginning of steamboat traffic yielded raw materials which did much to make Nashville the outstanding metropolis of Tennessee. The packets on the upper river lasted for a century and prolonged the life of the steamboat traffic for nearly ten years after that on most other rivers had died a natural death. In the heyday of its existence, 1890 to 1912, it was worth $10,000,000.00 annually to Nashville.

The glory of making the first voyage from Nashville to Point Isabel belongs to Captain E. S. Burge in command of the packet *Jefferson*, a Nashville built boat, launched in 1832. According to the National Banner and Nashville Daily Advertiser, the *Jefferson* arrived in Nashville from the junction of the North and South forks of the Cumberland River (Point Isabel) seventy miles above Creelsboro on April 13, 1833 with a cargo of tobacco. It had taken only fourteen short years for steamboats to conquer the Cumberland from Smithland to Burnside, a total distance of 516 miles.

Prior to the historic trip of the *Jefferson*, steamboats had been pushing their way to other points on the upper Cumberland. In the early stages of steamboating packets had ventured above Nashville only as far as Haysborough and the Hermitage. By 1825 they had pressed to Gallatin Landing and in 1828–29 boats had reached the mouth of the Caney Fork at Carthage. The spirit of adventure had begun to take the packets all the way to landings at what are now known as Gainesboro and Celina. Around 1831 and certainly not later than 1832 smaller packets were making fairly regular runs to all points on the upper river as far as the Kentucky line. At the beginning of 1833 we know from newspaper items the *Rambler*, which was owned by Johnson and Rayburn of Nashville, went up the river as far as Burkesville, Kentucky. Then on March 3, 1833, the *Tom Yeatman*, a fairly large packet, in command of Captain James Irwin, made a trip all the way to Creelsboro, Kentucky. This preceded the historic trip made by the *Jefferson* to Point Isabel by only a few weeks.

To those living in the upper reaches of the river, steamboats meant a new lease on life. In this era there were no roads in that section over which products could be taken to market. With the advent of the packets, this was changed. The hardy people of the upper Cumberland were elated and for years to come they showed their appreciation by shipping vast quantities of freight by their favorite packets. Nashville became a natural junction and transfer point for the upper and lower river traffic, something she was not to give up so long as steamboats operated on the Cumberland.

The river was not yet ready for such things as regular packet schedules. Definite trends, however, were pointing toward these improvements. The Cumberland was still open territory to all boats, both large and small, and no matter from whence they came. The packets, after a fashion, were "home" wherever there was any business. This explains in large measure why a boat making a trip to New Orleans from Nashville, instead of returning to Nashville, would next be reported as far east as Pittsburgh. This roving spirit which seemed to be a part of all the inland waterways, had much to do with the opening up of new frontiers and vast trade areas touched by the rivers. By 1835 the Cumberland was recognized as one of the main arteries of river traffic and Nashville became the chief point of distribution to the southeast.

In making any attempt to fix the amount of annual tonnage on the Cumberland during any given period the length of the season must be taken into consideration. Over a period of ten years the river would have two or three seasons when traffic was foreshortened on account of shallow water. This was the greatest handicap to the steamboat business on the Cumberland although at times ice in the Ohio and Mississippi hindered the free flow of traffic from these rivers. There was never any shortage in cargoes for the boats either coming or going.

With a view of giving some indication of the enormous increase in traffic on the river and at the same time dispelling any doubts concerning the estimate of tonnage further along in this chapter, there is submitted in Appendix "C" a summary prepared verbatim from the National Banner and

Nashville Daily Advertizer covering the period March 18, 1833 to April 29, 1833, approximately forty days, showing the names of the boats arriving and departing from Nashville.

There is also included, as a basis of comparison, in the Appendix, another summary prepared verbatim from The Nashville Whig five years later, beginning March 7, 1838 and ending April 4, 1838, a period of thirty days, giving the names of the boats arriving and departing from Nashville.

It will be seen from checking these summaries that during the busiest month of 1833 twenty-three different packets tied up at Nashville and in 1838 there were twenty-four, an increase of but one boat. At first glance this seems to indicate but a very slight growth in traffic. Just the reverse is true when the situation is analyzed. For example, the twenty-three packets in 1833 made less than two trips per month on the average while in 1838, after five more years of operational experience, the twenty-four boats made an average of nearly four trips per month. In steamboat parlance the arrival and departure of a packet constituted two separate trips. To put it another way and to make the comparison even more obvious, the twenty-three boats in 1833 made only forty trips in forty days while those in 1838 made a total of eighty-eight trips in thirty days.

Not only were the packets by 1838 rendering more efficient service, but thanks to increase in size they were carrying larger cargoes. Some of the big packets coming up to Nashville carried from 400 to 500 tons of freight and on leaving increased this figure by several hundred tons. Nevertheless, due allowance must be made in figuring tonnage for the many smaller packets which seldom carried more than 250 tons upstream and 450 tons downstream. In estimating the tonnage for this period and in order to be conservative, I have chosen to take these latter figures. There can certainly be no doubt concerning their accuracy, since the record will reveal there were more larger packets than smaller ones.

Suppose, for example, we give the tonnage handled by the *Rocky Mountain,* a fair sized packet and that of the *John Randolph,* one of the largest. On February 15, 1838, according to The Nashville Whig, the *Rocky Mountain,* in command of Captain T. Gilbert, left Nashville with the following cargo; 158 bales of cotton, 222 hogsheads of tobacco, twenty-four tons of pig metal, 304 barrels of flour, 715 sacks of corn, and various miscellaneous package freight. Figuring a bale of cotton at 500 pounds, a hogshead of tobacco at 2,200 pounds, a barrel of flour at 196 pounds and a sack of corn at 140 pounds, and the miscellaneous freight at fifty tons, the *Rocky Mountain* on this trip was carrying approximately 450 tons of freight.

On March 9, 1838, the *John Randolph,* according to the same newspaper, arrived in New Orleans from Nashville with the following cargo; 440 Hogsheads of tobacco, 333 bales of cotton, 851 bags of corn and 120 miscellaneous packages of freight. Using the same weights as above, this grand old packet was carrying 630 tons of freight downstream, figuring the miscellaneous package freight at three tons minimum.

While the smaller boats did not carry as much tonnage as the larger boats, they made up for the difference by making more trips. They were able to do this because they could navigate the river on a very low "tide," a factor which must not be overlooked in making any estimate of the total freight transported in any given season.

Assuming that the above figures are accurate, the twenty-four boats listed above as having made eighty-eight trips in thirty days in 1838, transported up to Nashville 11,750 tons of freight and from Nashville 18,450 tons of freight, or for the entire month, both coming and going, a total of 30,200 tons of freight. If the operational season was seven months, the total tonnage for the season of 1838 amounted to 211,-400 tons of common carrier commercial freight. It should constantly be borne in mind that this tonnage is not the total tonnage for the entire river, for such places as Eddyville, Canton, Dover, Palmyra and Clarksville on the lower river were receiving and discharging freight in huge volumes which never saw Nashville. In addition such towns as Gallatin, Lebanon, Carthage, Burkesville, Creelsboro, Waitesboro and Point Isabel on the upper river were coming into their own and some freight between these towns never came to Nashville.

A matter of more than passing interest in the operation of the old-time steamboat packets is that of freight rates. According to the Republican Gazette of February 12, 1831, the prevailing freight rate for a bale of cotton from Nashville to New Orleans was $4.00; a hogshead of tobacco, $7.50, and other freight $1.00 per one hundred pounds. Applying these rates to the cargo handled by the *Rocky Mountain*, and assuming that the entire tonnage was transported to New Orleans, the charges for handling the freight on board would be above $3,800.00, not including packaged freight or freight from way stations.

These figures are misleading unless further analyzed. It is highly probable that all of the freight taken on at Nashville was not transported to New Orleans and, therefore, proper deductions should be conceded. Nevertheless, if we assume that some of the freight taken on at Nashville was dropped en route, it is also fair to assume that a fair amount was taken on. Articles in contemporary newspapers indicate that this was the usual practice. Furthermore, the prevailing freight rates on articles coming up the river were higher than those downstream, and it can be assumed that while the cargo was less, the packet on the return trip from New Orleans to Nashville would take in as much revenue as on the trip down. The gross revenue from all sources in the operation of this boat from Nashville to New Orleans and return would be not less than $7,000.00 per trip.

If the *Rocky Mountain* made a minimum of only one round trip per month for six months, the gross revenue would be $42,000.00. In this figure are included an average of thirty cabin passengers to New Orleans at the prevailing rate of $25.00 each, and a like number from New Orleans to Nashville at the rate of $30.00 each; twenty to thirty deck passengers taken on at Nashville at the prevailing rate of $5.00 each and a similar number from New Orleans to Nashville at $10.00 each. It would also include other cabin and deck passengers taken on at intervening points. A total revenue of $42,000.00 for one season might appear excessive, but by the time this figure is reduced by the expense of operation, the average packet did not make as much money as might be expected. Here are a few estimated expenses per month, which had to be met:

Captain	$ 100.00
Chief Clerk	75.00
Second Clerk	60.00
Third Clerk or "Mud" Clerk	40.00
Chief Mate	90.00
Second Mate	75.00
Two Pilots ($100.00 each maxium)	200.00
Chief Engineer	90.00
Second Engineer	75.00
Six to eight Firemen ($40.00 each)	240.00
Steward	60.00
Carpenter	50.00
Watchman	30.00
Twenty Deck Hands ($20.00 each)	400.00
Fifteen Deck Hands ($15.00 each)	225.00
Cabin Crew, including Cook, Pastryman, Chambermaids, etc.	300.00
Food supplies—thirty days @ $60.00 per day	1,800.00
Wood—not less than twenty cords per day @ $2.00 per cord (Maximum)	1,200.00
Total	$5,110.00

Thus, a packet making one round trip per month, and taking in a gross revenue of $7,000.00 would have operational expense of $5,110.00, leaving a net revenue of $1,890.00 per trip. If the operational season lasted for six months, the packet, with good luck, would make $11,340.00 for its owners. All of this would not be net profit on the basis of good accounting practice, because such figures do not include deductions for depreciation, insurance, repairs and replacements.

The claim is not made that these figures are absolutely accurate. They are the best obtainable after years of research. They serve to illustrate a point frequently overlooked, that steamboats even during this early period, when operated by men who knew the business and were willing to risk the hazards, with a modicum of luck thrown in, received very excellent returns on their investments. From old accounts, most steamboat owners, after laying aside a tidy sum "for keeps," invariably used their boat's earnings to buy another packet, which would "far surpass any steamboat on the Western Rivers." I might add in concluding this part of the discussion that most packets were operated on a cash basis. They had no bills and there was practically no litigation.

This was not a day and time of rigid law enforcement and safety measures. Such rules as were in common use were more customs than anything else, and in this era of great development, one wonders why there were not more accidents, with resulting loss of life and cargo. This is a tribute to the fine old steamboat pilots. Many, if not all, of the early steamboats ran both day and night without a let-up. Many over-zealous pilots frequently ran in fog and mist in an effort to post better running-time between points on the river. Such foolish tactics often resulted in serious accidents and greatly injured the steamboat business.

Let us not forget also that all of these early steamboats were wood burners. All up and down the river, there were large stores of wood cut to suit the needs of the boats and hundreds of woodsmen earned a respectable living from this business. The burning of wood in the fire boxes of the early boats, which obtained draft from the tall, black smokestacks, was a constant threat on account of the sparks and embers. Despite the greatest care and attention, they would light on the roof or about the various decks and cause a fire unless quickly discovered and smothered.

Before the advent of electric lights, pilots on the earlier packets, while running at night, frequently used "fire pots," hung along the guard rails. These were filled with pine knots, and during later days, with cannel coal. When lighted they would reflect a dim glow and the pilots would receive sufficient illumination to give them an outline of the banks.

Pilots, however, did not depend as much on this antiquated system as they did on the markings up and down the river, and especially at danger points. These markings may have been an old tree or outline of the trees on either bank, the top of a hill, some other natural contour of the land, or in some instances, shadows and reflections. Furthermore, the pilots on the packets had various markings for all the different stages of the river. They also noted any changes in the channel caused by such things as floods, and after years of experience could draw a diagram of the bottom of the river. In this way, many of the pilots, knowing the draft of their boats, could tell in advance exactly what places in the river would or would not give them trouble.

The silence which so frequently pervaded the pilot house gave the man at the wheel an opportunity to study the river and they took great pride in some new marking or sign that would make it easier to navigate their boats. In the earlier days many of the pilots took boys and young men to "learn" them the river. These youngsters were referred to as "cub" pilots or "steersmen." During the easier stretches of the river, the pilot of the packet would turn the wheel over to the "cub" and after an apprenticeship of not less than two years, the youngsters would apply for their license, if they received the required recommendations. The life of a cub pilot was by no means an easy one. Many youngsters broke under the strain of the rigid discipline and training. But the pilot and the "cub" nevertheless had many peaceful hours to themselves in the pilot house. It was during these interludes that the pilots related their fantastic stories of the river to the "cubs." These stories, oft repeated, grew in stature and have been handed down to posterity as "tall tales."

Even in this day and time, when modern aids to navigation have been erected, it is no easy matter to navigate a sizeable boat on the river. It is not a job for the inexperienced or faint hearted. It takes courage and intelligence. Those who have stood at the wheel or controls of modern boats, aided by every conceivable device, including such things as air control and powerful searchlights, are utterly amazed at the exploits of the old steamboat pilots. Their originality, courage and skill will ever remain an outstanding accomplishment. Mark Twain fortunately has preserved old times on the river in his "Life on the Mississippi."

Life on board one of the packets during this particular period was truly colorful. Drinking of hard liquor was often abused and this was a disturbing influence, which might have been handled better. As for drinking water, it was served to the people directly from the river and was enjoyed by all. No one knew about germs at this time. The early boats were famous for the good food served on board. Meals were charged into the passenger fare and they formed the basis of the social life on the boats. There was much gambling.

The impression should not be given from the discussion of the *John Randolph* and the *Rocky Mountain,* that the only cargo handled by packets consisted of cotton, tobacco, corn and flour. There are many accurate accounts of cargoes brought into and leaving Nashville during this particular period. From them we find, for example, that on March 20, 1833, the *Memphis* under command of Captain C. M. Bradford arrived from New Orleans, carrying 164 hogsheads of sugar, 200 barrels of molasses, sixty sacks of coffee, sixty-six plows, twelve tons of iron, 1 box of furs, fifteen pieces of castings. Incidentally, the Hon. James K. Polk was on the *Memphis* when she arrived in Nashville on this trip.

The *Rambler* arrived from Creelsboro in the upper reaches of the Cumberland on March 30, 1833, under command of Captain Stratton, with a cargo of 103 hogsheads of tobacco, 131 barrels of whiskey, thirty bales of cotton, 109 reams of wrapping paper, and a large assortment of feathers. On April 10th of that same year, the *T. Yeatman* arrived from Indian Creek, Kentucky, with ninety-nine hogsheads of tobacco, sixty barrels of whiskey, 150 reams of paper, and three tons of hemp. The *Harry Hill,* on April 17th, with Captain Davis in command, arrived from Kanawha in the Ohio trade area with 1,100 barrels of salt. The *Pacific* as early as March 9, 1831, arrived with 302 tons of freight, represented by 2,466 packages.

The law of supply and demand had thus created a "pay load" for the boats both to and from Nashville.

During this decade there was a general awakening to the great possibilities of river transportation all over the State. In the latter part of the thirties the State considered legislation looking to the improvement, not only of the larger rivers but of the smaller ones. Some of these were the Duck, Elk and Caney Fork, well known in Middle Tennessee. The towns on these rivers were very anxious to have the channels improved so as to gain the advantages of river transportation.

During this period there was unending discussion as to what was the best means of making such improvements and of raising the necessary funds. The question was constantly argued as to how far the State should go on matters of this kind and what, if any, help could be obtained from the Federal Government. This was but a natural result of a confused situation. There was as yet no concerted plan or definite scheme for Federal aid, although on July 17, 1832, the River and Harbor Act did provide a small appropriation for channel work on the Cumberland. The tremendous increase in traffic, particularly during this period, on all the Western Rivers, gave increased emphasis to Governmental aid for such projects. Very little, relatively speaking, was done about it by either Federal or State Government. Many Tennesseeans believed that substantial State aid should be voted for the rivers regardless of any nice questions of constitutional law concerning their regulation by the Federal Government. This resulted in a small appropriation from the State.

This period was notable for another reason. It produced the first effort to finance railroads in the state. Few, if any, of the boat operators envisioned what this new competitor would mean to their business. During the latter part of this period, there was much general agitation throughout the State for some well devised plan to cover all internal improvements. Tennessee was developing so rapidly that overland transportation was fast becoming a pressing problem. In other States, notably New York, this problem had been met by the Erie Canal. In Tennessee this method was out of the question. In addition, enterprising citizens had heard of the successful operation of railroads in other States, and were of the opinion that Tennessee, as a matter of public policy, should render material assistance in developing this method of travel.

In 1836, the first general system of internal improvements was established by an Act, which among other things, provided that when two-thirds of the capital stock of any company organized for the construction of a railroad or turnpike within the State had been subscribed, then the Governor could, in behalf of the State, subscribe the remaining one-third and issue 5¼ per cent bonds to cover the State's subscription.

In addition, the paltry sum of $300,000.00 was appropriated for the improvement and navigation of rivers, to be divided equally between the three grand divisions of the State. This was certainly not very generous of the politicians since the rivers were transporting nearly sixty per cent of all commercial freight in Tennessee at the time. The intentions of the State for internal improvements, when put into actual operation by politicians, soon resulted in the State being heavily indebted, with very little improvements made. A total of $1,500,000.00 was issued to infant railroads under this Act, and $800,000.00 to turnpikes. The $300,-000.00 appropriated for rivers was diverted and not more than $150,000.00 actually went to the improvement of any of them. Approximately $30,000.00 was actually spent on improvements for the Cumberland River. This was hardly sufficient to pull up snags in the main channel.

While the people of Tennessee were keenly alive to the advantages of railroad transportation, better roads and other internal improvements, they quickly revolted against the misuse of the State's funds by politicians, and by the end of 1839, reaction had set in to such an extent that the Act of January, 1840, repealed former appropriations, except on work already started. The result of all this financial manipulation was a black eye for both the politicians and the early railroads. All of this will be referred to later.

The manufacture of iron along the Cumberland River continued to be one of the leading industries during this period. Steamboats rarely, if ever, made a trip without large cargoes of pig iron and kindred products on board. Under the guiding hand of Messrs. Yeatman and Woods of Nashville, the Cumberland Iron Works near Dover, among others, had increased in capacity to such extent that they had cornered the market in the Nashville area for making nails, chains, shovels, castings and other foundry products.

The Nashville Republican on December 26, 1834, brought the gratifying news to Nashvillians that the Tennessee Rolling Mills located on what is now known as Rolling Mill Hill just north of the present City Hospital, were ready for business. Messrs. Baxter, Hicks and Ewing were the proprietors, and had already paid more than $70,000.00 for the machinery. When completed, they expected to produce 2,500 or 3,000 tons of iron annually for the residents of Nashville.

Steamboats not only brought the raw material to the mills, but in turn carried the finished products to other points on the inland waterways.

In 1835, A. W. Van Leer, another prominent Nashvillian, took over the Cumberland Furnace on the lower Cumberland. Daniel Hillman assumed the management of the business, having previously in 1832 formed a partnership with VanLeer and John Sullivan in the operation of still another furnace at Big Richland Creek. From this time on, the Cumberland Furnace became one of the most successful projects on the river, and one very closely identified with the steamboat business.

Van Leer around 1839 next began to center his attention

on the Tennessee Rolling Mills. He finally purchased Ewing's interest in them, which gave him a competing market in Nashville with the Cumberland Iron Works. Then in 1838, Van Leer, Hillman and R. Baxter opened up the Clay Steam Forge at Betsytown on the Cumberland, in connection with the Cumberland Furnace. This, of course, added additional cargo of freight to the steamboats.

Daniel Hillman and Van Leer also became interested in the iron ore mines in Trigg and Lyon Counties, Kentucky. At the close of 1840 they purchased a large tract of land and a one-half interest in the Empire Furnace in Trigg County. This assured them of a continuous supply of ore and ultimately led, as will be seen from succeeding chapters, to the development of one of the largest iron industries south of the Ohio River.

Another industry on the lower Cumberland came into existence during this period. Messrs. Seay and Shepherd, during 1835, erected the Sycamore Mills, about four miles north of Ashland City, and a short distance from the Cumberland River. They first operated a grist mill, but soon developed a sawmill, flour mill, cotton factory and finally the manufacture of gunpowder. In 1840, they were receiving large shipments of raw products by steamboats coming up the river and exporting their finished products to Nashville and other cities.

Many citizens of Nashville at this time will be surprised to learn that as early as 1832, there were paper mills in operation on the upper Cumberland, and that steamboats brought all of their output down the river to market. In 1840 there was a paper mill in Davidson County and one in Sumner County, Tennessee. They were rather small affairs and their entire production was consumed in Nashville. Prior to 1840, the paper brought down the Cumberland by steamboat, insofar as can be ascertained, came from across the line in Kentucky in the vicinity of Creelsboro and Waitesboro.

The Cumberland in 1831 made another notable contribution to Nashville. In that year the City built the municipal waterworks and from that time on the faithful Cumberland has continuously supplied the water essential to the daily need of its residents.

Nashville, with a population of nearly 7,000, was taking on the aspects of a real city. Its many schools, colleges and churches had already given it an atmosphere of culture and refinement far beyond most towns which only twenty years previously had been typical frontier villages. From the standpoint of political importance it was outranked by only a few in the entire nation. Andrew Jackson was first inaugurated president in 1829 and for eight years thereafter the Hermitage became a second White House and was frequently more newsworthy than the White House itself. Jackson dearly loved his home on the river and during the later years of his life spent much time there. Important visitors, many arriving by steamboat, frequently came to see "Old Hickory," who was never more sparkling than when at home at the Hermitage. For thirty years Nashville had basked in his political limelight, a distinction which proved of inestimable value in more ways than one, not the least of which was excellent publicity.

Jackson was by no means the only political figure in Nashville and Middle Tennessee during these early days. Newton Cannon, William Carroll, Sam Houston, "Lean Jimmy" Jones, Aaron V. Brown, and James K. Polk, Cave Johnson, Gustavus Henry, John Catron, Abraham and Robert Caruthers, Peter Turney, William B. Campbell, William Trousdale, William Hall and many others had gained deserved recognition in public life and were destined to add their share of glory to the State and Nation. In the history of Tennessee there probably never were more Tennesseeans in the political limelight than in this period.

Of course the Cumberland was not directly responsible for this remarkable political prestige nor for all the financial and civic virtues of Nashville and other towns along its course. It can hardly be denied, however, that since the river was almost solely responsible for the industrial growth and wealth of every city and town in the Cumberland Valley, it deserves some degree of credit for other virtues which ordinarily flow from such material assets. One may well ponder what would have been the lot of Nashville and Middle Tennessee without the Cumberland and its steamboats. Without the steamboats, cotton, iron, tobacco and other products no doubt would have reached the market but in far less volume. In the final analysis, therefore, the Cumberland and the packets by 1840 had made the difference between a people still struggling against frontier life and a people who were able to capitalize on progress under the most favorable circumstances.

CHAPTER THREE

The Golden Age of Steamboatin' Begins

Period 1840–1850

This period marks the beginning of the "Golden Age" of steamboatin' on the Western Rivers. Whether we base this conclusion on the actual number of boats built and operating, their gross tonnage, or the amount of freight transported, makes but very little difference—the steamboats on all of our inland waterways were entering upon an era of unprecedented success and one which had much to do with the future development of our country.

The steamboat packets were the best, and in many cases the only, means of commercial transportation between the interior industrial centers of our country and the vast and rich resources west of the Mississippi and south of the Ohio. These great water highways, fortunately, extended east and west as well as north and south. No other country in the world can boast of so many natural waterways. The Mississippi, Ohio, Cumberland and Tennessee were ideal traffic arteries leading to the industrial centers of our country. To the west of the Mississippi, the Missouri, Arkansas, and Red Rivers, to mention only a few, spread like fingers into the fertile and undeveloped land of promise which was to make the nation self-sustaining. Through the medium of these inland waterways and the steamboat packet, the raw materials so badly needed for an industrialized nation were being transported to market and manufactured articles in turn distributed to remote hamlets.

While many obstacles remained, by 1840 the steamboats on the Western Rivers had passed the experimental stage altogether. Marine architects, ably assisted by steamboat owners, who always had their eyes on more business and the demands of the traveling public, had not only increased the overall dimensions of the boats but had also improved their looks externally and added every known refinement internally. It was during this period that the larger packets were referred to as "floating palaces," which was no exaggeration.

It must be admitted, however, that many steamboat owners in this day and time were over zealous about the looks and size of their boats. They should have paid more attention to their operation. According to the official records of the Steamboat Inspection Service there were 1656 steamboats operating on the Western Rivers in 1849, just three years prior to the enactment by Congress of the more stringent laws regulating the inspection and operation of steam vessels. Of this number no less than 168 were destroyed by boiler explosions alone. This terrible record does not include many others which were destroyed by fire or collision. Assuming each of the 168 boats referred to were worth only $15,000.00, the property loss would amount to $2,520,-000.00.

If there is any comfort to be gained from such a record, it is in the fact that only one life was lost in every 55,714 passengers carried in 1849. Incidentally, there were approximately 8,000,000 paid passengers in that year. By way of comparison, in 1882 there was only one loss of life in each 1,726,827 passengers carried. In that year more than 20,000,000 people rode the packets. Any doubt concerning the splendid service rendered by the alert and highly competent Steamboat Inspectors after the Act of 1852, should be dispelled by this excellent achievement.

Many of the accidents were the direct result of carelessness on the part of captains and pilots. Fortunately, the Cumberland was not suited to some of the abuses frequently indulged in. The river was too narrow and tortuous for even the most daring pilots to engage in such dangerous pursuits. Nevertheless, there were races, most of them against "time," which always thrilled the public. For example, in May, 1843, the *Nashville* under command of Captain Joseph Miller, one of the best known and best educated men on the Cumberland, made the trip from New Orleans to Nashville in six days and thirteen hours. When this record was publicized, the second *Talleyrand,* a new boat owned by the famous Yeatman family and in command of Captain Jacob Hunter, set out to better it. In the same month she pulled into Nashville from New Orleans in five days and twenty-three hours. Stunned by this remarkable record, which clipped fourteen hours from its previous time, the *Nashville,* on May 23, 1843, made another record run of five days and twenty-two hours.

Still in a racing mood, Captain Miller, on June 12, 1843, once more astounded the people by piloting the *Nashville* from New Orleans to Nashville in five days and nineteen hours. This meant an average speed of 8.8 miles per hour up stream, including all regular listed stops, over a distance of 1,226 miles, a record which even in this day and time of modern boats and aids to navigation, is something to talk about.

Remarkable as the record of the *Nashville* may seem, it was only short lived. On May 29, 1849, the famous *America,* one of the most pretentious packets to ply the Cumberland, under the command of the veteran Captain Jesse Johnson, arrived in Nashville from New Orleans in the record-breaking time of five days and seventeen hours. As far as I know that record still stands after more than a century. The Nashville Daily American of May 30, 1849 credited the *America* with making the trip in five days, fifteen hours and thirty minutes, but two other papers, the Nashville True Whig and the Nashville Daily Union reported the time as first stated, so the preponderance of the written evidence is in favor of the longer time. The *America,* on this great run, averaged nine miles per hour, including all stops or in river parlance "landings." If we cast aside the danger involved and consider the fact that it was made in 1849, it is an achievement that may well rank side by side with that of the *Robert E. Lee* which beat the *Natchez* in a race between New Orleans and St. Louis twenty-eight years later in the phenomenal time of three days, eighteen hours and thirty minutes over a distance of 1,210 miles, for an average speed of 13.26 miles per hour. That famous race rocked the country from one end to the other and became the greatest sporting event of Reconstruction Days. Millions of dollars were bet on the outcome and the progress of the boats up the Mississippi was minutely reported by telegraph to all the principal cities. People in London and other European capitals also anxiously awaited the outcome.

The Nashville True Whig editorialized the record-breaking trip of the *America* as follows:

"This magnificent steamboat reached our wharf Tuesday morning last—having left New Orleans the preceding Wednesday evening, making the trip, including all stoppages (and there were two or three, caused by fogs embracing several hours) in five days and seventeen hours —'the quickest trip on record.' We suppose the *Bostona* did not pass the *America* 'under full headway' this trip. We have noticed in the Louisville papers a very remarkable fact connected with the history of steamboats built at Louisville. For instance take two boats built there by the same architect, after the same model and with the same power, and first one running in the Louisville trade and the other in some other trade, and the one running in the Louisville trade will be the fastest boat, even ceteris partibus, as we learn from the Louisville papers. This is a strange 'anomaly' and we hope our friends of the Louisville press will elucidate it. Perhaps steamboats, when they are sundered from the trade of their Louisville alma maters, take the 'studs' as fine race horses sometimes do, and 'won't run', or perhaps it is just an 'old habit' the Louisville boats and papers have got into of 'beating' all competition in their respective 'callings.'"

By way of explanation, the "Bostona" mentioned in the above editorial was a rival packet in the Louisville and New Orleans trade. It is of interest to note that the *America* was a new packet built in New Albany, Indiana (considered the same as Louisville to steamboat men), at a reported cost of $60,000.00 by the well-known owner and designer, M. D. F. H. Brooks, familiar to all Nashvillians of this period. She was of 1,600 gross tons and the Louisville Journal, in an excellent description, had this to say about her general appearances:

"This immense floating palace went over the falls yesterday. She is, both in magnificence and magnitude one of the finest boats that were ever launched on the bosom of the Ohio. Her hull was built by Jones and Hungary, and is 260 feet long on deck. Her breadth of beam is 49 feet and her depth of hold is 9½ feet. The extreme length of her cabin, which was built by Hart and Story, is 222 feet. They are very spacious, airy, light and comfortable. The gentleman's cabin has a range of 36 staterooms. The ladies' cabin contains twelve capacious staterooms, together with two beautiful bridal chambers. It is superbly furnished with a splendid carpet, rich curtains, superior linens and blankets from the large and well-known establishment of Messrs. Bent and Duvall. If any lady travellers are not happy in such a cabin, they must be squeamish indeed. In addition she has a ladies' dressing room and bath house, and a large pantry. She has five boilers, 52 inches in diameter and 32 feet long; 25 inch cylinders, 10 feet stroke; 32 foot wheel and 14 foot buckets."

While it must be admitted that the *America* was one of the finest of all packets engaged in the Nashville trade during this or any other period, there were many others which must not be overlooked. For example, there was the majestic *Marshal Ney*, in command of Captain John Carlisle, who was her principal owner. This steamer was just short of 265 feet long and had a gross tonnage of 1,000 tons. No more popular boat plied the river. Then there was the *North Carolina*, under Captain Gordon Runyan and Charles W. Anderson; the *Tennessee* under Captain H. T. Yeatman, which brought President-elect Zachary Taylor to Nashville on February 8, 1849, and the *Daniel Boone,* on which he left for Louisville. The *Belle of Clarksville*, owned principally by Canton, Kentucky interests, arrived in Nashville on February 14, 1843, under command of Captain W. Gerard. She was a very elegant boat for her size.

The *Paragon*, which sank ten miles above Eddyville on June 29, 1843, under command of Captain James Lee, was another well-known boat. There was a *Belle of Nashville* during this period, operated by Captain John Crouch and a *Burkesville* owned by Captain Tom Harmon. The *John Marshall* was a favorite packet for years between New Orleans and Nashville. She was owned and operated by Captain Thomas Gilbert. The *James Dick,* under Captain Thomas Bellsnyder, was an exceedingly large packet and did a thriving business in the Nashville trade. She was built in 1845 and was named for a well-known New Orleans businessman. On May 5, 1850 this fine packet burned at the Nashville wharf. Other fine boats were the *Smithland,* built at Smithland, and the *Old Hickory*, captained by James Lee; the *W. Newton* and *Susquehanna,* both captained at various times by James Miller; the *Charles Carroll,* a very large and powerful boat, owned by Captain S. D. Farnsworth, John J. Shield and Thomas F. Marshall of Nashville and R. F. Harrison of New Orleans; the *W. Tennessee* and the *Governor Jones,* both captained by M. D. F. H. Brooks; the *Harry Hill* one of the outstanding packets and one of the most popular, with Captain Thomas H. Newell, Robert Graham, Alexander Jenkins and William Crockett listed as owners; and the *Colorado,* which saw extended service on the Cumberland under Captain T. C. Reeder.

The only race between boats, as distinguished from races against "time," on the Cumberland, oddly enough did not take place until near the turn of the century. The *R. Dunbar,* a new Ryman Line packet under command of Captain Tom Ryman, Jr., raced the *Will J. Cummins,* an Independent Line packet under command of Captain W. S. Bowman from Nashville to Burnside in 1896. The *R. Dunbar* came off with the laurels, it being reported that Ryman ran the *Dunbar* with its safety valves weighted down with a keg of nails and fed the boiler fires with pine knots, bacon and lard until the smokestacks were red hot. He also mounted a small cannon on the deck of the *Dunbar* which was fired to clear the river and arouse interest. After this race, the *Dunbar* sported the famous "antlers," emblematic of such victories.

This race aroused considerable interest both in Nashville and other river centers. Those who knew the rivalry existing between the packets on the upper river and the intrepid Ryman were not astonished at this dangerous combat. The remarkable thing is that both boats came out unscathed. The aftermath of the race is interesting. Ryman had his license revoked for a relatively short time, but despite very rigid laws, was never prosecuted. Bowman's friends insisted that the *Dunbar* won the race because it skipped regular landings. It was necessary to make such stops to keep within the law. Members of the crew of the *Cummins* also insisted that Bowman did not carry an excessive head of steam.

Many of the catastrophes which took place in the packet business were unpardonable. Some captains and pilots, intent upon building up names for themselves in an effort to break speed records, took desperate chances. The same thing happened in the early days of railroading and again in the early days of automobiling. The conclusions to be drawn are simple. The operational end of the steamboat business suffered from a lack of trained personnel and rigid rules and regulations were too long in coming. The traffic had grown beyond expectations and naturally some irresponsible men had infiltrated into the business. They exacted a heavy toll.

Aside from racing, this period continued to represent an era of adventure in steamboating. There is a news item that Captain A. L. Davis, on December 17, 1846, took the *Caney Fork* up the Caney Fork River as far as Oakland, which was some fifteen miles overland from Sparta. This was by no means the first boat to ply the Caney Fork as will be presently shown. The *Madison* on March 16, 1839 also reached Columbia, Tennessee on the Duck River, and the *Union* went up the Elk River to Fayetteville on April 26, 1850. While the latter two trips were made by boats operating on the Tennessee, they are inserted here to show the spirit of adventure and the eagerness with which these earlier steamboat men sought new fields to conquer.

Life on the steamboat packet of this era was peculiarly characteristic of the people who were making America. It typified a young and struggling nation at the crossroads between industrial development and expansion of its frontiers. Both of these were essential to the life of our nation and the steamboat packet was the connecting link. It has been truthfully said there was something about a steamboat which exuded the spirit of frontier progress and yet gave an air of confidence in the future. Like the average American, they were self-reliant, powerful, adventuresome, rough and ready. Like the people of 1840, they often hit a snag or bumped a rock, but still they delivered their cargo. In short, they could and did "take it." Thus it often happened that passengers who did not like to hear the squealing of the hogs on board these boats, or the smell of cattle, tolerated such nuisances and accepted them as part and parcel of the spirit of progress.

There were 190 new boats that plied the Cumberland River in this decade. Their names are given in the Appendix. This represented an increase of fifty-nine boats over the period of 1830 to 1840. They came from all parts of the country and traveled all of the inland waterways. River traffic was not localized in any sense of the word.

In addition to the 190 new boats seen on the river for the first time, a careful check shows that of the 131 boats that came on the river from 1830 to 1840, fifty-four continued to ply the Cumberland. Adding the fifty-four old boats to the 190 new ones, we have a total of 244 boats plying the Cumberland during this ten-year period.

In 1841 there were forty-two boats that came to Nashville during the season, and of these thirty-six were making regular schedule runs. During the season of 1850, the number of boats had increased to fifty-two, and on March 30, 1850, according to the Nashville True Whig, there were no less than fourteen packets tied up at the wharf in Nashville. With one notable exception, which will be mentioned in a later chapter, this is the largest number at Nashville on a single day in a given season. These boats were the *Clipper, Cumberland No. 2, American Star, Sligo No. 2, James Dick, Harry Hill, Nashville, Colorado, Lady Madison, Josephine, Brooklyn, Jamestown, Tennessee* and *Dover.*

In order to estimate the seasonal tonnage handled by the packets coming up to Nashville alone during this period, it has been determined that the number of boats at the wharf during the average season was forty-five. Many of these made more than three trips per month during the season. Nevertheless that number of trips is accepted as a fair average. In order to be conservative it is assumed that the average packet carried minimum payload cargo of 300 tons per trip. If the average season lasted seven months, the forty-five boats at Nashville during each season carried 567,000 tons.

In the period 1830 to 1840 the tonnage for the average season at Nashville was 211,400 tons. Therefore there had been an increase of 355,600 tons, or better than two and one-half times that of the previous ten year period. This remarkable increase more than anything else proves that the steamboat business had entered its "golden era" on the Cumberland.

The above calculations, it should once more be emphasized, do not include the total tonnage for the entire river.

All of the towns on the lower river, relatively speaking, had enjoyed an increase in business similar to Nashville, while the upper river had blossomed into a veritable steamboat paradise, at times originating more freight than the packets could handle. Any estimate, therefore, of the total seasonal tonnage transported by steamboats on the Cumberland would be mere guesswork. The figure would certainly be very close to 750,000 tons of commercial freight and that estimate is still conservative when we consider the value of the river tonnage as estimated by an authority such as V. K. Stevenson of railroad fame whose figures will be referred to shortly.

Since the upper Cumberland during 1840–1850 became an unexcelled steamboat empire, it deserves further comment. This great region, as previously stated, was peculiarly adapted to steamboat transportation. In fact this method of transportation remained the only practical one available for a century. During this period there were still very few if any turnpikes capable of handling heavy loads or connecting the scattered towns and settlements with a market. From Carthage to Point Isabel many sections would have been completely isolated except for steamboats. It was one of the last frontiers in the Eastern United States, unexcelled in beauty and unadorned by any semblance of modern improvements. Rich in raw materials, peopled by the finest stock of pioneers and unperturbed by advancing civilization all around it, here was a prize that caused many steamboat captains to gasp for breath. Best of all, it was a prize which, when possessed, was destined to remain in the hands of the packet owners without any serious competition. Even the railroads could not conquer the deep ravines and endless hills of the Cumberland Plateau and find the hidden wealth along the banks of the river.

It was not until the arrival of the motor trucks and automobiles that packets gave up the ghost. These pesky inventions could wind and twist, wiggle and crawl over hitherto unconquered territory. Competition with them proved futile when modern highways were finally completed in the late nineteen twenties. But, before the packets left, they had established a record for continuous service covering one hundred years and had annually brought to market raw materials valued at millions of dollars which might otherwise have remained untouched. They had also transported to the upper river communities from Nashville and other industrial centers every conceivable commodity or product so essential to rural life.

The robust business directly resulting from the upper Cumberland packet trade was a rich blessing to Nashville. With her commerce now opened in every direction and her trade area increased and extended by a water highway 325 miles long, Nashville was ready to make her bid for industrial fame, thereby adding another link in the chain of her many virtues.

The first town of importance above Nashville was Gallatin, served by a landing which from the early days of steamboats could always be counted on for an abundance of river freight. Gallatin was named for Albert Gallatin, Secretary of the Treasury. It was made the seat of Sumner County in 1804, the second county erected in Middle Tennessee and named for General Jethro Sumner of Revolutionary War fame. Thomas Sharp Spencer, known as "Big Foot" Spencer on account of his huge feet which scared many an Indian into believing a giant was at large, had planted corn in Sumner County as early as 1778. The first settlement was made at Bledsoe's Lick, later called Castalian Springs, by Colonel Isaac Bledsoe and his brother Colonel Anthony Bledsoe and their families in 1779, a year before Nashville was founded. Just above Gallatin on the river was another well-known landing, first called "Ca Ira," later called Cairo. It was first designated as the county seat in 1796 but the law was later repealed.

Long before the advent of steamboats, the early settlers of Gallatin and Sumner County were shipping products out by keel boat and barge. Gallatin served a very large trade area and was located in an excellent agricultural section. It contributed large cargoes of corn and tobacco to the Cumberland packets. Sumner County boasted of a paper mill and large cargoes of its output were also transported by the packets to Nashville.

The next large town above Gallatin was Lebanon, served by a landing at Hunter's Point, six miles north of the town. Lebanon was erected in 1802, three years after Wilson County, of which it became the county seat. The county was named for Major David Wilson, a North Carolinian who was speaker of the first Territorial Assembly. The first settlement in the county was made at Drake's Lick on the Cumberland River in 1797 by John Foster and William McClain. So long as the packets plied the river, the landing at Hunter's Point was an important stop. In addition to the usual agricultural products and barter, boats were particularly favored with large shipments of hogs and cedar lumber.

Some twenty miles above Hunter's Point was a landing for Hartsville, first settled in 1799. It became the seat of Trousdale County, erected in 1870 and named for Governor William Trousdale of Tennessee. Hartsville is mentioned time after time in the early days of steamboatin'. Up until 1830 it was usually the last landing touched by the average packet plying the upper river. The most notable cargo taken on by steamboats at Hartsville was burley tobacco. In later years it contributed its share of familiar upper river cargo.

Carthage, located on the right bank of the river slightly below and across from the mouth of the Caney Fork, largest tributary of the Cumberland, was first settled by Colonel William Walton about 1787. Walton blazed the famous trail named for him from Kingston in East Tennessee across the mountains to the Caney Fork. From this point it followed the general course of the Cumberland to Nashville. Smith County, of which Carthage was made the county seat, was erected in 1799 and was named for General Daniel Smith, Secretary of the Southwest Territory and United States Senator from Tennessee, succeeding Andrew Jackson. Carthage was established in 1804.

In addition to Walton, some of the first settlers were Daniel Burford, Richard Alexander, Peter Turney, grandfather of Governor Peter Turney, William Saunders, Tillman Dixon, founder of Dixon Springs settlement, Micajah Duke, William McDonald, William Goodall (there is still a Goodall's Island in the Cumberland which he owned), Armistead Flippen, James Hodges, George T. Wright, Arthur S. Hogan and Samuel M. Fite.

The name or exact date of the first steamboat to reach Carthage is unknown. However, as indicated by listings in old newspapers, we know that by the season of 1829 a few packets had gone up the river that far. Prior to that year barges and flatboats had moved down the Cumberland from both Carthage and points on the Caney Fork. By 1833 Carthage was a full-fledged river town, and a favorite haven for packets seeking more adventuresome trips farther up the Cumberland.

Since Carthage was on the Walton Road, near the Caney Fork, and also an ideal stop-over spot for steamboats, it early gained strategic importance in the upper river packet business. As the years rolled by, the Caney Fork River contributed its part to the growth and prestige of steamboat traffic. This tributary, however, was afflicted with a shallow channel depth.

The first steamboat of record to ply the Caney Fork was the *Harry Hill*. The timber for her hull had been hewed out by Sam Caplinger and William Christian at Caplinger's Mill on South Fork near Carthage in 1832. The hull was floated to Nashville where machinery was installed. She then returned to Carthage in the same year and made her historic trip up Caney Fork on a huge tide to Sligo Landing, fifteen miles by land from Sparta. In due course she became a leading packet on the Cumberland.

While Carthage was always rated a good river town, it shone brightest in the field of politics. It has cradled many distinguished judges, congressmen, governors, soldiers and statesmen. Even today, that record is kept intact. Cordell Hull, world statesman and America's most beloved Secretary of State, lived there for a number of years and it was still home to him when he came to Tennessee. Incidentally, Cordell Hull's interest in the river, as will be pointed out later, was not that of a bystander. He came from a family long identified with the timber and rafting industry on the Cumberland.

Carthage was in the center of several other busy landings in that area. Dixon Springs, 23 miles, and Rome, 15 miles below Carthage, as well as West Point, 10 miles, and Granville, 24 miles above, were all exceedingly well-located in the heart of rich river-bottom land, and were settled by outstanding pioneer families. Few packets passed up these landings.

Gainesboro, about fifty miles above Carthage, was the next town up the river, and was located near the mouth of Roaring River, a nonnavigable tributary of the Cumberland. It was named in honor of General Edmund Pendleton Gaines of Revolutionary War fame and was established in 1817, as the seat of Jackson County, which was erected in 1801 and named for President Jackson, then serving the state as a judge of the Superior Court of Law and Equity. Years before Gainesboro was established, a frontier fort had been built on the Cumberland several miles by river between the future town site and above what is now called Upper Holliman Island. It was named Fort Blount in honor of Governor William Blount.

Gainesboro, while never a large town, was a prosperous one. It served an extensive trade area covering several adjoining counties which were not fortunate enough to be located on the river. The trade area served by Gainesboro is significant and worth emphasizing. Many of the towns and landings on the upper Cumberland were very small places and yet, like Gainesboro, they had a very large packet business resulting from an extensive trade area. This explains why the steamboats did such a thriving business in a section which had very few large towns actually located on the river. Fully two-thirds of the freight going and coming at the landings did not originate or terminate at them. The real value of a landing was the territory it served and not its size, a point which should be remembered in any discussion of the upper river.

Twenty-three miles above Gainesboro is Celina, seat of Clay County. The scenes along the river between the two towns are considered by many the most beautiful on the Cumberland. There are high bluffs, wooded hills, low river bottom land, deep pools, sand and gravel bars, island chutes and an endless number of little streams to gaze upon. In this period, there was still plenty of game to be seen along the banks. In more modern times this region produced several good oil wells. The oil boom which followed did not last very long and very little if any of the oil found its way to traffic on the river.

Celina is located at the mouth of the Obey River, one of the largest navigable tributaries of the Cumberland. It sits somewhat back from the junction of the two streams and was named for the daughter of Moses Fisk, an outstanding early educator of Tennessee who founded Fisk Female Academy at Hilham in 1806. Clay county was named for Henry Clay and was not created until 1870. Besides Celina, the county had two other prosperous steamboat landings, Butler's Landing and Bennett's Ferry.

Celina was in the heart of the hardwood timber belt which later on contributed so much to the wealth of Tennessee and the prosperity of steamboats on the Cumberland. This fact has led some to minimize the nature and extent of other and earlier products shipped out on the packets. Celina at a very early date contributed an enormous volume of typical up-river cargo to the steamboats, excelling in hogs, corn, poultry, eggs, hides, furs, molasses and meats. It also served generally as the river landing for Jamestown, county seat of Fentress County, and Byrdstown, County seat of Pickett County, a fact which greatly augmented its river trade.

The Obey River, which I shall mention again in connection with the lumber industry, was of no great importance as far as river tonnage was concerned during this decade. The possibilities for packet trade were recognized, but owners were chiefly interested in conquering the upper Cumberland. Barges and rafts were already moving out of Obey and no doubt some fearless pilot during this era turned his boat up the stream to see what it looked like. Perhaps one of these days this belief may be verified by another student of the river. If Obey had not been "stirred up" by a packet by 1840, it was unique not only among the rivers of Tennessee, but among those throughout the eastern United States.

In 1840, there were twelve principal river landings and towns on the upper Cumberland in the State of Kentucky. These were in order, going up-stream, Martinsburg, Mc-Millin's Landing, Black's Ferry, Cloyd's Landing, Burkesville, Bakerton, Albany Landing, Creelsboro, Rowena (Wild Goose), Mill Springs, Waitsboro and Point Isabel.

Martinsburg, in Monroe County, Kentucky, was just budding into a good river landing and was the first sizeable village across the Tennessee line. McMillin's Landing, also in Monroe County, is of interest to all Tennesseans because it bears the family name of Governor Benton McMillin, who came from this part of Kentucky before migrating down the Cumberland, to become one of the best beloved citizens of Smith County and his adopted State. He was an ardent friend of the river, as will be brought out later on. McMillin's Landing became one of the best on the upper Cumberland. It frequently surpassed all others, especially in tobacco, hogs and corn. Steamboats coming up from Nashville always "got shed" of an abundance of freight at McMillin's. Black's Ferry, last of the larger landings in Monroe County, served Tompkinsville, county seat of that county, and did a flourishing business.

Cloyd's Landing was a favorite stopping point for the packets and remained so until the steamboats left the river. Its most successful years came after the War Between the States. Bakerton, on the other hand, while a very small place, was an excellent landing during the early days of steamboatin', but lost prestige after the War and never recovered.

Burkesville, seventeen miles above Cloyd's, was incorporated in 1810 as the seat of Cumberland County and was named for Samuel Burke, an early settler and prosperous tavern keeper. At a very early date it became one of the leading river landings on the upper Cumberland, being located in the heart of the Kentucky timber belt and in a good farming section. A large trade area also helped Burkesville grow and prosper. In 1834 citizens built the *Burkesville,* which became a favorite steamboat in the upper river trade. Burkesville for more than a century annually shipped out a never-ending tonnage of upper river cargo. This small town is of peculiar interest to Nashvillians. It was the original home of Colonel Joel Cheek of Maxwell House Coffee fame. He was the son of Dr. James H. Cheek, long time respected citizen of Burkesville, and made his first trip to Nashville on a steamboat.

Albany Landing, which served Albany, county seat of Clinton County, Kentucky, at a very early date assumed a position, along with Burkesville and Point Isabel, as one of the "big three" in steamboat traffic on the upper reaches of the Cumberland. Albany, named for Albany, New York, was one of the largest as well as one of the oldest towns in southeastern Kentucky, having been established as a settlement in 1790. Like most other neighboring villages, what few roads ran to Albany were unsuitable for commercial transportation and steamboats were not only the favorite but the only means of satisfactory transportation.

The principal cargoes shipped from Albany were similar to those previously mentioned. In later years and particularly after the first railroad reached Point Isabel, sizeable quantities of freight which normally flowed from Albany Landing to Nashville were given to the local boats operating in the area. Nevertheless Albany, year in and year out, was considered one of the best steamboat towns on the river from the standpoint of the Nashville packets.

Twelve miles above Albany Landing was the little town of Creelsboro. Rowena, near the famous Wild Goose Shoals, was twelve miles further up the river. It appears from contemporary newspaper notices and announcements that Creelsboro was a very prominent river landing during this era. Almost every boat received a large cargo there. Rowena was near the western terminus of the coal belt in southeastern Kentucky and also in the heart of the virgin hardwood timber belt. Mill Springs, the next small hamlet, was located in Wayne County, Kentucky, thirty-seven miles above Rowena and reached its greatest prominence during the War Between the States. General Zollicoffer, beloved Nashvillian as hereafter noted, was killed near there while leading Confederate forces in one of the earliest and bloodiest battles of that war. Waitesboro, eleven miles above Mill Springs, was the last landing before reaching the head of navigation on the river. While all of these four towns in 1835 were hardly more than settlements, they contributed a surprising amount of cargo to the early packets and in later years helped maintain the two-way pay load freight so essential to the steamboat industry. In return for raw materials they received manufactured goods from Nashville in great volume.

Point Isabel, the last and by far the most important town on the Cumberland in Southeastern Kentucky, was the leader in the upper Cumberland packet business. It frequently enters the picture and will be referred to as the occasion demands. Point Isabel was one of the oldest settlements on the Cumberland and one of the most beautifully located. According to modern survey it is 325 miles by river from Nashville and is situated in Pulaski County, Kentucky, on a high bluff overlooking the Cumberland at the junction of the Big South Fork. Point Isabel during the War Between the States became the headquarters of General Ambrose Everett Burnside of the Federal Army and changed its name to Burnside in his honor.

Turning our attention once more to the lower river, one of the more interesting features of this period was a proposed lock and dam on the Cumberland River three miles above Nashville. The chief purpose of the project, according to the Nashville Whig of November 26, 1842, was to create water power for manufacturing purposes and slack water during the dry season. The cost was not to exceed $150,000.00. Albert Stein, a well-known engineer, was to be in charge of the work. A canal leading from the dam was to be constructed to Nashville, along which industries could be located. It was emphasized that the dam would not interfere with navigation. This venture seems to have ended as quickly as it started. Sixty-three years were to pass before any lock and dam was erected on the Cumberland. By that time the steamboat business was definitely on the decline.

During this decade most of the larger packet lines had succeeded in working out reciprocal agreements with connecting lines thereby inaugurating the first through or trunk line transportation system for the general good of the public. Shippers in this way could get through bills of lading from point of origin to point of destination even though several lines handled the freight. In like manner passengers could obtain through tickets, were permitted stopovers and had the choice of several packet lines. It was distinctly a day of readjustment. Old methods, many of which were slipshod and tactless, were dispensed with. Perhaps no other ten year period in the history of the river was marked by a more earnest effort to curry favor with the shippers and traveling public.

Practically every large city and town on the river increased and improved their wharves and terminal facilities. Commodious wharf boats were erected and wharf masters employed. Packet lines vied with each other in expediting the loading and unloading of both passengers and freight. Drays and busses met the boats which were beginning not only to publish schedules but also to maintain them with regularity.

By 1845, passengers with ease and comfort could go from Nashville to New Orleans and back in fifteen days. They could make a restful round trip to St. Louis or Memphis in ten days and to Pittsburgh in twelve. The navigable course of the Cumberland from Smithland to Point Isabel could be covered on a good tide in six days with a stopover for one night in Nashville.

There were many entertaining events arranged for the passengers, such as orchestra recitals, dances and social games. The most interesting interludes were the frequent landings, when all would line the decks to exchange pleasantries with the throngs along the bank, or watch the husky roustabouts amid the shouts of clerks, load and unload various types of cargo. For those on board who felt the urge of strong drink, a convenient bar was provided with every popular brand of whiskey and wine. Card games consumed the time of many male passengers, some of whom found out to their sorrow that the benign looking "gentleman" who had won the stakes was a gambling shark plying his trade as regularly as the packet.

Another event of absorbing interest to all of the people of Tennessee and one which was to be carefully watched by the steamboat interests, was the Act of the Legislature of December 11, 1845, authorizing the construction of a railroad between Nashville and Chattanooga, which was known later on to all Tennesseeans as the "Nashville, Chattanooga and St. Louis Railroad." Engineering parties were put in the field for survey purposes as early as 1847. The first rails of the railroad were laid in South Nashville in 1848 and were brought to the city by steamboats.

When the Nashville & Chattanooga Railroad was chartered it was not expected to compete with the Cumberland River packets. On the contrary, the chief talking point for the building of the road centered around the point that the advent of the road into Nashville would greatly increase river business by opening up traffic to the southeastern states and the Atlantic seaboard. Nashville, as the natural river and rail terminus and feeder would ultimately be the largest city in the South.

Contrary therefore to general and popular belief, when the first railroad was built into Nashville there was no resentment on the part of the steamboat owners against it.

Most all river men believed it would increase business. It was not until many years later that matters so changed that a "live or die" competition developed between the two systems of transportation.

A very noted Civil Engineer, John Edgar Thompson, made the first survey of the railroad between Nashville and Chattanooga and his report was submitted to the Commissioners of that railroad in February, 1847. This is truly one of the most interesting documents of transportation history in the State of Tennessee. Thompson served as Chief Engineer of the Pennsylvania Railroad, and later became its President. The following paragraph from Thompson's report is a concise statement of the aims and aspirations of the proposed railroad.

"That there will be a connection between the South Atlantic Coast and the great West at an early period, no one, acquainted with the extent and importance of the interests to be beneficially affected by it, can for a moment doubt;—and that the route of your road is the most advantageous for such a communication, is equally clear. Through the Cumberland it brings the mouth of the Ohio, —the heart of the West,—more than 700 miles nearer the Atlantic, than by any of the present avenues of commerce, an advantage which must claim for the line, a large share of the travel and transportation of the products, and consumption of the Mississippi Valley. It would seem unnecessary, however, to go beyond the country, which now makes Nashville its market, to find ample business, to justify the construction of this railroad— opening as it does to Middle Tennessee, a direct route to consumers of her present products, distributing them through Alabama, Georgia, Florida and Carolina, by means of the network of railroads, diverging from Atlanta,—the Atlantic end of the Georgia State railroads,— leaving out of view the foreign market for Indian Corn, her great staple, which will find at Charleston and Savannah, a cheap and ready transit to Europe."

V. K. Stevenson of Nashville was perhaps the most ardent advocate of the Nashville and Chattanooga Railroad. One of the most forceful advocates of the railroad in South Carolina was John C. Calhoun. Stevenson, who was later to become the first President of the Nashville and Chattanooga, realizing the public would want statistics before investing money, proposed to Calhoun that he obtain statistical information regarding the amount of freight expected on the southern end of this railroad line. Stevenson would do the same for freight that could be counted on at Nashville. Statistics were submitted by Stevenson to Calhoun, in a letter dated December 12, 1845. The historical and factual value of this letter is tremendous, for it definitely proves that steamboat traffic on the Cumberland River created one of the chief selling points for the building of this railroad. The whole plan revolved around the accomplishment of the steamboat business in Nashville, and by a mutuality of interest, it was anticipated that traffic on the river would be greatly increased, which would inure to the benefit of the railroad. There appeared to be no idea of competition between the infant railroad and the steamboats.

The figures which Stevenson submitted were obtained by the most reliable sources available at the time. It may be assumed they are accurate and represent for the first time a correct appraisal of the enormous steamboat traffic on the Cumberland River. Through these figures obtained from an independent source, we have strong reason to believe that at the close of 1846, $12,642,576.00 worth of freight annually passed through Nashville. Of this amount, it was estimated that one-half was hauled from Nashville and one-sixth from Clarksville by boat, or two-thirds of all the freight, valued at $8,428,384.00. The other one-third balance was hauled and driven to the south in wagons and other vehicles. According to Stevenson, the following freight went out on the Cumberland River alone, namely: 30,000 hogsheads tobacco, $1,500,000.00; 50,000 bales cotton, $1,666,666.00; 500,000 sacks corn, $400,000.00; 350,000 hogs, $1,995,000.00; 21,000 cattle, $420,000.00; 30,000 horses and mules, $1,820,000.00.

Concerning the following freight, the letter said: "the largest part was shipped on the Cumberland River,":—Cotton goods, $200,000.00; Cotton seed and products, $400,-000.00; Wagons and carriages, $116,000.00; Cedar and lumber, $166,000.00; Iron, $3,075,000.00. In arriving at the above figures respecting iron Stevenson mentions that in the area to be served by the railroads, there were twenty-one blast furnaces, eleven forges and three rolling mills, one of which produced iron valued at $800,000.00 annually.

The balance of the freight was represented by the following commodities:—600 tons hemp, $48,000.00; Feathers, $161,000.00; Wool, $187,000.00; Whiskey, $120,-000.00; Cut stone, etc., $360,000.00; also poultry, beeswax, ginseng, flax seed, dried fruit, peas and beans, brandy, furs, saddles, harness, machines, cotton gins, etc.

The ever careful and analytical Stevenson further significantly pointed out that New York State, with a population of 2,626,000 produced agricultural products valued at $57,-685,400.00; that Ohio, with a population of 1,760,000, valued its agricultural products at $57,899,394.00; and Tennessee with only 910,000 population, produced agricultural products valued at $57,551,820.00.

He further pointed out that the Cumberland River is south of the freezing weather, which annually afflicted the steamboat business on the Ohio and Upper Mississippi Rivers, and for this very pertinent reason, the season on the river was longer, and Nashville might well become a distribution point for a vast amount of freight supplying the lower Mississippi River as far as New Orleans. Stevenson concluded his report as follows:—

"With this slack water and our railroad, the Charleston and Savannah, finished, our system of internal improvements would be complete; so our river is south of the point where water freezes hard enough to impede navigation; it also empties into the Ohio below that point, which now give us great advantages over our more northern neighbors, when other rivers are frozen over, and ours open, in supplying New Orleans at full prices." (Underscoring is that of the author.)

It was during this ten-year period that Clarksville became the center of the dark-fired tobacco industry on the lower river. Of the 30,000 hogsheads of tobacco mentioned by Stevenson, fully 20,000 were shipped to New Orleans from this thriving and growing city. The balance of the tobacco was burley grown on the upper Cumberland from points as high up as Burkesville, Kentucky. It also went to New Orleans.

The manufacture of iron which had reached enormous proportions, deserves further mention. All of this iron was being manufactured on the lower Cumberland. In 1841, Messrs. Van Leer and Hillman were making excellent iron at the Empire Furnace just above the Tennessee line in Kentucky on the Cumberland. In 1844, Dan Hillman and Dr. Samuel Watson erected the Center Furnace in the same area and put it in blast. During this same year Hillman decided to convert all of the furnaces into making charcoal bar iron. This foresight and decision were soon to yield rich dividends. In the meantime, Nashville, as well as Clarksville, was doing a very large rolling mill business. In 1845, Hillman and VanLeer, together with Dr. Watson and B. M. Runyan, a well-known steamboat man, and C. E. Hillman, bought out the Tennessee Rolling Mills at Nashville, which they immediately dismantled and placed on barges and floated down the Cumberland to Lyon County, Kentucky. For more than ten years, these mills were successfully operated, and their products distributed in large retail stores under the Hillman name at Nashville and Clarksville. These products also reached the larger cities on the Mississippi and Ohio. The iron manufactured by these mills was peculiarly suited for boiler plates.

The Tennessee Rolling Mills were not the only manufacturers of iron on the lower Cumberland. There were twenty other furnaces in actual operation, the principal one in Tennessee being located at Cumberland Furnace. Practically every steamboat during this period plying the Cumberland River could boast that some of its cargo consisted of the "famous" Tennessee iron and kindred products, such as nails, horse shoes, plows and spikes.

Through the medium of the iron industry, aided and assisted by the steamboats, Nashville became an outstanding hardware center. Steamboats were carrying those vital materials to rural sections so that citizens could build their homes and plow their fields, and in turn brought back agricultural products needed for the industrial life of the city.

The Sycamore Mills on the lower Cumberland were continuing to contribute in no small measure to the steamboat business. In 1844, Dr. Samuel Watson bought an interest in them and towards the close of 1850, or shortly thereafter, they were operated under the name of Cheatham-Watson & Company. In addition to making a very fine powder, they were gaining a wide reputation in the manufacture of cotton goods and cloth.

Work on the State Capitol began on January 1, 1845, which emphasized the importance of Nashville as the seat of our State Government. It also gave the city a certain amount of political "flare."

One of the worst floods that ever occurred on the Cumberland River took place in March, 1847, when the river rose to a height of 54.9 feet. This flood was near its crest for a full week, the weather was unusually cold and it worked a tremendous hardship throughout the city and adjacent territory. A steamboat crossed the Gallatin Pike at the foot of the bridge in what is now known as East Nashville. The water at the corner of Broad and Market Streets was six feet high, and two steamboats were tied up near the warehouse of Yeatman and Armistead in that general locality.

The previous highest floods recorded in the history of the Cumberland were in 1806 when the river rose to a height of 54 feet, and in 1826 when it rose to a height of 52.1 feet. All of this took place, of course, before the present erection of locks and dams and when our roads had not been elevated above the flood stage of the river. These three floods compare favorably with the great flood of 1927, when the Cumberland rose to an all-time high of 56.2 feet. It is doubtful whether the flood of 1927 did any more damage than the floods of 1847, 1826 and 1806.

In speaking of some of the hardships encountered by steamboat men, such as floods, freezes which have occurred on the Cumberland River from time to time should not be overlooked. The worst freeze took place in 1832, when wagons and teams drove across the river for a week. As most steamboat men will agree, a freeze in the river is far more dangerous than a flood, although not so unpleasant to the public in general. Other data concerning floods and freezes in the river are mentioned in the Appendix.

During most of this period, however, there was an atmosphere of happiness and prosperity not only in Nashville, but throughout the length and breadth of the Cumberland Valley. The six hotels operating in Nashville received excellent patronage from travelers all over the country, most of whom arrived on packets. Almost every week there was a fancy dress ball or a banquet in honor of some distinguished visitor. There were concerts and recitals. The "Nashville Theatre" was in full swing and such dramas and tragedies as "The Irish Lion," "Married Rake," and "The Hole in the Wall" were holding audiences spellbound. Soon Jenny Lind was to arrive in Nashville on a steamboat, the *W. Newton,* and thrill a big audience with her first concert in the city.

After the theatre, or on a balmy summer day, young men and their ladies sought out their favorite meeting place and partook of the "newly discovered and delectable soda-water, richly flavored with either chocolate or vanilla, to which is added a spoonful of the choicest ice cream—all for the price of five cents." Thus was ushered in another American institution, the "chocolate ice cream soda," which unlike steamboatin' on the Cumberland, was to meet and defeat every competitor.

But, while prosperity prevailed for most of this period, catastrophe struck near the end of it and greatly upset steamboat and all other kinds of business. In July 1850, one of the worst cholera epidemics in the history of the State spread its wings of death over Tennessee. There were 911 deaths resulting from the disease in Nashville alone, bringing the percentage of deaths among the inhabitants to an all-time high of 7.9%, being one for every 12.6 inhabitants of the city. Steamboat traffic, however, did not suffer to the extent of other businesses, because the season had just about ended.

President James K. Polk, who thoroughly enjoyed riding on steamboats, left Nashville on February 11, 1845, on the steamboat *China* en route to his inauguration in Washington. In leaving by steamboat on this memorable occasion, he followed a precedent set by his friend, General Andrew Jackson.

Nashville remained a city of great political importance. President Jackson died in 1845. For nearly thirty years he had brought uninterrupted national political importance to the City and State. President Polk was to carry on this task for several years more. Nashville's educational and religious institutions were providing a marked degree of culture and refinement. Steamboatin' had just about reached the peak of its success and popularity.

CHAPTER FOUR

Ugly Clouds and a Devil on Wheels

Period 1850–1860

During this fascinating period the golden age of steamboatin' grew to full maturity and swept over the Western Rivers in a blaze of glory. Never before had there been anything like it in the history of transportation. Even the growing rumblings of an ugly war failed to dent the steamboat business. No previous decade could match and very few if any in the future could surpass the number of packets plying the rivers, their registered tonnage or the tonnage transported.

The Cumberland, already considered one of the major water highways of America, found itself crowded with packets from every port. There were big ones and little ones, stern-wheelers and side-wheelers, tramp boats and tow-boats, coal barges, lighters and rafts. Wharves were not large enough to accommodate the increase in traffic.

The growth of the packet business on the Cumberland is best illustrated by the increase in number of new boats which came on the river up to Nashville. There were 281 such boats which have been positively identified and which are listed in the Appendix along with other data. To these boats should be added sixty packets of the last decade which continued to ply the river. It results that 341 different packets are known to have landed at Nashville during this decade. Such a phenomenal record was so astounding that it raised serious doubts. It has been checked and double checked, however, and its accuracy has been verified. Only the years 1862–1864 exceeded this record, but they were abnormal years due to the War. While amazing, this record does not do the river justice since it omits scores of packets that plied the river, principally the lower part, and did not come up to Nashville.

If a guess might be made as to the total number of different boats which plied the entire river from 1850 to 1860, 400 would not be far wrong.

With the beginning of this period the registered steamboat tonnage on all the inland rivers was 126,278 tons whereas that of United States ships on the Great Lakes and the Atlantic Ocean combined was only 93,716 tons. The annual registered tonnage of steamboats that took out their papers in Nashville and called Nashville their "home port" was the highest recorded and compared favorably with that of Louisville and other large Ohio ports. The value of the 341 boats on the river was $5,115,000.00, assuming each was worth the small sum of $15,000.00.

There were thirteen separate packet lines operating in Nashville in 1854, employing twenty-two packets. That in itself constitutes some kind of record for a city which had a population of less than 20,000 people. No accurate record can be found of the number of passengers using these lines. Passenger traffic was considered one of the most lucrative parts of the steamboat business. People loved to travel on their favorite boats, selected chiefly on account of a kindly captain or other officer. The fare remained reasonable, the cuisine as good as the best and the staterooms commodious and elegant. Passenger traffic on the river above Nashville was particularly good in this and each succeeding period. There was still no other satisfactory transportation open to the people above Carthage.

One Nashville squib, commenting on the increase in travel, among other things said—"There are so many boats at the wharf that passengers get confused. All should be sure to get on the right boat. The other day a sober gentleman went to sleep thinking he had taken a packet for

Smithland. Next morning while about to partake of a hearty breakfast, he discovered he was riding a packet bound for Burkesville. Unable to eat, the gentleman explained the mistake would lose him several hundred dollars in a business venture, the nature of which was not stated."

This amusing but no doubt truthful incident may be hard to understand in this day and time when the Nashville wharf is shorn of packets. At the time it was written, there were possibly ten or twelve of the larger packets at the wharf and the scene was one calculated to confuse even a "sober" gentleman. The modern metropolitan railroad station has some slight resemblance, but could not hold a candle to a busy wharf in 1860,—with its boats, freight piles, drays, busses, gangplanks, smoke, whistles, bells, lines, sweating roustabouts, squealing hogs, bleating sheep, moaning cattle, cursing mates and clerks.

Quite a few of the packets were built in Nashville, notably the *Rock City, Hartsville* and *Luella,* all of which were among the smaller of the lot. Most were built and launched along the Ohio, principally Jeffersonville, Cincinnati and Pittsburgh, where the largest shipyards were busy year in and year out and where boilers, engines and other materials were more accessible.

If a present day Hollywood publicity agent had seen the more palatial packets on the Cumberland around 1855, he would have described them as "marvelous, stupendous and colossal—the most superb yet envisioned by the American public." Yet, this description was not an exaggeration. This is saying a good deal and yet with one or two exceptions, when taken singly or as a group, there had never been any finer packets on the Cumberland. Any one of the larger boats, such as the *Nashville, H. R. W. Hill, James Johnson* or *Red Rover,* was especially outstanding.

Suppose we take a longer glance at some of the more prominent packets. The *Nashville* of this period was built in 1849, was of 500 tons burden and ran regularly between Nashville and New Orleans. Captain Tom Bellsnyder was her master and he was almost as famous as his boat. The *Nashville* was nearly 200 feet long, could accommodate 100 cabin passengers with ease and was noted for her refinements and excellent hospitality. We know from old newspapers that "she was well decorated, but not gaudy, trim but not fragile, a tribute to the city whose name she bore." The new edition of the *Clarksville*, under command of the intrepid and ever popular Captain Jacob Hunter, was 192 feet long, neat and agile, with elegant promenade and a sheer that made her the delight of any steamboat man. She was referred to by one glib writer as the "daisiest boat on the river." Her regular run was to New Orleans.

One of the largest packets was the *Humboldt*, built in 1855, by Captain William Strong, John D. Taylor, William Wyatt, Matt T. Martin and Captain Calvin G. Cabler. All of these men were well known in Nashville. Strong and Cabler were outstanding steamboat operators for years. The *Humboldt* was 512 tons gross, "a sight to behold, powerfully and superbly built, manned by officers who were courteous and popular." She was a distinct addition to the Cumberland. Disaster struck the *Humboldt* in 1857, when she sank in the Mississippi near Ozark Island below Memphis. The size and value of this fine packet may be surmised by the loss sustained, her owners estimating it at $250,000.00, which included 750 tons of freight. Seventeen slaves and several other lives were lost in this horrible disaster.

Despite the loss of the *Humboldt*, her old owners and a new partner, Frank Shackleford, almost immediately built the new *Red Rover* to take her place. This packet like its predecessors became a favorite. She measured 249 feet 6 inches, had a beam of 37 feet 4 inches, and a depth of seven feet. Her gross tonnage was 625 tons. She ranked as one of the very best and did a tremendous business.

Then there were the *James Johnson* and *James Wood*, two palatial side wheelers. The *Johnson* was 220 feet overall, and the *Woods* slightly longer. Captain Jesse Johnson, whose name was known wherever steamboat men gathered, H. P.

Shaw, R. L. Wheatley and A. J. Cole owned the *Johnson.* Captain William Boyd, A. Hamilton and William A. Longworth built and owned the *Woods.*

From the standpoint of size and capacity one of the largest packets to ply the Cumberland was the *Atlantic*—captained by E. D. Farnsworth who later became a steamboat Inspector at Nashville. This great boat measured 265 feet in length, thirty-six feet across the beam and had a depth of nine feet. Some estimate of her size can be obtained for those who cast an eye at the Cumberland by imagining the *Atlantic* straddling the river under the Sparkman Street Bridge with her bow snubbed to one pier and her stern made fast to the other. In this position she would have a clearance of only thirty-five feet between the piers. The *Atlantic* was capable of carrying 1200 tons of freight and for obvious reasons did not ply the Cumberland except on very high stages of water.

Many other boats could be mentioned in more minute detail, but there must be an end to all good things. The *B. M. Runyan*, for example, owned by Captain James Miller, George Stacker of Clarksville, and B. M. Runyan of St. Louis, cost $40,000.00 and was over 230 feet in length; the new *Talleyrand*, more beautiful than ever, measured 234 feet long and was owned by Benjamin Duffield and N. D. Elliot; the *Ella*, not so large but extremely popular, was commanded by James Loring; the *H. R. W. Hill*, captained by Thomas Newell and as fine as they made them, was 600 tons burden and was owned by Thos. Hamilton of Nashville and James Dyas of New Orleans; the *John P. Tweed* was owned by Captain R. L. Dismukes, J. H. Couch and J. W. Lovell, who were active in the packet business for nearly fifty years; the *E. Howard*, one of the largest, was captained by R. Y. Northern; the *C. E. Hillman* was a side-wheeler which was named for one of the three Hillman brothers; the *Joseph Savage*, built at Paducah, was owned by Captain Owen Davis, James Davis and Jonas Martin and had a burden of nearly 500 tons; the *Scotland* came out in 1855 and ran the river for many years and was exceedingly popular.

The *Minnetonka,* under command of Captain John Dashiel, while smaller, was a splendid packet and had a big following. The *Charter,* owned by Captain Elijah Carroll and James Carroll and the *Blanche Lewis,* captained by James Lee, were other packets which were outstanding despite their comparatively small size of 200 tons.

The Cumberland had not only carved a niche for itself among the Western Rivers because of the number of packets plying its waters, but also because of the many able and competent owners and licensed officers in charge of them.

In addition to those whose names I have already mentioned there were many others. For example, Owen W. Davis, Wiley Sims, Joseph Ambrose, J. V. Scyster, A. L. Davis, W. T. Yeatman, R. B. Baugh, W. C. Henegar, Jesse Joiner, J. V. Throop, John B. Davis, Charles Ryman, James Irwin, William Dix, Sam Milliken, J. C. Leake, L. T. Armstrong, W. J. Harmon, Charles & John Ryneman, and a host of others. Practically every old newspaper during this period at some time or another contains a reference to their marked ability, courtesy and friendliness.

In 1852, Congress enacted drastic laws, protecting the safety of both passengers and cargo. This was the beginning of the first step to organize a modern Bureau of Marine Inspection and Navigation. There were many bridges to be crossed in connection with this legislation and it was really not until the Act of Congress of February 28, 1871, that all of the differences were very logically and conclusively settled. But, this period marked the beginning of a step in the right direction and the public was to receive great benefits from it. Uniform Pilot Rules were adopted and inspection of steamboats more rigidly enforced.

The movement started at the close of the last period to operate steamboats on regular schedules and to have regular stopping places where cargo and passengers could be transferred under reciprocal arrangements, was proving highly successful. There was less confusion and far more efficiency in the handling of passengers and freight.

While better passenger and freight service was the chief

contributing factor toward the establishment of reciprocal agreements, there were other reasons. In this connection, the "tramp" steamboat traffic, which was quite extensive during the last period, continued to be just as prevalent throughout this one. These boats, which did not run on regular schedules, continued as in the old days to go anywhere and everywhere they could pick up any freight or passengers. They frequently undercut prevailing freight and passenger rates. This had a tendency to unstabilize passenger and freight rates for the larger steamboat companies and owners. To offset these evils, steamboat operators tried to build up local pride in the ownership of the steamboat business. A clear manifestation of this is indicated by the large number of regular packet lines operating in Nashville.

Steamboats in this period more than ever before became identified as "A Nashville packet," or "A Louisville packet." Captains were also identified with their boats, and took great pride in that fact. Freight and passenger service became highly personalized and strong friendships were made in the industry. In general, it was felt that the Nashville boats were entitled to the Nashville business in return for the service rendered and the capital invested. Very strong pressure was brought to bear by the Nashville interests to use Nashville boats, even though they might in fairness choose one of several different packet lines owned by Nashville citizens.

A similar feeling was felt in such centers as New Orleans, St. Louis, Cairo, Louisville, Cincinnati, and Pittsburgh, and this helped to crystalize a general spirit of competition between the local owners and "tramp" boats. Steamboat owners in Nashville, therefore, enlarged their agreements with regular packet owners in other ports and worked together as never before in handling passengers and freight, in wharfage facilities, and in many other ways. It was the first serious attempt to adjust and regulate rates and standardize services.

Packet companies also began to extend privileges and

grant exclusive rights. This brought on other evils and hurt the business. In return for these rights, either in respect to passengers or cargo, certain concessions were made. A merchant at a small landing was told if he saw that all of the freight and passengers went by certain packet lines, he would personally receive extraordinary courtesies, either in outright pay or passes on the line. In some instances, agents were appointed to get business away from competitors. This practice continued to some extent until the end of the packet business on the Cumberland River. Owners would agree on certain tariffs and they would be published. But in their eagerness to get business, captains, pilots and mates would frequently negotiate a side agreement reducing rates, or make other concessions.

As to the average seasonal tonnage transported by steamboats to and from Nashville during this great era of the packets, we are not in the dark. Thanks again to various newspapers of the time, we find that in 1850 there were fifty-four different packets which plied the river and tied up at Nashville. Some of these plied the stretch between Nashville and Point Isabel on the upper river, but the vast majority made runs to New Orleans, Memphis, St. Louis, Evansville, Louisville, Cincinnati and Pittsburgh. From this latter majority at least fifteen during the average season were on regular schedules and were operated by recognized packet lines.

In 1851 there were a total of fifty-three different packets; in 1852—sixty; in 1853—sixty-two; in 1854—sixty-one; in 1855—sixty-nine; in 1856—seventy; in 1857—sixty-six; in 1858—sixty-nine; and in 1859—seventy-two. This makes an average of sixty-three boats which came to Nashville in the average season from 1850 through 1859. Available records disclose that each of the boats during the season, which in this decade averaged seven months, made a minimum of three trips per month to Nashville. Many of them, particularly the regular packets, averaged four trips and often brought seven or eight hundred tons of freight to Nashville and left with five or six hundred tons. However, the smaller boats must be considered. Therefore, once more it is assumed each of the packets made three trips a month and carried an average minimum both going and coming of three hundred tons each trip during the season. On this basis the average seasonal tonnage at Nashville for the period would be 793,800 tons, or an increase of 226,-800 tons over the preceding period.

The above figures indicate that the Cumberland was one of the four or five major water highways of America at the close of 1860. More freight than ever before was transported on the Cumberland which never saw Nashville. Clarksville, for example, during this busy decade was the best known tobacco center in the United States, with the exception of New Orleans. In 1859–60 more than 13,000 hogsheads of tobacco, valued at $1,625,000.00 left for New Orleans. In addition, there were 2,500 hogsheads of strips and dried leaf, valued at $350,000.00, which also went by packet, and 700 hogsheads of stems valued at $24,-500.00. It should be stated that 1859 was not considered a "banner" year. During this same season Clarksville also shipped out 17,000 barrels of flour and 16,000 hogs. These are only a few of the many items of Clarksville exports which were shipped direct to New Orleans and other points, and therefore were not included in the tonnage at Nashville. If the Clarksville outbound and inbound tonnage was also counted it would be immense, for this lovely town was serving a most extensive and lucrative trade area. Clarksville, however, was by no means the only town on the lower river that was handling an enormous river tonnage. Smithland, Eddyville, Canton and Dover were enjoying an excellent steamboat business during this decade.

The total tonnage of iron transported by packets on the lower river and shipped direct to Pittsburgh, Louisville, Cincinnati and other industrial centers was near its peak. Large quantities of burley tobacco also passed through Nashville from points on the upper river, destined for New Orleans, as well as axe handles, staves, shingles, furs and meats. This freight was in addition to that included in the

H. R. W. Hill. One of the largest packets on the Cumberland prior to
1860.

l. to r. *Blanche Lewis* (1855), *James Johnson* (1856), *B. M. Runyan*
(1858), *Tempest, Scotland* (1855) and *Grand Turk.* Nashville Wharf
about 1860.

strictly Nashville tonnage. Also not included in the above tonnage was that shipped in barge load lots. There was considerable coal being brought down the river and much more brought up the river from the Ohio. There has been no attempt to calculate this tonnage, although it existed in abundance.

If, therefore, all of this tonnage is taken into consideration, it is certain that for the first time in the history of Steamboatin' on the Cumberland, more than 1,000,000 tons of strictly commercial pay load common carrier freight was transported annually on the river and it was conservatively valued at close to $40,000,000.00.

In retrospect, it may be difficult for some to believe that Nashville, Clarksville, and the smaller towns and landings along the river could support so much steamboat traffic. The secret rests in the fact that the Cumberland River at the close of 1860 was not merely an artery of transportation for the people along its banks, but was actually the major transportation system for a large part of Kentucky, with Smithland and Eddyville the principal outlets to the West, Clarksville, Dover and Nashville in the center, and Burkesville, Albany and Point Isabel to the East. This was by no means all. Thanks to Muscle Shoals, which remained an impassable barrier on the Tennessee, the Cumberland, with Nashville at the apex of its east-west curve, gave the merchants and farmers living to the south and southeast—as far away as Northern Alabama and Georgia—a market and distribution point for their goods and products.

It was not unusual in this decade for whole caravans of wagons loaded with cotton, corn and every other variety of agricultural products, to wind their weary way to Nashville from Murfreesboro, Columbia, Pulaski, Fayetteville, Decatur, Athens, Gunters Landing, Rome, Dalton and many other towns still hampered by muddy roads and minus any outlet for their goods. These same wagons on their return trips would be loaded to the hilt with the manufactured articles supplied by Nashville concerns.

Nashville, to use a modern slang expression was "riding

the crest of the wave" and Tennessee as a whole was enjoying undreamed of prosperity which was based on sound economic principles. She had vast raw products to sell and when they were sold, she became a sizeable buyer with plenty of money. The Cumberland River and its packets were a necessary part of this set-up for the obvious reason that without them there could be no delivery of raw materials sold or manufactured articles bought. As long as such a situation existed, steamboat business would be ideally situated.

During this particular decade, Tennessee was one of the top-flight States in the production of cotton, corn, tobacco and iron, all of which were eagerly sought by the rest of the United States. Cotton in particular was a great river cargo, closely followed by the others, all ranking about the same. All freight was plentiful, but cotton was the "King." Steamboats left Nashville and other points on the Cumberland with their decks frequently flattened out with hundreds of bales of this product.

In 1840, Tennessee ranked first in the nation as a corn producing state, the yield amounting to 44,986,188 bushels. It was still going strong in this period. In 1860, Tennessee grew 43,000,000 pounds of tobacco, and in 1850, it became the largest hog producing state in the South. It is stated that in 1840, Tennessee raised over 4,500,000 bushels of wheat and unlike many other states which were short on flour, Tennessee produced a large surplus of this valuable commodity.

No other period in the history of Tennessee represents a greater advance in the production of iron than does this ten-year era. In 1854, the rich iron resources of the Western Highland Rim were yielding 37,282 tons of pig metal and castings in the State of Tennessee alone. J. M. Safford, in his "Geological Reconnaissance of the State of Tennessee," published in 1855, lists twelve furnaces in Stewart County, seven in Montgomery and six in Dickson, all of which depended primarily on steamboats for transportation of their iron to market. These furnaces produced more than 30,000 tons of pig metal and castings out of the total yielded for the entire state.

The outstanding manufacturer of iron and kindred products on the lower Cumberland, however, continued to be the Tennessee Rolling Mills in Lyon County, Kentucky, which until 1854, had been operated jointly by A. W. Van Leer, Daniel Hillman, Dr. Samuel Watson, C. E. Hillman and B. M. Runyan. In the fall of 1854, Daniel Hillman and his two brothers, George and C. E., bought out the other partners and paid them a reported $500,000.00 cash for their one-half interest.

By the purchase of the Tennessee Rolling Mills, these three brothers became the outstanding iron manufacturers on the Western Highland Rim, and one of the best customers of the packets. One reliable account states that at the outbreak of the War Between the States the Hillmans were producing nearly three-fourths of all of the iron manufactured south of the Mason and Dixon line.

Now let us turn our attention to the railroad situation during this period.

The Nashville and Chattanooga Railroad had been chartered in 1845 and a small portion of its tracks had been laid in 1846. The advent of this road was to give Nashville access to the southeastern states as far as Charleston. Steamboats which had brought the first rails to Nashville also brought the first locomotive. It was placed on an improvised track made up of sections, was then hauled ahead by teams, sometimes using its own power, and proceeded up Broad to Cherry Street (Fourth Avenue), and out that street to the present Nashville & Chattanooga crossing, where it was placed on the main track. The name of the first locomotive was the "Tennessee," and it came in the form of a Christmas present, arriving on December 25, 1850. It took four days for the "Tennessee" to go from the wharf to the main track. Other locomotives were brought into Nashville by steamboat and were hauled to the nearest portion of the tracks.

The first Nashville and Chattanooga train to run covered

the meager distance of eleven miles from Nashville to Antioch. That memorable journey was taken on April 15, 1851. On July 4, 1851, the first train reached Murfreesboro. In February, 1854, the main line was completed to Chattanooga. The cost was approximately $4,000,000.00, of which Nashville subscribed $500,000.00; Murfreesboro, $30,000.00; Charleston, $500,000.00; and the Georgia Railroad and Banking Company of Augusta, $250,000.00. Other towns along the road also subscribed to the stock and the State of Tennessee underwrote the bonds of the company issued from time to time on completed miles of road. Everyone in Nashville and vicinity welcomed its advent.

On March 5, 1850, the Kentucky Legislature passed an Act under which the Louisville and Nashville Railroad Company was incorporated. In May, 1851, several engineers started surveying a proposed roadway from Louisville to Nashville, and the steamboat interests at Nashville and other points on the Cumberland River became instantly alarmed. They figured, and correctly so, that this railroad was destined to cut off freight moving down the Ohio, particularly at Louisville. They were not long in recognizing that while the Nashville & Chattanooga started out as a friend, the Louisville & Nashville was a foe from the beginning. Furthermore, when the two connected at Nashville both were sure to give the steamboats no end of trouble.

By October 1, 1858, the Louisville & Nashville had extended its railroad line south to Gallatin, there connecting with a line leading to Nashville. Finally, on November 1, 1859, the road was opened for through business from Louisville to Nashville, the railroad having spanned the Cumberland in that year with one of the finest railroad bridges in the United States.

Thus was established the second railroad into Nashville, and thence forward the Louisville & Nashville and the Nashville & Chattanooga Railroads were to dominate this type of transportation. In like manner, in a period of approximately five years, Nashville had been connected by railroad not only with the southeastern territory, but northward to the Ohio River, one of the best of all steamboat empires.

The entry of the Louisville & Nashville into Nashville naturally continued to create profound unrest among the steamboat men, and for the first time the seriousness of railroad competition dawned upon them. It marked a definite trend detrimental to the traffic on the river. There was an obvious reason for this feeling. Louisville was situated strategically in one of the richest agricultural sections of what was then the Midwest. It was on one of the truly great inland waterways of America. It was close enough to such cities as Cincinnati and Pittsburgh to the northeast, and to such western cities as Evansville and Owensboro to intercept an extensive amount of "pay-load" freight that had normally flowed down the Ohio into the Cumberland.

The annual shipment of freight from these points on the Ohio constituted a goodly portion of the freight by steamboat to Nashville. It was now possible to haul this freight by a direct overland route and, of course, it was contemplated that when it got to Nashville it would be taken by rail to the southeast over the Nashville & Chattanooga. Furthermore, all freight coming in to Nashville from the seaboard and the southeast over the Nashville & Chattanooga Railroad could be shipped over the Louisville & Nashville Railroad, whereas this freight had always been shipped by steamboats.

Such a state of events could be fatal to steamboats. When the Nashville & Chattanooga entered Nashville, there had been a few misgivings, but no real apprehensions for the reasons already mentioned. At that time it did not appear to be a competitor. The Louisville & Nashville had created an entirely different situation and a very serious one. When the railroads connected at Nashville river traffic could be by-passed.

The terminus of the Louisville & Nashville Railroad into Nashville was at what is known as "Link's Depot," two blocks north of the Public Square. The Nashville & Chattanooga depot was below Eighth Avenue, between Church and Cedar Streets, and passengers were taken by carriage from one depot to the other.

In addition to the Louisville & Nashville, the steamboat industry faced expectant competition from other infant lines by the end of this period. There were three of these— the Nashville & Northwestern, the Nashville & Decatur, and the Edgefield & Kentucky. They had been designated under the acts of 1852 and 1854 for State aid and were to become serious competitors after the shock of the War Between the States had been somewhat absorbed.

V. K. Stevenson, President of the Nashville & Chattanooga, who has been mentioned in a preceding chapter, in his Annual Report to the Stockholders in 1860, in speaking of the proposed Nashville & Northwestern, made this statement:

> "Our Road is *mainly dependent for permanent and profitable business upon this extension (connecting Nashville with Johnsonville on the Tennessee River, and Hickman Kentucky, on the Mississippi River), which, if made, will give us uninterrupted communications all the year,* with the trade and travel of the upper and lower Mississippi and country beyond." (Parenthesis supplied by author.)

It is of particular interest to observe that Stevenson referred to the Nashville & Northwestern as an extension, and while a separate entity, its destinies from inception were controlled by the Nashville & Chattanooga. Stevenson was its first President, and it was partially completed under Michael Burns who also served as President of the Nashville & Chattanooga.

No attempt at this time will be made to further discuss this statement by Stevenson other than to emphasize that from a railroad standpoint, he again proved to be a man of keen vision and had correctly sized up the situation. If the plan went through, the Nashville & Northwestern would intercept freight on the Mississippi and the Tennessee, in the same way the Louisville & Nashville was doing at Louisville and Cincinnati on the Ohio. Neither the plan nor the competition, however, presented an acute problem in 1860. From a practical standpoint, it did not seriously threaten as a competitor to steamboats until 1869. The War Between the States intervened and partly postponed work on the roadway, which extended only as far as Kingston Springs in 1862. During the War this line was extended as far as Johnsonville on the Tennessee River by the Federal Armies. In 1869 it was leased by the Nashville & Chattanooga and Stevenson's plan finally materialized in 1872 when the Nashville & Chattanooga then purchased the road at foreclosure. By that time, through various connections, its western terminus was at Hickman on the Mississippi.

The Nashville & Decatur Railroad, which was chartered around 1852, was to connect with Decatur, Alabama, to the South. There it was to join with other railroads and ultimately lead south to Birmingham, Mobile and New Orleans. When this was done it would complete a through line from the Ohio River to the Gulf of Mexico, and in that way, practically preclude any shipment of freight by river between New Orleans and Louisville, Cincinnati and Pittsburgh on the Ohio, and Nashville on the Cumberland. This railroad, first conceived as early as 1836, was completed to Decatur in 1859, and its Nashville depot was located near the old City Cemetery.

Work on the Edgefield & Kentucky Railroad was started in 1857 and was expected to connect Nashville with the Evansville, Henderson and Nashville Railroad, which was started about the same time. These roads when completed would trap freight moving from Kentucky and the Ohio River basin in the direction of Clarksville and Memphis. This line was calculated to tap the rich mineral wealth of Western Kentucky and Tennessee and rob the steamboats of the iron and coal business. By 1859 the road was completed to Springfield and by 1860 it had connected with the Louisville and Nashville at Guthrie, Kentucky, and with the Memphis, Clarksville and Louisville at Clarksville, where a bridge across the river was completed in the same year.

Like a spider in its web, the railroads were catching their prey.

The apprehension of the steamboat industry concerning the railroads was lessened to some extent because of the infancy of the new competitor. The railroads in the south in this period were an unknown quantity. Not even the railroads themselves expected such rapid success as actually took place.

In 1852 the Nashville & Chattanooga had three locomotives, two passenger cars, one package car, seven box cars, eighteen platform cars, nine repair cars, and one hand car, and the gross freight revenue was $40,912.00. In 1854 the gross freight was $163,426.11. When the main stem from Nashville to Chattanooga was completed in 1855 revenue from the freight jumped to $235,662.44. At the close of 1860 gross revenue from freight amounted to $347,-217.97, of which $145,068.50 originated at Nashville. When the main stem of the Louisville & Nashville was completed to Nashville this meant a large increase in freight to the Nashville & Chattanooga. These figures, while promising, were so out of proportion to the enormous gross revenue taken in by the steamboats during the same interval, that even they helped allay any fears of the steamboat men concerning the future of their business.

There were other cogent reasons why some steamboat men refused to be alarmed over the railroads. At the beginning of 1855 there were only 9,021 miles of railroad in the entire country, and by the close of 1860, there were only 30,635 miles, including spurs and switches. The locomotives and cars were very light affairs, utterly incapable, both on account of power and the grade of the roadways, of hauling any heavy burden of freight. It takes but a glance at an old-time locomotive and cars to substantiate these facts. Many steamboat men also felt, with the development of Nashville, more freight would originate on the river, particularly the upper stretches, for transshipment northward to Louisville, which was already becoming a large tobacco market. In this they were correct, and many years later Captain Tom Ryman—"steamboat tycoon"—was said to have used this up-river traffic to reach an understanding with the Louisville & Nashville Railroad regarding competition.

One of the chief difficulties of the railroads was the lack of any standard gauge. It seems almost incomprehensible to us at the present time that cars on one railroad could not be interchanged with those of another because of a different gauge in the tracks. Nevertheless this was exactly the situation.

Major John W. Thomas, President of the Nashville & Chattanooga Railroad, in 1901 speaking at a banquet honoring the Fiftieth Anniversary of the services of Major James Geddes, first to be so honored, who was one of the Civil Engineers who constructed the L. & N. railway from Louisville to Nashville and later became Assistant to the General Manager, said:

> "The decade, 1850–1860, can appropriately be termed the 'noninterchangeable decade,' as the roads were of different gauges, four feet, eight and one-half inches, four feet, nine inches, five feet, and six feet, and in many cases there were no physical connections between the roads, but freight and passengers were transferred by wagons from one road to the other, and each road was operated independently and without reference to any other road."

It was not until 1886 that all railroads south of the Ohio River changed over to the standard gauge of four feet, eight and a half inches, thereby making unnecessary the transfer of freight by outmoded methods.

All of these factors lessened the apprehensions of the steamboat operators. There seemed to be no way open for the formation of "trunk" lines. In this period the general trend was to build short lines of railroads without regard to the all-important question of success based on "pay-load" freight. During the period 1852 to 1857, the political leaders in Tennessee, as in many other states, were enthusiastic over state aid to railroads. The State, under the guise of so-called progress, passed enabling acts for many railroads that had no justification for existence. Many Legislators coming to Nashville had the foolish notion that a railroad should be erected in their section of the state but could give no sane reason for such conclusion. The state having underwritten the bonds of one railroad, was placed in the untenable position of lending financial aid either directly or indirectly to every "jerk water" railroad that applied for a charter. Many of these "railroads" under the enabling act of 1852 and subsequent acts received financial backing to the extent of $10,000.00 per mile of track. There probably never was such an era of unmitigated disregard of Tennessee's finances.

Credit is due those leaders in the organization of the Nashville & Chattanooga and the Louisville & Nashville, and other major railroads in the State, who kept their roads from over-extension. These roads, in contrast with many others, had been built upon sound economic principles.

Some historians have inferred that the War Between the States was the chief cause of the financial disaster that descended upon many of the railroads. The facts do not always justify such conclusions, but the War did play a part in the debacle. At this point it is sufficient to say that very few railroads had been completed in Tennessee when the War began and the "jerk water" species were, for the most part, not completed and, therefore were not hurt.

At the close of this period all of the steamboat owners on the Cumberland, however, knew that if the major railroads were successfully financed and they connected their lines so as to create a network leading to focal points on the rivers, there would ultimately be a battle for existence. This was a matter which provoked the thoughts of the steamboat industry during this period, rather than prompting them to concerted action.

Amidst the confusion incidental to the organization of the railroads and the political graft and corruption which afflicted the State, the steamboat owners stuck close to their business. Much to their credit, they refused to join the public cry of "subsidy" when State aid was so badly needed by their competitors. Instead of bemoaning the turn of events the steamboat operators turned their attention to such things as better service. It is paradoxical, but true, that the financial assistance rendered many railroads by the State, City and County Governments rose to smite their progress. Some were never able to cast aside the yoke of indebtedness. Many became strangled and it was necessary for the strong to absorb the weak. By this process, the steamboats and their operators received a very long and protracted respite from an inevitable conflict. It gave them time to prepare.

The State Capitol building at Nashville was completed in 1855, and a new Courthouse adorned the Public Square, replacing the one burned in 1856 by the fire which destroyed the old Nashville Inn and many of the ancient landmarks in that vicinity. The city boasted a splendid water works, which had been greatly enlarged and the first gas for light and heat had been manufactured in May, 1851. Much of the coal for these enterprises was brought to Nashville by barges towed by steamboats. The Post Office had been moved to Church and Cherry Streets.

Nashville seemed to have everything in her favor. A sudden rise to industrial prominence had been added to her fame as a center of culture and refinement. But, in about two years, Federal gunboats opened fire on Fort Donelson below Nashville on the Cumberland. War had come, and with it impoverishment and blasted dreams.

CHAPTER FIVE

War is Hell—Gunboats Prowl

Period 1860–1870

The events immediately preceding and subsequent to the War Between the States, as well as those during that conflict, make this period one of the most interesting and important in the long career of the Cumberland.

It is difficult to discuss the part played by the Cumberland during the War without mentioning the parts played by other Western Rivers, principally the Ohio, Tennessee and Mississippi. Almost every incident on one of these rivers had a bearing on the part played by the others. For this reason, and in order to preserve continuity, it has been necessary to enlarge upon the main story. In that way only is it possible to give a complete picture of the service rendered by the Cumberland during this turbulent decade.

The early recognition by the Federal Government that the Western Rivers, including the Cumberland, could be used and maintained both as supply lines and as offensive weapons, played a large part in the outcome of the War. This fact has been greatly minimized by most historians.

The use of the rivers early became one of the component parts of the grand strategy of the Federal Government. It would be unfair to say that the Confederate States did not also recognize the immense value of the rivers, but delicate questions of diplomacy involved in the neutrality of Kentucky and the lack of proper materials delayed whatever plans were entertained and rendered them almost useless.

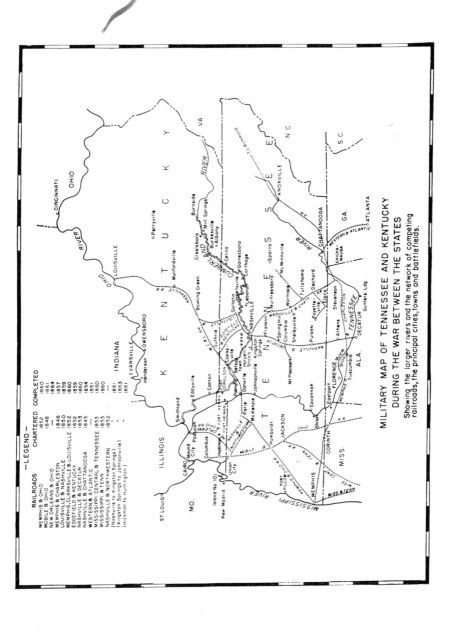

MILITARY MAP OF TENNESSEE AND KENTUCKY
DURING THE WAR BETWEEN THE STATES

Showing the larger rivers and the network of competing
railroads, the principal cities, towns and battlefields.

—LEGEND—

RAILROADS	CHARTERED	COMPLETED
MEMPHIS & OHIO	1852	1860
MOBILE & OHIO	1848	1861
NEW ORLEANS & OHIO	—	1864
MEMPHIS & CHARLESTON	1846	1857
LOUISVILLE & NASHVILLE	1850	1859
MEMPHIS, CLARKSVILLE & LOUISVILLE	1852	1860
EDGEFIELD & KENTUCKY	1852	1859
NASHVILLE & DECATUR	1853	1860
NASHVILLE & CHATTANOOGA	1845	1854
WESTERN & ATLANTIC		1851
MISSISSIPPI CENTRAL & TENNESSEE	1853	1860
MISSISSIPPI & TENN	1853	1860
NASHVILLE & NORTHWESTERN	1852	—
(Nashville to Kingston Springs)		1861
(Kingston Springs to Johnsonville)	"	1863
(Hickman to Huntingdon)	"	1861

With the exception of Mobile and New Orleans in the deep South, at the opening of the War, there were no immediate facilities available for the construction of heavy armament. In addition, the South, an agricultural section of the country, was peculiarly short on other kindred materials. Practically all steamboats then operating on the Western Rivers were manufactured in northern cities along the Ohio.

After the secession of South Carolina on December 20, 1860, steamboat business on the Cumberland did not immediately show any ill effects. The year 1860, all things considered, had been very prosperous from the standpoint of the steamboats. However, when Mississippi, Florida, Alabama, Georgia and Louisiana seceded during the month of January, 1861, closely followed by Texas on February 1st of the same year, it was apparent that such an upheaval in the affairs of the country would soon disrupt traffic on all the rivers.

When the Confederate Congress met for the first time on February 4, 1861, at Montgomery, Alabama, one of the most serious problems for discussion was whether the Mississippi and its tributaries could be kept open for peaceful traffic between all States. What would be the attitude of the Confederate Government toward the use of these great rivers by non-seceding states? Would they be blockaded, tolls collected on boats and each state independently create its own tariff and custom laws? What would happen to foreign commerce coming to New Orleans in the South, and routed over the Mississippi and Ohio to Pittsburgh in the North? These were but a few of the many questions involved which would affect commerce on all the large rivers.

In January, 1861, the State of Mississippi caused batteries to be erected at Vicksburg. Steamboats operating from the northern and northwestern states immediately claimed their boats were detained by such batteries and searched. On the other hand, Mississippi contended the batteries had been erected solely for the purpose of keeping the river open. On January 26, 1861, Louisiana seceded and forthwith expressed her intention to erect similar batteries and for similar purposes.

Public anxiety, however, was somewhat relieved when the Confederate Congress, by one of its first Acts, declared, "that the peaceful navigation of the Mississippi River is hereby declared free to the citizens of any State upon its borders, or upon the borders of its navigable tributaries." The immediate effect of this temperate Act on the steamboat business was to encourage a renewal of transportation on the Western Rivers. It seemed, for the time being at least, that the steamboat traffic on the Cumberland might continue without interruption. The wharf at Nashville in the spring of 1861 remained a thriving transportation center.

On the very day that the Confederate Congress met, Tennessee voted four to one against secession. This added additional hope among its citizens that the tragedy of war might be averted. The hope thus aroused was soon to be dispelled. Great pressure was soon exerted upon Tennessee to join one side or the other. Overt acts by parties on both sides took place, which made it apparent that the State would be drawn into the conflict if it came. These acts were political and militaristic. They were numerous and inflammatory as will be pointed out shortly.

Fort Sumter fell on April 14, 1861, and President Lincoln on April 19, 1861, issued his Proclamation calling up troops. The War thereby became a reality, and steamboat owners along the Cumberland almost to a man sided against the North. The fall of Fort Sumter and the tragic events which immediately followed, however, did not completely disrupt transportation on the Cumberland. The State of Tennessee was still officially neutral, and from a legal standpoint at least, boats operated by her citizens enjoyed the benefits, such as they were, of a neutral State. Any such legal technicality, however, was soon dispelled.

Shortly after the fall of Fort Sumter the Federal Government also issued directives to curb the transportation, by river or rail, of arms, ammunition, and many other commodities to the seceded States. Tennessee was included in the Directive of May 8, 1861, to the Surveyors of Customs along the rivers. This action, taken before Tennessee had seceded, greatly incensed the citizens of the State, and particularly the steamboat owners. Almost immediately there sprang up an undercover traffic on the river which brought in more supplies than ever before. The Directive also helped to crystalize public opinion against the North.

Even before such action, traffic along the rivers was demoralized. On April 26th, the *C. E. Hillman,* a well known Cumberland River packet, was stopped at Cairo and a large quantity of powder and lead belonging to the State of Tennessee for delivery at Clarksville and Nashville, was seized. The Clarksville Chronicle of May 3rd referred to this incident as an "Act of Piracy" and proudly proclaimed it had already provoked retaliation at Helena, Arkansas, where two Cincinnati boats bound upstream from New Orleans were detained and one held. A Cincinnati boat had also been fired into and badly damaged at Napolean, Arkansas. This was by no means the only retaliation. Governor Isham G. Harris of Tennessee forthwith seized the funds deposited in Nashville banks in the name of Jesse Thomas, then United States Surveyor of Customs. These deposits amounted to $74,460.00 and, needless to state, such action further kindled the fire of mutual distrust.

Search and seizure of steamboats at Cairo, St. Louis, Louisville, Evansville and Memphis continued during the hectic months of April, May, June and July of 1861. Blockades were erected at many if not all of these places. Although both North and South diligently tried to explain that such acts had been first instituted by the other, it was obvious to all steamboat men by June of 1861 that the steamboat business on the Western Rivers as it existed in the days prior to the fall of Fort Sumter was a thing of the past.

On May 21, 1861, the Confederacy in retaliation against Lincoln's directive of May 8, 1861, placed an embargo on shipments to the North, and on July 4, 1861, Tennessee seized all rolling stock of the L. & N. Railroad in the State.

Thereafter no trains ran over this line into Tennessee until the Federal Army entered Nashville on February 24, 1862.

Most of the boats at Nashville before the end of the 1861 season were forced into retirement and awaited developments. During the summer of 1861, the *James Johnson, James Woods, Nashville, Sam Kirkman, C. E. Hillman, Red Rover, Minnetonka, B. M. Runyan, Umpire* and the *General Anderson,* among others whiled away their time. The Nashville Patriot of June 1, 1861, in referring to the *General Anderson* had this to say:

"The *General Anderson* retired from busy life yesterday, and went into Summer headquarters at Edgefield, there to rot out the remainder of her life. Old Abe's blockade has ruined our steamboat trade and thrown hundreds out of employment. The *General's* reputation was co-extensive with the navigable world, and her friends will miss her accustomed whistle. She went to the 'boneyard' in gallant style, colors flying and her band playing 'Dixie.' Gibraltar's fleet now lies at Edgefield doomed to many months of ignoble inactivity."

Tennessee voted once more on the question of secession on June 8, 1861, and this time the vote was two to one in its favor.

As early as April 17, 1861, James B. Eads of St. Louis, one of America's distinguished engineers, had been notified by President Lincoln to hold himself in readiness for service in connection with the defense of the Mississippi and Ohio rivers. On April 29, 1861, he submitted a plan, which was soon approved, to blockade the Mississippi and Ohio Rivers at Cairo by the use of land and river batteries.

In July, 1861, while details of this proposed blockade remained to be worked out, Eads was given a contract to build seven iron-clad gunboats for service on the Western Rivers, namely, the *St. Louis, Cincinnati, Carondelet, Louisville, Mound City, Cairo,* and the *Pittsburgh.* At a slightly later date, he was authorized to build the *Benton,* another powerful iron-clad. All of these were in service by January, 1862, giving the Federal Government a squadron of gunboats and iron-clads aggregating 3,600 tons, and mounting 117 guns. The building of these boats was a master stroke of strategy, and they had much to do with the outcome of the war, as will be brought out as this story of the War unfolds.

These were by no means the only plans of the Federal Government for the use of the larger rivers. On May 16, 1861 Lieutenant John Rodgers of the U. S. Navy was directed to report to General George B. McClellan, then in command of the Department of Missouri. He was authorized to purchase and place in immediate commission three gunboats. Rodgers forthwith bought three average size packets and converted them into side-wheel gunboats with iron casements and heavily reinforced oak bulwarks. Each mounted a battery of several guns. By late August 1861 two of them, the *Lexington* and the *Conestoga,* had been commissioned, followed by the *Tyler* in September. These were the first gunboats on the Western Rivers, and cost a total of approximately $100,000.00 when completed.

On August 25, 1861 the *Lexington* seized the steamboat *W. B. Terry,* lying alongside the wharf at Paducah, Kentucky, on the single excuse that she was a "Rebel." From that moment on, the Federal Government's attitude toward free trade on the rivers was manifest. The *Lexington* delivered her prize to the Federal authorities at Cairo. Shortly thereafter the *Samuel Orr* of Evansville was seized by Kentuckians sympathetic to the South with a cargo valued at $25,000.00.

The *Terry* was a short lived prize. She was later captured on the Tennessee near the mouth of Duck River on August 31, 1862 by a reputed force of 200 Confederates who then burned her. The *Samuel Orr* served as a hospital ship at Fort Henry in 1862 and was also burned on the Tennessee to avoid capture by the *Lexington, Tyler* and *Conestoga* as they proceeded up that river after the fall of the Fort.

The Federal Government also increased its armed forces

at such key points as Cincinnati, Evansville, Cairo and St. Louis. General Henry W. Halleck, with headquarters in St. Louis, was given command of the Department of Missouri with general supervision over Western Kentucky and Tennessee. Major General Don Carlos Buell shortly opened headquarters at Louisville in command of the Union forces in Kentucky east of the Cumberland. Brigadier General U. S. Grant was brought out of retirement to command the armies at Paducah and Cairo. Commodore A. H. Foote, who had been in charge of the New York Navy Yards, was made Flag Officer of the Western Flotilla on August 30, 1861. Oddly enough, he was under command of Halleck, although he was a naval officer. The two never did get along together as might have been expected.

While these activities were taking place, the Confederate States, with equal foresight, but with far less material to work with, were preparing for the defense of the rivers. Tennessee, however, because of the continued neutrality of Kentucky, was peculiarly hampered in her own defense. If Kentucky remained neutral , it was obvious Tennessee would bear the brunt of the first offensive directed at the deep South by the Federal armies which were gathering in the Ohio River Valley and along the northwestern extremity of Kentucky.

Governor Harris, an ardent secessionist, and the Tennessee representatives in the Confederate Congress constantly pointed out the grave difficulties involved in building fortifications for the protection of its three main rivers, the Mississippi, Tennessee and Cumberland, as long as Kentucky remained neutral. Most historians now agree if Kentucky had joined the Confederacy it might have spelled victory during the War, because the plan of the Federal Government to close the Western Rivers and to take up an offensive against the South absolutely depended upon Kentucky remaining in the Union, or at least neutral.

Her failure to join the Confederacy was one of the greatest afflictions which struck the South. President Davis of the Confederacy and Governor Harris of Tennessee did all in their power not to tread on her toes, hoping she could be finally won over. In fact, they were so careful to avoid any overt act against Kentucky's avowed neutrality that it seriously impeded the defense of Tennessee.

Shortly after Tennessee seceded, Governor Harris promptly ordered the construction of river forts on both the Cumberland and Tennessee. General Daniel S. Donelson, a nephew of General Andrew Jackson's wife, was assigned the duty of selecting the locations of the forts. Due to the situation in Kentucky, General Donelson was unable to select the sites which admittedly were the most advantageous—that is, in Western Kentucky where the Cumberland and Tennessee Rivers were approximately three miles apart. As the next best he selected Dover, seventy-five miles below Nashville on the Cumberland, and a site twelve miles due west from Dover on the Tennessee.

In a short time work was undertaken to fortify the two locations, the one on the Cumberland being named Fort Donelson for General Donelson, and the one on the Tennessee, Fort Henry, named for Gustavus A. Henry of Clarksville, at the time a Senator from Tennessee in the Confederate Congress. From a military standpoint both sites were badly located. Fort Henry proved to be incapable of defense during high water and was built without regard to possible land attack. The west bank of the Tennessee River across from Fort Henry was in Kentucky, fringed with high hills which could not be fortified because they were on neutral soil.

Fort Donelson was also badly located according to most military experts. Brigadier General John B. Floyd, who later defended it, had this to say:

> "It was ill conceived, badly executed and still worse located. I consider the place illy chosen, out of position and entirely indefensible by any reinforcements which could be brought there to its support."

Despite this highly disparaging description by Floyd, whose opinion is of doubtful value in light of subsequent events, the consensus of opinion among his contemporaries was that Donelson was a far better located fort than Henry because it was on high ground and its riverward guns could bring a merciless fire against gun-boats. While the land side was not anything to brag about, it offered fair protection against any ordinary assault when sufficiently manned in the outer works.

Colonel A. Heiman of the Tenth Tennessee Regiment was assigned the task of building Fort Henry and in early July reported that he had mounted the first gun. It was near the middle of October before any work was done at Fort Donelson. Colonel R. W. McGavock was directed to build the fortifications and he took three companies of Tennessee troops to Dover, but was handicapped by lack of equipment and labor. When General Albert Sidney Johnston arrived in Nashville on September 14, 1861 as supreme commander, he immediately conferred with Governor Harris of Tennessee and ordered the completion of both Fort Henry and Fort Donelson at the earliest possible moment. General Lloyd Tilghman was assigned the overall task of speeding up the work and locating the guns.

General Johnston, not satisfied with the location and the reported progress of their construction, next sent Major J. F. Gilmer, his chief engineer, to inspect the works. On November 3, 1861, Gilmer reported there was no necessity of making any vital changes in the locations since the forts were already under construction. Johnston, still apprehensive that the work at the two forts was not progressing as rapidly as possible, next assigned Captain Joseph Dixon to make a thorough examination of the forts and to take any steps necessary for their completion. He was also directed to make any additional defenses and to complete them without delay.

During the construction of Forts Henry and Donelson, all steamboats on both the Tennessee and Cumberland Rivers were turned over to military authorities and they did their part in carrying men and equipment to the two locations. Senator Henry, on November 1, 1861, in a letter to General

Johnston reported that while Fort Henry was in fine condition for defense, Fort Donelson "was in very bad condition and no work had been done on any account." Henry even intimated that Major Gilmer, when he completed his inspection, might decide to fortify Lineport, some distance below the Fort, rather than Donelson. This suggestion indicates the unsettled state of affairs existing in the construction of the forts.

Gilmer and Dixon, instead of changing the site of Fort Donelson, did all in their power to complete it, and in addition, they sank old barges and flats loaded with rocks at Ingram Shoals, a few miles above Eddyville. They reported these would obstruct the river for the passage of gunboats on any rise less than twelve feet over a low stage of water. This proved of very little consequence as most any experienced river man might surmise.

Some of the guns for Fort Henry and Fort Donelson, according to the contemporary Clarksville Chronicle, were manufactured at Clarksville by Messrs. Whitfield, Bradley & Co., and were transported to the forts by steamboat. Still more guns at both forts came from the Norfolk Navy Yard which had been surrendered to the Confederacy, and some were made at Nashville. In all, there were fourteen guns mounted at Fort Henry, nine of which faced the river and five protected the fort from a land attack. At Fort Donelson, there were ten light guns mounted, one large columbiad and one rifle gun. All were trained on the river.

The forts, it is now agreed, were not completed as planned before they were assaulted. This failure cannot be attributed to Johnston or Harris. No one can say they did less than humanly possible to complete the forts. The engineers may have been dilatory, but they too probably did the best they could. It was due probably more than anything else to the unpreparedness of the South for a war.

Fort Henry and Fort Donelson were not the only forts erected for the defense of the Cumberland. The citizens of Clarksville erected Fort Defiance near the city, with three guns and another fort a short distance up Red River, which boasted two guns. These inadequate defenses, however, surrendered to the Federal forces after the fall of Fort Henry and Fort Donelson without firing a gun.

The citizens of Nashville, in February 1862, had erected Fort Zollicoffer six miles below Nashville. This fort was situated on a high bluff about 130 feet above the river and mounted thirteen heavy guns. When General Johnston was compelled to surrender Nashville all of these guns were spiked. One of the larger guns at this fort was a six inch rifle weighing 9,490 pounds and was manufactured by the Tredegar Iron Works of Richmond, in 1861. Another six pounder was manufactured in Rome, Georgia, and another by Ellis & Co., of Nashville.

These were all of the fortifications erected for the protection of the Cumberland River. The State of Tennessee also sought to protect its line along the Mississippi River by the erection of defenses at Island No. 10 at the northwestern extremity of the State, and at Fort Randolph and Fort Pillow above Memphis. When the fighting started none of them, except Island No. 10 was sufficiently strong to withstand the assault of the enemy. When it fell the other two forts were evacuated.

One of the first steps taken by the Confederate Congress was to organize a Navy and included in the overall program were a number of ironclads and ram type gunboats for service on the Western Rivers. Construction of the two powerful ironclads *Mississippi* and *Louisiana* was undertaken at New Orleans, and contracts for two ironclad rams, the *Arkansas* and *Tennessee,* were let at Memphis. In addition to these very powerful gunboats, which were being built primarily to combat those of Admiral Foote, the *Manassas*, which was an ironclad ram, had been built at New Orleans, and the *Eastport,* another ironclad gunboat, was being built on the Tennessee River at Florence. In size and firing power it was anticipated all of these gunboats and rams, when completed, would equal if not surpass those in the Western Flotilla.

Commodore G. N. Hollins of the Confederacy, who was in

command of the Mississippi River Squadron at New Orleans, also had under his command six gunboats which included the *McRae, Livingston, Maurepass, General Polk, Ivey, Pontechatrain,* and the *New Orleans,* the latter being termed a floating battery. As fighting units these particular gunboats were not in the same class as those built by Eads.

On January 9, 1862, the Confederate Congress also appropriated $1,000,000.00 for the purpose of buying, converting and fully equipping eight rams to be known as the Mississippi River Defense Fleet, unattached to the Confederate Navy. These boats when acquired became the *General Van Dorn, General Price, General Beauregard, Colonel Lovell, General Jeff Thompson, General Bragg, Sumter,* and the *Little Rebel.*

It will be seen from this brief review of the facts that the Confederate Government, while seeking to protect the Mississippi River by constructing gunboats, rams and ironclads, had done nothing whatsoever along similar lines to protect the Cumberland River, although it was at the front door of the enemy.

As a matter of fact, the number of gunboats, rams and ironclads of the combined Confederate Navy, and the Mississippi River Defense Fleet, exclusive of the vessels operating on the rivers in and around Mobile, which played no part in the operations here under discussion, consisted of a total of only thirty-six vessels. Of this number, by the end of December 1862, no less than twenty-nine had been sunk or burned to avoid capture, leaving only seven for service during the year 1863, and of this seven there was not a single survivor after April 1863. Six of the gunboats falling into the hands of the enemy were repaired and later used against the South.

On the other hand, the Federal Government by the close of 1861 had placed the *Tyler, Lexington,* and *Conestoga* in commission and in early 1862 had added all eight of the powerful gunboats built by Eads. By the close of 1862, the Western Flotilla could boast of a total of forty-eight gunboats, ironclads, tinclads, rams and armored vessels and a mortar fleet of considerable strength.

In addition, Colonel Charles Ellett USA had organized his Ram Fleet, one of the most novel military units to serve during the War. This ingenious outfit, originally composed of eight ram-type gunboats, was created for the express purpose of running into enemy gunboats and sinking them in that manner. The crews were hand-picked by Ellett. Later on, other armored vessels were acquired which carried mounted troops, and were known as the Marine Brigade. It was used extensively to break up small bands of Confederate soldiers, make raids, and prevent movements across the rivers. One of the most notable achievements of the Ram Fleet took place at the fall of Memphis in 1862. The Marine Brigade, however, was not popular with the Western Flotilla or the Army.

In 1863 the Western Flotilla was increased by thirty-two additional armored vessels of great strength and in 1864 by another twenty-four. By the close of the War, the Flotilla was the largest and the best equipped river navy ever assembled in the world, and it was used wisely and effectively.

One final effort was made by Nashvillians on their own accord to obtain gunboats for use on the Cumberland River before actual hostilities occurred. On December 5, 1861, about two months before the attack on Fort Donelson, Ex-Governor Neill S. Brown and W. G. Harding, a distinguished citizen, addressed a letter to General Johnston suggesting the propriety of constructing "a" gunboat on the Cumberland River. Governor Harris approved this idea unhesitatingly and it was favorably endorsed by Johnston. Then, on December 14th, at the instance of Brown, Mayor R. B. Cheatham of Nashville presented a letter to the Secretary of War, urging the construction of gunboats on the Cumberland and Tennessee Rivers. Brown, in urging the construction of gunboats, expressed the prophetic opinion that the City of Nashville was in imminent danger.

On December 25, 1861, S. R. Mallory, Secretary of the

Confederate Navy, belatedly authorized Lieutenant Isaac N. Brown of the Navy, then stationed at Nashville, to purchase the *C. E. Hillman, James Johnson, James Woods,* and the *B. M. Runyan,* familiar Cumberland packets, for approximately $110,000.00, and forthwith convert them into gunboats. Apparently ignorant of the lack of materials for doing this work, Mallory estimated that the boats could be converted into gunboats in from thirty to fifty days.

As a matter of fact, none of the four was completed in time to see service. Work had been started on the *James Johnson* and *James Woods,* and the rolling mills below Nashville were doing their best to complete the iron casements needed for their conversion when Fort Donelson was attacked. When Nashville fell, in order to avoid capture, the *Johnson* and *Woods* were sunk across from the present wharf at Nashville. Old time rivermen have stated to me that Charles Gallagher, father of Captain Tom Gallagher of Nashville who will be mentioned again later on, set the two boats on fire. For some years their superstructure was visible at very low stages of the river. Thus, there was not a single gunboat available to defend the Cumberland.

When General Albert Sidney Johnston arrived in Nashville to assume his duties as Commander of the Confederate Forces in the West, he was fifty-eight years old and headed the list of full generals in active service. This distinction in itself affords ample proof of the esteem in which he was held. He was perhaps the best qualified military leader on either side of the War. His arrival in Nashville was hailed with delight throughout Tennessee and the deep South. Prior to his appointment there had been criticism, officially and otherwise, for the failure of the Confederate Government to give Tennessee more support in men and materials for her defense. His arrival stopped all this.

When Kentucky failed to cast her lot with the South, Tennessee became the first line of defense and offense. She could be compared to a great viaduct with springboards sticking out from every side. In the hands of the Confederacy Tennessee could defensively represent gilt edge security as a "buffer" against penetration of the Deep South and offensively she could be a menace to the entire Ohio Valley. In the hands of the North she could be used as a wedge, splitting the heart of the South in two parts, turning the left flank of the Confederacy, interrupting commerce and industry and finally bringing an end to hostilities. Thus Tennessee, with its rolling hills, rivers and railroads, sprawling farms and growing industries, was the key to many military problems. No one appreciated these facts more than General Johnston, a superb officer and one deeply conscious of his responsibility.

While the Confederacy, during the early days of the War, was criticized and may have seemed indifferent to forwarding the men and tools of war to Tennessee as expected, this was not due to any lack of appreciation of the state's military importance. It should be remembered that the Confederacy was an infant republic which at the start of the War had no army or navy, and it seemed a necessary obligation of each southern state to arm and protect itself pending the organization of a central government. Such a course of action was naturally adopted by the seceding states which clung to the traditional doctrine of "State's Rights." It had many faults. For example, every state, no matter how far removed from actual danger, nevertheless, considered it essential to first protect its own borders. Such difficulties would be overcome, but they required time and patience.

It did not take very long, however, for other states and particularly those like Tennessee whose geographical position brought them automatically on the firing line, to ask the central government for immediate military assistance. Such pleas were not born from any lack of enthusiasm among the people. Tennessee was peculiarly blessed in her leadership. Governor Harris was considered one of the ablest governors in the Confederacy. Largely due to his vigorous and outspoken administration, the state early became aroused despite the fact that a large portion of East Tennessee remained loyal to the Union. Large armies were raised, industries were rapidly converted into munitions plants, cannons were turned out and uniforms manufactured. But the truth remained that Tennessee, like all the rest of the South, was utterly unprepared to fight a war.

It took the trained eye of Johnston only a very short time to see that Tennessee was defensively very weak, and that any immediate offense was out of the question. His combined military forces, when he assumed command, were about 20,000 men. Most of these were untrained and without modern arms. Shot-guns, muskets, flint-locks and made-over rifles were the predominating types of guns in use. Artillery was scarce and heavy guns for the most part untested and manned by inexperienced men.

Johnston's command extended from the Appalachian Mountains to the Kansas border. On his way down to Nashville he had ordered General Felix Zollicoffer, with 4,000 untrained troops, to Cumberland Gap. After conferring with Governor Harris, he decided to visit his roommate of West Point days, General Leonidas Polk, who had already moved to Columbus, Kentucky, the northern terminus of the Mobile and Ohio Railroad. Polk's decision to occupy Columbus finally dispensed with the delicate questions involved in the neutrality of Kentucky. Polk, known as the "Fighting Bishop," because he was a bishop in the Episcopal Church, had thus automatically created the western terminus in the line of defense. Johnston established the center of the line on Bowling Green, Kentucky. He then ordered Brigadier General Simon Bolivar Buckner to that point with 4,000 troops, thereby controlling the L. & N. Railroad leading south to Nashville, Clarksville and Memphis.

After repeated warnings to the Confederate Government that his position was untenable without additional troops and proper arms, Johnston, by calling on the governors of Tennessee, Alabama and Mississippi finally managed to establish garrisons at Hopkinsville, Russellville, Canton and Eddyville in Kentucky, and at Union City, Clarksville and Jackson in Tennessee.

These raw and untrained troops did not exceed 5,000 in

number. He also managed to place small contingents at Fort Henry and Fort Donelson, numbering altogether not over 4,000 raw recruits. To strengthen his center he finally procured an additional 4,000 troops under General William J. Hardee, who had been stationed west of the Mississippi. These were sent to Bowling Green. By the end of December 1861 they were augmented by other troops, mostly inexperienced Tennesseeans, which made a combined force on all fronts of approximately 37,000 men. Johnston personally assumed command of the center and sought to arm and train his men.

Opposing Johnston were Halleck and Grant on the left flank, who combined had approximately 50,000 men. Grant's forces alone, in the vicinity of Cairo, approximated 20,000. Opposing Johnston's center at Bowling Green was Buell with 40,000 troops and opposing Zollicoffer on the right was General George H. Thomas with not less than 10,000 well-trained men.

The perilous position confronting Johnston was called to the attention of the Confederacy time after time. By January 1862 Johnston knew he would be attacked at some point along his thinly held line of defense. All that prevented such an attack had been the failure of the Federal commanders to know the true situation regarding his troops and their disposal. He could hardly be expected to keep this information from the enemy much longer. Through various movements, however, he tried to give the impression that he might take up the offensive and was much stronger than he was. This game of bluff, he knew, could not last much longer. As a matter of fact several armed "brushes" had already taken place.

The opening skirmish on the Cumberland took place October 18, 1861, at Canton, Kentucky, between the *Conestoga* and the cavalry forces under Lieutenant Colonel Nathan Bedford Forrest. The ever alert Foote had constantly employed the *Tyler, Lexington* and *Conestoga* to reconnoiter the Tennessee and Cumberland Rivers, and it was one of these routine trips that led to trouble. Forrest arrived at

Canton ahead of the *Conestoga* on this occasion and carefully concealed one piece of artillery on the outskirts of the
town in a wooded point. When the *Conestoga* approached to
a distance of fifty yards, one shot was fired which did very
little damage. The *Conestoga* was rounded to and its stern
gun used so effectively that the Confederate battery removed to a more distant point where it continued to fire.
While this was going on, Forrest's troops kept up an incessant fire with small arms, shooting into the portholes of the
Conestoga. The gunboat was driven away with no loss of
life on board, but with a disabled smokestack. This engagement was the first between a gunboat and land based artillery. Thanks to the ingenious Forrest, there were to be many
more.

The next engagement involving the Cumberland was far
more serious. It took place January 19, 1862, on Johnston's
right flank on the far upper reaches of the river at Mill
Springs, Kentucky, between the forces of General Zollicoffer
and those of General Thomas. Zollicoffer was a distinguished Nashvillian, a newspaper editor, and one of the
most beloved of the many leaders produced by the South.
He was very short, however, on military experience. Contrary to the orders of Johnston, Zollicoffer moved his entire
command across the Cumberland where he was attacked
by the superior forces of Thomas and compelled to stand
his ground with the river at his back. General George B.
Crittenden, who had been appointed to relieve Zollicoffer,
arrived on the scene before the battle. Finding Zollicoffer
had already crossed the Cumberland, he decided, after a
conference with the general officers, that it was too late to
alter positions.

In this engagement, which was one of the bloodiest in the
entire war, Zollicoffer lost his life and his army was completely routed. Only remnants finally succeeded in recross-
ing the Cumberland, thanks to a worn-out steamboat, the
name of which still remains unknown. The effect of this
unfortunate battle, which should never have been fought,
was instantaneous. Johnston now had no available troops to

send to East Tennessee to replace those of Zollicoffer, and it left his right flank completely unprotected.

Hardly had Johnston received news of Mill Springs before he was informed of activity on his left flank along the Cumberland and Tennessee Rivers in Western Kentucky. While he was pondering the question of future movements, Halleck, Grant and Buell answered it. They had determined on a campaign which, if successful, would compel him to change his entire line of defense, not just a part of it.

The Federal plan, like the one suggested by Eads for the Ohio and Mississippi, among other things involved the blockade of both the Cumberland and Tennessee, but was to be executed in an entirely different way. Grant was to swoop down from the vicinity of Cairo and Paducah with a force of approximately 20,000 men and attack Fort Henry and then Fort Donelson, in conjunction with the Western Flotilla, under command of Admiral Foote. Grant's troops would be moved by steamboats in order to give an element of surprise to the attack. The powerful gunboats would be deployed near the forts and bring their heavy guns to bear and reduce them. In the meantime, Buell, who had been heavily reinforced, would press Johnston's center at Bowling Green and prevent his forces in that sector from being diverted to protect the forts.

At first it had been difficult to get complete cooperation from Buell. In addition Foote desired to attack Fort Donelson as the first objective, whereas Grant desired to move on Fort Henry. Buell was lukewarm toward the plan, because he had overestimated the size of Johnston's army. He did not visualize the offensive power of the gunboats and the tremendous assistance which they could render. He had not had an opportunity to observe their work. Unfortunately Buell and Grant also were admittedly not fond of each other, which did not help matters.

Halleck, in emphasizing that the plan should be put into effect as soon as possible, pointed out to Washington that the fall of Fort Henry and Fort Donelson would weaken the whole arc of Confederate fortifications in Kentucky. If successful, he rightfully contended it would be impossible for Johnston to retain possession of Columbus, Island No. 10, and Memphis or defend the Mississippi River all the way to Vicksburg. Fort Henry and Fort Donelson, Halleck correctly surmised, being to the rear of such fortifications, would be the entering wedge that would divide the forces of Johnston on the east with the rest of his army west of the Cumberland and Tennessee Rivers.

Grant and Foote left Cairo on February 2nd, proceeded up the Ohio and turned into the Tennessee on the same day. Grant had three divisions of approximately 18,000 men being transported by more than forty steamboats—more than ever before assembled in one place anywhere in the world. They had come from all the larger river ports held by the North and their rendezvous was at Cairo. They were accompanied by seven gunboats heretofore referred to, under command of Foote. The river was at a good stage for the work to be undertaken. Without the use of steamboats it would have been impossible to have moved an army during mid-winter over the muddy roads of Western Kentucky. Grant, therefore, had correctly assumed he might to some extent catch his opponent by surprise.

Some of the more familiar Cumberland packets used in this maneuver were the *City of Memphis, Iatan, Chancellor, B, Emerald, Aleck Scott, January, Fanny Bullitt, Minnehaha, Hannibal, G. W. Graham, Rob Roy, Prairie Rose, Wilson, Empress, White Cloud, Fairchild, Baltic, Adams* and *Tutt.*

The transports and gunboats arrived at Bailey's Ferry within gun shot of Fort Henry on the morning of February 4th. There they were discovered by a lookout. He was indeed observing a novel sight. Steamboats had been used for many various purposes, but never before in an amphibious military operation to transport an entire army.

Grant, with 12,000 troops, stayed on the Tennessee side of the river, and General C. F. Smith, with 6,000 troops, was detached to the left bank to take Fort Heiman opposite Fort Henry. Smith and his troops had little to do since Fort Heiman had not been completed and was un-occupied. By sundown on February 5th, all the troops had been landed. The gunboats had taken a position some three miles below the fort. Here they remained until 1 A.M. the following day when they steamed up the river within sight of the fort.

Admiral Foote was personally present to direct and deploy his gunboats. These included his flagship, the *Cincinnati*, the *Corondelet*, and the *St. Louis*, each with thirteen guns, the *Essex* with five guns, and the *Tyler*, with seven guns, the *Lexington* with six guns, and the *Conestoga* with four guns. They presented an awesome sight on the muddy river which was on a seasonal rise.

Despite the heroic defense of the Southern forces under General Tilghman, the fort surrendered to Foote on February 6, 1862, after a bombardment lasting one hour and eight minutes. The fire of the gunboats was terrific. The stage of the river permitted them to level their guns directly against the batteries of the fort. Foote had struck at exactly the right time to make his gunboats most effective.

The Confederate batteries, although inexperienced, wreaked considerable damage on the gunboats. Tilghman, in the final stages, manned one of the guns himself. The *Cincinnati* received thirty-one shot, the *Essex* fifteen, the *St. Louis* seven and the *Corondelet* six. There were seven killed on board the *Essex* and twenty-six wounded. Twenty-eight of these casualties resulted from steam scalding on the *Essex* which received a direct hit in her boilers. This type of hit was most feared of any. In addition there were five reported missing and these were assumed to be dead. This made a total of thirty-eight casualties.

Foote, taking advantage of his victory, directed the *Tyler*, *Conestoga* and the *Lexington* to move further up the Tennessee to Florence, Alabama. The Confederate gunboat *Eastport*, heretofore mentioned, was captured and taken in tow, and a large quantity of quartermaster provisions was confiscated. Several steamboats, including the *Appleton Bell*, *Lynn Boyd*, *Sam Kirkman*, *Julius* and *Time* were burned by their southern owners, rather than be captured. In addition, the steamer *Dunbar* was sunk, and the *Muscle* and *Sally Ward* captured.

The untried gunboats had done their work well. Grant, hampered by rain and mud, was unable to bring his forces to bear against Fort Henry, and 2,500 of the Confederate troops were evacuated to Fort Donelson. Grant and Foote now turned their attention to that fort twelve miles to the east and on the left bank of the Cumberland.

In the meantime, General Johnston, suddenly faced with a possible defeat bordering on a catastrophe, held a hurried conference at his headquarters in Bowling Green with members of his staff. These now included General P. T. G. Beauregard lately transferred from Virginia. Something had to be done quickly, and those critics of General Johnston who later arose to condemn him for the loss of Nashville failed to consider just how overwhelming the odds were against him at the moment. He had neither the arms nor men, and certainly not the gunboats available to meet Grant and Foote, and at the same time protect his own army against Buell, who greatly outnumbered him.

It was obvious, if Fort Donelson fell, all of the Confederate forces in Western Kentucky and Tennessee would be separated from him and Nashville would be within easy reach of the Federal armies. He therefore decided to defend Nashville by making a stand at Fort Donelson. Polk at Columbus was directed to take all but a small part of his troops down the Mobile and Ohio Railroad into Tennessee. Bowling Green was to be evacuated south along the Louisville & Nashville, and Brigadier Generals John B. Floyd, Gideon J. Pillow and Simon Bolivar Buckner were directed to move all available troops under their commands to Fort Donelson or that vicinity for the battle that was impending. General Charles Clark was ordered to take his command to Clarksville. Colonel Nathan Bedford Forrest was assigned to the scene of battle with his cavalry. These were all the available troops except those at Bowling Green directly facing Buell. If these had been diverted Buell could take Nashville with a corporal's guard.

Leaving out the details of the military operations which took place on land at Fort Donelson and any comment upon the strategy employed by those in command on either side, both of which have received much attention by historians, it is sufficient here to say that the Fort fell to Grant on February 16, 1862, after a joint land and naval battle. As a result, severe criticism was directed against General Johnston on the ground that he himself did not go to Fort Donelson, but had assigned three generals, Floyd, Pillow and Buckner, of equal rank and nearly the same seniority, to defend the stronghold. None of them seemed to have the power of decision so indispensable in battle and have left the impression of surrendering the Fort too hastily, despite admittedly heavy odds against them.

All of the troops at Fort Donelson were captured, except Forrest's Cavalry, whose able leader had refused to surrender, and a small contingent under command of General Floyd. Grant refused anything less than unconditional surrender.

Commodore Foote had again accompanied his fleet of gunboats to Donelson, which included the flagships *St. Louis, Carondelet, Louisville, Pittsburgh, Tyler,* and the *Conestoga.* During the battle he was injured in the foot, which later led to his retirement from service with the fleet. None of the gunboats was sunk, but several were seriously damaged. Suppose we take a deeper look at this battle from the standpoint of the river.

Actually the Western Flotilla at Fort Donelson was thoroughly whipped by the land batteries. No one knew this better than Foote and it took much explaining on his part to cover up that fact, which he never quite succeeded in doing.

The gunboats opened the battle by attacking at 3 P.M. on February 14th, less than 400 yards from the fort. Here they were greeted with a tremendous blast of guns from the fort, which had purposely withheld their fire. Things were quite different from Fort Henry. Soon the river was filled with the sound of cracking timbers and metal. The *St. Louis* received a shot through her pilot house, which was completely carried away, and the tiller lines on the *Louisville* were disabled, rendering these two boats unmanageable. They soon drifted down the river. The batteries at the fort also struck the *Pittsburgh* and *Carondelet* between wind and water, which compelled them to drift downstream.

By sunset the batteries had gained a splendid victory and a great rebel cheer broke out as the gunboats withdrew. The *St. Louis* alone received fifty-nine shots and there were a total of fifty-four killed and wounded in the attack. The *Carondelet* in less than two hours had fired one hundred and thirty-nine shells into the fort. The loss of life among the batteries was nothing in proportion to that of the men on the gunboats.

All of the gunboats withdrew with exception of the *Tyler* and the *Conestoga,* which remained beyond the range of the fort. Admiral Foote, after checking over the serious damages to his fleet, left the fighting to the land forces under Grant who received the surrender.

After the victory, Grant joined with Foote in asking permission to move immediately on Nashville. Halleck refused permission to take the undamaged gunboats any further than Clarksville. This caused Foote to intimate that Halleck was jealous and their relations thereafter were severely strained.

Unfortunately, during the first day of the battle at Fort Donelson, the citizens of Clarksville and Nashville had been given to understand by both military and civil authorities that the situation was satisfactory. This was due in part to the reports of the first day's rout of the Federal gunboats by the land batteries which did not take into account the bad situation which had developed in the land fighting. The newspapers had printed highly encouraging dispatches. Even General Johnston, due to the blundering reports of his subordinates, had been advised on the night before the surrender that the operations at Donelson were progressing favorably.

The optimism of the people had been raised by all types of wild rumors, including one to the effect that Commodore G. N. Hollins, with his entire fleet, had fought his way from Memphis and was steaming up the Ohio and Cumberland to engage the Federal gunboats. As a matter of fact, on the day Fort Donelson fell, Hollins was busily engaged on the Mississippi with his fleet, with no thought of the battle at the Fort. He had been fighting near Island No. 10 and had received an urgent request to return to the defense of New Orleans.

On February 19th Foote and Grant arrived at Clarksville, accompanied by two gunboats, the *Conestoga* and the *Cairo*. They received the surrender of the city without bloodshed and issued a proclamation assuring the people that no harm would be done if they remained peaceful. The railroad bridge had already been burned before the gunboats arrived.

In the meantime down at Nashville panic seized the people and everything was in utter confusion. The suspension bridge and the railroad bridge, built by the Louisville & Nashville Railroad, were both burned. Immediate preparations were taken to remove the seat of government, and the military authorities hastily prepared to evacuate all of the supplies and provisions. The Nashville & Chattanooga Railroad placed all of its equipment at Johnston's disposal and rendered valiant service in transporting the large quantities of southern supplies to points of safety.

Johnston arrived in Edgefield across the river from Nashville on February 13th. From this point he watched his army under Hardee pass over the river to Nashville. Here he heard the first favorable reports of the battle at Fort Donelson and later the tragic news of its surrender. Moving over to Nashville on February 17th, he witnessed some of the depredations committed by the bewildered populace, including the plundering of warehouses loaded with Confederate supplies. Down on the wharf one or two steamboats had been loaded with supplies for the men at Donelson. The frenzied population ransacked these boats and dumped large quantities of meat and produce into the river.

Just as soon as Floyd arrived from Dover with his weary troops, most of whom came in by steamboats, Johnston directed him to take over the city and restore order. Forrest and his little band of cavalry arrived in Nashville over the Charlotte Pike about the same time and materially aided in this work. Plundering and other acts of violence were checked without any great bloodshed.

The names of the faithful steamboats that brought Floyd and his command from Donelson have not been preserved, but a good guess would be either the *C. E. Hillman, B. M. Runyan* or *Minnetonka*. They were all on the river at the time and are known to have rendered valiant help. According to one old version, the *General Anderson,* previously mentioned, had arrived at the Fort with four hundred reinforcements just in time to be included in the surrender.

Johnston remained in Nashville long enough to advise with all civil authorities. He later joined his army at Murfreesboro, having first assured all concerned that he would not defend Nashville in a battle with Buell or Grant. Each he knew had a larger army than his own, and both were expected to arrive simultaneously. This decision saved the city from bombardment.

The loss of the two Forts and Nashville brought General Johnston face to face with still another painful situation. As soon as the loss was reported he was subjected to criticism by prominent officials of the Confederacy and of the separate southern states, including those of Tennessee. He was abused for almost everything. Some of the "second-guessers" requested President Davis to remove him.

Davis, on the contrary, unequivocally stood by his general. During these hectic days Johnston exhibited the fine qualities of his character. In his official reports on what had transpired he stated the facts as they were and never sought to cast the blame on anyone else. He informed Davis that he would welcome a change in command—even suggested Davis himself—and then observed that the best way for a soldier to overcome the criticism was to wage a successful campaign against the enemy. This campaign was not long to be delayed and for audacity, organization and conception was destined to prove that the confidence reposed in Johnston was not misplaced. According to the southern viewpoint, at Shiloh it fell one stray bullet shy of a decisive victory which might have suddenly changed the outlook of the War.

The expected surrender of Nashville did not occur until February 24, 1862. By that time some of the frantic excitement had subsided and the people were more calm. Only one gunboat, the *Cairo*, came up to Nashville, arriving on February 25. She was under command of Lieutenant N. C. Bryant and convoyed seven steamboats up the river with General William Nelson's army aboard. The Sixth Ohio Regiment, attached to Nelson's command, formally occupied the city upon arrival. Mayor Cheatham, in the meantime, was assured by General Buell that no wanton destruction of life or property would take place. This materially helped to overcome the fears of the people, who, for the first time began to realize the hardships of war.

The loss of Nashville had a paralytic effect upon the Confederacy, politically, psychologically and from a military standpoint. Its loss not only demoralized the civilian population but also had severe repercussions in the Confederate Government. A speedy investigation was undertaken to determine the responsibility for the debacle. While this responsibility is even now subject to debate, the effect of it on the trend of the war is not. The suddenness with which Nashville had fallen and the bottling up of both the Tennessee and Cumberland Rivers, as well as the railroads at Nashville, all of which could be henceforth used by the Federal Government, changed the entire aspect of the war. Never during the war was the South to recoup its losses so quickly yielded. In the light of subsequent events there is substantial support for the belief that the loss of Henry, Donelson and Nashville more nearly lost the war in the Deep

South than any other battles fought in that section. The suddenness in the turn of events caused many to misjudge the seriousness of the situation.

Andrew Johnson, twice elected Governor of Tennessee, shortly before the war, arrived in Nashville on March 12, 1862, to assume his new duties as Military Governor. He was received with mingled emotions. By some Johnson was considered to be liberal and tolerant. He had managed to win the Governorship of Tennessee in 1855 against Meredith P. Gentry largely because of support of religious freedom and tolerance. If Johnson ever had any intention of being tolerant, it was soon forgotten. His acts and deeds while Military Governor were exceedingly harsh and remain difficult to explain. After the war, as successor to Lincoln, he was liberal in the treatment of the South. His conduct as a whole therefore has remained enigmatic.

Upon arrival in Nashville, Johnson declared all appointive and elective offices vacant until officials approved by him were appointed. Many authorities who had sons and relatives fighting against the Union, and many others with high principles resented such high-handed tactics. They were arrested and many prominent men were sent to the penitentiary. Civil administration sunk to a new low and thereafter Nashville was ruled with an iron hand.

All newspapers and publications, even religious periodicals, were suspended. Several of the outstanding ministers of the city were arrested and placed under military surveillance. Freedom of speech was a thing of the past. Public schools were partially closed and rendered ineffective.

"Steamboatin' on the Cumberland," until after the War, was conducted by the Federal Government and its carefully selected agents. Every boat on the river was seized and put in use by the Union forces. Nashville citizens, in the twinkling of an eye, lost their fortunes in steamboats and equipment.

Johnson, thanks to the various raids of Forrest and Morgan, became obsessed with the idea that Nashville might be retaken by surprise. Already suspicious of everything and everybody, he began to fortify the city. This having been done very thoroughly, he then procured a garrison to defend the city, which, from time to time, ranged from one thousand to several thousand troops. With due regard to the more refined methods of controlling public opinion, the military authorities also organized a secret police force. This built up a spirit of unrest and suspicion among the people.

As the war wore on, and the wounded were brought to Nashville, practically every church and school was converted into a hospital. With all its pride, culture and wealth, Nashville had become the first large Southern city to surrender. It was a city of suppressed hate and mistrust. Its plight was prophetic of the future trend of the War and its surrender not just an ordinary loss, but a full-fledged catastrophe.

General Buell, upon arrival in Nashville from Bowling Green, seemed in no hurry to carry out any plans he may have had. The partial destruction of the Louisville and Nashville Railroad by Hardee's retreating troops and the burning of the railroad bridge across the Cumberland before Buell's arrival made traffic very difficult and helped to delay him for a week. The bulk of Buell's supplies and equipment soon started coming in by steamboat. Familiar packets from the Ohio came up to Nashville in a never-ending stream. The wharf was once more piled high with freight, but this time it was ammunition and army supplies. Traffic soared to a new record and the faithful Cumberland henceforth served the North for the duration of the War.

Johnston, having withdrawn to Murfreesboro, wasted no time in reorganizing his army. Great activity was evidenced everywhere. Discipline became more rigid. Preparation was started for a movement to a new location "somewhere south of the Tennessee." This turned out to be Corinth, Mississippi, at the intersection of the Mobile and Ohio Railroad running north and south, between Columbus, Kentucky, and Mobile, Alabama, and the Memphis and Charleston Railroad, running east and west, connecting Memphis, Chattanooga, Atlanta and Richmond. At Corinth, Johnston expected to form a junction of his forces so suddenly severed and attack Grant before Buell could march to his assistance.

Leaving Morgan's cavalry in the rear to befuddle Buell and delay his pursuit, Johnston left Murfreesboro on February 27th. The army by forced marches arrived at Corinth on March 22nd. There Johnston made his junction with the troops of Beauregard and also General Braxton Bragg, who had brought 10,000 men from Pensacola. Polk and Breckenridge also arrived with their forces. General Earl Van Dorn was expected to arrive with 20,000 more troops from west of the Mississippi. With Van Dorn, Johnston might amass an army of 60,000 men.

In the meantime General Halleck over in St. Louis had received very little advice about events taking place on the Cumberland. Neither Foote nor Grant had kept him posted in detail. Grant, never long on making official reports, made none at all to him in the waning days of February. Halleck, with a view of protecting his gains and striking another blow if that seemed advantageous, had wired Grant on March 1 to move his army up the Tennessee. If Grant received the message he took no official notice of it. Finally Halleck, still not hearing from Grant, found out that he had left his own military district and had proceeded to Nashville within the military jurisdiction of Buell. In desperation and righteous indignation, he suspended him and placed General C. F. Smith in command. This indeed was a novel situation. Grant had received the plaudits of Congress for his victories in one breath and relieved of his command for insubordination in the next. This entire episode has never been satisfactorily explained. Which man was right is a matter of opinion. Neither had any love for the other.

Smith immediately moved the bulk of Grant's army, bivouaced in the vicinity of Fort Henry and Fort Donelson, up the Tennessee River. On March 10th, with the assistance of an immense fleet of steamboats of every description, Smith and the army arrived near Savannah, Tennessee. On the next and succeeding day nearly 20,000 troops disembarked on the east bank of the river at landings close as possible to the little town only thirty-one miles from Corinth, the point of Confederate concentration. The rest of Grant's army, numbering another 20,000 men, for the most part came in by steamboats in the next few days from Dover, Clarksville, Cairo and Paducah.

The number of steamboats used from time to time in these movements counting gunboats totalled not less than forty and no doubt some were overlooked in checking available records. It is safe to say this maneuver has never been equalled, and it remains a bright chapter, but one seldom mentioned in the history of steamboat transportation. By the use of steamboats most of Grant's army, free from mud and fatigue, had arrived at its destination twelve full days ahead of Johnston. Steamboats under way were always to be seen, often several at one time.

Shortly after arrival of the army in the vicinity of Savannah Grant was restored to command. He almost immediately transported his forces across the river in gunboats and steamboats to Pittsburg Landing, at the foot of a high tabletop plateau and nine more miles in the direction of Corinth. On that plateau in the vicinity of a little country church called Shiloh, Grant ordered his men to pitch camp and await orders.

For some inexplicable reason Grant refused to pay attention to reports of impending danger. The two gunboats *Tyler* and *Lexington* which Foote had thoughtfully left at Grant's disposal, patrolled the river daily. Their skippers had reported to Halleck the movement of Confederate troops all along the Tennessee in the vicinity of Corinth. They had skirmishes with Confederate outposts near Pittsburg Landing even before the Federal army moved to that point. They went so far as to state the number of Confederate troops and their commanding officers, including Johnston. Grant, however, still did nothing. No earthworks were built, no trenches were dug as Halleck suggested. With his usual laxity he failed to even keep Halleck or Buell fully advised.

If Grant was willing to sit idly by and do nothing, General Buell, now moving from Nashville to his assistance, was not. Moving slowly but surely overland from Nashville, he was doing his best to join the complacent Grant. The roads were bad, things went wrong, but day by day he was getting closer.

Johnston opened the Battle of Shiloh at 5 A.M. on Sunday, April 6th, a clear, crisp spring day. He had struck just before Buell arrived. By mid-afternoon Grant was hurled back in complete disorder. Johnston had been riding close to the front lines all day. As he approached his own right flank in early afternoon, he perceived stiff fighting in the direction of Pittsburg Landing. Quickly organizing his troops nearby for a charge against Federal troops under General Stephen A. Hurlbut which he sensed might complete a decisive victory, he then gave the order to advance and sat on his horse to watch the result. He never knew the outcome. A stray bullet mortally wounded him. The battle went on until darkness set in and then Beauregard, his next in command, called off the conflict for the day. Buell, in the meantime, came up with reinforcements and with the aid of steamboats hurried to the scene and the faithful *Tyler* and *Lexington* crossed the river to Pittsburg Landing. As the next day dawned Grant, with Buell's fresh troops breathing new life into his ranks, stormed across the blood-soaked plateau and what had seemed a great victory for Southern arms resulted in a draw followed by a well organized but heartbreaking retreat to Corinth.

In all nearly 20,000 troops, about equally divided between the North and South, was the cost of Shiloh. Neither side made claim to a victory on the sanguine field of battle, but unfortunately that is not the only evaluation which must be placed on its outcome. In the light of history it ranks with Gettysburg as one of the significant turning points in the War Between the States and, like that great battle, a stunning blow to the South. At Shiloh the Confederacy, above all else, was seeking a decisive victory. Johnston, like Lee at Gettysburg, could ill afford less. Thus Shiloh, from the standpoint of the South, is not only an epic battle, but a reminder of what might have been had Fate been less unkind.

Johnston vindicated his reputation as a great general. He made no mistakes on the battle field. Grant, according to some historians, fought the poorest battle he ever fought and was lucky to get a draw. Beauregard received his share of criticism for calling off the battle after Johnston's death. The Southern view still condemns him for a blunder which he strongly denied.

Foote and the Western Flotilla won still more fame and glory as a result of Shiloh. The *Tyler* and *Lexington*, under command of Lieutenants William Gwinn, Jr. and James W. Shirk, respectively, hovered near the battle during both days. No less an authority than Grant himself reported the two gunboats prevented a collapse of Hurlbut's position on the left flank guarding Pittsburg Landing. If his position had been taken, Buell's fresh troops might not have crossed over. They had great trouble in doing so even though Hurlbut held on.

Grant is not the only one who paid tribute to the gunboats. Leonard Swett, personal representative of President Lincoln, arrived at Shiloh shortly after the firing was over and he reported "that the *Tyler* and *Lexington* saved our army from defeat" and recommended a promotion for Gwin and Shirk.

Such is the Northern viewpoint. On the other hand the South has always contended that the bombardment by the gunboats was ineffective and if Johnston had lived he would have stormed Hurlbut relentlessly. He had plenty of troops, saw Hurlbut's weakness and knew he could not be reinforced at the time. Johnston would have been thoroughly justified in expending the necessary men to gain a position which assured him of a decisive victory, and he was in the act of doing so when he was mortally wounded.

Regardless of which viewpoint is accepted, one thing cannot be overlocked. The two gunboats under Gwin and

Shirk added greatly to the prestige of the Western Flotilla and from that time on Foote and other commanders received as many gunboats as they asked for.

In the wake of Shiloh lurked many dangers to the South. Some of these were obvious, including the fact that it sapped the available manpower. The entire South was stunned and grieved. And why not? A valiant Southern army, after a courageous stand and on the threshold of victory, had been forced to retreat. Grant and Buell, with huge armies, now stood at the back door of Island No. 10, Fort Pillow, Memphis and Vicksburg, ready to strike another offensive blow at the very heart of the South. They were in control of Nashville and its railroads and every other railroad in Western Kentucky and Tennessee, except the Memphis and Charleston. The Cumberland and Tennessee Rivers were completely bottled up and the Mississippi was threatened. Henceforth, supplies from the industrial centers of the east and mid-west could be transported without any serious interruption to the invading enemy. The Confederate left flank had been turned and the arc of defense as originally conceived shattered beyond repair. Johnston, reckoned as one of the best generals on either side, had been killed on the field of battle.

More trouble soon arrived and some bordered on disaster. Suppose we leave the Confederate Army under Beauregard at Corinth, whither it had retreated from Shiloh, and take a brief glance at some of the events directly related to the rivers, including the Cumberland, which almost immediately struck the South with paralyzing effect.

On the same day that hostilities started at Shiloh, April 6, 1862, Island No. 10 in the Mississippi River just below the Tennessee line, and one of the strongest Confederate fortifications in the whole chain of defenses on that river, was under assault by the Federal Army ably assisted by the *Pittsburg* and the *Carondelet* of Foote's Western Flotilla, and the newly completed mortar boat flotilla. On April 10th, the fighting was all over at the Island, and once more Foote and his Squadron received the plaudits of the Federal Government. They deserved it, for Island No. 10 had withstood all assaults by the Army until the gunboats arrived on the scene.

New Orleans fell in a surprising victory for Admiral Farragut on April 28, 1862. This was strictly a naval victory. It closed a major port and shattered the last chance the Confederacy had to organize any river navy to combat the now powerful Western Flotilla. It sealed the doom of the lower Mississippi. In this engagement, the ironclad gunboats *Mississippi* and *Louisiana,* which at the time were under construction at New Orleans and considered far superior to any gunboats serving under Foote, were destroyed by their own crews to avoid capture. This was a shattering blow. In addition, the *Manassas,* which was a powerful converted ironclad, was sunk below New Orleans, together with the gunboats *Defiance, Bienville, General Quitman, Governor Moore, Jackson, Resolute, Pamlico, McRae,* and the *Carondelet* (Confederate) as well as many others of lesser importance. The loss of all these vessels at the time almost destroyed the Confederate Navy on the Western Rivers.

On June 4, 1862, Fort Pillow, fifty-five miles below Columbus, Kentucky, was evacuated. If Memphis and Vicksburg could now be reduced by the Federal forces, the Mississippi River, as well as the Ohio, Cumberland and Tennessee, could be freely used as transportation facilities and by constant patrol of the Mississippi, the Confederacy would be cut off from the supplies so badly needed from the Western States.

Admiral Foote, who had received a severe injury at Fort Donelson, was forced to retire on June 12, 1862. He was succeeded by acting Rear Admiral C. H. Davis. Before Foote left his command, he had succeeded in building and capturing several more gunboats, and in converting other steamboats into naval vessels.

On June 6, 1862, six days before he relieved Foote, Memphis fell to Davis. The ram fleet under Ellett, who received a fatal injury in this engagement, ably assisted Davis and the

Western Flotilla. Ellett employed the ram *Switzerland* as his Flagship and the rams *Queen of the West, Monarch, Lancaster, Dick Fulton, Horner, Mingo,* and *Lioness.* Davis' vessels in this action consisted of the Flagship *Benton* and the *Carondelet, Cairo,* and the *St. Louis.* None of these vessels received serious injury. The Mississippi Defense Fleet proved a tough foe for Davis and Ellett at Memphis and it succumbed only after a spectacular battle. The *Lovell, Beauregard* and *Price* were sunk and the *Thompson* blew up. In addition the *Bragg, Sumter* and *Little Rebel* were captured. The *Van Dorn* managed to escape. The famous *Arkansas* had not been completed and had been towed up the Yazoo for safety, but the Confederate Navy as such on the Western Rivers was finished off in this battle.

Rear Admiral D. D. Porter succeeded Davis on October 15, 1862, as Commander of the Western Flotilla, and separated the Cumberland, Tennessee, Ohio and Mississippi Rivers into districts. Porter, after the War, became Superintendent of the United States Naval Academy, and was an excellent organizer. He soon saw the great good that could be accomplished by a constant patrol of the rivers. He began to systematically increase the number of gunboats on the rivers, and in this he had the hearty cooperation of the authorities in Washington. Porter had helped Farragut in the capture of New Orleans and, shortly before he was given command, the Western Flotilla had been transferred to the Navy Department. Thereafter the Flotilla became known as the Mississippi Squadron.

But let us return to the Confederate army at Corinth. General Beauregard, who had been joined by the Army of the West numbering nearly 16,000 men under General Earl Van Dorn, evacuated Corinth on May 29, 1862, much to the disgust of Halleck, and established Tupelo, Mississippi as the future base of operations. Halleck had assumed personal command of the armies led by Buell and Grant and had braggingly assured everybody that he would destroy Beauregard. His failure to do so made him appear ridiculous, as he outnumbered Beauregard two to one.

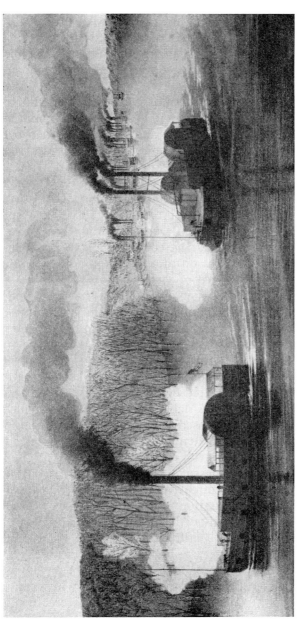

BATTLE OF SHILOH

The gunboats *Tyler* and *Lexington* supporting the National troops by firing up the ravine back of Pittsburg Landing. Sketched by A. F. Mathews, 31st Regiment G.V.U.S.A. (Courtesy of Library of Congress)

On June 27th, differences having arisen between Beauregard and President Davis, General Braxton Bragg succeeded to the command of the Army of Tennessee, which gave him practically the same duties as General Johnston had before his death.

In the meantime, Halleck, to the consternation of his immediate subordinates, had gone to Washington as commander of all Federal forces. Grant and Buell had taken over their respective independent commands. Buell was soon ordered to East Tennessee. Grant remained in front of Bragg to protect Western Tennessee and Kentucky and to keep a watch over Mississippi and Vicksburg. Collectively they commanded forces of approximately 100,000. A split in their forces offered the only chance Bragg had for another bit of strategy. What he could not do to Grant and Buell combined he might do to either separately, namely, attack with a fair chance of victory.

The Confederate forces in East Tennessee were under command of General Edmund Kirby Smith, a graduate of West Point and one of the ablest leaders on either side in the War. He had gathered together about 20,000 troops and they were officered by men who, as later events proved, were far above the average. Smith also was a keen observer.

On July 20th, Smith wired Bragg that Buell (whose army was then near Stevenson, Alabama, where the Nashville & Chattanooga Railroad crossed the Memphis and Charleston Railroad) was in a threatening position. He indicated it might be a propitious time to cooperate and move on Buell. No sooner had this message been received than Bragg started figuring on an offensive campaign.

The campaign in question had no connection with the Cumberland and is mentioned for the purpose of indicating the help rendered the Confederacy by another river. It started at Tupelo and was to be a combined movement of Bragg and Smith against Buell to regain Nashville and Middle Tennessee. It finally wound up as an invasion of Kentucky. Bragg, following Grant's tactics of creating an element of surprise, moved most of his army by train to

Mobile, then by steamboat up the Alabama to the juncture of the Atlanta and West Point railroad and thence to Chattanooga. Buell was busily repairing the railroad as he moved West and this river-rail movement so surprised him that it gave Bragg a tactical advantage.

The "Kentucky Campaign" should have succeeded. Most historians place its failure on Bragg's own stupidity. He had Buell at his mercy and all of his supply lines cut. Bragg had moved his army with great ability over a long and tedious route. Smith had cooperated to the fullest extent. Once more the stage was set for a decisive Southern victory. But Bragg, with all the facts before him, faltered and stumbled and did not follow up. Buell escaped and again a valiant Confederate army with victory in its grasp retreated—to wait and ponder. Thus, what was a well conceived plan and a well executed one up until the final moments, turned out to be another lost opportunity.

At the moment of Bragg's fatal mistake in the Kentucky campaign, the star of the Confederacy was shining brightly despite the severe blows sustained. General Robert E. Lee had just defeated Pope at Second Manassas and was crossing the Potomac, the Deep South was still intact, many political and diplomatic problems had been solved. Vicksburg seemed secure and everybody in Kentucky except Bragg was positive Louisville, and even Cincinnati, would fall into his hands.

After the battle of Perryville, Kentucky, on October 8, 1862, which ended the campaign in that state, Bragg returned with the Army of Tennessee to Murfreesboro, arriving on October 28, 1862. Buell also gathered up his army and returned to Nashville where he was relieved by General W. S. Rosecrans.

Rosecrans, a very careful and deliberate man, early came to rely upon the Cumberland River as his principal transportation artery to the North. The daring raids often made by General John Hunt Morgan and others on the Louisville & Nashville Railroad in Kentucky, his only other important line of supply, so disrupted transportation on that

road that Rosecrans worried about any offensive move
unless the Cumberland was kept open. But he seemed unable to make his superiors understand the seriousness of
the continued raids on that railroad. This led to some bitter
words and accusations by Rosecrans concerning the cooperation he received. The truth is that Morgan's raids were
astonishingly effective during Rosecrans' stay and he was
correct about the importance of keeping the river open at all
costs.

The Federal Army, during the late winter and spring of
1862–63, received the major portion of its supplies by
steamboat up the Cumberland River to Nashville. There is,
of course, no possible way to determine just how many
steamboats were used in the movement of these supplies.
Troops also came in on transports guarded by the ever-
present gunboats of the Western Flotilla.

After the Battle of Murfreesboro on December 31, 1862,
which was savagely fought and resulted in a stalemate,
Rosecrans became gravely concerned lest his line of supplies and communications be disrupted. Morgan was then
loose in Kentucky and Generals Forrest, Wheeler and
Wharton were on the rampage, attacking supply and communication lines in Tennessee. Washington was also urging
that Rosecrans take up the offense against Bragg at the
earliest possible moment, so as to relieve possible pressure
on Grant, who was expecting to assault Vicksburg. Rosecrans felt he could not do this unless his supply lines were
assured.

Even before the Battle of Murfreesboro, Fleet Captain
A. M. Pennock of the Western Flotilla at Cairo received an
urgent request from General H. G. Wright, stationed at
Cincinnati, to transport supplies to General Rosecrans at
Nashville under convoy of gunboats. Pennock immediately
instructed Commander Le Roy Fitch, who had been placed
in command of gunboats patrolling the Ohio and Cumberland Rivers, to render all assistance possible.

This officer carried out these instructions and all subsequent tasks assigned him with zeal and ability. He is another of the lesser known officers who deserve far greater

credit than history has so far accorded for the part he played in the victory of the North. He was the officer who did more than anyone else to keep the Cumberland open.

Fitch took action immediately by ordering the *Fair Play*, *St. Clair* and the *Brilliant*, three of his best light draft gunboats, to Smithland, where they were assigned to regular convoy duty up the Cumberland to Nashville, making two trips each week. It was not uncommon for forty or fifty steamboats to reach Nashville weekly. This was more traffic on the river than ever before recorded. It was never exceeded in the future.

The apprehension of Rosecrans regarding this vital convoy system, however, was aroused by the sinking of the army gunboat *Slidell* at Harpeth Shoals by General Wheeler on January 10th, together with four transports. As a result, he asked for additional vigilance. Fitch thereupon took more gunboats off the Tennessee and ordered them to the Cumberland, even though he had received reports that Bragg was moving to cross the Tennessee.

On February 4, 1863, forces under Generals Wheeler, Forrest and Wharton attacked Fort Donelson, garrisoned by troops under Colonel A. C. Harding. Wheeler and Forrest were not in unanimity regarding such a movement even before it started, and the attack was neither well conceived nor well carried out. The fort remained in Federal hands and Forrest became very bitter toward Wheeler and blamed him for the failure. This attitude continued during the War and neither willingly served together thereafter.

It is doubtful if the capture of Fort Donelson could have resulted in a complete blockade of the river, but it would have had a tremendous psychological effect upon the people of the South. It would have had a most depressing effect at this particular time upon Rosecrans who thought he was facing a disruption of his entire line of supplies and communications. With the Fort still in Federal hands, supplies continued to move at will during the balance of the navigable season on the Cumberland.

Commander Fitch did not arrive during the attack on Fort Donelson in time to render any real assistance. In the waning hours of the fight, however, he came up with the gunboats *Robb, Tyler, Silver Lake, Lexington, Fair Play, St. Clair,* and the *Brilliant,* and ineffectively shelled the retreating Confederate troops. The gunboats also convoyed reinforcements to the Fort which was never seriously threatened thereafter during the War.

After this skirmish, Fitch reported to Pennock that he had returned to Smithland from Nashville, having convoyed forty-five steamers up the Cumberland, making a total of one hundred in all since the river had been navigable. This report proves the great service rendered by the river to Rosecrans at such a critical moment.

Always skeptical, Rosecrans however was not satisfied with the help thus rendered by the gunboats. On February 11, 1863, he telegraphed President Lincoln personally, asking for definite instructions to the Navy to cooperate. On February 12th the President called in the Secretary of the Navy, Secretary of War, and the General and Chief of the Army, and obtained their promise of cooperation, and he added in a reply to Rosecrans, "I cannot take it into my own hand without producing inextricable confusion."

Not only was Rosecrans begging for help on the Cumberland, but he also urged assistance in keeping open the Tennessee River. His anxiety concerning the Tennessee had been greatly increased because of the movement of Confederate forces under General Van Dorn in the direction of Florence, Alabama, in an effort to join the forces of Bragg. Fitch immediately directed gunboats up the Tennessee River, but never succeeded in cutting off Van Dorn because the river was not navigable up to or beyond Florence, where Van Dorn finally crossed.

Still not completely satisfied with the way things were going, Rosecrans next requested assistance from Fitch on the Cumberland above Nashville. In this way he hoped to prevent enemy troops from crossing the river and striking his flank. Gunboats soon were patrolling the river up to Carthage when the "tide" was sufficient.

Despite all of these fears by Rosecrans, only once were

any gunboats or transports lost or damaged on the river during the spring of 1863. On April 3rd the gunboat *St. Clair*, engaged in convoy duty, was shelled by Confederate artillery at Palmyra on the lower river, and nearly sunk. Three transports, the *Luminary*, *C. Miller*, and the *J. W. Kellogg*, were also badly damaged. As a result of this attack, Fitch sent other gunboats to Palmyra to shell the little hamlet. He later reported to Admiral Porter that not a single house was standing. Such destructive tactics were employed by the Western Flotilla on many occasions and excused on the grounds that "guerrillas" and not organized Confederate troops were firing on the gunboats.

By the end of the navigable season, Fitch was still in complete control of both the Cumberland and Tennessee. Rosecrans, despite the damage to the Louisville & Nashville Railroad, had gathered together a splendid army and abundant supplies. He was at last ready for an attack on Bragg. Nashville during this same interval had become a fortress city second to none in the country, with a garrison estimated at nearly 12,000 troops.

Rosecrans also had some tricks up his sleeve concerning his adversary's supply lines. One of these is here mentioned because the Cumberland was involved. Having had ample opportunity to observe the tactics of the Confederate Cavalry, Rosecrans authorized a campaign to send Colonel Abel D. Streight into Northern Alabama and Georgia in an effort to cut Confederate communications. Accordingly, on April 11th, Streight left Nashville with 2,000 men and 700 mules on eight steamboats accompanied by gunboats. He bivouaced at Palmyra until the steamboats could proceed down the Cumberland and Ohio, and up the Tennessee to Fort Henry. There he joined them once again. From that point he proceeded by steamboat to Eastport, where he met General Granville M. Dodge. This latter movement was a screen to the real threat into Alabama and Georgia. Rosecrans once more called upon Admiral Porter for assistance to protect Streight while he crossed the Tennessee. This time Porter, who had already sent him every available gunboat that could be spared, ordered Colonel Ellett and his Marine Brigade to assist Fitch, but they were of very little help due to low water.

Fully two weeks after Streight arrived in Alabama, General Forrest was put on his trail and as usual that meant no rest or letup for his antagonist. The pursuit lasted until May 3rd, when Forrest overtook and received the surrender of Streight and his entire command at the little town of Lawrence, about twenty miles southwest of Rome, Georgia, which was the destination of the Federal expedition. So ended a venture which once more combined a movement by land and water, through three states and on two rivers. It doubtless never would have been undertaken except for the faithful steamboats.

Rosecrans, after much prodding from Washington, finally took up the offense against Bragg, moving his army southeasterly in the general direction of Chattanooga. All during the hot summer months both Bragg and Rosecrans were sparring for position. A decisive battle, everyone knew, was in the making.

On September 19, 1863 the two armies met in the Battle of Chickamauga. Rarely, if ever, had there been such a military spectacle. Both armies fought with the courage and patriotism which had always characterized their battles. While they were fully engaged, a sudden gap appeared in the right flank of the Federal lines, due to the removal of certain troops by Rosecrans and the failure to give clear orders for their replacement. General James Longstreet on the Confederate left noticed the breach and ordered General John B. Hood to advance with his five divisions. This movement was quickly and skillfully accomplished. The Federal troops, upon seeing Hood's men on their flank and to their rear, became disorganized and could not be rallied. This resulted in a serious break-through and caused the Union forces to retreat in hapless fashion. General Thomas, on the left flank, by standing like "The Rock of Gibraltar," saved Rosecrans from a disastrous defeat or even annihilation and earned for him the sobriquet of "The Rock of

Chickamauga." But even so, most experts agree that Bragg, by following the retreating Union army and striking at once, could have won a complete victory.

Once more Bragg, as in the Kentucky campaign, had brought himself to the brink of greatness but would not take the plunge to gain it. The Confederacy thereby missed another opportunity. Nearly 20,000 Confederate soldiers died or were wounded on the bloody field at Chickamauga. This was too high a price for a partial victory even though Rosecrans lost nearly 16,000 men and was bottled up in Chattanooga. There he was relieved of his command.

Bragg lost the confidence of his officers and of his men and he also was to lose his command. Instead of a coup de grace being administered the Union Army, it retreated to Chattanooga and emerged once again as an even better fighting force.

General Grant by this time was in high favor with Lincoln after his great victory at Vicksburg. The fall of Vicksburg gave the Federal Government absolute control of the Mississippi and ended all hope the Confederacy had of obtaining supplies from the west. Another great loss had been sustained and one which could never be remedied. The victory at Vicksburg could not have been attained without the aid of the Mississippi. Steamboats, convoyed by gunboats, were used to transport all of Grant's army across the river below Vicksburg. Such an amphibious movement first involved the risk of running many batteries along the river. Grant took the risk and was enabled thereby to place his army in a striking position never anticipated by the Confederate generals. He readily admitted this great victory could never have been won without the aid of the Western Flotilla and the steamboats.

On October 16th, Grant was made Supreme Commander of all Union Forces west of the Alleghenies to the Mississippi, referred to as "the Military Division of the Mississippi." He arrived in Chattanooga after a hard journey over the mountains from Jasper. The same order appointing Grant as Supreme Commander also relieved Rosecrans and placed General Thomas in command of the Army of the Cumberland.

Upon arrival Grant immediately undertook steps to relieve the siege which had been inflicted by Bragg on Chattanooga. Federal troops were near the point of starvation by mid-October because the Confederates held all lines of supply except the tortuous pass over which Grant had just arrived. The situation was acute, but once more Grant received extraordinary help from a river and its boats. This time the Tennessee and the now famous "Cracker Line" would help bring him more laurels.

The Nashville & Chattanooga Railroad, the only supply line from Nashville, was open to Grant as far as Bridgeport, Alabama, twenty-five miles by turnpike from Chattanooga and some forty miles by river to Kelly's Ferry. From the ferry there was a good level turnpike six miles into the heart of the city. It so happened there was stationed at Bridgeport a young and ingenious quartermaster named Edwards and a former Lake Erie shipbuilder named Turner. Both were attached to General Joe Hooker's Corps of 10,000 men recently sent from the East to reinforce Grant. These two soldiers conceived the idea of building a small steamboat at Bridgeport to carry supplies to Kelly's Ferry. From an old saw mill and other wreckage there emerged the cadaverous but successful *Chattanooga*, the flagship of the now famous *Cracker Line*. It took less than thirty days for this little boat (resembling a cracker box with a smoke stack) to be built. Thereafter she daily, under cover of darkness, towed two barges to the ferry loaded with food for the starving army in Chattanooga. Thus was born the *Cracker Line* which helped save a starving Union Army, ably assisted by the Nashville & Chattanooga and mule wagons.

Other steamboats were soon added and by the ensuing spring four small tinclads, the *Grant, Sherman, Thomas*, and *Burnside* were plying the river to help prevent any future interruption of supplies or troops. Later on as the Confederate Army moved toward Atlanta they patrolled the river all the way from Muscle Shoals to Chattanooga.

The Cumberland, too, ought to receive some credit for the part it played in relieving the Union Forces in Chattanooga. The Louisville & Nashville Railroad (due to incessant raids) could not handle the supplies and later the equipment wanted by Grant. The Western Flotilla sent half a dozen gunboats up the Cumberland to Nashville and they took turns convoying into the city the usual forty boats a week, during the navigable season, all loaded to the guard rails. Their cargo, like that coming in on the L & N, would then go by rail into Chattanooga, where the aggressive Grant would get them.

Things were going to move rapidly in Chattanooga. Sherman, with his Army of the Tennessee, arrived at Bridgeport from Mississippi on November 14th. To save time they had gone by steamboat up the Mississippi from Vicksburg to Memphis. Thus one more army had received the blessings of river transportation. It took them five days to make this part of their trip and forty-six days to go from Memphis to Chattanooga. Halleck, chief of staff, had directed Sherman while en route to make "needed" repairs on the Memphis and Charleston Railroad. None had to be made on the steamboats.

On November 23 Grant began military operations to break the strangle-hold which Bragg held on Chattanooga. The Battles of Lookout Mountain and Missionary Ridge resulted and Grant again emerged victorious. President Davis reluctantly removed Bragg, "the great disciplinarian," from his command in the field, but refused to part company entirely. He was given the job of Military Adviser to the President, which involved matters of the most confidential nature, and gave Bragg further and unlimited influence on military policies. It was the most unfortunate appointment Davis ever made, in view of the known bias and prejudice which Bragg maintained toward so many of the leading generals in the army. His dislike for Forrest, who was not a career or regular Army man, was particularly uncalled for. General Joseph E. Johnston succeeded Bragg on December 2, 1863.

The Army of Tennessee in its retreat from Chattanooga had stopped at Dalton, Georgia. Here Johnston, one of the most beloved of all Southern generals, restored confidence in his army. He granted furloughs and ordered clothing. In all, "his boys" totalled nearly 60,000 men and most of them were veterans. No one knew better than Johnston how matters stood. If either Grant or Sherman "licked" his army, the war in the Deep South was over, and it might spell doom to Lee in Virginia. Johnston, under such conditions, determined to draw the adversary away from his supplies and to fight him only under favorable conditions and on a battlefield carefully selected.

On March 18, 1864 Sherman relieved Grant as Supreme Commander of the Military Division of Mississippi. Grant, in the meantime, was made a Lieutenant General and had gone to Washington on March 1 to assume the position as Commander-in-Chief of all the Union forces in the field.

Before leaving Chattanooga, Grant and Sherman had reached complete accord on the forthcoming spring and summer campaigns. Just as soon as the weather permitted Sherman would strike at Johnston with Atlanta as his goal and Grant simultaneously would strike Lee with Richmond and the rich Shenandoah Valley as his goal. Sherman's army, with Thomas, McPherson and Schofield as corps commanders, numbered close to 90,000 men. He would be fighting in enemy territory and against one of the ablest generals on either side, but Sherman felt confident.

One thing bothered both Grant and Sherman about the Georgia campaign, namely, the supply lines, and the possibility of attacks by Forrest against such lines. The fastest line of supply was over the muchly-raided Louisville & Nashville Railroad from Louisville on the Ohio to Nashville, where supplies could be re-routed over the badly abused but still operable Nashville and Chattanooga Railroad to Bridgeport, Stevenson and Chattanooga. Supplies could now also be shipped to Nashville over the Nashville and Northwestern Railroad from Johnsonville on the Tennessee or over the Nashville and Decatur Railroad from Nashville to Athens and Decatur, Alabama, where it joined the Memphis and Charleston Railroad into Chattanooga.

All of these latter railroads were usually in such bad repair that Sherman, like Buell and Rosecrans, refused to rely upon them alone. The other supply lines were the Cumberland River into Nashville, which in season would handle a minimum of five times more freight of all kinds than the railroads, and the Tennessee River, which in season was navigable up to Johnsonville, with rail connection there to Nashville, where freight could be re-routed to Decatur over the N. & D. or to Chattanooga over the N. & C. (See the accompanying map.)

Sherman had carefully built large supply depots at Paducah, Smithland, Nashville, Johnsonville, Athens, Decatur, Pulaski, Stevenson, Bridgeport and Chattanooga. In order to further protect his lines, Sherman had stationed General Hurlbut in Memphis, with an army of 20,000 troops to protect Northern Mississippi and Western Tennessee. At each supply depot there were garrison forces calculated to withstand minor assaults. At Nashville there were about 5,000 soldiers available for such service and at Chattanooga nearly 3,000, while in Paducah there were 2,500 and at Cairo 2,000. What Sherman wanted was to keep all of these supply lines open, but he knew he had to have both L. & N. and the N. & C. railroads and the Cumberland River up to Nashville open during any offensive he undertook.

Grant had set May 5 as the day for the simultaneous attacks in Virginia and Georgia. Sherman had certainly been vigilant in his preparations, but there still remained the one big question—Where was General Nathan Bedford Forrest? The absence of any activity on his part since Grant had broken out of Chattanooga was a source of great worry. All other Confederate generals were pinned down and accounted for. Sherman surmised that Forrest as usual was busy getting ready to strike somewhere to his rear and harass his supply lines.

Forrest had become enraged with Bragg after the Battle of Chickamauga for various reasons. Nearly all of his veteran troops had been placed under General Wheeler, whom he greatly disliked. He had refused to serve under Bragg and had gained permission of Davis to go into Western Tennessee and Northern Mississippi to recruit a new cavalry unit. "Old Bed," still with fire in his eyes, arrived in Okolona on November 15th with only 279 men and four guns, a very small army for a major-general's command. In twenty-one days he had raised an army of over 4,000 men and was ready to strike again. For the first time he was also to receive good cooperation from young General Stephen D. Lee, who was now his Department Commander.

During the month of January, 1864, Forrest was stationed at the little town of Oxford, Mississippi. Sherman had already received news on December 3rd that he was ready to "ride again." As a matter of fact, he had played a serious game of hide and seek with Hurlbut, inflicting much damage. Above all else, however, Forrest had equipped his men and by various deceptive movements had created the customary psychological fear in his adversary.

The reports about Forrest brought on a renewed correspondence between Grant and Sherman and Admiral Porter of the Mississippi Squadron. The Admiral was notified that Forrest was going to strike at both the Cumberland and Tennessee and that every possible precaution must be taken to avoid any interruption of traffic on these rivers.

Grant also requested that Fitch be sent up the Cumberland as far as Point Isabel, (Burnside), Kentucky, to deliver much needed supplies to General Ambrose Burnside and to protect him from a large number of guerrillas said to be gathering in that section. Fitch assigned Acting Lieutenant H. A. Glassford with the gunboat *Reindeer* to go with the *Silver Cloud* up the river to quell such forces, if any existed.

Some of the other steamboats and armed transports employed in this mission were the *Silver Lake, Pioneer, Marmora, Hazel Dell, Mariner, Hartupee, Victory,* and the *Newsboy.* The expedition was fired on at various points on the river beginning at Hartsville, but with little success, and reinforcements were delivered to the garrison at Carthage. Southern sympathizers between Hartsville and Celina were driven off and the gunboats proceeded to intimidate the residents of these places and other small hamlets by shelling them on the theory that "guerrillas" were sniping at the boats.

Another expedition under Glassford with the gunboats *Reindeer* and *Victory* was made up the river at Grant's insistence during the latter part of January, 1864. On this occasion a thousand troops were convoyed into Jackson County. The gunboats once more terrorized the countryside above Carthage and as far up as Celina.

Other familiar boats on the Cumberland River serving the Federal Government one way or another in the spring of 1864 were the *Emma, Nannie, Nettie, Ollie Sullivan, A. Baker, Alpha, Echo No. 2, Duke, J. W. Cheeseman, Lilly, Anna, Venus, Kenton, City of Pekin, Prairie State, Gennie Hopkins, Aurora, Mollie Able, Liberty, Lawrence, Savannah, Norman, Duke of Argyle, Shreveport, Prima Donna* and *War Eagle.*

Fitch, who by this time was a veteran of many gunboat engagements, had worked out and completed a system of convoying which had surpassed anything he had hitherto accomplished for Buell and Rosecrans. The wharf at Nashville during the winter and spring of 1863–1864 was so congested with freight that boats could not unload for days at a time. The depots at Nashville and Chattanooga and at places like Athens, Decatur, Pulaski, Stevenson and Bridgeport were overflowing. Not a single transport was lost on either river during the navigable season. That was an accomplishment which should be credited to Fitch.

In the meantime, while Forrest had made no attacks against the gunboats and convoys, he had been very busy in West Tennessee. Sherman knew better than anyone that when Forrest struck it would be strongly felt. This was putting it mildly. During the winter of 1863 and spring of 1864 he met and outfought some of the ablest generals the North could offer, including Generals Hurlbut, Benjamin H. Grierson, William Sooy Smith, S. D. Sturgis, A. J. Smith, Cadwallader C. Washburn and others. With a skill akin to genius, he struck with brilliant success at Okolona, Paducah, where he held the town for 10 hours, destroyed a transport and obtained supplies, Fort Pillow and won a dazzling victory in the Battle of Brice's Cross Roads, which is considered a model for all students of military science. Since none of these with the possible exception of Paducah involved any river activities, they will not be further mentioned.

These activities by Forrest from December, 1863, through June, 1864 were most exasperating to Sherman because he had seemingly left no possible loophole open in his plans to press against Johnston and Atlanta. Now, if he advanced farther south, it was with the full realization that Forrest was in his rear, moving all over Northern Mississippi and West Tennessee with perfect abandonment and knifing his lines and depots to pieces. What chagrinned him most was the fact that none of the officers he had selected to crush Forrest had inflicted serious injury upon him, although they had many more troops. There was always one excuse after another.

After the victory at Brice's Cross Roads on June 10, 1864, Forrest counted noses and found that his army consisted of nearly ten thousand men divided in three cavalry divisions under Chalmers, Buford and Roddy, and an infantry division under Lyon. These troops were now all veterans, well fed and well disciplined. Every Federal general whom Sherman personally selected to "handle" Forrest, had felt the devastation of his attacks. Sherman issued orders that Forrest must be annihilated regardless of the sacrifice it might entail.

By the first of July, Forrest was in the best possible position to aid Johnston by striking a decisive blow to the river and rail supply lines in Western Kentucky and Tennessee. He could then move directly into Middle Tennessee. If lucky he might even regain Tennessee with some help.

His effort to help Johnston was not to be realized although Johnston had urgently requested Davis three or four times to authorize it. Governor Brown of Georgia had made a similar request on July 5th. Other officials had done the same thing but Davis, still listening to Bragg, refused to permit such a campaign.

Thus, while the roads were good and Forrest could move more boldly and with more men than ever before, he was unable to do what everybody else in the Confederacy, except Davis and Bragg, wanted him to do and what Grant and Sherman were sure he would do. To make matters worse Bragg visited Johnston during June with the intention of ascertaining how much longer "Old Joe," as Johnston was affectionately called, expected to retreat before fighting it out with Sherman. This visit, which had some aspects of a spying trip, naturally infuriated Johnston, who informed Davis he was doing all he could with what he had and he was not going to fight a crucial battle until the odds were favorable. He refused to be stampeded by Bragg or Davis or to change his plan of campaign.

On July 1st Johnston was relieved of his command and General Hood was appointed to succeed him. The soundness of this decision will here not be discussed, but it is sufficient to state it shook the entire South. Johnston, according to his account, was about to launch an attack on Sherman, who had made the mistake of splitting his armies around the Chattahoochee River and Peach Tree Creek. This was what Johnston had been waiting for. He could at last hit Sherman's armies separately and in a favorable location.

Hood fought the battle on July 20th which some insisted Johnston had planned, but without his touch and the usual enthusiasm of the army. The battle was unsuccessful due to many factors—including delay. Hood claimed his generals had failed to attack either as directed or with vigor. Hardee, whose loyalty to Johnston was a religion, received the worst criticism and he was detached from Hood's army. The road was now cleared for the final attack on Atlanta.

In the meantime Forrest had rested in Mississippi. He was somewhat exhausted and disconsolate. Hot weather was on and he had eased up a bit. However, Lee, his commanding officer, was disturbed. General A. J. Smith, better known as "Baldy" to distinguish him from "Sooy" Smith, was moving on him with about 15,000 men. There was a battle to be fought and this time Lee as senior to Forrest would be in command although Forrest was on the field. Forrest disagreed regarding the place of battle. Smith and Lee met shortly at Harrisburg, Mississippi, in mid-July. It turned out to be a full-fledged battle and before it was over Smith had won a sanguine victory. As Forrest saw his gallant men dead and wounded on the field, he was livid in his criticism of Lee. This battle is an excellent example of what happens when there is disagreement among the top officers. Smith was overjoyed with his victory and received congratulations from all the Federal top brass—particularly Sherman.

Soon after Harrisburg, General Lee was ordered to report to Hood where he was assigned to command a corps. This he did with great gallantry. He was succeeded by General Dabney Maury, whose appreciation of Forrest was genuine and resulted in complete cooperation. Henceforth Forrest was not to be harassed in any way and he was to exercise his best judgment.

Sherman's elation over the affair at Harrisburg was soon to be dispelled. Forrest had hardly met Maury before he was gathering his troops for a campaign in Tennessee, right where Sherman would resent and feel it most. Smith was still encamped between Mississippi and West Tennessee. This would compel Forrest to go around him. This he did after leaving Chalmers near Oxford to mislead Smith, who was planning to move South on August 17th. On August 18th Forrest moved out with 1,500 men and of all things, towards Memphis, which was the headquarters of General Washburn, Commander of the District.

On an early Sunday morning Forrest appeared in Memphis and his brother, Colonel Jesse Forrest, stormed into the Gayoso Hotel, Federal Headquarters, and finding Washburn had suddenly departed, came off with the General's pants. These were later returned by General Forrest. By the 29th

Forrest was back in Oxford. Sherman, in disgust, ordered Smith back to Memphis. The city was thrown into complete confusion and very few, if any, of the Federal generals escaped censure. The value of this raid did not amount to much from a military standpoint, but psychologically it was unsurpassed. Sherman was receiving all sorts of information about Forrest. One minute he was in Memphis grabbing a General's breeches and the next in Chicago and the next in St. Louis.

Atlanta, however, fell to Sherman on September 2nd. Hood then withdrew his army to the west of the city and on September 28th Davis arrived in Macon to pay him a visit. Almost immediately Hood presented a new plan of campaign. If agreeable to Davis, he would move his entire army to the rear of Sherman and cross the Tennessee River as rapidly as possible, thereby compelling Sherman to either retrace his steps to protect his supply lines or divide his army. If Sherman retraced, Hood would be no worse off and if he split his army the units could be attacked separately. The plan was approved and it had considerable merit.

The conception of the ensuing campaign was excellent, and in many respects very well executed by Hood. He now had approximately 35,000 troops and if he could get back into Tennessee ahead of Sherman or any divisionary forces, he might repossess Tennessee and Kentucky, to say nothing of cutting Sherman's supply lines. The plan was appealing to the army composed largely of Tennesseans. They would welcome a return to home soil.

After the plan was agreed to, Davis, in Hood's presence, made a long speech to the army. Among other things he "detailed" the campaign which Hood was to make. This blunder was immediately reported to Sherman and Grant who refused to give it credence, thinking it was a ruse. Nevertheless it had the effect of putting them on notice.

Hood was not the only one who had a new campaign up his sleeve. Now that Atlanta was reduced, Sherman could make his suggestion about a future campaign to Grant with

United States Steamer Peosta (Courtesy of Library of Congress)

a lighter heart. It was to be known as "The March to the Sea." It would bisect the Deep South, and if successful, he could eventually strike Lee in Virginia from the rear while Grant was pressing him from the front. Grant finally gave Sherman approval, but it was conditioned on Thomas being given sufficient men to handle Hood.

Sherman's only difficulty was his supply line. It still remained the one problem he could not solve. Grant had already warned him to get it out of the way before he did anything else. Forrest was still loose in Tennessee and, if Hood could carry out his plans, he might destroy these lines entirely and then try to regain Tennessee. This was something to be considered. Nevertheless neither Grant nor Sherman seriously thought Hood would cross the Tennessee to give battle. They thought Chattanooga was his real object and he would try to take that "rail head," then cut the vital supply line south and strike in the direction deemed best. He would be at the back of Lee and might even form a junction with him if necessary.

Just two days previous to Davis' speech, General Thomas had arrived in Nashville minus his own famous corps which Sherman decided to keep in Georgia. Thomas did not like this, but what irked him most was that Sherman and Grant still failed to realize the full import of Hood's forthcoming campaign or the danger of further activity by Forrest. Both kept informing him that Hood had no intention of trying to recover Tennessee and engaging him in an all-out battle. Thomas flatly refused to believe such prattle about Hood. If Chattanooga was the goal, why was he moving toward Tuscumbia? Thomas, now assured of the correctness of his position, called for immediate reinforcements and from the time he arrived in Nashville began to strengthen his garrisons at all the railroad and river points within a radius of 100 miles of the capital. In this way he was also hoping to keep Forrest somewhat contained.

All of this took men and Thomas had none to spare at the moment. Steedman in Chattanooga had 7,000 in his command and Schofield and Stanley, when they arrived at Pulaski, would have 27,000. By pressing into service the clerks and quartermaster employees in Nashville, he could muster another 5,000. Wilson, his chief of cavalry, had only 3,500 effectives, but would have approximately 8,000 men when and if he could get mounts. To make sure of everything, Thomas was promised a corps of approximately 14,000 under A. J. Smith and if they arrived from Missouri by steamboat he could breathe easier.

Thomas also sent hasty and urgent communications to Admiral Porter of the Mississippi Squadron asking his complete cooperation. Porter in turn alerted Fitch and Shirk, his gunboat commanders on the Cumberland and Tennessee Rivers, respectively. The "tide" of both rivers was low and their work limited, but Thomas wanted everything in readiness.

The gunboats and tinclads were all spruced up, discipline was enforced and the guns inspected.

Thomas was aware that his immediate concern was Forrest who could soon be expected to strike again. But he would also keep a sharp eye on Hood. Forrest could only raid with his small army. Hood, with thirty-five thousand veterans, could fight and win a battle.

While Hood, Sherman and Thomas, in the late summer of 1864, were all working on their campaigns, General Richard Taylor in early September had succeeded Maury as Departmental Commander over Forrest. Taylor and Forrest happily struck it off together and almost immediately put into effect a campaign to help Hood. They both were intent upon hitting the enemy before he was fully prepared, regardless of what Davis or Bragg might now have to say.

Forrest repaired to Corinth and at that point gathered all of his troops. He was promised that Generals Wheeler and Roddy would give him assistance. Wheeler had arrived back to Middle Tennessee from a disastrous campaign to cut Sherman's communications in Georgia. Forrest met Wheeler at Tuscumbia on September 20th and found Wheeler had less than 1,000 men that could be turned over. Roddy was sick but he was able to return three regiments of

900 men. These, added to the other divisions, made a small but compact and highly trained army of about 5,000 men now available to Forrest. They had two great assets—a wonderfully clever and resourceful leader and courage born of experience under fire.

On September 22, 1864, four days before Thomas actually took command in Nashville, Forrest crossed the Tennessee at Shoal Creek, six miles down the river from Florence. This placed him within a short distance of Athens and Decatur. Both of these were main supply depots and fortified towns of considerable importance. Forrest, with his usual foresight and daring, proceeded quickly to reduce the fortifications at Athens and then attacked Decatur, burning blockhouses and capturing 1,200 prisoners, together with a large amount of supplies. Forrest rightly figured this would knock out the N. & D. railroad for a considerable time.

He next moved against the railroad trestle across Sulphur Branch, and burned and destroyed the bridge and its block houses, taking 1,000 prisoners, a large number of guns, small arms, ammunition, stores and wagons. He then continued minor raids into the heart of Middle Tennessee and after approximately three weeks, moved on Eastport toward the Alabama line.

On October 10th the gunboats *Key West* and *Undine*, convoying the *City of Pekin, Aurora* and the *Kenton,* with approximately 1,200 infantrymen and several artillery pieces aboard, under command of Colonel George B. Hoge, approached Eastport, where they were greeted by Forrest's ever alert batteries. The light draft gunboats escaped after receiving some damage, but two of the transports, the *Aurora* and the *Kenton* were knocked out and drifted down stream. The *City of Pekin* managed to pick up most of the Federal troops along the river banks.

Hardly stopping long enough to take a deep breath, Forrest next moved to his favorite haunt in the vicinity of Jackson, Tennessee. Here he met Chalmers and Buford, two of his trusted and most gifted officers, and with full cooperation from Taylor, planned his next move to help Hood.

After careful deliberation, he decided to disregard the danger of an attack on his rear from the Federal forces in the direction of Memphis, and in the latter part of October moved to Fort Heiman, across the Tennessee from Fort Henry. Placing one battery there, he mounted another one five miles further up the river at Paris Landing, the idea being to trap Federal gunboats and transports moving between the two batteries. The plan was immediately successful, resulting in the capture on October 26th of the steamboat *Mazeppa* and her barge with a large cargo of quartermaster's and subsistence stores. After the supplies were removed, the boat and barge were burned. Some of the supplies on the *Mazeppa* consisted of blankets and shoes, which were badly needed by Forrest's men.

On October 30th the gunboat *Undine* and the steamboats *J. W. Cheeseman* and *Venus*, bound from Johnsonville down the river were observed between the batteries. After a protracted fight, the *Undine*, somewhat disabled, was captured, together with her valuable signal book. The *Cheeseman* and *Venus* were next captured. The *Undine* and *Venus* were repaired by troops under Forrest, but the *Cheeseman* was found to be badly damaged, and after being unloaded, was burned.

At this point Forrest exhibited his usual ingenuity by organizing certain of his troops to man the *Undine* and the *Venus* for service under the Confederate Flag. This was Forrest at his best.

Lieutenant Colonel William Dawson was put in command of the *Venus* and Captain Frank M. Gracey, who had served as a pilot before the war on the Cumberland River, was given command of the *Undine*. Captain Gracey after the war was very active in the affairs of the Cumberland and was a distinguished citizen of Clarksville, Tennessee.

Having found the hunting for gunboats and steamboats very good, Forrest turned to Johnsonville where the game was bigger and better. Johnsonville at the time was one of the largest river and rail supply bases in Tennessee. Supplies could be transferred by rail to Nashville or stored until high water in the Tennessee, and then moved to Florence, Athens and other strategic points, for reshipment over the Memphis & Charleston Railroad to Chattanooga and thence to Sherman in Georgia.

On November 2nd, Lieutenant E. M. King, with the gunboats *Key West* and *Tawah* left Johnsonville, going down the Tennessee. Some five miles below that point he met the gunboat *Undine* and the steamboat *Venus*, now in Confederate hands, steaming up the river. The *Venus* was carrying two twenty pound Parrott guns. King opened fire and the *Venus* was disabled and abandoned, but the *Undine* steamed down the river. The *Venus* was towed to Johnsonville. On November 3rd, the *Undine* came up the river near the head of Reynoldsville Island, little more than a mile below Johnsonville. By this time the *Key West* and *Tawah* had been joined by the gunboat *Elfin* and they moved down to attack the *Undine*. King, however, sensing there was a trap to bring his gunboats under concentrated fire, returned to Johnsonville.

On the morning of November 4th, the *Undine* was again discovered lying at the head of the Island, and the skippers on the *Tawah*, *Key West* and *Elfin*, not being able to forbear the insult of seeing one of their own gunboats under the enemy flag, decided to move down the river and engage her. This was a most unfortunate decision. The gunboats were immediately met with a merciless fire from the well-placed batteries which Forrest had secreted in the most cunning manner along the river banks. It was like shooting ducks on a pond for the experienced gunners under Forrest, and all of the gunboats were put out of action.

Commander Fitch, hearing the firing, pulled up to the foot of Reynoldsville Island on board his flagship, the *Moose*, accompanied by the gunboats, *Fairy*, *Paw Paw*, *Curlew*, *Victory* and the *Brilliant*. From his position, it was impossible to render assistance to the *Key West*, *Elfin* and *Tawah*. The narrow channel, between Reynoldsville Island and the bank of the river, was infested with five guns of masked Confederate batteries under Forrest and he dared not run past them. The guns had been so placed as to bring point blank fire against any boat passing in the channel, but were not vulnerable to fire from Fitch's gunboats. Looking in both directions, Forrest immediately sensed what was going on. As soon as he knew Fitch would not approach he quickly changed some of the batteries so as to bring them directly against Johnsonville Landing and the large number of Federal Troops, steamboats and quarter-master's stores. The *Tawah, Key West,* and the *Elfin,* by this time were also tied up at the bank at the landing.

The three gunboats continued firing until they were completely disabled, when King ordered them to be abandoned and burned. For fear of the steamboats falling into Confederate hands, these were also burned. Forrest, by concentrated fire, demolished the levee and warehouses, and by the following morning, November 5th, left the scene of destruction. He noted in his official report that on this expedition his forces had destroyed four gunboats, fourteen transports, twenty barges, twenty-six pieces of artillery, valued at a total of $6,700,000.00, and in addition, had captured approximately 150 prisoners. Neither the victory nor the damage was seriously denied by the Federal Government. For sheer audacity the engagement remains unsurpassed in the military annals of the war.

This campaign on the Tennessee had a double barreled effect. It not only disrupted transportation on the Tennessee, but rendered the Nashville & Northwestern Railroad useless and it also left Thomas at Nashville doubtful of the future use of the Cumberland, which was so badly needed by him. It was one of the two supply lines now left open and the best one. The situation was so serious that both Thomas and Sherman took immediate steps to overcome it. Once more they urgently requested cooperation of the gunboats in protecting the Cumberland, which they emphasized was absolutely essential to their plans.

Fitch had temporary command of the Ninth District in

At Nashville Wharf, December, 1862.

l. to r. *Rob Roy, Belle Peoria, Irene, Revenue, Palestine, Lizzie Martin* and *Mercury.*

the absence of Lieutenant Commander James Shirk. He immediately notified headquarters in St. Louis that in view of the destruction wrought by Forrest on the Tennessee, he was moving the remainder of the tin clad gunboats to the Cumberland for fear transports moving supplies and troops on it might suffer the same fate. "The Cumberland must be kept open at all odds," he stated. He thought he could do this "provided one or two iron clads were given him." Commander Shirk, on November 9th, upon returning to duty, complained that due to the loss of the tinclads *Undine, Key West, Tawah* and *Elfin,* he had only the *Peosta* and the *Paw Paw* remaining in the Ninth District, which included the Tennessee River from Cairo to Muscle Shoals. Forrest, as will be seen by all these admissions, had "played hell" with all the pompous gunboats of the so called invincible Mississippi Squadron. He had "scared the daylights" out of Thomas, Sherman and Grant.

Admiral S. P. Lee succeeded Porter as Commander of the Mississippi Squadron on October 26, 1864, and once more Sherman and Thomas pleaded with him to protect both the Tennessee and the Cumberland, particularly the Cumberland, against any further attacks by Forrest. Thomas was particularly demanding because he knew that Hood had arrived at Tuscumbia on October 30th with an army of approximately 35,000 troops and was expected to pass over the Tennessee River at almost any moment.

Fitch, thanks to Admiral Lee and all this urging by Sherman and Thomas, soon had his fleet, consisting of the *Moose, Curlew, Brilliant, Fairy* and *Victory,* plying the Cumberland.

Of utmost importance to Thomas was the arrival of General A. J. Smith's army of 14,000 men from Missouri, who were coming in by steamboat to Nashville. Thomas was also short on cavalry, and almost every boat was bringing in a few horses for Wilson, the young cavalry commander. There was not even a mule to be found in Middle Tennessee, let alone a horse. In such a situation it was obvious to him that if Forrest could make a daring assault on the Cum-

berland and blockade transportation as he had done on the
Tennessee, it might result in the loss of the impending battle with Hood before it was fought. He also believed that
despite all precaution, the Louisville and Nashville Railroad
to Nashville might be demolished again. If this occurred,
then his as well as Sherman's supply lines would be completely out.

The big question in Thomas' mind, therefore, was: Would
Forrest join Hood or be reinforced and left to ravage his
supply lines from the rear? In such a situation, Admiral
Lee, like his predecessors, was quick to take action to assist
Thomas. He immediately assigned the *Carondelet, Neosha*
and the *Peosta,* powerful ironclad gunboats, to reinforce
Fitch on the Cumberland, and promised him other ironclads, including the *Cincinnati,* in an effort to keep the
river open.

By late November Commander Fitch had the *Carondelet,
Neosha, Peosta,* ironclad gunboats, and the *Moose, Fair
Play, Silver Lake, Brilliant, Springfield, Reindeer* and the
Victory, less powerful gunboats, to safeguard the Cumberland. These constituted the greatest fleet of gunboats
ever to appear on the Cumberland during the War. They
played no small part in the ultimate victory of Thomas
over Hood, as will be pointed out hereafter. Above all else
their appearance indicates the respect which Thomas,
Sherman and Admiral Lee had for Forrest.

Hood did not cross the Tennessee until November 21,
1864, after a delay of nearly a month. He has been severely
criticized for this seeming blunder, which he attributed to
the failure of Forrest to join him. The orders, however,
were delayed in transit to Forrest, who always contended he
left as soon as he received them. The delay, regardless of
who was at fault, was extremely costly to Hood from a
military standpoint, for it gave Thomas the necessary time
to receive the needed reinforcements and supplies and for
Schofield's army to be placed as a buffer in front of Hood.

In less than a week after his successful assault on Johnsonville, and while Thomas and Sherman were still worry-

ing as to where Forrest would strike their supply lines next, Forrest received his orders to join Hood. This he did on November 14–15th. The greatest single anxiety afflicting either Sherman or Thomas at the time was thereby removed. Now Thomas had but one target—Hood. It was exactly what he wanted to happen, but never expected. Upon arrival at Hood's headquarters, Forrest became commander of all cavalry, but it is doubtful if he had more than 8,500 well-disciplined and effective troops in his command at any one time. No longer would this ingenious leader be left to harass Thomas. Henceforth he would be a unit of a big army taking orders.

Thomas knew where Forrest was. If he remained with Hood, the supply lines could be kept open. Forrest did not have enough cavalry to march with Hood and at the same time seriously harass the Federal supply lines. Besides, in another two weeks, Thomas, thanks to the gunboats and the Cumberland, would have plenty of supplies and Smith's corps would be in Nashville.

For several weeks prior to Forrest's juncture with Hood gunboats under Fitch had been patrolling the Cumberland, both above and below Nashville. Admiral Lee came down from Cairo to personally supervise matters on the flagship *Cincinnati*, which on account of low water remained at Clarksville. He was in constant communication with General Thomas. According to contemporary accounts, Lee even sent a floating hospital ship, the *D. A. January*, to Nashville to take care of casualties.

General H. B. Lyon, attached to Forrest's command, marched into Cumberland City with a sizeable cavalry force on December 9th. With the aid of Grace's battery, three Federal steamboats were captured. He then crossed the river into lower Kentucky, marching east to Burkesville, recrossed the river at that point and again crossed back into Tennessee through Sparta, to the utter consternation and dismay of Thomas, Lee and Fitch. Lyon finally rejoined Hood's army after the Battle of Nashville.

This flying raid by Lyon was a belated and desperate attempt made under Hood's orders to destroy Thomas' lines of communication and supply to Nashville and to create a diversion of Federal forces. It was the move which Thomas so greatly feared would be made by Forrest only in greater force, before reinforcements and supplies reached Nashville. It turned out that Lyon's well-executed raid came too late to do any real damage to Thomas' plans. He simply did not have the men and the hour to strike had passed.

In his official report, General Lyon stated he destroyed property, including steamboats, estimated at $1,000,000. He claimed he had caused to be withdrawn from Nashville McCook's entire division of cavalry consisting of 3,000 veteran soldiers and also detained at Louisville Wilder's brigade of 1,500 cavalrymen. This was a diversion of 4,500 troops from General Hood. While Lyon may have been guilty of exaggeration to some extent, this exploit proved the vulnerability of the blockade of the Cumberland River by Lee and Fitch. It stands to reason that Forrest, with adequate forces, could have dealt Thomas a severe and timely blow if he had been permitted to strike before reinforcements reached Nashville.

Around December 1st Colonel D. C. Kelly, one of Forrest's most trusted commanders, was assigned the task of holding the bluff near Bell's Mills 12 miles below Nashville and cutting off supplies coming up the river. This battery, located some four miles by road from Nashville, was also a constant threat to the right flank of Thomas' line of defense. On the day before Kelly arrived at Bell's Mills, Fitch and his gunboats had safely convoyed all of General A. J. Smith's army of 14,000 men to Nashville by steamboats. Once again, the hour to strike had passed, yet the gallant Kelly, known as the "fighting parson," proved what even a small force in gifted hands could do to supply lines and all the fine gunboats sent up the Cumberland.

Fitch was assigned the duty of silencing Kelly's Battery. Early on December 3rd Kelly had captured the transports *Prairie State* and *Prima Donna* and was engaged in removing the supplies on them, when under cover of darkness,

Fitch moved down and opened fire. In the ensuing fight, Fitch succeeded in recapturing the two transports. He again tried to run past Kelly's battery with a convoy on December 6th, but Kelly's fire was so terrific that the convoy was sent back to Nashville and the superstructure of the iron-clad *Neosha* damaged. Not to be outdone, Fitch went back a second time on the 6th, taking the *Carondelet* and the *Neosha*, and once more engaged Kelly. Again Kelly ran them back up the river, the *Neosha* being struck over one hundred times.

No other engagement took place near Bell's Mills, or on any other part of the river, between the 7th and 15th, but during this interval the tinclads, *Brilliant* and *Springfield* had gone up the river as far as Carthage on patrol duty. At daylight on the morning of the 15th, Fitch again took the *Neosha, Carondelet, Moose, Reindeer, Fair Play, Brilliant* and the *Silver Lake* down the river to Bell's Mills, where he attracted the attention of Kelly's Battery. In the meantime a Federal Cavalry division, under Brigadier General Richard W. Johnson, was moving to the rear of the battery to attack Kelly. Kelly's Battery during this last affair was tearing the gunboats to pieces when he was forced to retreat. This gun play really opened the Battle of Nashville on the 15th.

Hood's advance into Middle Tennessee during the memorable days of November and December, 1864, which led to the battle of Nashville, has been traced by historians almost foot by foot. Schofield was somehow permitted to slip between his fingers at Spring Hill, which in turn brought up the disastrous battle of Franklin. Then with a depleted army Hood marched to Nashville, where he was crushed by Thomas and forced to retreat. Only the superb fighting qualities of the soldiers and the brilliant protection afforded by Forrest to the retreating army remained to soften the disaster which once more befell the Confederate cause in the Battle of Nashville. The end was now plainly visible.

The victory at Nashville was complete in every detail.

Thomas had won the type of victory which the North had been seeking for four years without success. In effect, it left only Lee with an army capable of fighting another major battle.

Thomas, however, even in victory carried a deep wound in his heart not caused by an enemy bullet. Grant had exhibited a total lack of confidence in him. He had even gone so far as to approve his removal on the eve of battle. Fortunately, this absurd order was never delivered, for Thomas, biding his time, had struck and won beforehand. Grant, it is now known, had completely misunderstood Hood's campaign from its inception and so had Sherman, whose obsession was his "March to the Sea." Furthermore, Grant, although fully advised, failed to analyze the situation at Nashville after the Battle of Franklin. He was misled by the relatively minor raid of Lyon and the disposition of Kelly's Battery. He thought these movements meant that Hood was preparing to move into Kentucky. Grant failed to understand that it would be suicidal for Hood to cross the Cumberland and march into Kentucky with one-fifth of his army out of commission and twelve generals killed or wounded as a result of the Battle of Franklin. How could he have crossed the river and where? He overlooked the threat of Murfreesboro to Hood. He refused to take any notice of the freezing weather in Thomas' plans.

In later years Grant could ponder these mistakes, but before the Battle of Nashville his conduct toward Thomas was reprehensible. He was second-guessing on a man who deserved his greatest confidence. It was Thomas, not Grant nor Sherman, who had diagnosed the situation and made sure of victory. It was Thomas who had won the first decisive victory.

Federal gunboats engaged in no other activities on the Cumberland River during the remainder of the War. Admiral Lee and the Mississippi Squadron, however, continued to assist General Thomas in his effort to prevent Hood from crossing the Tennessee River on his retreat. Lee personally took charge of this activity in the waning days of

December, 1864. They were unsuccessful in preventing Hood's escape into Alabama on the day after Christmas. Forrest and his cavalry later crossed the river near Florence. The gunboats, according to Admiral Lee, were unable to get over Muscle Shoals and were thereby prevented from doing Hood and Forrest any further damage.

Thus we come to the close of the part played by the Western Rivers in general, and the Cumberland in particular, during the War Between the States. Any doubt about the importance of the contribution made by the rivers and the steamboats may be dispelled by a few simple facts. Fort Henry, Fort Donelson, Shiloh, Island No. 10 and Vicksburg all fell as a result of joint land and river strategy. None of them would have capitulated at the time they did except for such strategy. Memphis and New Orleans surrendered to the Mississippi Squadron and the Navy respectively, without any assistance from the army whatever.

Buell's seizure of Nashville without a fight was due to the work of Grant and Admiral Foote at Fort Donelson. Rosecrans, in his campaign against Bragg, used the Cumberland River as his chief supply line, because of the raids on the Louisville and Nashville Railroad. Sherman and Thomas, like Rosecrans, relied upon both the Cumberland and Tennessee for a large part of their supplies. Thomas, before the Battle of Nashville, received most of his heavy supplies over the Cumberland. Due entirely to the steamboats he was reinforced by Smith's corps of 14,000 men from Missouri in the very nick of time. Gunboats also patrolled the river from Smithland to Carthage to protect Thomas' flanks.

How many corps and armies were moved by steamboats is hard to ascertain. We know that three of Grant's armies at least were transported by steamboats, one from Cairo to Fort Henry, a second from Fort Donelson to Shiloh and a third in order to successfully attack Vicksburg. Bragg moved a large portion of his army from Tupelo partly by railroad and partly by river to Chattanooga just before the "Kentucky campaign."

There should be little wonder that Buell, Rosecrans, Grant, Sherman and Thomas, each paid highest tribute to the rivers and gave their thanks to the Mississippi Squadron and its admirals. These thanks were not mere formalities, but were richly deserved. The service rendered by the river and its boats was often a distinct and decisive factor in military victory.

The surrender of General Robert E. Lee at Appomatox occurred on April 9, 1865. Traffic on the Cumberland for the most part thereafter consisted of the movement of troops and supplies. The surrender of General Joseph E. Johnston to General Sherman came on April 26, 1865. The Mississippi Squadron as such went out of commission in August of that year when Admiral Lee hauled down his Flag on the 14th of that month aboard the flagship *Tempest.* Gradually all of the gunboats of the Mississippi Squadron were withdrawn and by the beginning of a new season, September, 1865, a few privately-owned steamboats were back in the trade.

As might be expected, however, a return to normal traffic on the river took considerable time. All of the steamboat owners on the Cumberland had lost their fortunes as a result of the War. In addition the Mississippi Squadron and the Federal Army between them had bought or taken over a vast majority of all boats. Many of them were put up and sold directly after the war and almost immediately entered the packet trade. In this manner the steamboat business received aid in staging a comeback. It took some time to perfect a changeover, but the work was carried on with great rapidity and marked success.

No attempt has been made to estimate the average number of steamboats operating on the Cumberland during this period because of the War. There were more than one hundred boats which were included in former periods that continued to operate on the Cumberland at various intervals during this decade. Contemporary newspapers and other sources have furnished the names of two hundred and ninety-seven additional boats which at one time or an-

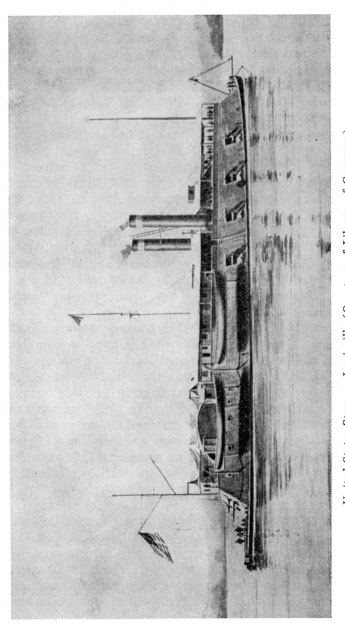

United States Steamer Louisville (Courtesy of Library of Congress)

other plied the River. This would make a total of approximately four hundred known steamboats that operated on the river during this period up to Nashville. There were doubtless many others since army transports were not always carried in the listings found in newspapers.

The Nashville Times of March 9, 1864 carried a statement that "The river and levee presented a lively appearance yesterday, there being nearly fifty boats in port." So far as can be ascertained this is the largest number of steamboats reported at the Nashville wharf in a single day. This, however, while interesting, is not a fair basis of comparison with normal years, since the vast majority of these fifty boats were Federal transports and supply vessels.

Immediately after the fall of Nashville in 1862, a strict embargo was placed on all private shipments of freight and high charges collected for its transportation. Before commercial freight could be shipped during the war, it was necessary to obtain a priority permit, which carried a high tax. The surveyor of Customs Office in Nashville collected these taxes and issued the permits. It soon became one of the busiest places in the city. Old records at this office prove that the merchants of Nashville, despite the intervention of War, continued to do a relatively good business during the occupation of the city by the Federal Government.

The Nashville Dispatch of January 5, 1866, announced the establishment of the St. Louis & Nashville Packet with the steamer *Imperial*, H. G. McComas, Master, and two Louisville & Cincinnati Packets with the side-wheeler *Rebecca*, under command of Captain Sam Hildreth, and the steamer *Bertha* under command of Captain Piersel. A month or so later another packet was operating under command of Captain James F. Miller; also one from Nashville to Burkesville, and still others to Memphis and New Orleans. This was an excellent beginning in view of the many difficulties confronting the steamboat business.

The railroads running through the battle zones in the South with two or three exceptions had been terribly mutilated. The Louisville & Nashville was one of the exceptions. It was so important to the Federal armies that after every interruption of traffic, it was immediately and generously repaired. Except for the first two and a half years of the War, when traffic was on several occasions completely destroyed by raids, the Louisville & Nashville remained open thanks to a round-the-clock vigil by the military.

Some histories prefer to say that the Louisville & Nashville Railroad, like Kentucky, adopted a strict policy of neutrality. This is neither the time nor place to discuss that matter. It is sufficient to say that the railroad was confronted with many grave problems for several months previous to and all during the War. Tennessee requested transportation of war materials over its line as soon as the State seceded. Thereafter such requests became demands. In fairness it should be stated that due to the neutrality of Kentucky, if the railroad had met such demands it would have been accused of transporting contraband goods to the Confederacy, which might have subjected it to drastic action by the Federal Government.

The State of Tennessee and the Confederate Government did all they could to destroy the roadway and equipment after the fall of Nashville. This was never done permanently as already explained, and, as matters turned out, the Louisville & Nashville was in an exceedingly prosperous condition at the close of the War. It was from birth a major competitor with the steamboats on the Cumberland.

With the fall of Nashville, the Nashville and Chattanooga Railroad, contrary to its own Southern sympathies, whenever possible, was taken over immediately by Federal troops. It remained in hostile hands until September 15, 1865. Many battles were fought up and down its lines. Much of its equipment was moved out before the invading army arrived. Some was sent to the far South and later into the Carolinas. The railroad acted as a supply line to the Southern armies so long as they held it. When force of circumstances changed the picture, it was then used as the chief railroad supply line from Nashville to the armies of Buell, Rosecrans, Grant and Sherman.

When the Nashville and Chattanooga was turned back to its owners at the close of the War, the Federal Government presented a claim of $1,600,000.00, bearing interest at 7.3%. This claim was based on the ground that it represented improvements to the railroad which had greatly increased its value. After extended negotiations the claim was finally settled by paying $1,000,000.00, although the Nashville and Chattanooga, according to its annual report of 1868, actually lost $128,773.28 invested in slaves, $922,-552.00 in Confederate bonds and $126,429.00 due from the Confederate States. It also claimed the Federal Government had collected $900,000.00 from passengers during the War.

The Nashville and Decatur Railroad had a hectic career throughout the War. It was used only in a limited way and suffered severe damage to all of its component parts, consisting of the Tennessee and Alabama Central from Decatur to the Tennessee line, the Central Southern to Columbia, and the Tennessee and Alabama to Nashville. During the War, whenever possible, it was a main artery of supply to the Union Armies south of Nashville. At the end of the War, it was evident that unless financial assistance could be obtained, the Nashville and Decatur would go under the hammer like so many other lines. There was this difference, however. It was the most direct line south to Birmingham, where there were rich iron fields, and to New Orleans, the chief port of Dixie. Both the Louisville and Nashville and the Nashville and Chattanooga would soon eye this railroad with jealousy.

The Edgefield and Kentucky Railroad was not in operation at the close of the War and its two proposed connecting lines, the Evansville, Henderson and Nashville and the Memphis, Clarksville and Louisville were also in great financial trouble. But this little span of railroad was not to be cast aside. Through "hell and high water" it was going to be built and to become a competitor with the majestic two-stackers then plying the lower Ohio and Cumberland. The process was to be painful, but here was the beginning of competition in the St. Louis and Cairo area of the steamboat business. This could not be overlooked.

The Nashville and Northwestern Railroad, another promising steamboat competitor, was in a bad state of repair when the War ended. It had wended its way by various connections to Hickman, Kentucky, on the Mississippi. Under proper management and financial backing, soon to be obtained, it became a serious and early competitor with the packets.

Steamboats, unlike railroads, which had been severely damaged by the War, were able to make a quicker recovery. There were no roads to be repaired or bridges to be erected over their routes, and it did not take as long to repair them. Steamboats under private ownership were soon operating and affording Nashville a transportation system of inestimable value. They had taken advantage of their good points and by 1870 had almost completely restored transportation on the Cumberland. What is far more important, they retained the confidence of the public.

On the other hand, the railroads had many obstacles to overcome besides badly needed repairs. Whereas a good packet could be purchased at a cost of $15,000.00 to $25,-000.00, this was a mere drop in the bucket compared to the millions required by the railroads for the purchase of equipment and the rebuilding of their roadways. Then, too, the damage to the railroads already built, while a great affliction, was nothing compared to the dismal and ugly financial situation which surrounded their corporate set-ups. The corrupt administration of Governor William G. (Parson) Brownlow, publisher, preacher and politician, who succeeded Andrew Johnson as Post-war Governor in 1865, ushered in a new era of graft under the guise of progress and internal improvement which has never been paralleled in the history of Tennessee.

In addition to the aid already extended to the railroads,

which was mentioned in preceding chapters, an additional $4,000,000.00 was split among fifteen railroads in 1867. Many of these were on the threshold of bankruptcy. During the last two years of Brownlow's administration the "pie was really cut" when another $14,000,000.00 of state bonds were issued to railroads, many of which were already defunct.

When Brownlow left the Governorship for the United States Senate in 1869, he was succeeded by D. W. C. Senter. His administrational was an improvement, but it did not stem the tide of "easy money." The damage had already been done. More than $34,000,000.00 of state aid had gone to the railroads between 1852 and 1869 and if city and county aid is added, the total would be about $50,000,-000.00.

Most of the good railroad men revolted against such slipshod methods in our State finances. The tragedy of this era soon developed a very strong public sentiment against such methods and resulted in the repeal of all the enabling acts. The new Constitution of the State, adopted in 1870, prevented a recurrence of such practices. These evils did more than any other one thing to retard the development of railroads in the State of Tennessee, and most certainly detracted from their ability to compete with the steamboats. During this unfortunate period, the steamboats stuck close to business and received the thanks of the shippers and passengers quite similar to pre-war days.

The "straw house" which had been erected by the politicians and unscrupulous railroad promoters toppled over in 1870. Amidst the wreck and ruin the State found on its hands twelve bankrupt railroads to which $20,502,684.00 had been advanced. When these were finally sold by judicial sale, they brought $6,698,000.00, leaving a loss of $13,804,684.00 to be absorbed by an already war-torn state.

When the time came, the stronger railroads, such as the Louisville and Nashville and the Nashville and Chattanooga, became interested in the outcome and sale of certain afflicted railroads. For example, the Louisville and Nashville, after first leasing, purchased the Memphis, Clarksville and Louisville, which gave it a direct line from the Ohio south to Memphis on the Mississippi. In this manner, too, the rich and fertile territory on the lower Cumberland was to be first bisected and ultimately cut into small parts by branch lines.

The Nashville and Chattanooga first leased and then purchased the Nashville and Northwestern, and thereby procured access to the Mississippi at Hickman. This provided through transportation from the Mississippi to the Atlantic Seaboard and the expanding southeastern part of our country.

It can be seen, therefore, that through a very early policy of wise acquisition, the Louisville and Nashville and the Nashville and Chattanooga continued as the leaders of the railroad business in Tennessee. There were soon to be other developments and acquisitions which would have an important bearing on the competition between steamboats and railroads. These, however, did not take place during this decade and will be referred to as the story progresses.

While the State, Counties and Cities were furnishing financial aid to the railroads, the river during the same period had received no State aid and very little, if any, from the Federal Government. It was still supreme in transporting such raw materials as tobacco, hay, wheat, corn, lumber, whiskey, horses, mules, iron and foundry products, hardware, wagons, hides, meats, furs, lard, flour, and what little cotton was shipped after the War. By 1870, it had developed the upper Cumberland territory into one of the richest and most lucrative trade areas on the Western Rivers. For more than fifty years the merchants of Nashville, thanks to the steamboats, would receive an annual estimated $10,000,000.00 in trade from this one section of the river, and for thirty-five years it would not be penetrated by the railroads.

Nashville, while receiving the richest blessing from steamboat traffic, was no more grateful than Eddyville, Clarksville and Dover on the lower river and many other towns and hamlets on the upper river. At every landing packets were greeted by a war-weary but courageous people. The familiar packets epitomized the return of a real friend in an hour of great need. In many cases the captains of these old packets knew every man, woman and child at the smaller landings by their first names. Perhaps they had a ribbon for Mary or a bottle of cough syrup for Aunt Liza. If Hank was sick he would be taken to the nearest doctor. A pretty cousin from the city might come aboard and ring the bell. In many other ways, the steamboats and the men who ran them were not mere symbols of our American way of life, but the way of life itself.

On account of the War an accurate estimate of the freight tonnage handled by steamboats on the river during this period cannot be made. The wharves at Nashville and Clarksville were once more teeming with business remindful of the "Golden Age" of steamboatin'. The six or seven packets in the Nashville trade in 1866 had increased to fifteen by 1870 with a registered tonnage of 5,175 tons, valued at $230,000.00. These were all making regular scheduled trips on both the lower and upper river. Packets had established regular connections at such points as Smithland, Paducah, Cairo, St. Louis and Evansville. There was a gradual tendency to split up the territory and protect it from "tramp" steamboats, thereby precluding a freight warfare. However, the Cumberland during this decade remained open territory and many Ohio and Mississippi steamboats continued to ply it.

Nashville's wholesalers, retailers and manufacturers in 1870 did an aggregate business of $41,869,000.00.

On July 24, 1866, Tennessee was re-admitted to the Union. The Supreme Court started regular sessions after a lapse of four years due to the War. Gradually civil government returned.

The original Ku Klux Klan was organized in 1866–67 and created a somewhat mystical atmosphere in the midst of a distressed people.

The year 1870 marked a real return to normalcy. In that

year more than $2,500,000.00 had been spent on building projects in Nashville alone. The famous Maxwell House, owned by Colonel John Overton, was completed in 1869 at a cost of $400,000.00. This famous hostelry, with its two hundred and forty rooms heated by steam, "served by an elevator," with a bath and "water closet," as advertised, on each floor, was destined to entertain future presidents and other celebrities. It still remains a reminder of its glorious past when no Nashville debutante was officially welcomed to society until she had "tripped the light fantastic toe" at one of the annual Maxwell House balls.

Nashville was released from the infamous "Carpetbag" Government in 1868, and a grateful public took a new lease on life.

The University of Nashville continued to be a leading institution in the South and had added a law department. Ward Seminary was founded in 1865 and in a short span of four years more than one thousand young ladies from all over the South had matriculated. Many of Tennessee's loveliest matrons have attended this institution, which finally merged with Belmont College a generation ago to give Nashville the widely known Ward-Belmont College, now, once again, Belmont College.

As further evidence of its progress, Nashville boasted three distinct street railroad companies whose cars were all drawn by horses. The South Nashville Street Railroad was the first, completed in 1866, and ran out Cherry Street (Fourth Avenue) and College (Third Avenue), from Cedar to Franklin Street. Its entire length of roadway was four and a half miles. It was the proud owner of forty-three head of horses, eight cars, five of which ran regularly, and it employed nineteen persons. The North Nashville Street Railroad, known as the McGavock and Mt. Vernon, ran from the Public Square north on College Street to Jefferson Street, thence west to Summer (Fifth Avenue), thence north to the vicinity of St. Cecilia Academy. It had a roadway of two and a half miles and was completed in 1867. The Church and Spruce Street Railroad ran from the corner of Church and Cherry out Church to Spruce Street (Eighth Avenue) to the city limits, a distance of two and a half miles. One of the pleasant ways to spend a summer afternoon in 1870 was to go riding on the "street cars." It took an hour to go from the Maxwell House to the present city reservoir on Eighth Avenue South.

Tennesseans once more could enjoy the full benefits of a free and enlightened press. There were four daily newspapers in East Tennessee, two in Middle Tennessee and four in West Tennessee. In addition there were forty-three weekly newspapers published in the various county seats all over the State. In Nashville, The Republican Banner and the Union American, both of which had been suspended during the War, were published daily and had a large circulation.

In no uncertain terms Tennessee had served notice on the rest of the country of her intention to be the first of the seceding states to completely recover from the rigors of war. The Cumberland River and the faithful steamboats as never before stood ready to make this intention come true despite any threats of competition from the railroads.

CHAPTER SIX

Reconstruction and Slow Poisoning

Period 1870–1880

Before we enter into the main discussion of this very interesting decade, certain governmental agencies which have had much to do with the development of the river and its traffic should be mentioned.

The Nashville Office of the Collector of Customs, U. S. Treasury Department, with a Deputy Collector or Surveyor, as he was designated for many years, dates back as far as 1837. It is probable that such an office was in the city some years previously, but no records are available. It is one of the oldest governmental agencies in Nashville, and through it were issued all licenses to steamboats claiming that city as home port.

The records of this office enable those who are interested to obtain the date when a steamboat was built, the place where it was built, its tonnage, length, breadth and depth, as well as its owner and master. Such records are invaluable, but since steamboats from practically all ports on the Western Rivers plied the Cumberland, it has been necessary to examine every available newspaper published in Nashville from 1818 to the present time to obtain an accurate list of the many boats which plied the river. This task was finally completed and will be found in the Appendix. It has been checked against all available records, including those of the Collector of Customs and those of various governmental agencies connected with the river.

The records in the Nashville Customs office are priceless aids in determining the ownership and dimensions of the old-time steamboats. Without them much historical information would have been left unrecorded.

The next oldest governmental agency connected with the river in Nashville was the Bureau of Marine Inspection and Navigation, which was placed under the United States Coast Guard shortly after the outbreak of World War II. Among the steamboat fraternity it is better known as the Steamboat Inspection Service. Under the Act of 1871, its duties and functions were greatly enlarged and its powers extended. The Sixth Supervising District, composed of Nashville, Evansville, Louisville and Memphis, compared favorably with any in the service. The Annual Meetings of the Board of Supervising Inspectors are on file in the office of the Local Inspectors, beginning with the year 1872.

Among other duties, this Service is concerned with the inspection of boilers on steamboats, their hulls, the examination and issuance of all licenses to Masters, Mates, Pilots and Engineers, the enforcement of the Pilot Rules as enacted by Congress, and the promulgation and publication of rules and regulations for navigation. It has very great supervisory power and is authorized to reject, revoke or suspend licenses. Its publications are the most authoritative on safety methods to be found. Its personnel is highly respected by all river men and is entitled to great credit for the part played in the improvement of navigation on the Inland Waterways.

Much of the detailed information relating to the old-time masters, mates, pilots and engineers, the accidents to the boats and the little incidents given in this book, were obtained from the Annual Reports of the Steamboat Inspection Service.

On May 2, 1873, the first of the post-war (1861–1865) District Engineers, known among all river men as "The USED," came to the Nashville District. Since that date, until the present time, no other agency has done so much to help the Cumberland River overcome its own natural disabilities. The Engineer Department has had direct supervision over the problem of channel clearance, channel depth, obstructions, permanent improvements and maintenance, locks and dams, flood control, aids to navigation (until assumed by the Coast Guard) and surveys. These are but a few of its many activities. They will be mentioned from time to time as the occasion arises.

The Annual Reports of the District Engineers at Nashville are filled with facts and figures on every phase of the river. Statistics are found in abundance, and are not only complete, but accurate for any designated period of time.

The Engineers maintain a "work fleet" on the Cumberland and are in a position to give expert information on channel depth at any given period or part of the river. They make valuable suggestions respecting hazards, whether pertaining to floods or navigation, and what equipment should be used. They know every facility for handling cargo on the river and in this manner are called upon for suggestions that often save thousands of dollars. All parties connected with the river have come to realize not only the importance of consulting with the Engineer Department respecting difficult problems, but the necessity of doing so. From the great mass of statistics acquired over a period of many years, such problems are often overcome automatically.

It would be impossible to over-estimate the work of this agency or its achievements. It has done much on comparatively little. Many new businesses using the river have come to Nashville and other points in its vicinity after consulting the Engineers and getting their candid opinion relative to water transportation. No hand is left unturned to accommodate river traffic and to aid those in trouble by every legal means available.

This period also saw the beginning of another governmental agency which has been of great benefit to all those using the river or in any way affected by it. It is now known as the United States Weather Bureau, Department of Commerce. It is of peculiar interest to all Tennesseans, because Senator William B. Bate sponsored the Act which created the Bureau, and his relative, H. C. Bate, became the first Observer at Nashville. Prior to 1870 The Service was under the War Department, United States Signal Service. It was little known in this immediate period, and little used until around 1900. Its chief function is to keep records and issue reports. No service has been more faithful or diligent and it early gained popular favor. Rivermen depend on the forecasts to help them in their transportation plans. Now The Bureau can prophesy the rise of the river with uncanny accuracy, after taking their old records, so painstakingly kept on precipitation, and other factors, into consideration.

Here in Nashville, as elsewhere, the public fails to appreciate the work of this particular Bureau unless the river gets at flood tide, perhaps freezes over, or some other emergency exists. This is not true of the people who use the river or live on it. They have long since learned to rely upon the wily gentlemen who constantly study figures and get reports from various observers and after careful study, proclaim "that the river will fall at Nashville and rise at Clarksville, and the crest of the flood will pass Eddyville on next Friday night or early Saturday morning."

All of these agencies have cooperated with each other and with the public. Their record of service is peculiarly praiseworthy because they have remained outside the portals of politics and attended strictly to business. While this has not been conducive to publicity, it has encouraged great confidence in their work. The author heartily recommends their annual reports to all students of the river. They are most illuminating.

While there were few, if any, visible indications of impending danger, looking at the situation in retrospect, the close of this period marked the beginning of real and deep-seated trouble for "Steamboatin' on the Cumberland." One must go completely behind the scenes to understand the situation. To the average steamboat man of 1870–1880, such pessimistic utterances would have been "treasonable," for oddly enough, during this entire period, the packets on the Cumberland were enjoying an unusually good business. But the owners and those financially interested in the packet business knew, even if they would not admit it in public, that great changes were taking place, chiefly because of railroad competition. The storm was still far away, in fact, many years distant, but thunder could be heard by those who had their ears close to the ground.

First, however, let us momentarily skip over the gloomy aspects of the picture and recount the bright spots of steamboatin' during this decade.

At the end of 1870, steamboats on the Cumberland were still the outstanding transportation facility in Tennessee. They had fitted into the reconstruction in an ideal manner. To the impoverished Southern people along the banks of the Cumberland they were affording transportation based on low freight rates and were moving the type of cargo so badly needed. The men who operated these sturdy boats gladly landed at muddy river banks or any other place where they were hailed, to pick up or deliver their cargo. Thousands of tons of freight which would not otherwise have been moved found their way to market solely because of the packets.

While the major railroads were busily engaged in straightening out their finances, buying up defunct roads and making necessary repairs, the steamboat business, by its zealous work and clever management, was maintaining supremacy as a transportation facility.

Shortly after the opening of this period Nashville-owned boats were rendering through passenger and freight service to every point on the Western Rivers. Most of the packets were as "elegant" and "majestic" as those on the larger rivers. There were boats leaving daily for such points as Paducah, Evansville, Louisville, Cincinnati and Pittsburgh on the Ohio and Cairo, St. Louis, Memphis and New Orleans on the Mississippi. In addition, when there was sufficient water, at least three packets were making daily trips on the upper Cumberland, frequently going as far as Burnside, Kentucky.

Steamboat operators, with due regard to the demands of the public, once and for all abandoned the practice of haphazard schedules. Packets were leaving and departing on time. Freight was transported with greater care and attention and passengers were extended every courtesy and consideration. Perhaps no other era in the history of the packet business produced such a marked change in improved service to its patrons. In these and other ways, the steamboat men retained all of the grandeur of the packet business of the past, but gave it the added touch of more modern service demanded by the public.

In this ten-year period, eighty-one more named boats plied the waters of the Cumberland. Many were owned by Cumberland River operators residing in Nashville. The average boat during the navigable season made not less than one trip into and out of Nashville each week. Some of the better packets made an average of two trips a week, depending, of course, on their point of destination. The average number of boats operating per month was twenty-five, an increase of nine or ten over 1870, which proves conclusively that the business on the river at the close of 1880 was increasing steadily.

It is revealed by contemporary newspapers, and by personal conversations with old time captains and pilots, that the average Cumberland River packet during this period carried not less than 400 tons of freight, coming and going. If the navigable season on the river lasted only seven months, twenty-five boats making an average of five trips per month during the entire season would transport 700,-000 tons of commercial freight into and out of Nashville annually.

The boats on the lower river, especially up to Clarksville, were carrying more cargo than ever before. It is not only possible, but highly probable, that the entire steamboat tonnage for the Cumberland River, at the close of 1880, had again soared to considerably more than 1,000,000 tons annually. No other business in Tennessee after the War made a quicker or more complete recovery.

All of this traffic was taking place with very little material aid from the Federal Government or the State. Only $150,-000.00, according to the old records, was spent by the Federal Government on the Cumberland River from 1870 to 1880, and that was all expended on channel clearance which might be termed of an emergency character.

At the close of 1880, there were at least twenty-seven packets running regularly from Nashville. Their names will be found in the Appendix and it will be seen that many of them bear the names of prominent Nashvillians and citizens of Middle Tennessee.

This particular decade also marked a definite trend toward the establishment of trade areas for the packets. This resulted from the many reciprocal agreements between connecting packet lines on through passenger and freight service. Regular Cumberland River packets on the lower river were now inclined to stay within the territory between Cairo, Evansville, Paducah and Nashville, which roughly speaking, was that consigned to their trade area. Fewer Nashville boats plied beyond this area and fewer Ohio and Mississippi packets were seen in Nashville. Nevertheless, there still remained a large number of "tramp" steamboats which cut in heavily on the regular packets.

One of the greatest afflictions of steamboat traffic was the absence of terminal facilities. Unloading and loading still presented a serious drawback. Nashville, for her size and prestige, had very meager wharf facilities and no steamboat terminal at all. Despite improvement along many other lines, the Cumberland River packets were still plagued by muddy banks, steep inclines and long delay at landings. Such hardships were a menace and costly. At an early date, the railroads took advantage of this situation and lured shippers and travelers away from the packets solely because they maintained better terminal facilities and avoided drayage charges. But, this is getting ahead of the story for this period.

This decade marks the beginning of what might be termed a new generation of post war steamboat owners and operators on the Cumberland. Many of the founders of the steamboat business and famous captains and pilots had not lived to see the end of the War.

At Paducah the Fowler brothers were the leading lights in the packet business. As early as 1859, Captain Littleton Augustus Fowler was the owner of the *Silver Star*, a packet which plied between Evansville and Paducah. During the War, Captain J. Wythe Fowler, brother of Captain Gus, distinguished himself on the *Little Rebel*, the flagship of the Mississippi River Defense Fleet, and another brother, Captain Dick Fowler, helped construct the *Arkansas*, a Confederate ram which was referred to in Chapter Five. After the War, the three Fowler brothers resumed their steamboat business.

Beginning around 1876, the Fowlers either owned or had an interest in the following boats: the *Pat Cleburne, James Fiske, Jr., John Gilbert, Gus Fowler, Silver Cloud, Joe Fowler, Red Cloud, Dick Fowler, Robert Mitchell, John S. Hopkins* and *Rapidan No. 1*. The *Joe Fowler* was generally considered the most majestic of all the Fowler boats and her career extended until around 1920, after being made over into an excursion boat with her name changed to the *Crescent*.

Captain Dick Fowler lost his life on the *Pat Cleburne* when she sank in May 1876. Old-time steamboat men agree that he was one of the best steamboat men on the river.

The lower river also boasted of another family of splendid steamboat men whose boats for many years were identified with the Cumberland, although their home port was Evansville. The patriarch of this family was Captain Joshua V. Throop, who started on the river as early as 1830, and continued until the outbreak of the War Between the States. John Throop and George S. Throop succeeded their distinguished kinsman after the War, and their boats during this period brought heavy cargoes of grain and other commodities from the rich Ohio Valley section up to Nashville.

At Clarksville, Captain Frank Gracey and his brother, Matt Gracey, became the leaders in the packet business at the close of the War. Captain Gracey has been briefly mentioned heretofore as an outstanding officer in Forrest's Cavalry. He was a pilot on the *America* before the War and with his brother gave up active piloting to become the head of the lucrative river business in Clarksville. For years Captain Gracey controlled the wharf boat at Clarksville and the drayage companies that handled drayage of the freight. Shortly after the War, he and his brother operated one of the largest tobacco warehouses in Clarksville, and he also became the agent for the Louisville & Nashville Railroad.

There were many other splendid citizens, such as Gracey Childers at Clarksville and Captain Ben Egan at Paducah to mention two of many who helped build up the packet business.

At Nashville, during this period, we find such steamboat owners and operators as the Lovell Brothers, Thomas Ryman, Sr., James S. Tyner, Charles Yarbrough, Thomas and Will J. Harmon, Pink Dews, William Dix, James Hughes, the three Armstrongs, A. T., T. H. and Major L. T., Shep Green, Tom Gallagher, W. D. Cowleshaw and his son Albert, better known as "B," Isaac T., Jas. A., Jas. F., and Madison M. Leek, and Ben Goad, to mention only a few more who were to spread their fame throughout the steamboat business on the Cumberland. There were other men in Nashville who were not captains and pilots, but who had an interest in the steamboat business and were to contribute much to its success from a financial standpoint. For example, there were B. M. Runyan, John Lumsden, B. G. Wood, Nat F. Dortch, Alex Kendall, J. J. Odil, B. H. Cook, J. R. Handly, H. W. Buttorff, and last but by no means least, B. S. Rhea and his son, I. T. Rhea. All were financially interested in the ownership of steamboats or as shippers. Each had a boat named for him and each played an important part in steamboatin' on the Cumberland during this and subsequent periods. For this reason, as the story progresses, further comments will be made about many of them.

In view of the fact that Captain J. W. Lovell and his family as operators of the Lovell Line, and Captain Ryman and Captain Tyner as operators of the Ryman Line, were to be keen competitors and the dominant steamboat operators on the Cumberland River for the next succeeding twenty years, a brief outline of their background will be given at this time.

Captain James W. Lovell, best known of the Lovell family, was reared in the Dixon Springs Community on the upper Cumberland in Smith County. He became a pilot before the War Between the States and a master as early as 1862. According to old time river men he was the personification of sobriety and honesty and one of the best pilots ever to stand a watch at the wheel of a steamboat. He had two brothers, William H. and Ben F. Lovell, who sustained excellent reputations and became Pilots and Masters of great ability. From these three brothers sprang a whole family of steamboat men who were known from one end of the river to the other. In all there were not less than nine Lovells who were either licensed officers or owners. Among these I might here mention, W. E., Will, Ton, Frank, Dock, Earl, and C. E. whom I recall.

With the possible exception of Ryman, Captain James W. Lovell owned more steamboats than any other of the old-time packetboat operators on the Cumberland. His first boat was the *John P. Tweed,* which he purchased in 1861. His last boat was the *John W. Thomas,* which was still operating at the turn of the century.

"Captain Jim," as J. W. Lovell was known, contrary to most of the upper Cumberland River captains, was notoriously careful and prudent in the operation of his boats. This characteristic, however, did not dim his courage and boldness in times of emergency. It has been truthfully said that he could safely take his boats through hazardous channels when other pilots would have quaked in their boots. His "light" touch on the big "wheel" was the envy of every pilot. As head of the famous "Lovell Line," he required and received strict obedience to his orders without any show of physical violence. His boats were kept in first class condition and cleanliness was his watchword. He was by far the most popular of any of the many steamboat captains to run the river between Nashville and Burnside. Unlike so many other packets, his boats never failed to stop for the small shipper, and space would be saved for their cargo even though it meant a loss financially.

Captain Lovell was a picturesque figure as he stood in the pilot house or on deck and greeted his many friends whom he counted by the thousands. He came up the hard way. Financially he was most successful with his boats, and during the long drawn-out competition with Captain Ryman for control of the upper river, he had sufficient cash to put up a fight which forms one of the most absorbing stories in connection with the packet trade on the Cumberland.

Captain Thomas G. Ryman was born in 1841, and his partner Captain James S. Tyner was born in 1847. At the end of this period, therefore, both were in the prime of life. If there ever were two self-made men, in the literal sense of the word, they were. Like their competitor Captain Lovell, from the time of their birth they had lived on the river and both loved it with characteristic zeal. They were to become the Damon and Pythias of the Cumberland.

In his early youth, Captain Ryman had engaged in commercial fishing in Chattanooga with his father, John Ryman, who for many years had been a fisherman. With the outbreak of the War, the youthful Ryman moved down the river to the vicinity of Decatur where he organized a prosperous fishing trade. After remaining at this point for a short time, he moved certain of his equipment down the Tennessee River to Fort Henry, where he sold large quantities of fish to the Confederate soldiers. We next find him moving to Nashville and later engaging in a similar business on the Cumberland at Fort Donelson.

At the outbreak of the War, Captain Tyner volunteered in the Confederate Army as a drummer boy and served under General Zollicoffer in East Tennessee. He was discharged in the Spring of 1862 because of his tender age.

After the Battle of Shiloh, Captain Ryman came to Nashville and went into the commercial fishing business with Captain Tyner. Tyner, incidentally, I am informed, had previously worked for Ryman in Chattanooga.

Commercial fishing during these years was a flourishing enterprise and Ryman and Tyner soon began to make good money. Tyner would go up and down the river, pick up the fish caught by fishermen and bring them to points around the wharf where they would be sold by Ryman. By the close of the War, Captain Ryman and his younger associate Tyner had definitely established themselves in a growing and prosperous fishing business.

The boys were honest and industrious, had pleasing personalities, knew how to deal with the public, and by saving their money were comparatively independent at a very early age. Young Ryman was more venturesome than Tyner and he began to look around for more fertile fields to conquer. He had an excellent knowledge of the river, knew all of the boat owners and believed he could make money in the steamboat business. Accordingly he purchased his first steamboat, the *Alpha*, which was brought up from New Orleans, probably in 1869 or 1870. It was by no means palatial, but it was a good boat and had seen some service as an auxiliary or transport during the War. From the very first, Ryman made money in the operation of the *Alpha*.

Tyner, in the meantime, had conducted the profitable fishing business and did not enter the steamboat business until three or four years later. Ryman, still venturesome, next acquired the *Bermuda*. Again meeting with success, he branched out and between 1875 and 1880 either bought or built six additional boats, some of which were extraordinarily fine packets and made considerable money for their owner.

Finding the steamboat business profitable, it was but natural that Captain Ryman would get his bosom friend, Captain Tyner, into the business. When Captain Ryman obtained the *Eddyville*, Captain Tyner, who had procured his pilot's license, became her pilot and ran on it for many years between Nashville and Paducah. From this time on the official records reveal that all of the thirty-odd boats operated by the famous Ryman Lines, with but few exceptions, were jointly owned by Captain Ryman and Captain Tyner. It is highly possible, because of the confusion and irregularities in the official records, that Captains Ryman and Tyner between them owned four or five more boats which are not accounted for. They owned and operated more steamboats on the Cumberland than any other men in its history.

Not only was the friendship between Ryman and Tyner enduring, but it also yielded rich dividends. As they grew older, Ryman became the financier of the business, and the partner who dealt intimately with and had the confidence of the shippers and men of affairs in Nashville, while Tyner, the other partner, was the skillful, energetic, hard-working and practical type of man who had no superior when it came to the actual operation of steamboats on a profitable basis. Both men had two great blessings in common—inherent honesty and good habits. They were in business together for more than forty years.

One of the highlights in the colorful career of Captain Ryman occurred in 1881 during one of the many visits paid to Nashville by the evangelist, Sam Jones. During a revival, Captain Ryman was converted, and from that time on, he was leader in the religious activities of Nashville. Many of his acquaintances who did not really know the man were led to believe, on account of his zeal, that he was a religious fanatic. On the contrary, he was far from a fanatic, but did believe in Christianity as a practical solution to human troubles. He joined the Elm Street Methodist Church and then contributed the tidy sum of $20,000.00 towards the Union Gospel Tabernacle, which was later named the Ryman Auditorium. When this building was erected, it was Captain Ryman's idea that it would become a meeting place for all interested in the furtherance of the Christian religion regardless of denomination.

John Galt (1857), *Eddyville* (1871) and *Dora Cabler* (1877). Seen at the Nashville Wharf 1879.

Captain Ryman after his conversion maintained an ever-increasing religious fervor. He was always a man of excellent habits and to those close to him he particularly expressed a distaste for the drinking of liquor. Rumor has it that after he was converted by Jones he immediately left the revival meeting, went down to the wharf and personally destroyed all of the barrooms and liquor on his boats. This is not true. What actually happened was that he talked the matter over with certain of his friends and as the leases for the concessions expired, he refused to renew them. In this way he once and for all rid his boats of bars which meant a serious financial sacrifice. If we accept the word of his trusted friend and business associate, Captain Tyner, as well as many of his other friends who knew him best, Captain Ryman's religious beliefs were genuine and sincere and were a very active and vital force in his make-up.

As we look back on the events of this period, it seems peculiarly unfortunate that at one and the same time, the Cumberland River and the steamboat business could be richly blessed with such men as the Lovells, Armstrongs, Ryman and Tyner, and all the rest of the fine steamboat men mentioned, and yet at the same time because of their own strength, courage and hardheadiness, there would be differences of opinion which would lead to a devastating competition among themselves. This competition, however, during this particular period had not become so acute as to affect the packet business. For this reason, it can be passed over for the present without further comment. It was not long in coming, however, and when it did come, it seriously crippled the steamboat business while it was desperately fighting for its life.

One of the most hopeful signs on the river during this period was the coming of such men as Hugh Kyle, M. C. Gore, "Uncle Billy" Hull, father of Cordell Hull, Ed Myer, Benton McMillin, John A. Fite, Arch P. Green and David Hughes to the booming trade of the upper Cumberland. In the area from Nashville to the head of navigation at Burnside, the steamboats found it difficult to handle the cargo. While on the surface there appeared reasons for optimism on the part of the steamboat owners and business was very good, certain dangers were looming on the horizon. Let us turn our attention to these.

First among the worries of the steamboat operators was the loss of cotton shipments. Prior to the War cotton had been the largest and best cargo handled by the packets. This great money crop was peculiarly suited to the packet business for more reasons than one. It was, for example, carried to market during the best months of the navigable season and it was a "long haul" freight item, going as a rule all the way to New Orleans. It was an excellent "on board" cargo and handled easily and in great quantity.

After the War Between the States, cotton as a cargo on Cumberland packets simply ceased to exist. The abolition of slavery left the cotton planters in this section without any help to cultivate and gather the crop. Middle Tennessee became more and more a diversified agricultural region and in the turnover, cotton was displaced by corn, oats, hay, wheat, cattle, tobacco, hogs and poultry. The reconstruction of the South required food as never before and this fact added to the growing tendency of the large land-owners to split up their crops.

The loss of cotton shipments was a serious blow to the steamboats. This fact, however, was overlooked by many in the business, who "saw no further than their noses." On the other hand, to the old-timers and owners came the realization that the first "big" loss in pay cargo had come about and it would be extremely difficult to find a replacement.

There were other worries. In 1875, the iron and rolling mill business on the lower river, which had yielded a rich revenue to the steamboats since 1829, was on a rapid decline and by 1880 it had shifted to Birmingham, soon to be dubbed "The Magic City." Most of the iron magnates in the Western Highland Rim of Tennessee and Kentucky had moved or were beginning to move to what appeared to be better locations served by railroads.

The lucrative iron industry, founded by such men as Montgomery Bell, A. W. Van Leer, Dan Hillman, and others, which has been mentioned in previous chapters had been severely damaged by the War. The Hillman interests, after trying to operate for a limited time, found the rich ore of the Birmingham area, which they had explored, to be of a quality and quantity equal to any in the country. After the death of Dan Hillman, his two sons, T. T. Hillman and J. H. Hillman, were to emerge as worthy successors to their distinguished father, but not as iron producers in Tennessee and Kentucky. T. T. moved to Birmingham and became the founder of the steel business in that city, while J. H. migrated to Pittsburgh and became an outstanding figure of the industry in that city. C. E. Hillman, Dan Hillman's brother, remained in Nashville and headed his own prosperous business for many years.

The Tennessee and the Cumberland Rivers did not lose this great iron business in a month or a year, but by the close of 1880, it was gone insofar as the packets were concerned. Once again, the more thoughtful of the steamboat owners grew apprehensive. Iron was another heavy cargo and a "long haul" pay load type of freight peculiarly adapted to steamboat transportation with thousands of tons going all the way to Pittsburgh.

There was another grave situation resulting from the possible partial loss of tobacco. With cotton definitely removed from steamboat transportation as early as 1870 and iron rapidly declining by 1880, tobacco by 1880 constituted the third great freight cargo which gave definite signs of being weaned away from the packets. Tobacco, however, was not to leave as rapidly or to the extent of either cotton or iron, and for this reason, its connection with the packets must be carefully analyzed. This particular money crop, unlike cotton and iron, did not leave the river because of any change in the economic situation of our country or because farmers did not plant it as in the case of cotton. As a matter of fact, there was very little if anything which the steamboat owners could do to prevent the loss of cotton and iron as cargo. In the case of tobacco, the steamboat industry on the Cumberland felt it had a fighting chance to keep this crop for the river, particularly in the section between Nashville and Burnside. This feeling was not without merit, principally because the railroads were not to penetrate that section for another twenty-five years.

On the other hand, there were unmistakable signs very early in this period which by 1877 turned into definite convictions that on account of the railroads the tobacco shipments on the lower end of the Cumberland would soon be nothing as compared with the past.

Such a situation with all of its gloomy ramifications can be traced to the partial shifting of the trade from New Orleans to the East. This was brought about by the ever-increasing "trunk line" development of railroads and the fact that New York presented a better and closer port to the foreign markets then buying the dark fired tobacco grown in the counties contiguous to the Cumberland River in Western Tennessee and Kentucky. Such a shift in the trade was to help destroy steamboat transportation but on the other hand was to help the dark fired tobacco industry tremendously. By 1887 Clarksville became the second largest tobacco market in the United States, the Tobacco Board of Trade announcing that more than 20,000 hogsheads of the ever popular product had been handled in that year alone. Such a record may have made Clarksvillians forget the familiar sound of the steamboat whistles and the contribution which the packets had made to the industry from 1819 to 1870. Without these boats in that period, the great tobacco crop would not have reached the market and soared to fame.

The Louisville & Nashville, toward the end of this decade, had rapidly developed not only a main line through Clarksville leading to Louisville and thence to Cincinnati but a trunk line to New York. It was also preparing to criss-cross and bisect the entire western part of Kentucky with its own branch lines. Eventually, about the only tobacco left for the packets on the lower Cumberland was grown so close to the river that a railroad could not find it. All of this was brought into Clarksville and constituted a short and not a long haul cargo. Before that date, and while New Orleans was in its prime, the packets had taken the entire dark fired crop each year to that metropolis on the Gulf, and it was a long haul (1,200 miles) pay-load freight. From 1850 to 1861, the Clarksville warehouses handled an average of 11,000 hogsheads and from 1866 to 1870, nearly 15,000 hogsheads, annually. It takes a lot of steamboats to carry such a load such a far distance.

Dark fired tobacco has always been raised principally along the lower river and in the western section of the State, whereas burley is grown on practically every farm in the Cumberland Basin but in great abundance from Nashville to Burnside, Kentucky. For this reason, the burley crop was always referred to as an upper river cargo by steamboat operators. Prior to 1870 the burley crop like the dark fired crop had always been transported by Cumberland packets on the long haul to New Orleans. This great seaport, therefore, had the distinction of being the center of both the dark fired and the burley export trade.

During this period and almost simultaneously with the shifting of the dark fired trade from New Orleans, there was also a shift in the burley market to Louisville, Kentucky. This shift was also due to the railroads and was felt immediately by steamboats on the upper river. Henceforth, the burley crop would be a short haul cargo. Instead of carrying the burley to New Orleans it would be dropped at Clarksville or Nashville, depending on whether it was grown in the lower or upper section of the river basin, and then trans-shipped by the Louisville & Nashville to Louisville and later on to nearby Lexington, which became the big center for the burley crop. Nashville, however, always got its fair share from the boats and processed it.

Thus, because of the railroads, the steamboats had to be content with a short haul on both dark fired and burley tobacco. So long as packets ran, however, they always carried some tobacco on both the lower and upper river. During bumper crop years, burley remained one of the best revenue cargoes handled by upper river steamboats and the shift to Louisville in this trade was not felt as keenly as that of the dark fired to the East. The lower river in particular, which had lost cotton and was about to lose iron, could ill afford another loss such as the long haul on dark fired tobacco.

All of these adverse developments were bad enough for the steamboat business, but they were nothing compared to the one which had arisen in respect to grain and kindred products. For more than fifty years grain had been the largest and most lucrative cargo handled on the river. It was generally conceded that grain was the exclusive cargo of the steamboats. Now, as though to add coal to the fire, certain events had taken place which indicated this end of the steamboat business was in great danger. Such a state of events was enough to cause even the most rabid river man to quake in his boots. As in the case of tobacco, railroad competition was the moving force behind the fear.

Long before there were any rail connections between Nashville and such mid-west river points as Cincinnati, Louisville, Evansville, Paducah, Cairo, St. Louis and Hickman, the Cumberland River packets had brought vast amounts of grain and kindred products to Nashville. Before the Nashville & Chattanooga Railroad was extended to Chattanooga and there connected with Atlanta, the southeastern cities such as Charleston, Savannah and Atlanta did not have access to the rich crops of corn and wheat abundantly grown in southern Ohio, Indiana and Illinois.

It had long been the dream of the Nashville & Chattanooga, as well as other railroads, to connect the Atlantic Seaboard with the progressive cities along the Western rivers. The first link in the chain was the construction of the Nashville & Chattanooga, but as I have previously observed, when it was originally conceived, such a gigantic trunk line seemed remote, and while its founders may have had such a plan in the back of their heads, every one, including steamboat owners, thought they were merely building "castles in the air."

Nevertheless, in 1872, less than twenty-odd years after the first train ran between Nashville and Chattanooga, and despite the intervention of a devastating war, the Nashville & Chattanooga Railroad, through the acquisition and reclamation of the Nashville and Northwestern Railroad, had connected Hickman, Kentucky, on the Mississippi River with Charleston on the Atlantic Coast. Prior to that acquisition, the N. & C. railroad had never been interested in how grain moving from the midwest reached Nashville from points on the Ohio and Mississippi Rivers for transshipment over its roadway to the southeast. Such shipments had been within the exclusive control of the steamboat packets. Beginning, however, in 1872, the Nashville & Chattanooga became vitally interested in such shipments and had completed plans to capture them, if possible, before they were even made available to the steamboats at midwestern river crossings.

The acquisition of the Nashville & Northwestern was the first step in the plan. Next, large grain elevators were erected by the railroad at Hickman on the Mississippi and Johnsonville on the Tennessee. The use of these conveniences was free to shippers and it was expected in a short time large shipments of grain normally flowing into Nashville by packet would go to these elevators for transshipment by rail. Such was not the case, however, chiefly because Hickman was too far removed from the center of the grain trade, and the overall river and rail rate from the Wabash, Ohio and Mississippi River crossings by way of Hickman and Johnsonville to Nashville proved to be higher than the all-river rate promulgated by the steamboats. In fact, it was so much higher that the railroads could not compete.

Turning to other possible solutions, the Nashville & Chattanooga, while not abandoning its hopes at Johnsonville and Hickman, decided on the somewhat novel plan of granting to Nashville grain dealers what was to be commonly referred to as "reshipping" or "rebilling" privileges, throwing in "milling in transit" privileges for good measure. These privileges were to continue for more than forty years and finally resulted not only in taking the grain business away from the packets but a long-drawn out legal battle between Atlanta and other complaining southeastern cities, and the Nashville, Chattanooga & St. Louis (formerly the Nashville & Chattanooga) and the Louisville & Nashville Railroads. This case was first heard by the Interstate Commerce Commission, next the Commerce Court and at last, the United States Supreme Court. It was contended the privileges above referred to were illegal devices, making it possible to transport grain, etc. at less than applicable freight rates and giving Nashville dealers an undue and illegal preference and advantage over her competitors, chiefly Atlanta. The case was finally decided in 1913. The milling in transit privileges were not involved, because they had already been extended to southeastern cities by the railroads.

At this point it is sufficient to say that the decision of the Supreme Court was adverse to the railroads, and it annihilated the grain business in Nashville as it existed under "the privileges." The rebilling privileges by which the railroads hoped to corner the shipment of grain to Nashville are described in the opinion of the Commerce Court rendered in the above case, found in 197 Fed. Reports 58, and are so vital to "Steamboatin' on the Cumberland" that I quote them verbatim, as follows:

"On grain, grain products and hay shipped to Nashville by rail from or through Ohio or Mississippi River crossing points such as Louisville, Evansville, Hickman, Paducah, Cairo, etc., the L. & N. and N. C. & St. L. R. R. charged the full local freight rate from said crossing points to Nashville. These shipments may then be stopped at Nashville for a period not exceeding six months during which time they may be rebilled or reshipped to destinations in southeastern and Carolina territory, and on such reshipments so rebilled, the freight charges into and out of Nashville are readjusted so that the total transportation charge on any one shipment from any given Ohio or Mississippi River crossing via Nashville to any given destination in said territory shall exactly correspond with the transportation charge legally assessable on that shipment had it been billed and moved through from its point of origin at the Ohio or Mississippi River crossing points to its final destination without having been stopped in transit at Nashville."

The practical effect of the rebilling privileges is described in the opinion of the Supreme Court in the same case, cited in 235 U. S. Sup. Ct. Reports 245, in which the Court said:

"For example, the local rate on grain from Evansville, on the Ohio River, to Nashville, is ten cents per 100 pounds, and the local rate from Nashville to Atlanta is seventeen cents per 100 pounds. The joint rate from Evansville to Atlanta is twenty-four cents or three cents less than the sum of the locals. Under the reshipping practice the joint rate of twenty-four cents is protected when the shipment has been stopped in transit at Nashville. The local rate of ten cents from Evansville to Nashville having been paid at the time of the shipment into Nashville, an adjustment of the total transportation charge is made when the reshipment to Atlanta occurs, so that the shipper in the end pays upon the shipment the joint rate instead of the combination of local rates into and out of Nashville."

Cities like Atlanta claimed that the "rebilling" and "milling in transit" privileges were nothing more than a subterfuge to give Nashville grain merchants a through rate rather than a local rate on grain stopped in Nashville and later forwarded to southeastern markets. Nashville was an ideal stop for grain in transit to the southeast and early gave promise of its future greatness as an elevator and storage point. Under "milling in transit" privileges, a miller in Nashville could process grain into flour or meal which he had received by rail under rebilling privileges, and by holding his bill of lading on the grain, in turn ship his finished products in equal weights on that same bill of lading to southeastern points on the through rather than the local rates. The milling in transit privileges obviously contributed to the success of Nashville as one of the largest flour and meal centers south of the Ohio.

While the rebilling privileges actually did not lower the railroad rates, they nevertheless gave to Nashville dealers the priceless advantage of a six months stop-over privilege on grain and also gave them the advantage of the through freight rate not only on reshipments to southeastern cities in large quantities, but on less than car load lots. This latter feature helped Nashville to accommodate the small dealers as well as the large ones, and had much to do with its popularity as a distribution point. In future years, as might be expected, some of the dealers in the southeast claimed they were forced to look to Nashville to supply their demands. Practically every dealer in that section wound up by buying grain in Nashville. Nashville in the next twenty years, and not Cairo, Evansville, Louisville and Paducah, became the center of the grain trade. The midwest remained the center of grain production, but Nashville was to become the center of grain distribution, and flour and meal manufacture, in the South.

There were certain other advantages which the railroads exerted over the steamboats not connected with the privileges mentioned above. First of all, they were able to make delivery at the doors of the dealers, thereby cutting out the expense of unloading and drayage, which prevailed on shipments via steamboat. This saving helped to shave the difference in the freight rate. Secondly, the packets generally handled grain in sacks, but the railroads took it unsacked or in bulk. This amounted to a saving in the time consumed in loading and unloading and was considered by many dealers as the safest way to handle grain. This latter theory is still a matter of debate.

In 1877, the Louisville & Nashville followed the example of the Nashville, Chattanooga & St. Louis, and extended the rebilling and milling in transit privileges on grain moving from Louisville and other midwest river crossings touched by its lines. By 1882 these connected with St. Louis on the Mississippi. Previously in 1871–72 the Louisville & Nashville had leased the Nashville & Decatur and by other acquisitions had extended its lines all the way to New Orleans.

After this there were other slight fill-ins, but to all intents and purposes the ring of steel around the Cumberland had been completed.

The long anticipated battle for existence had begun in earnest for the packets on the lower river. With cotton gone, iron leaving, tobacco converted to a short haul—well, if grain left, so would the majestic and elegant packets. In the words of one venerable steamboat pilot of the times:—"Hell had really busted loose and it was time to quit sittin' 'round and wondering what would happen next. Damn, if it didn't look like the railroads were slow-poisoning us by putting out the fire under our boilers while we sat in the pilot house blowing a toot or two on the whistle." This old timer hit the nail on the head—the railroads were "slow-poisoning" the packets. The lower Cumberland, like many of the other Western Rivers, had been caught in the jaws of a vise and from now on, the railroads would be closing in slowly at first, but faster and faster as time went by.

Fortunately for the river and the gallant men who ran the steamboat business, the various plans of the railroads did not make a sudden inroad upon the grain trade enjoyed by the river. For this reason, the packets during this entire period continued to enjoy a very good business on the lower river while those on the upper river were doing more business than ever before. Such a state of affairs naturally created an optimism which distracted the attention of less thoughtful steamboat men from the serious trends and dangers which were striking at their business. Just how far this distraction permeated the scene is difficult to determine, but whether one liked to admit it or not, the steamboat men on the lower river during this period were overconfident, cocky and fussed too much among themselves. Many of them admitted to me at a much later date as they turned back their memories that they paid little attention to erection of free elevators at Hickman and Johnsonville. When these failed to immediately affect the grain trade on the river, they forgot there might be other successful plans adopted. Others stated they never took the time to investigate the real meaning of such things as "rebilling" and "milling in transit" privileges. They were complicated and it was like speaking in an unknown tongue to describe them.

There were many steamboat owners and other friends of the river, however, who visualized what was going on. They knew the lines were being drawn tighter and tighter. They saw the railroads had big and powerful guns and of a long ranged variety. The steamboat owners, on the lower river, like Ryman and Tyner, knew "it was time to quit sittin' around and wondering what would happen next."

Contrary to expectations, the steamboat men as the battle grew closer began to fight among themselves. This and many other tactless blunders did much to hurt the river and its traffic. The packets, however, during this period, remained a powerful and potent facility and one which was rendering a vital and valuable service to the people. This was especially true in the Nashville to Burnside trade, where it had endeared itself to thousands of merchants and farmers who so far knew nothing of, and cared less, about the railroads. An enterprise so deeply entrenched for so long in the life of the people in that area was not easily toppled over as will be noted as this story of the river progresses.

"Slow poisoning" was a new and unheard of weapon, but, for a business handling approximately 1,000,000 tons of freight annually, it seemed fair to assume that future dangers might well take care of themselves.

New boats were being built. Nashville was fast becoming one of the largest hardwood lumber centers in the country, thanks to the virgin timber being cut on the upper river and transported down to Nashville by steamboats and rafts. Flour mills were booming. Cattle and hogs handled by the steamboats were pouring into Nashville's stockyards. The people were happy in the Cumberland Valley, now that the war was over and there was corn in the crib and bread in the cupboard. Steamboat operators found it difficult to express concern for their business when all appeared so bright on the surface. Look at the present, let the future take care of itself. Unfortunately such an attitude would be insufficient to meet the dangers facing the packets which were hovering just beyond the horizon.

CHAPTER SEVEN

Sudden Merger—The Cumberland Compromise

Period 1880–1890

The period of 1880–1890 was destined to be one of the most hectic in the long career of Steamboatin' on the Cumberland. In one way or another this was the result of railroad competition. Unfavorable trends and undercurrents in river trade had now become realities.

Railroads generally were beginning to extend their empires through the medium of trunk lines and consolidations. Perhaps no other period produced more railroad mergers. The larger roads were buying up the weaker ones. It was a day of consolidations, interlocking directorates and pyramiding of wealth. Big business knew no restraints. Men like Morgan, Vanderbilt and Rockefeller were beginning to amass huge fortunes. The people craved speed and excitement. More gold-headed canes and patent leather shoes were appearing on Main Street. America had just about outgrown its frontier days. Great cities were taking shape as more and more laborers were leaving the farms.

Into this cycle of progress, bordering upon complete transformation, the railroads seemed to fit perfectly. They were to this era what the steamboats had been to the early days of the nineteenth century. They had taken transportation away from the muddy banks of the rivers. Despite the elegance and charm of the old-time packets they were now too slow for the average passenger, dazzled as he must have been by such crack trains as the "Cannon Ball Express" or "The New York Limited." Business and mercantile firms were reluctant to turn their backs on the steamboats, but were forced to gradually yield to the more modern system of delivering freight to the very door of the store or warehouse. More and more railroads were erecting good terminal facilities, including commodious freight houses and spur tracks. These were lucrative and of particular value in competing with the steamboats which still maintained cheaper freight rates.

There was no longer any doubt in the minds of the steamboat men on the Cumberland about the gravity of the situation. The fireworks opened on January 17, 1880, much sooner than even the most alert steamboat men expected. On that memorable day the daily newspapers of Nashville announced that the L. & N. had purchased a majority of the stock of the N. C. & St. L. This deal, which brought about control of Nashville's best beloved and locally owned railroad, fell like a bombshell all over the South. One daily paper referred to it very properly as "The Great Railroad Scoop." It caused more discussion than any other business transaction in Tennessee up until that time. It has had as much to do with the industrial life of Nashville as any other one single event.

While the Nashville papers bemoaned the fact that the "consolidation" of the L. & N. and the N. C. & St. L. had destroyed competition and dealt a death blow to the industrial and commercial life of the City and had made it a "one railroad town," no one seemed to visualize its effect on another Nashville blessing—i.e. river transportation.

Prior to this stock transaction the L. & N. and the N. C. & St. L. had been engaged in spirited competition and a real battle royal had taken place to see which of the roads would first get into St. Louis, then recognized as the gateway to the west, with the shortest and fastest rail line. The L. & N. had a line completed from Nashville to New Orleans and the N. & C. had one from Nashville to Charleston. For obvious reasons, Nashville held a strategic position, since all midwestern railroad freight, whether it came from river crossings on the Wabash, Ohio or Mississippi or as far west as St. Louis or Chicago, had to come first to Nashville.

While this fight was under way, such financiers as V. K. Stevenson, John Stanton and Russell Sage, who had strong financial interests in the future of the N. & C. and the southeast, made an effort to block the L. & N. in the acquisition of the through line to Birmingham. If this had been successful, Stevenson and his friends had hoped to divert the rich iron, steel and coal to Chattanooga which they envisioned as the "magic city" and not Birmingham. The L. & N. disliked this meddling and made no bones about it.

As the fight to get into St. Louis grew hotter, what rankled most in the minds of the men in control was, that all realized the two roads had to deal with each other because of their connections at Nashville. In other words, it was inevitable that much of the freight would be split, some going over the N. C. to the southeast and some over the L. & N. to the Gulf, Nashville being the intermediary point.

The N. C. & St. L. had a line to Hickman and it was hopeful of getting connections from there into St. Louis. The L. & N. was hopeful of acquiring a direct line from Nashville to Henderson, Evansville and thence to St. Louis. It was at this point that the stock transaction took place and it does not take a magician to understand why. Its wisdom can hardly be denied on any grounds except one of sentiment. At any rate, shortly after the transaction and consolidation, the L. & N. did acquire a through connection to St. Louis and in a relatively short time thereafter the N. & C. had its line into St. Louis also. But, instead of fighting and fussing over who would get the freight, the L. & N. got it all through ownership of the N. & C.

While all of this was going on the steamboats operating on the lower river were hauling three times more grain from the mid-west than the railroads. Steamboat men now saw the whole picture. They knew perfectly well that the

l. to r. *B. S. Rhea* (1886), *J. P. Drouillard* (1881), *J. H. Hillman* (1882). Clarksville, Tennessee, June 22, 1889.

D. H. Pike. Originally *Benton McMillin* (1883)

goal of the railroads was to corner the one remaining heavy long haul freight and the best paying one-namely-grain. The railroads had tried free elevators at Johnsonville and Hickman, they had acquired rail connections to such points, they had put into effect "the privileges" on grain to Nashville, but now they proposed to penetrate the very heart of the grain kingdom itself.

There was no sudden or immediate effect upon grain shipments coming up to Nashville by packets. By 1885, however, the strong resentment of the public over the stock transaction was beginning to subside, despite the warm feeling almost every one had for President E. W. (King) Cole, of the N. C. & St. L. who had guided the destiny of this home-owned railroad for many years. Many felt he had received bad treatment at the hands of his stockholders, especially since he had almost won the fight against the L. & N. to enter St. Louis. The able and popular Cole was succeeded by Ex-Governor James D. Porter and the L. & N. promptly announced that it had no intention of abolishing local and separate management of the N. C. & St. L. This had the effect of blunting the blow of the consolidation and distracting attention from the future absence of competition. The policy of local management remained until just recently when the L. & N. took over the operation of the N. C. & St. L. in all respects.

The railroads not only were hauling more and more grain by 1885, but they had other devious ways to cut in on the packets. For example, all the grain dealers now had spur tracks to their warehouses and elevators. While the river rate on grain from the river crossings into Nashville was considerably less, as will be mentioned later, part of this differential was eaten up by drayage from the wharf or landings. Also, grain shipped in by rail could be shipped out by rail. Free terminal facilities were being erected at the larger towns on the Ohio and Mississippi so that packets not in the Nashville trade could dump their grain cargoes at such points where it could be transhipped by rail to Nashville.

Toward the end of this particular period all of the packet operators in the lower Cumberland trade realized that something drastic had to be done. If they lost grain it would be tantamount to going out of business in this section. The freight from Nashville to Ashland City, Clarksville, Dover, Canton, Cadiz, Kuttawa, Smithland and Paducah had fallen off to a shadow of its former self and none of the packets was making money on the downriver haul and if grain left, the packets could not stand it.

For a very special if somewhat paradoxical reason, however, the railroads as well as the packet owners were gravely concerned about the possibility of the packets leaving the lower Cumberland. This reason was due to the fact that "the privileges" which the railroads had extended on grain shipments by rail to Nashville were granted solely because of steamboat competition between Nashville and the river crossings in the mid-west grain belt.

When the railroads granted "the privileges" they were unknown in railroad circles and were an experiment. As a result of "the privileges," however, the grain business mushroomed beyond all expectations in Nashville. "The privileges" had grown to be as much a part of that business as the grain itself and for this reason the railroads were willing to do anything within reason to protect them.

When "the privileges" had first been granted the railroads had in mind the complete annihilation of steamboat competition. Certainly by the end of this period, if not a few years before, it suddenly dawned on them that such an intention must be altered or it would result in "killing the goose that laid the golden egg." If, for example, the railroads so cornered the grain shipments, that not enough were left for the steamboats, and they went out of business, the sole basis of the granting of "the privileges" in the first place would cease to exist. This indeed would be a catastrophe and in fact this was exactly what ultimately became the basis of the litigation and the adverse decision by the Supreme Court as heretofore noted. There was something else to consider, namely, if it was found necessary to reduce the rail rate on mid-west grain, the reduction would also apply to every other commodity handled by the railroads from that section. It was this latter consideration that chiefly concerned the railroads in this decade. Any complaint by Atlanta, Macon and other cities had not developed and was more a matter of legal than practical significance.

Whether the railroads liked it or not it was therefore essential to the preservation of "the privileges" that steamboat competition continue and that no rate warfare take place. In a way the railroads had made their own bed and now they were forced to lie in it.

Ryman, in 1890, was beginning to be the dominant steamboat man on the lower Cumberland. He was shrewd, direct in his manner and a good executive. In addition to Ryman, there were two other steamboat and grain men in Nashville who were greatly interested in grain shipments coming into Nashville from the mid-west. They were B. S. Rhea and his son I. T. Rhea, who owned the Rhea river-rail terminal in East Nashville served by the L. & N. and which they had recently erected and also owned the St. Louis and Tennessee River Packet Company on the Tennessee River. They also had a large warehouse and elevator on the N. C. & St. L. located in south Nashville. Ryman Line boats unloaded practically all of their mid-west grain at the Rhea terminal.

The Rheas were not primarily interested in competition between Ryman and the railroads. They were, however, vitally concerned in getting as much grain up to Nashville as possible and in having it unloaded at their terminal. The St. Louis and Tennessee River Packet Company boats operated on the Tennessee and Mississippi and dumped their grain shipments at the free elevators owned by the railroads at Johnsonville and Hickman, where it was transhipped over the N. C. & St. L. to Nashville.

Ryman and the Rheas were good friends and as might be expected, Ryman had complete cooperation in the use of the Rhea terminal. The Rheas, however, zealously refrained from any further activity which had to do with competition on the Cumberland. The wisdom of this stand will be better understood as subsequent events proved.

Ryman had much at stake in this situation. In fact, he could lose his entire steamboat fortune if he made a wrong move. He had the choice of three alternatives.

First, he could reduce the rate on grain shipments which was already 3¢ under the rail rate. If he did this he had every reason to expect a long drawn out rate fight with the railroads and there was no particular reason for him to believe he could win. Besides he was barely breaking even on the present rate and there was no indication his boats would get any more grain. This was a hope, but one based on speculation.

Secondly, Ryman might start converting his palatial packets into towboats, buy modern barges and enter contract hauling. This was not anything new on the Western Rivers. In fact, some few towboats had entered the Cumberland. At first glance this might have appeared to be Ryman's best solution. But Ryman was not a towboat type operator to begin with. Neither was Tyner. Their steamboats were beautiful, well appointed and particularly suited for the packet business. It was almost sacriligious to think of dismantling one of their packets. Still another thing, could they get sufficient private towing to make up for the cost of dismantling and the purchase of fifteen or twenty modern barges suited to dry cargo?

In later years, Captain Tyner and other good friends of Ryman told me that he had made a confidential and personal check among his many friends in Nashville and had become convinced that he could not get enough contract hauling to warrant the change. These friends also added that Ryman, as early as 1890, was convinced the railroads had caught the lower river in a vise of steel and it would be only a short time before they would completely capture the mid-west grain. This latter prediction proved to be correct, however, it took longer than Ryman anticipated. A few towboats entered the lower Cumberland grain trade under charter and did a fair business for several years after he died in 1904—notably the *Lotus Sims, Belle Calhoun* and *John B. Heckman.*

The third alternative and the one which Ryman decided to adopt was by far the most logical but the most difficult for him to have undertaken. He would enter the Nashville-Burnside trade area on the upper Cumberland in a big way and endeavor to get as big a slice of this trade as he could, while still keeping one or two packets on the lower Cumberland. There is no great mystery involved in this decision, although it was to have all kinds of repercussions. For years, Ryman had needed greater volume of freight in order to make any money. This volume was not available on the lower river. However, Ryman did not wish to part company with this part of the river just yet. His boats were still getting considerable grain and if he got a break in tobacco, hogs, cattle or lumber, which seemed possible, he might hold on in a limited way for a considerable time. He also knew that the railroads wanted competition on the lower river because of "the privileges." This might be of help to him in any dealings he might have with them.

The Nashville-Burnside trade was the nearest and best place Ryman could get business. He had been eyeing it for a number of years and he knew it had great possibilities. It was the one remaining area which Ryman could enter in a big way and at the same time and without too much money and trouble carry on his competition with the railroads on the lower river. If he could get a fair amount of this upriver business it would prolong if not completely save his business even if the lower river was abandoned. In addition, if he was highly successful he would have a big say in any future agitation over river-rail terminal facilities in Nashville. This last prognostication turned out to be no idle pipe dream.

Ryman had first entered the up-river packet business in 1875. This venture consisted of operating two packets in that area for about two years. Even this "trial balloon" had met with severe criticism and very keen competition from the steamboat men already in that field. These included at the time among others the Lovells, Armstrongs, Hughes and Dix. They openly stated that Ryman was an interloper. While they personally liked him, they considered him an opinionated, extremely ambitious man who had first cast his lot on the lower river and they felt he ought to remain there and not try to "horn in" on them. In brief, they wanted Ryman to mind his own business and that meant stay on the lower river.

Ryman did not at this time press his rights to a conclusion, but instead proposed and later agreed with his competitors to organize the Peoples Line. This line consisted of a pool of boats owned by the competitors, but separately operated. The owners agreed to fixed rates and published them. The papers announced the "war was over."

No sooner had this Line been organized, before other lesser lights in the field opened up with independent boats. These became a thorn in the side of the Peoples boats and after another round of rate warfare the Peoples Line folded and the boats in the pool were sold and the proceeds returned to the owners. This was to be the last and only time Ryman and the owners on the Upper Cumberland ever tried to get together. In 1879–1880, the section from Nashville to Burnside was declared open territory and remained that way. When and if a fight ever again arose, Ryman knew from this rugged experience that his advent up-river would be most unwelcome to say the least. In 1875 Ryman was operating his packets on the lower river most successfully. His entry in the upper river territory at that time was more of an adventure than it was a necessity. Conditions were quite different now.

There is little wonder that there would be some action taken which would affect the principals involved in this confused situation and subsequent facts bear this out.

It is doubtful if any outsider ever knew the exact date or what actually took place. The real facts have probably gone to the graves with the very fine gentlemen who faced the situation.

From time to time and over a long period I have discussed this matter with men who not only knew all the principals, but who were directly related, one way or another, with it. These included Captains Tyner, W. E. Lovell, C. E. Lovell, William T. Hunter, Shep Green, Tom Gallagher, "Preacher" Gann, W. S. and Bridges Montgomery, and grain dealers, including John A. Tyner, S. S. Kerr, Duncan McKay, H. H. Hughes; James Tyner, a former mate on Ryman Line boats; T. A. Clarkston, formerly secretary of the N. C. & St. L. R. R. and the Nashville & Decatur R. R.; Major E. B. Stahlman, railroad executive and publisher, and many others.

I have also had occasion to read a transcript of the evidence and the briefs filed by all parties before the various courts, including the Supreme Court of the United States, in the case heretofore mentioned wherein "the privileges" were declared discriminatory.

From the information gained and subsequent events, it seems that the first important decision was that there would be no rate warfare on grain shipments up to Nashville. The steamboat rate would remain. Ryman would continue his competition on the lower river and he would have continued access to and "friendly" use of the Rhea terminal in Nashville, and the railroads would concentrate on procuring shipments of grain in great bulk from the larger midwest river crossings and leave those at the smaller river landings alone. In this way Ryman hoped it would insure sufficient grain shipments to keep his boats profitable. Ryman knew, however, that such a hope was not well founded and certainly the railroads knew it. Ryman no doubt let it be known that he was unwilling to risk the future of his business solely on such a hope and therefore, for reasons already explained, he expected to enter the upper Cumberland trade. If he did this, it would be a difficult, mean and long drawn out fight. Ryman wanted the railroads' friendly influence in this fight, in return for his toward them on the lower river. He especially wanted such action from the L. & N. since it was his chief competitor in the grain belt in which his boats operated and it also controlled the tracks to the Rhea elevator on the banks of the Cumberland at Nashville.

Just what action was taken as between the railroads and

Ryman as heretofore indicated is buried under all kinds of rumors and gossip, but the events which took place on both ends of the river during the last years of this decade and on up to Ryman's death in 1904 shed light on the situation.

Beginning around 1889, Ryman had completed his plans for all-out competition in the Nashville-Burnside trade. He had built three brand new packets and had published new tariff rates and landings and announced that he would issue through bills of lading via L. & N. R. R. If Nashville merchants desired, their freight into the city could be unloaded at the Rhea terminal and then carried by the railroads to their warehouses. If they wished to load freight or receive it at the wharf that could be done. His boats would be punctual and stop at regular landings.

It did not take long for open warfare to break out on the upper Cumberland. The Lovells, Armstrongs, Greens and at a somewhat later date, Handly, Kendall, Parmenter and others, with one accord rose to meet Ryman, whom they accused of "cooperating" with the railroads solely to destroy their business. These hardy operators especially resented the implication which was rumored about that Ryman had saved "the privileges" for Nashville grain dealers by his "so called" competition on the lower river. They pointed out with much truth that the competition he was offering was exactly what it had always been and as a matter of fact Ryman was pulling his punches and offering nothing but token competition as a camouflage to protect "the privileges."

His competitors claimed Ryman was already losing money on the lower river and would not have been justified in building several new boats, manning and operating them, without something more than "cooperation." They contended he was being backed by the railroads and there would never be a satisfactory river-rail terminal in Nashville. Ryman was quick to deny all such accusations as were the railroads.

These claims and counter-claims enlivened the community, but it certainly did not help the steamboat business. It grew to such an extent that in the upper Cumberland a person was forced to identify his favorite—Ryman or the Independents. People became hot headed. Competition was strictly of the dog-eat-dog type and no quarter given. If Ryman built a new boat his rivals built one. If he cut rates the others would cut even further. If a Ryman Line packet left the wharf in Nashville, there would be another one just ahead or behind. Freight rates dropped from 15¢ to 10¢ to 5¢ a hundred, but still both sides held on. It was utterly impossible to negotiate any form of compromise. Venom took the place of legitimate criticism. This went on until all of the "battlers" were gone.

Ryman strenuously insisted that he received no financial backing from the railroads or their officers. His good friend and trusted partner, Captain Tyner, told me Ryman never received any such help. Others claimed just the opposite. Tyner contended with much merit that Ryman had no other choice except to enter the Nashville-Burnside trade if he expected to stay in business and Ryman was in excellent financial condition and he could get all the financial help he wanted without asking aid from the railroads or any one else. This was one side of the picture, but the independent operators were never convinced he was entirely on his own in either offering "token" competition on the lower river or in trying to corner the packet business above Nashville. It must be admitted, however, that Ryman had a perfect right to protect his business and subsequent events proved that Ryman did this for a number of years by entering the upper-river trade. Ryman had everything to gain and nothing to lose—except a lot of sleep over the criticism directed toward him.

Since the packets had no outside competition in the trade above Nashville, the competition between Ryman and the independent operators did not in any way diminish the volume of freight going or coming. Whether the cargo went by Ryman Line packets or by an independent packet made no difference in the fabulous volume of freight handled. The steamboats got it all anyway and every year the volume increased until it amounted to some $15,000,000 annually.

This was sufficient to support not only Ryman packets but all of the others, too. It explains better than anything else how the two factions were enabled to carry on their fight. Neither was able to run the other off the river, because both were making good money. It further explains why the wharf at Nashville, despite a near collapse of packet business on the lower river, was teeming with all types of freight and as many packets as usual. This was due primarily to the upper-river trade.

One is liable to forget something else in discussing this situation. Personally, I have felt that the Nashville-Burnside packets represented to the 400,000 people in their trade area something more than transportation, as valuable as that was. I refer to the sentiment and confidence which existed between the operators and their customers. The coming of a packet up to a landing was a big event in the lives of these sturdy Anglo-Saxons. The packets were in many sections the only glimpse they had of the outside world. They brought them the necessities of life such as wire, hardware, stoves, roofing, drugs, cloth, knives and farming implements to mention but a few. In return they took to market meat, butter, furs, molasses, tobacco, hogs, cattle and other products indigenous to the section.

Whenever the melodious whistle of a friendly packet resounded in the hills, old grandpappy would grab his walking stick, Aunt Molly would put on her favorite sun bonnet and even the old hound dog would crawl out from under the house.

I shall never forget the thrill of watching an old time packet "making" a landing at some small community on the upper reaches of the Cumberland. It seemed impossible for so much freight to be put off and taken on as often occurred at such out of the way places. After the usual friendly greetings and discharge of freight, I have seen as many as 5 or 6 hogsheads of tobacco, 100 sides of hog meat, 50 or 60 stands of lard, 30 or 40 coops of chickens, 20 or more cases of eggs, 300 or 400 hides, 100 gallons of molasses, several lean steers and 200 or 300 hogs taken on. This would continue at almost every landing until the guard rails of the packet would be licking the water. It is almost beyond words to describe the nerve-shattering trip down the river on a high "tide," with a pilot at the wheel trying to make the Nashville wharf in time to eat supper with his wife and kids on Saturday night. There never will be a more carefree or adventuresome type of life in all the world than that on board one of the old time packets.

When Col. M. T. Bryan, one of Nashville's most enthusiastic river men, organized the Cumberland River Improvement Association in 1889, it planned to increase traffic through the erection of locks and dams by the Federal Government. It was the first organized voice seriously raised in many years by the public in behalf of the river. For this reason, if none other, it deserves highest praise. There had been talk of such improvements for a number of years.

Colonel Bryan procured the cooperation of many outstanding river men in Indiana, Illinois, Kentucky and Tennessee. At the first meeting of the Association, held in the Amusement Hall on Broad Street in Nashville, such distinguished citizens as Gov. Robert L. Taylor and Congressman Benton McMillin made enthusiastic addresses.

The Association, in 1890, after most arduous work, procured an appropriation of $290,000.00 from Congress and thereafter other sums which were considered sufficient to complete Locks 1 and 2 in the vicinity of Nashville on the river. Prior to 1889, the total appropriations made by Congress for such improvements amounted to $275,000.00, although the Rivers and Harbors Committee had approved a complete lock and dam system for the Cumberland, which was to cost $6,000,000.00.

At the meeting of the Association in 1891, Colonel Bryan went all out in his enthusiasm and predicted that both Locks 1 and 2 might be completed within a year. It was my great pleasure to have known Colonel Bryan and because of his deep interest in the river and what he did for it, his memory shall always be cherished, but, in this instance his prediction was so grossly wrong that he must have been emotionally upset while speaking. At any rate, Lock 1 was not thrown open until 1904 and Lock 2 not until 1907 and they finally cost $395,634.45 and $340,241.65, respectively. The Association, Colonel Bryan, Benton McMillin, Congressman John Wesley Gaines and the very excellent U. S. Engineers stationed at Nashville deserve great credit for their ultimate completion.

The Cumberland River Improvement Association was an excellent idea as far as it went. Locks and dams were only a small part of the river's trouble. If Colonel Bryan and the Association, or any other similar organization, had directed their energies to such matters as railroad competition and the building of a modern river-rail terminal at Nashville, it might have resulted in great and immediate benefits. Such projects, however, were loaded with dynamite. The vital question of competition was forgotten in favor of all year round traffic supposed to be provided by the proposed locks. It took thirty years to get a municipal river-rail terminal at Nashville. Ryman by that time had been dead 16 years, both the Rheas had died, and so had the packet business on the Cumberland River. But a terminal was finally built, like the locks, too late. It was from the beginning and still is served by only one railroad—the Tennessee Central, which dared to enter Nashville early in the twentieth century. It was of no aid to the packets although it has afforded considerable aid to the modern style of river traffic.

During this period it is possible for the first time to give definite and conclusive figures on the amount of tonnage transported by the steamboats. Beginning in 1886, the War Department, through its Engineers stationed in Nashville, began to compile such statistics. Until boats locked through and a law was enacted by Congress making it mandatory to report tonnage, the War Department had difficulty in checking the freight handled by the packets. It was also next to impossible to check other tonnage handled by tramp steamers engaged in contract hauling. In this way items such as coal, barged up or down the river, fertilizer, and in a few instances, even grain, slipped by the diligent District Engineers. Such a thing does not happen under the present law. The reports of the War Department are the best available records and I have no doubt of their accuracy.

In 1889, despite all the trials and tribulations, the packets really made a remarkable record. In that year, which closes this period, the packets on the lower river handled 323,000 tons of commercial freight and those on the upper Cumberland 525,000 tons. The people of Nashville might well look back and ponder that achievement—875,000 tons of "reported" riverborne freight in one navigable season. This does not include coal and other unreported items. If these were added, the total tonnage would again jump to near the 1,000,000 ton mark.

Such a record was made although the Federal Government and the State of Tennessee together had spent less than $850,000.00 on the Cumberland since the "General Jackson" first tied up at the wharf at Nashville.

The year 1889–90 was one of the finest crop years in history for the territory served by the Cumberland. This was of great aid in making the above record. There were bumper grain and tobacco crops. The navigable season lasted seven full months on the upper river. As a result of this blessing, the packets on the river, among other things, handled 82,-033 tons of grain, 2,344 tons of flour, 522 tons of hay, slightly more than 25,380 tons of miscellaneous freight, which does not include eggs, poultry, bacon, lard and other barter; 10,331 tons of iron, better than 250 tons of brick, 18,121 tons of tobacco, nearly 9,000 head of livestock, and in excess of 22,000 barrels of salt.

In addition, steamboats and barges transported better than 40,000,000 feet (B. M.—Board Measure) of rough sawed lumber and more than 6,000,000 shingles. Other items included chickens and eggs, which were always hauled in great abundance; 15,000 head of hogs, sugar, coffee, molasses, walnuts, ginseng, furs, feathers, bacon and lard. There were better than 30,000,000 feet of timber (B. M.) rafted to Nashville. Such a record was never again to be approached so long as the packets ran. The Cumberland seemed to rise up and shake itself in the hopes of better treatment. It was a great record, coming as it did in the face of many difficulties. Most river men referred to 1889 as the last big year before the downward turning point in traffic below Nashville.

If the packets, however, were having a banner year in 1889, so were the railroads. Every year from then on was a bumper year for them. Their tonnage, especially that in competition with the steamboats, was increasing by leaps and bounds.

In 1875 the L. & N. on its main stem, from Louisville to Nashville, which was the only railroad line then competing with the river from the Ohio crossings, had handled only 66,694 tons of grain. The N. C. & St. L. had handled from Johnsonville and Hickman via Nashville & Northwestern a total of only 125,086 tons of freight, of which less than 30,-000 tons was grain. In 1875 the two railroads had thus handled less than 100,000 tons of grain into Nashville.

But, by 1889, the L. & N., with its lines to Evansville, Hendersonville and St. Louis completed, was bringing to Nashville corn totaling 299,025 tons, wheat totaling 75,403 tons, other grain 89,547 tons and hay 57,083 tons, making a grand total of 521,058 tons. In 1889 the N. C. & St. L. was bringing in an additional 190,338 tons of corn and wheat from Johnsonville and Hickman and another 30,287 tons of hay, making a total of 220,625 tons.

If we add the L. & N. and its subsidiary together, we have a total of 741,683 tons of grain and hay brought into Nashville in 1889. This was 3 and ¾ times more grain than was brought in by the steamboats during a banner year. These figures are eloquent testimony of what the railroads had accomplished. Another revealing sidelight shown by these figures is the established fact that Nashville received from both river and rail facilities almost 1,000,000 tons of grain and kindred products for distribution to the southeast or for processing into flour and meal.

In completing this chapter, it is pertinent once more to refer to the two major items of freight which the steam-

E. G. Ragon (1887). Loading tobacco at Cloversport, Ky.

boats were handling in ever-increasing amounts—lumber and live stock. While these two great cargoes were not to save the day entirely, they were to go a long way toward postponing the final departure of the Cumberland River packets.

So we come to the close of another period. The steamboat men were hopeful—they always were. The wharf at Nashville was still a busy place. Freight was piled in the familiar stacks. Roustabouts were just about as happy as ever. Captains and mates were cussing. Whistles were blowing and the bells ringing. Passengers were plentiful—more than 30,000 rode the Nashville packets in 1890.

One old mate who happened along did remark that the freeboard on some of the packets was showing more than usual. Funny how these old-timers had a way of expressing a sad thought. When a packet was "flattened out," that is, loaded to the point where you could play a tune on her hog chains, she had no freeboard visible to the naked eye and her guard rails licked the water. The time had not yet come by any means to count the packets out. Some of the finest boats on the Western Rivers could be seen at the Nashville wharf. A glance at the Appendix will reveal their names and ownership. There might be fewer than in the years gone by, but they had the old-time glamor and elegance. Steam was still up and they were 'raring to go.

CHAPTER EIGHT

Friction Dims the Golden Nineties

Period 1890–1900

Most historians of Tennessee who have written about the Cumberland—and they are few and far between—invariably fix the demise of the packet business on the river at the end of this period. This is not justified by the facts, and marks a failure to diagnose the true situation. While things were gloomy as compared to the past, the "Golden Nineties" held in store no such grief for the steamboats. Their obituary was not yet ready for publication.

Due to certain favorable circumstances, packets on the Cumberland were destined to carry on for a number of years. The "privileges" granted by the railroads on grain transported to Nashville, while cutting in heavily on the river grain traffic, had not yet annihilated it. Nashville packets on occasion were flattened out with the familiar sacks of grain picked up along the banks of the river or from small towns and landings not yet affected by railroad competition. Such places were getting scarcer, but quite a few were still left.

Other business on the lower river was in a precarious situation. The chief problem still was to obtain freight downstream from Nashville to points nearer the mid-west grain belt. If this could not be done, the boats would lose so much money that no amount of grain on the return trip could make it up.

In an effort to increase his pay load freight down river

from Nashville to Paducah, Evansville and Cairo, Captain Ryman and his partner, Captain Tyner, sought by every available means to procure more business from Nashville merchants and manufacturers. They published a very favorable rate on freight moving by river from Nashville to Ashland City, Clarksville, Dover, Smithland and Paducah. The Ryman Lines also gave excellent one-day delivery service on such freight and in that manner hoped to offer substantial competition to the railroads.

Nevertheless, by the close of this period business downstream from Nashville was still declining, and to make matters worse the larger towns on the lower Cumberland had welcomed another American institution, commonly referred to as the General Merchandise Store. Every town which was served by a railroad, whether main line or spur, boasted at least one "big" store, which handled everything from Lydia Pinkham's Compound to red flannel underwear. Traveling salesmen could be found on every train. Small town hotels could hardly accommodate these amiable gentlemen, known to all as "drummers."

While steamboats on the lower river in making trips from Nashville might have survived the loss of patent medicines and what can be termed "light freight," when the small town river merchants began to enter the field of wholesale groceries, flour, meal, hardware, stoves, furniture, wagons, leather goods and other "heavy freight," it cut deeply into the necessary two-way pay load freight. The Ryman Line for the first time, despite every effort and pressure by Ryman and Tyner, began to show permanent signs of recurring nonprofitable trips down river. Sometime between 1895 and 1900 the situation became critical, despite the fact that the boats were still handling quantities of grain on the return trip to Nashville.

There was a movement in America for better living conditions. Farmers had suddenly come to realize that it was easier and better to go into their county seats and look at merchandise at the big store, and buy it, than to write a letter to a Nashville merchant and order a base burner, for example, and have a steamboat deliver it at a landing on a muddy bank. Human nature being what it is, no could blame the farmer and since the railroads and general merchandise stores had teamed up and were doing a good job, it was inevitable that their business would increase.

Ryman, during this period, had anticipated a much larger flow of freight to his down-river packets from livestock. Beginning in 1890, he had attempted to build up a better river traffic in this field. Alex Perry of Nashville was a leader in this business. In 1891, Ryman had built and named a fine new packet for him. However, steamboats on the lower Cumberland never did receive the great benefits from it as anticipated or prophesied. On the other hand, the upper river greatly profited by it, in fact, at a later date it had a major hand in making Nashville a large livestock and hog center.

Ryman was also keenly disappointed when it became evident that the bulk of the sawed lumber coming into Nashville would go by rail, rather than by river packets, to such points as Evansville, Henderson and St. Louis. He had hoped he could get a large part of this heavy cargo to offset the loss of other freight on the down river haul below Nashville. Evansville was fast becoming an outstanding furniture manufacturing center and was ideally suited to receive such cargo. But, here again Ryman ran headlong into the inevitable fact that once a railroad gets its hand on freight it never lets go of it. This trade up until 1890 had seemed very promising but when the big saw mills in Nashville began to buy up rafts and rough timber and make it over into finished lumber, it was much easier to then load it in box cars and transport it to market than to skid it back down a river bank to a faithful packet—even if it could be transported at a cheaper rate. Ryman soon saw that cheaper rates did not always mean he would get the business. By the time labor charges were considered, cheaper rates were likely to disappear and it took a lot of man power to load lumber on a packet.

It turned out that lumber like livestock and hogs, belonged to the upper Cumberland and never did amount to much below Nashville. Once more the packets which were begging for freight on the haul below Nashville, had seen their hopes fade. It was a novel situation to say the least. The Cumberland River and its packets on the upper river had made Nashville into a great lumber center, especially for hardwood, by first getting the lumber down to the city, but the packets on the lower river could not find a stick of finished lumber to carry to market. It was the same old story on the lower river. Better facilities for loading and unloading and faster service, had given the railroads another victory.

In view of the continued diminution of his business on the lower river, due to all these factors, Ryman determined to go after the trade on the upper river with renewed zeal. Starting in 1895, he went all out in his efforts to gain control of traffic in this area and whether the up river steamboat operators liked it or not he would seek total victory.

As a result, the competition which had already flared into an open and incurable break by 1895, became even more intense as this period progressed. Under such circumstances it was inevitable that over and above normal or fair competition, open warfare would continue between Ryman on the one hand and all other packet boat operators on the upper river. During this period charges and counter charges continued to be hurled back and forth, freight rates were published and then thrown overboard, special concessions were given by both sides on the slightest pretext. Shippers began to bargain for the cheapest rate and some could not get their freight moved promptly without agreeing to move all of it over the same line. A few captains and mates were more interested in taking freight away from a competitor than holding on to and delivering their own. Small shippers were frequently passed up at landings.

The railroads in Nashville were having an era of unprecedented success while all of this was going on. They had undisputed control of transportation in every section of the Nashville trade area with the one exception of the

Nashville-Burnside packet trade. They had a hand in this business to a limited extent, thanks to Ryman and their rail connection to the Rhea terminal where Ryman Line packets unloaded. Everything seemed rosy for the railroads, but there was one big obstacle staring them in the face. Sooner or later they would be called upon to justify the granting of "the privileges" on mid-west grain shipments to Nashville. In 1887, the Interstate Commerce Commission had been created by an Act of Congress and the principal purpose of this Commission was to stop discriminatory practices and rate abuses, if any existed, under railroad management.

The Interstate Commerce Act was amended on several different occasions and in 1910 a new Act created the Commerce Court, to try cases coming within the jurisdiction of the Commerce Commission. This of course completed the heretofore unheard of method of not only regulating interstate commerce, but providing a special court to enforce such regulations.

Prior to the creation of the Interstate Commerce Commission, "the privileges," granted by the railroads, had coasted along without any serious or concerted effort to dislodge them as discriminatory. Every time there had been any rumblings of action some emissary of good will, with glib tongue and warm smile, had been able to smooth things over. But, certainly by the close of this period, the railroads, Ryman, the Rheas and every grain dealer in Nashville knew that sooner or later, "the privileges" would be attacked when a proper forum could be found to hear such practices. Just what moves and counter moves would be undertaken, however, belong to the next succeeding decade and will be fully disclosed in proper sequence. It is sufficient to state at this time that not only the packet trade on the lower river but also the entire grain business in Nashville was involved.

Directing attention once more to the Nashville-Burnside trade, it might be of interest to note the average annual shipments of freight to and from Nashville in this period. The following figures have been carefully checked from old newspapers, and from USED reports and also manifest rec-

Alex Perry (1891). Leaving Nashville Wharf.

R. Dunbar (1895). At Nashville "flattened out" with upper river cargo.

ords furnished by my friends among the old time captains, pilots and mates. In 1895 annual freight brought into Nashville from the upper river amounted to 10,000,000 feet of hardwood lumber; 3200 hogsheads of burley tobacco; 100,-000 pounds of cured meat and lard; 3500 head of livestock; 30,000 head of hogs; 30,000 tons of grain and hay; 150,000 full coops of chickens, turkeys and ducks; 60,000 gallons of molasses; 100,000 cases of eggs; several thousand tons of hides, walnuts, furs, ginseng and wild herbs; and 200,000 minimum of cross ties. There was also a large quantity of ax handles and staves.

Freight going by packet up river to various points would average nearly 400,000 tons and consisted of drugs, cloth and clothing, furniture, wire fencing, hardware, stoves and foundry products, farm implements, wagons, buggies, saddles, leather goods, harness, groceries, chewing and smoking tobacco, snuff, coffee, salt, sugar, fertilizer, seeds, boots and shoes, candy and every other article so badly needed by people in rural communities.

The diversity of the shipments from Nashville explains why so many packets were named for prominent Nashvillians. For example, the *Bob Dudley,* named for the president of Gray-Dudley which sold so many stoves to the upper river people, the *J. B. Richardson,* the *Henry Harley,* the *H. W. Buttorff,* and the *Sam J. Keith,* were all named for prominent Nashville merchants and shippers of goods in large quantities to the upper trade area.

Brief mention has already been made of the relation of timber and lumber to the lower river traffic. Let us now turn attention to its connection with traffic on the upper river. Rough hardwood lumber first came to the upper river in volume between 1870 and 1885. The largest tracts of accessible virgin timber at the time were to be found in Jackson, Clay, Overton and Fentress Counties, Tennessee, and across the Kentucky line in Cumberland, Clinton, Russell and Wayne Counties. There were other lesser tracts in Wilson, Trousdale and Smith Counties, Tennessee. It has been truthfully said that some of the finest cedar, oak, ash, poplar, beech, walnut and hickory in the United States is found in the area contiguous to the Cumberland. The sections around Gainesboro and Roaring River and that about Celina and Obey River in the early days of the timber business were both extensive and easily accessible to the packets. There were other large tracts up the Caney Fork near Carthage. In all there were 13,000,000 acres of this timber in the upper reaches of the Cumberland with an estimated value of $130,000,000.00.

Prior to the War Between the States very little of this timber had found its way to market. Sometime between 1870 and 1880 such men as Hugh H. Kyle, William Hull, Captain A. C. Dale, J. D. H. Hatcher, Captain Jim Davis, W. C. Keen, Pleas and Hob Harrison, Jim Gamel, Buck Baker, Clabe Beatey, and M. M. Smith of Celina; J. M. Stephenson and J. A. Vaughan of Rowena; Cas, Will Henry and L. C. Ross, Sam Smith, William Murley across the Kentucky line; Colonel M. L. Gore and George Birdwell in the Gainesboro area, and many other upper Cumberland timber men began to cut the virgin hardwood timber near the banks of the river and raft it down to Nashville or saw it up into rough lumber and take it down by packet. Kyle and Hull were pioneers in this business and made substantial fortunes from it. Later on Charles, M. J. and Frank Kyle joined their father, Hugh, and successfully carried on the business. By 1880 the timber business had increased to a point which now seems fantastic.

As early as 1874, Killibrew in his "Resources of Tennessee" estimated that 22,500,000 feet of saw logs came down the river. Of this amount he said 15,000,000 feet remained in Nashville and 7,500,000 went to points beyond. It is regrettable that he was unable to estimate the amount of sawed rough lumber brought down by the packets which was immense. We have authentic figures on the sawed lumber beginning in 1882. A. E. Baird, writing in the Southern Lumberman, under date, December 15, 1882, reported that lumber cut by Nashville mills in the past year totalled 56,-000,000 feet and included in this amount was 15,000,000 feet of roughly sawed lumber brought down by steamboats. There were 1,400 rafts tied up in the river at Nashville during this one year. At the close of the year it was estimated that the Nashville mills had handled lumber valued at $3,372,000.00.

In 1884, there were twenty mills at Nashville that handled 86,165,000 feet of lumber. Some of these were Prewitt-Spurr Company; Southern Pump Co.; Indiana Lumber Co.; Edgefield and Nashville Manufacturing Co.; Jacob Shaeffer & Co.; Lieberman-Loveman & O'Brien; Ewing & Wilkerson Co.; Norvell & Wallace Co.; Goldberg & Rich; Cheny O'Connor & Co.; Cumberland Lumber Co.; E. S. & G. C. Van Valkenberg; John Streight and William Sutherland. During this period John B. Ransom & Company was organized and then others like the Farris Lumber Company and the Nashville Hardwood Flooring Company.

This brief story of lumber and its relationship to the river will not be burdened with additional figures. It is not always possible to give accurate estimates. One fact seems to be beyond contradiction. Timber and lumber, as a cargo, reached its peak on the Cumberland between 1900 and 1904. During these years the total lumber handled by Nashville mills and kindred industries exceeded 100,000,000 feet. From all sources it yielded a gross annual income of better than $8,000,000.00 and Nashville became one of the outstanding hardwood lumber centers of America and by far the largest in the South.

It is but fair to say that the Cumberland River and the steamboats made this industry possible. By a queer twist of fate, however, the packets lost a large portion of the upper river rough lumber cargo long before that business reached its peak. For example, around 1895 many of the larger saw mills along the banks of the upper Cumberland went out of business completely and the timber men began to float their logs down to Nashville instead of sawing them into rough lumber. It was found that the big saw mills in Nashville could buy and handle the rafts and saw them into finished lumber. The timber men were rarely mistreated as to prices and gradually they adopted rafts as the best method of getting their timber to the mills. Thus by this change or evolution in the business, the packets lost large volumes of rough and sawed lumber, but the river gained an increased number of rafts.

A contributing factor to this evolution was the growing decrease in large tracts of timber along the Cumberland. After a period of ten years, the virgin timber which formerly adorned the river was cut. It then became necessary to invade the banks of such rivers as the Obey, Roaring and Caney Fork. During the summer and fall, these rivers would be filled with rafts of oak, ash, poplar and beech. When the proper tide came the Cumberland would receive its annual flow of rafts destined for Nashville. The banks of the river would be lined for several miles both above and below the city. But, the steamboats went begging for rough lumber which they so badly needed to make both ends meet.

Since the rafting of logs constituted big business and is a most fascinating enterprise, it is proper to mention some of its sidelights. Most of the upper Cumberland rafts were put together according to the number of feet of lumber desired. Some were calculated to contain 40,000 feet according to Cumberland River standards. Others contained as high as 80 and 90,000 feet. Length was variable, also width.

No logs were cut less than ten feet and the longest sixteen feet. An average raft was 200 feet long and in a single tier. Larger rafts were two or three tiers wide and reached a length of 250 feet. As a rule the average raft was manned by a crew of five men and a pilot. Three men were assigned to the bow oar and two to the stern oar. Old time helmsmen were paid fifty cents a day and upkeep. An expert pilot received $1.50 per day and food. It took five days to run a raft on a good tide from Celina to Nashville, a distance of 220 miles. In the early days most pilots tied up at night, but later on they ran straight through. This was treacherous business and resulted in many accidents and shakeups, not to mention verbal assaults with the packet boat pilots, who always, according to the raftsmen, tried to "hog" the channel.

Bringing a big raft down the Cumberland on a high tide was no easy matter. It took great physical strength to manage the sweeping oars and courage to stick by them in wind and storm. Pilots had to know every foot of the river and anticipate the hazards well in advance. Their orders to the helmsmen had to be accurate and instantaneously obeyed. It is one thing to watch with awe and admiration a big raft gracefully swing around the sharp bend of the river, but still another to steer and pilot one on its tortuous course. One of the greatest of all Cumberland River raftsmen was the faithful Negro pilot, Cal Hamilton of Celina, who worked for the Kyles. He seemed to have a sixth sense when it came to bringing a raft "home" through a bad stretch of the river. There were many others, but Cal was the joy and delight of all raftsmen for years and years.

Not only is there a knack in steering a raft, but in the way they are landed and tied up. Sudden rises and falls in the tide often caused an inexperienced raftsman to lose his raft by "buckling" or breaking in two. After all hands had gathered around for the last cup of coffee in the small "lean-to" or "shanty," always found in the middle of the raft, the pilot generally examined his lines to make sure of his position and safety. The "lean-to" was the center of all social life on the trip. It was here the hardy raftsmen slept on straw and ate their meals which, as a rule, were unusually well prepared, even though cooked on a small step stove or an improvised rock grate atop a hearth of mud and clay.

Those who have watched a raft leisurely passing down the river with all hands at rest, chatting and joking, might think such a life is the laziest in all the world. On the contrary, others who have had the happy fortune to have ridden one of these awkward affairs down the river on a high tide, and around such hazardous points as Brimstone, Turkey Creek, lower and upper Holliman, Billtown, Whitley's Rock and a number of others, are perfectly willing to let the raftsmen have all the peace they can find, knowing full well they deserve it. My good friend, Millard Kyle, now deceased, who brought many a big raft down the Cumberland, sized up the life of a raftsman with this quaint statement: "Rafting

James N. White (1893)

John W. Hart (1890) and *W. K. Phillips* (1892). Nashville Wharf

was like being married. You were either in hell or heaven. Many a fellow would swear one minute he'd die dead in his tracks if he ever rode a raft again. The next minute some joke would be told or he'd go over and light up his pipe and then he'd swear he'd never do anything else. It was tough but a good life."

Rafting was a life unto itself. It suited the independence and courage of the Anglo-Saxon men of the upper Cumberland who were born and reared in that uncontaminated stronghold of Americanism. In addition to those whom I have already mentioned, there were many others from the upper Cumberland territory who went forth to make fame and fortune, including, Cordell Hull, Secretary of State in the Roosevelt cabinet, one of America's outstanding statesmen and son of William (Uncle Billy) Hull; Judge John J. Gore, U. S. District Judge for Middle Tennessee, son of Col. M. L. Gore; Benton McMillin, Governor and Congressman; Sam J. Keith, Nashville financier; T. Harvey Butler, Secretary of State of Tennessee, and a host of others.

Mr. Hull, familiarly known in the upper Cumberland as Judge Hull, having served with distinction in the Circuit Court, rode many a raft down the river. His interest in the affairs of the Cumberland never ceased. When he returned to this section of the state he never failed to visit his old friends of river days. The story is told of the time "Aunt Polly" Williams, proprietor of the only hotel in Gainesboro who, exasperated with Judge Hull because he did not adjourn court immediately when she rang the dinner bell, came out on the square, rang the bell incessantly and shouted: "Court or no Court, Cordell Hull or no Cordell Hull, you better git over here in a hurry and eat my food while it's hot or you won't eat it at all." "Aunt Polly," one of the most beloved and picturesque characters in all the upper river country, was no respecter of persons and she said what she meant. She had a way of emphasizing her point with sufficient color not to be misunderstood. She also knew that nothing was more annoying than a bell when it is rung continuously. Thereafter at the first tap of the bell all proceedings stopped and court recessed without the slightest formality. The Judge for once had met his match. He either ate at "Aunt Polly's" or he did not eat at all.

Judge Gore and Judge Hull were law partners at Gainesboro in their earlier years. Judge Gore also rode rafts down the river. He was never happier than when he was discussing the days of rafting and boating. I recall most vividly one late afternoon in the early summer on a June rise I picked him up by chance at the landing at Gainesboro on my towboat, the *J. S. Hopkins*, and we made it up to "Seven Sisters Bluff" by sundown. There all hands turned in for supper. The moon came up while we were sipping our coffee on the bow deck. The Judge started talking about old times. I shall never forget his humor, his utter lack of self-consciousness and his simple philosophy. He loved the river and acknowledged his debt to it. He said it had taught him much, especially patience.

On the return trip Judge Gore got off at Gainesboro. As I lingered to say goodbye, he passed a word of wisdom to me. "Byrd," he said, "I'd watch the tide up here. You know it runs out mighty fast." That ought to have been sufficient. He knew his river. I should have "lit out hell-bent for election." Instead I foolishly took my time. In less than a few short hours I was hung up for the first time in my life on the treacherous bar at Billtown with a sixty-four foot tow boat, and I stayed there two full weeks.

Mention has been made of Obey River and Caney Fork River in connection with the timber and lumber trade. The Obey River also supplied the Cumberland packets with many other commodities. In the early days top-water steamboats plied this river and brought down large quantities of tobacco, hogs, furs, corn, fresh meats, lard, poultry, eggs, hoops, staves, axe handles and hides. The head of navigation on this deep but narrow tributary was Barnes Shoals, about 46.8 miles above its mouth, but Byrdstown Landing was considered the farthest stop for boats. In later years many a fair-sized packet ran up this river upon catching a good tide, grabbed its cargo and hurriedly retraced its course. In later years lumber was the principal cargo. Huge rafts were annually made up on the Obey and it was a veritable paradise for raftsmen during the balmy days of the Kyles and Hulls, who lived at Celina, very near the mouth of the river. The Obey River drains an area estimated at 922 square miles. It is the fourth largest tributary of the Cumberland. Mark Twain has made certain portions of the country around Obey River famous in his "Gilded Age."

The Caney Fork River was designated navigable for approximately sixty miles above its mouth or within thirty miles of the Falls near Walling. It is the largest tributary of the Cumberland, draining 3,294 square miles. It is one of the most beautiful rivers in Tennessee. Coming down this graceful river in the spring on a "freshet" is a thrilling event. There are times when, due to rains over its huge drainage area, it reaches enormous proportions. Only then is it readily understood how the Caney Fork, despite its beautiful bluffs and sharp bends, could yield a rich packet trade. Many large packets, picking the right time and tide, have gone up the Caney Fork after their favorite cargo of grain and other typical up-river freight.

Sligo was one of the largest steamboat landings on this tributary. As late as 1887, the *Nashville, William Porter, E. E. Bedford, Sam P. Jones, Matt F. Allen, John Fowler,* and *J. D. Carter* ran regular trips up the Caney Fork, the distance depending on the tide. Traffic seemed so good that the War Department spent $25,000.00 improving the channel. There have been several packets named for the picturesque Caney Fork. The name "Sligo" has also been used by several packets, thus preserving the name of the famous landing.

The Queen & Crescent (C. N. O. and T. P., now the Southern) Railroad entered Burnside in 1880. The event was carefully watched by the Nashville packet owners, who foresaw stiffer competition in that section of the river. Nashville packets always counted the section between Nashville and Burkesville, Kentucky, as their trade area. Many boats plied all the way to Burnside, but the territory beyond Burkesville, a distance of about ninety miles, was extremely hazardous and frequently unnavigable due to low water.

The Burnside packets in years previous to 1880 had never seriously threatened the Nashville packets, but had remained content with the trade above Burkesville, although many ran, when business justified, all the way down to Nashville. The big question now was, would the Burnside packets, with a railroad connection, seek to capture the rich trade to Celina, an added distance of forty-six miles below Burkesville, and Gainesboro, an added sixty-nine miles, or even Carthage, an added 119 miles. If they did undertake such a venture in whole or in part, there could be serious trouble, especially if Ryman and his competitors continued their fight and freight warfare.

The steamboat men in Nashville were not the only ones in the city disturbed. The L. & N. did not care to lose any trade to the Queen & Crescent or any one else. Nashville merchants and manufacturers were also aroused. They also wanted the river business.

Time often adjusts matters. It did in this case. The Queen & Crescent strongly backed the Burnside packets and in due time, as indicated by the Appendix, several large boats had been built and were running. What was far better, a modern river-rail terminal was erected and the packets were easily unloaded. By the beginning of this period things were getting in good shape at Burnside, but there was one catch. The packets leaving Burnside continued to be loaded light. Too much freeboard was showing as the old time mate would say. There simply was not enough freight from Burnside to down river points in later years to make a two-way pay load possible. This as usual spelled final doom.

Nevertheless, the Burnside boats and some other independent Nashville packets put into the trade to Burnside did a fair business for a number of years. One of these boats, the *Albany*, did a tremendous business and was a real money-maker. The Queen & Crescent Railroad had offered an outlet for such typical up-river barter as poultry, eggs and produce, which were shipped by fast freight to large centers such as Cincinnati and Chattanooga on a one-day schedule. Large quantities of hogs and tobacco were han-

P. D. Staggs (1893)

l. to r. *J. B. Richardson* (1898), *Bob Dudley* (1897) and *H. W. Buttorff* (1896). Three Ryman Line packets, Nashville Wharf (c. 1900).

dled. But, while this was gratifying, it did not induce the boat owners to venture much farther than Gainesboro and most of them during this period seldom went below Carthage. They were forced to make a short haul to protect the light intake on the downstream trip.

It thus came about that the Nashville packets did not lose any great amount of territory, or freight to the Burnside boats. To be exact, their territories overlapped for less than 90 miles and this over shallow and treacherous water most of the time. If Burnside had been large enough to support a packet line down river the story would have been different. It might have been different if there had been a really large city on the upper river between Nashville and Burnside. There was none; all the towns were very small and they looked to Nashville for their supplies. Burnside had its railroad and its terminal, but its trade was limited. Nashville would remain in the future as in the past, the one big metropolis on the Cumberland. The importance of Burnside, however, is such that I will mention it more in detail in a future chapter.

Captain Tom Ryman's *Shipper's Own* took the Queen & Crescent bridge span up to Burnside and the *Dora Cabler*, belonging to Captain J. W. Lovell, met the first train.

Major E. C. Lewis, identified with the business and social life of Nashville for a number of years, was one of the contractors in the construction of the Queen & Crescent around Burnside. This able gentleman later served as Director General of the Tennessee Centennial Exposition and as President of the N. C. & St. L. He was for a long time identified with the Cumberland and operated the Sycamore Powder Mills near Ashland City, and was frequently seen aboard the steamer *Sycamore*, which hauled the powder up to Nashville.

The mills at Sycamore, even before Lewis' ownership, were doing a large business. Directly after World War I new capital had been obtained and the Confederate Powder Mills at Augusta was purchased and brought to Sycamore. Under Lewis the mills prospered as never before.

Will J. Cummins (1895)

Henry Harley (1898)

With this period passing into history, we find another decrease in the number of packets on the Cumberland. In the previous period there had been twenty-six packets. Only twenty-three new ones had plied the river. The worst feature of all from a sentimental standpoint, was that every year some of the "old guard" were missing—some of the "old timers" who greeted you with a smile and a hearty handshake. Boats could be replaced, but not these veterans of the river. Yet, despite the feeling of melancholy which naturally follows the loss of a trusted friend, it must be admitted that what the river needed most was youth, new blood and new methods, someone to take hold and carry on; leadership, if you choose to call it that. After a fashion this was coming about, but it was a slow process.

A few steam towboats were entering the Cumberland and were getting a fair amount of trade, but they had not yet perfected a system of handling commercial common carrier freight. Barges were still relatively crude affairs. Only heavy freight which could withstand the weather was being shipped in volume by this method.

It was a self-evident fact that before the steamboats could compete with the railroads in the future, some new method of hauling freight, big volumes of slow-moving freight, must be found. Old methods must be discarded. Above all else the shippers demanded and were entitled to better terminal facilities.

The boats must haul more freight at one time than they had been doing. It could be done. Had the old timer's eyesight been dimmed? Perhaps it had, for right under his nose was a way out if he but knew it—barges, barges and more barges, covered barges, decked barges, cargo barges, square bow barges, model bow barges—but barges, and more of them. Lash two together, three or even four and one steamboat could push them all without great trouble and with very little increase in cost.

The past must be forgotten. A hurricane had struck. The only way out was to start rebuilding. It would take time and a new generation, but it would be done.

CHAPTER NINE

Packets Leave the Cumberland

Period 1900–1930

This chapter will cover thirty instead of the usual ten years in the long and colorful career of the historic Cumberland. This is necessary because many vital events overlapped one another and it is almost impossible to evaluate their significance without extending the time element sufficiently to reflect them in full glory. The period covered is filled to the brim with important events, and from a sentimental standpoint, it has no equal, because at long last the "majestic" and "elegant" packets, after 100 years of service, were to leave the river, never to return.

In order to clarify many issues and to avoid any possibility of confusing the events on the lower river with those on the upper river, the discussion will be divided accordingly.

First, then, let us turn our attention to events on the lower Cumberland, the stretch between Nashville and Paducah, a distance of some 200 miles. Paducah, home of the irrepressible humorist, Irvin S. Cobb, while not located on the Cumberland, being twelve miles below its mouth and on the Ohio, after the turn of the century, was always considered the terminus of the lower river packet trade. It was this former great trade area, Nashville to Paducah, that received the first big shock from railroad competition.

Despite everything that Ryman and Tyner tried, it was now apparent to them that the packets on the lower river would continue to lose money. It was not solely the loss of mid-west grain that brought this about. Actually the packets now were making the trip down river without enough freight to pay the salaries of the licensed officers. Many Nashville manufacturers whom Ryman had induced to remain with him were no longer able to give their freight to the boats. Their customers were now demanding that they ship by the more convenient and faster railroads.

Under such trying conditions Ryman was again confronted with a grave situation. It was rendered all the more difficult because it now not only involved Ryman's friendly relationship with the railroads, but also any number of grain dealers, who had stuck by him and knew what it meant to lose steamboat competition. One thing was certain. Ryman could not operate his packets on the lower river as matters now stood. Furthermore, he had no expectation of any improvement in the future.

The futility of Ryman's situation gave rise to gossip among steamboat men that Ryman might have made a serious mistake, years before, when he decided to stick to the packet business instead of converting his packets into towboats and operating them under charter or by private contract. The soundness of this type of river transportation was no longer debatable. In fact, right under Ryman's nose several more large towboats from the "big rivers" had entered the Nashville trade and seemed quite successful.

Nevertheless Ryman remained adamant and he refused to dismantle his packets. However, in 1900, he began to limit his packet business to two trips a week between Nashville and Paducah, using the *J. B. Richardson* and the *H. W. Buttorff*. During slack periods these packets would also make trips in the Nashville-Burnside trade. In an effort to ward off competition from larger towboats and to further maintain competition with the railroads on mid-west grain shipments, he also put into operation the *Bart E. Linehan*, a rather large towboat. This boat became a familiar sight on the Wabash, Ohio and the Mississippi and once more proved the ingenuity of Ryman as an operator. The *Linehan* proved to be "an ace in the hole" and for several years brought thousands of tons of grain to Nashville from the grain belt.

It should be quickly added, however, that Ryman never did reduce the river rate on grain up to Nashville. While it is true the limited packet operations and the roving *Linehan* offered some competition to the railroads, as did the other towboats under private contract, such competition was a mere token of what it was when the railroads had first granted "the privileges" on grain shipments to Nashville in 1871–2.

This new and limited method adopted by Ryman for the operation of his boats on the lower Cumberland once more subjected him to renewed and severe criticism among competitors on the upper river. They harped on his failure to do the one thing—namely, reduce the river rate on grain shipments—which they contended would have spelled out real competition with the railroads.

"Coal was added to the fire" about this same time when Ryman built a river-rail terminal on the east bank of the river, just north of the present Woodland Street Bridge, which was served by the L. & N. The Rhea elevator and terminal which was the only one in Nashville, had burned around 1900 and Ryman had received a "green light" to build a terminal of his own. The new Ryman terminal burned on March 30, 1905, as did the *Bart E. Linehan* which was tied up alongside the railroad tracks down to the river. This terminal was of great value to Ryman and particularly in his fight to gain control on the upper river. His competitors again took the position that all of this indicated complete cooperation and a tie-up between Ryman and the railroads.

Captain Tyner, who of course was in a position to know, scoffed at what he called this "scandalous" criticism. When queried years later, he insisted that when the Rhea terminal burned the Rheas had no particular need for it as they were bringing all of their grain into Nashville from Johnsonville and Hickman via the N. C. & St. L. RR. They did not wish to spend the money to rebuild and offered no objection to

Ryman building a new terminal. They were granted the privilege of using it just as Ryman had been extended the privilege of using the Rhea terminal. Tyner also related that Ryman, before he made the decision not to reduce the river rate on grain shipments, again made a thorough survey of his friends and shippers in an effort to determine if such a reduction would result in more grain shipments to his boats. This survey, like the one he had previously conducted, convinced him that such a move might lead to a rate warfare which would be disastrous and that the grain dealers were now so deeply entrenched with the railroads that it would be impossible to throw their grain shipments back to the packets even at a reduced rate. Drayage, loading charges, convenience of delivery were now pertinent factors, not merely rates.

Others connected with the situation have indicated that Ryman and the Rheas had a misunderstanding over the building of the terminal, but there is no substantial evidence of any open breach. The Rheas had an excellent grain warehouse and elevator in South Nashville where they unloaded their grain shipped in from Johnsonville and Hickman. This would bear out the contention that they did not need the river terminal for their own use and benefit and could be assigned as one reason for not offering any objection to Ryman building a river terminal.

Tom Ryman died at Nashville on December 23, 1904 at the age of sixty-three. He had been confined to his home for several months and had become somewhat incapacitated for two or three years due to injuries received in a collision with a heavy wagon while driving his carriage over the unfinished viaduct near the present Union Station.

There have been many other colorful steamboat men on the Cumberland, but it is doubtful if any surpassed Tom Ryman. He was known in all the business and social circles of Nashville, and was peculiarly beloved by the poor and underprivileged whom he always helped. In the waning years of his life, assisting and encouraging the needy became an obsession. Above everything, Tom Ryman believed the Christian religion compelled action. People who thought his frankness on religious matters was insincere did not know the man and his simple faith. He had a way of making rough men, cursing men and drinking men quiet down. He was a crusader for anything he believed to be right. He called a spade a spade and a crook a crook. He was fearless, sober, honest and, as one of his close friends said, "gave more to life than he took away from it."

Some estimate of the esteem in which Captain Ryman was held by the people of Nashville may be obtained from an editorial appearing in the Nashville Daily News of December 24, 1904, which read in part:

"Rich and poor, sinners and saints, the ignorant and the learned, all knew Captain Tom Ryman, for an honest man and earnest Christian, and all gave him their unmixed confidence and respect."

The evangelist, Sam Jones, who had converted Ryman in 1881, came back to Nashville to officiate at his funeral, which was conducted at the Union Gospel Tabernacle and attended by more than 4,000 citizens. The name of the Tabernacle was soon changed to that of Ryman Auditorium and still remains as a tribute to his memory.

When Captain Ryman died, there was only one other member of his family at the time directly connected with the river, Captain Thomas G. Ryman, Jr., his son, who had been master of several steamboats owned by his father. Paul Ryman, another son, was a gifted musician and later invested some money in a navigation company in which his brother, Tom, was the moving spirit. Tom Ryman, Jr., better known as "Little Tom," had owned an interest in several boats built by his father and was a master of recognized ability. When his father died, he was a young man thirty-two years old, generous by nature, friendly and notorious among river men for overloading his boats. He had his faults but he also had many friends. He was fatally shot on June 1, 1915, by Captain Wilson Montgomery, at Hartsville Landing on board the *Jo Horton Fall*. His death ended a

An excellent view of the Nashville Wharf—1903. Two large Mississippi packets—The side-wheeler *Lotus W. Sims* (second from the left) and the *Belle of Calhoun* (first on the right) are among the boats. Note the cargo of grain and lumber.

colorful career and severed the name of Ryman from the river. Montgomery was acquitted after an extended legal battle which excited great public interest.

The newspapers erroneously stated that Captain Tom Ryman had sold out all of his steamboat interests prior to his death. This is an error. The records of the Deputy Collector of Customs at Nashville show that at the time Ryman died he was the principal owner of the *Bart E. Linehan, J. B. Richardson, R. Dunbar, H. W. Buttorff,* and the *Bob Dudley.* Shortly before his death he had disposed of the *Chancey Lamb* and the *James N. White,* the former having been sold to the John B. Ransom Company and the latter dismantled.

While, as stated, Captain Ryman had not disposed of any of the five boats just mentioned, certain facts justify the conclusion that he had agreed to a deal with a new company to be known as "The Ryman Line, Incorporated," commonly referred to as "The New Ryman Line." On December 10, 1904 a charter of incorporation was granted to such a company, the incorporators being Matthew Gracey, B. F. Lester, Captain James S. Tyner, George Doubleday, T. M. Steger and H. W. Buttorff. The capital stock was $100,000.00. This was in effect a consolidation of many interests connected with the steamboat business. Matthew Gracey, a long-time friend of Ryman's, operated the Gracey Warehouse at Clarksville; Lester was in the livestock business in Nashville; Captain Tyner needs no further introduction; Doubleday was a farmer and merchant at Neptune on the lower river; Steger was well known in river circles and Buttorff was one of the founders of the Phillips & Buttorff Company, for years a large shipper of freight on both ends of the Cumberland River.

Mrs. Ryman, executrix of her husband's estate, not long after his death transferred her interest in all five of the boats, and the good will of the old Ryman Line to the new Ryman Lines, Incorporated, for $100,000.00 cash, the purchase price being the exact amount of the capital stock of the Corporation. Captain J. S. Tyner, in return for his interest in the five boats, took capital stock in the company, and other parties (Captain Tom Gallagher and Captain Thomas G. Ryman, Jr., who had a small interest in the boats) were paid off in cash.

Captain Tyner took an active interest in the new company for a short time and continued to operate the *H. W. Buttorff* as master. Captain Gallagher, while not having any financial interest in the company, was attached to it in some administrative capacity. Captain Thomas G. Ryman, Jr. did not go along with the company in any capacity, but became associated with W. W. Parmenter and organized a new company, known as the Cumberland River Steamboat Company, which later built the steamboat *Robert Rhea,* on which he served as master. He also served for a short time as master of the *Electra* which this company purchased from the Ryman Lines, Incorporated. The *Robert Rhea,* incidentally was always known as "Little Tom" Ryman's boat. In 1910 it was sold to the Ryman Lines, Incorporated and the *Electra* was sold to Mobile interests. Shortly thereafter, the affairs of the Cumberland River Steamboat Company were liquidated. Thomas G. Ryman, Jr., then became associated with his brother, Paul Ryman, in the Nashville Packet Company, which owned and operated the *Jo Horton Fall,* built in 1913. This boat was sold in 1919 to the Nashville Navigation Company, with Captain J. S. Tyner as master. It was the last Nashville packet and went off the Cumberland around 1928.

After the purchase of the above five boats, the Ryman Lines, Incorporated, almost immediately bought the *Electra, Red River,* and the *W. T. Scovell.* These were large cotton boats formerly operating on the Red River emptying into the Mississippi. They needed extensive repairs. The *Electra* was repaired and operated in Nashville for a number of years. The other two never saw any service in Nashville, but were sold to interests on the Mississippi. The *W. T. Scovell* later blew up. Captain Tyner, as a stockholder in the company, strongly opposed the purchase of the three last named boats and differences arose between him and other officers of the company. He sold his stock as a result, and took a severe loss.

At a later date, the Ryman Lines, Incorporated purchased the *Chancey Lamb,* and finally the *Henry Harley.* By the end of 1916, the Ryman Lines, Incorporated had almost ended its career. The *Bart E. Linehan* had burned at Nashville in 1905, as heretofore mentioned, and the *J. B. Richardson* had been sold and later burned at Paducah on November 18, 1913. The *Bob Dudley* had gone to a watery grave on December 20, 1916 at Nashville. The *H. W. Buttorff* had been sold to the Lee Lines at Memphis and had been renamed the *Princess.* On December 10, 1913 the *R. Dunbar* was sold to Ralph E. Gaches, Point Pleasant, West Virginia, where she became the *General Crowder.* The *Henry Harley* was blown on the wharf at Nashville on January 17, 1917, and later sank. The *Robert Rhea* and *Electra* had both been sold and moved to other ports. There was nothing left of the Ryman Lines, Incorporated, and it went out of business. So did the old time packet business on the Lower Cumberland.

Since Captain Tyner was also an integral part of the original Ryman Line, it is appropriate to give some additional facts on his splendid career. Captain James S. Tyner lived to be a very old man, having died on July 4, 1935, at the age of eighty-seven years. He was recognized as one of Nashville's outstanding citizens. After he sold his interest in the Ryman Lines, Incorporated, he bought a boat at Pittsburgh named the *Rose Hight* (*Rose Hite*) and brought her into Nashville where he changed her name to the *Gracey Childers* in honor of the veteran wharf master at Clarksville. This boat needed considerable repairing, and when it came up for inspection a year after her arrival in Nashville, the Steamboat Inspectors turned her down. The *Gracey Childers* later burned and then Captain Tyner became interested in and chartered the *Princess,* formerly the *H. W. Buttorff,* from the Lee Line in Memphis. He had served as master of this boat for many years. He did considerable business with the *Princess,* but after a few years because of poor business returned her to the Lee Line in Memphis.

Some time after this, and prior to 1917, Captain Tyner, with W. W. Parmenter, operated the *Nashville,* but this venture did not pan out so well, and thereafter he left the river except for short intervals.

Ryman's death did not immediately alter the situation on the lower Cumberland, but it was not long before the railroads and the grain dealers were confronted with a new danger. The new Ryman Line owners, (contrary to Captain Ryman's idea), had planned to overpower any "foreign" towboat competition on the lower river by the purchase of the *Electra, W. T. Scovell* and *Red River* previously mentioned. The idea was to operate these as towboats to haul mid-west grain and their other boats as packets on both the lower and upper river. This plan, as foreseen by Ryman, turned out to be a very costly venture and it was soon abandoned at a substantial loss. It was at this point that the railroads and the grain dealers both became greatly alarmed for fear they could no longer justify "the privileges," if they were attacked, there being no substantial steamboat competition.

There had been some additional grumblings from Atlanta, Macon, Augusta, Savannah, Valdosta and other southeastern cities shortly before Ryman's death. Now there was developing more and more concerted and definitely organized complaint and dissatisfaction over the alleged discriminatory privileges granted Nashville grain dealers. To meet this alarming situation the grain dealers organized the Nashville Grain Exchange in 1904 and my father, the late Byrd Douglas, who was a grain dealer, became its first president. He died in 1911 while still in office, but before the battle between the railroads and the southeastern cities over the validity of "the privileges" was decided. The Exchange was organized primarily for the purpose of preserving "the privileges" and to curb bad practices among the dealers in Nashville. It took note of all grain shipments, adopted a code of ethics and punished "bucket shop" operations. It was, all things considered, a very powerful organization, well knit together and well financed. In 1910 the membership had grown to 54 grain dealers representing a business with a gross annual intake of nearly $6,000,000.00. Some of the

other founders of the Grain Exchange were I. T. Rhea,
W. R. Cornelius, Duncan McKay, Hugh McGavock, R. G.
Work, Charles Jones, S. S. Kerr, G. P. Rose, E. M. Kelly,
J. W. Wilkes, Harry H. Hughes, John A. Tyner, J. H. Bell
and F. E. Gillette.

When it became evident that the new Ryman Line, operating two packets part time, was unable to continue as a
substantial competitor to the railroads in bringing mid-west
grain shipments up to Nashville, and that the Cumberland
River Steamboat Co. could only put one boat, the *Robert
Rhea,* into the field, some grain dealers in Nashville, on their
own initiative, chartered converted Ohio and Mississippi
boats to bring mid-west grain into Nashville on a cheaper
rate than the railroads. This was certainly an odd twist, for
it really meant these grain dealers were affording competition against the railroads who in turn had granted them
"the privileges." But, for self-evident reasons, the railroads
did not complain. Considerable grain reached Nashville in
this way from 1904 through 1910 and even later.

As time went by and the Interstate Commerce Commission began to take action against so-called rate abuses, it
became a matter of time before the railroads would be required to show cause why their rates on mid-west grain into
Nashville were not discriminatory. A petition was finally
filed in 1910. From then until 1913, when the Supreme
Court handed down its opinion, which from a legalistic
standpoint had the effect of extending "the privileges" to
the southeastern cities, but the practical effect of thereby
abolishing them as to Nashville alone, the railroads and
grain dealers were in a state of confusion. First the Interstate Commerce Commission ruled with the protesting cities. Then the Commerce Court on appeal ruled with the
railroads and then the Supreme Court reversed this ruling
and ruled with the Commission. It was a real legal battle.
The Grain Exchange intervened and employed Luke Lea,
K. T. McConnico and my brother, Lee Douglas, then a young
lawyer, to present its case.

A reading of the transcript of the evidence in the case is

most revealing. Much of it was documentary and contained an abundance of exhibits. Major E. B. Stahlman was a star witness for the L. & N. and Captain Tom Gallagher, known from one end of the river to the other, testified at great length concerning steamboat competition. Others who testified were Charles Barham, General Freight Agent for the N. C. & St. L.; J. H. Bell, J. W. Wilkes, E. M. Kelly and S. S. Kerr for the grain dealers.

The decision was a close one and a hard one to make in view of the recognized fact that an adverse decision to the railroads might annihilate a gigantic grain business which in good faith had accepted and continued to act solely as a recipient and not as an originator of some alleged discrimination. In other words, the grain dealers were innocent parties and yet they were the ones who would suffer the most. Such a situation was a hard nut for any court to crack without hurting the delicate kernel.

It appears to be a common misconception that the grain business left Nashville overnight as a result of the Court's decision. It would be better to say that the grain business based on the exclusive use of "the privileges" left Nashville. This was a severe blow, but Nashville still retains a very large and prosperous grain business. The practical effect of the Court's decision was to dislodge Nashville from its position on the top of the ladder as a foremost grain concentration and distribution point and leave it to compete on an equal basis with its sister cities to the southeast. This it has continued to do and it still remains a fine grain and milling center.

It remains very doubtful if Ryman could have altered this situation even if he had lived. The men who ran the new Ryman Line and the Cumberland River Steamboat Company were all good operators and had been connected with the river and boats for many years. It is purely second-guessing to say that Ryman would have succeeded where these men failed. It is much fairer to say that Ryman was vindicated by what took place.

Before concluding the story about grain, I think it should

be noted that one of the chief contentions raised by the railroads and the grain dealers in the fight before the Supreme Court, was, that if the "privileges" were held to be discriminatory it would immediately result in the bulk of the midwest grain shipments returning to the steamboats. The theory behind this argument was that the steamboats could reduce the rates far below the rates then prevailing and still make money. The effect would be to put the railroads out of the grain business, give it back to the steamboats, which in itself would be discriminatory.

They further insisted southeastern cities would not benefit by this move and in fact it might cause the mid-west grain to be concentrated at such cities as Chicago, Minneapolis, Louisville, Cairo, Indianapolis and Cincinnati, all of which were much closer to the center of the grain belt.

The decision of the Supreme Court had no such effect. There was no great revival of the steamboat business on mid-west grain. At the time the decision was rendered, the new Ryman Line and the Cumberland River Steamboat Co. remained as the only lines operating on the lower river. The Cumberland and Tennessee Transportation Co., the Burnside and Burkesville Transportation Co. and the Carthage Packet Co., to be referred to later, were all upper Cumberland operators, and did not get into the mid-west grain trade in any substantial way. There was one exception. The *Albany*, a B. & B. T. Co. boat, often roamed the lower river and brought grain to Nashville. Towboats from other rivers under charter tried to make a go of it, but despite cheaper rates returned to their home ports after a season like so many others in years past.

There was a considerable shift in the concentration of mid-west grain. Nashville minus the peculiar benefits of "the privileges" no longer was one of the chief concentration and distribution centers for mid-west grain.

It had taken one hundred years to wipe out the steamboat packet business on the lower Cumberland River. First, cotton had left, then iron, then tobacco and finally grain. In 1920 steamboats on the lower river were getting to be as

Lotus Sims. One of the largest side-wheelers ever at Nashville. Behind her is the *India Givens,* originally named *P. D. Staggs,* a Cumberland River packet. Photo at St. Louis.

The *Nashville*

scarce as the proverbial hen's teeth. But a new era was being born. To replace the "majestic two stackers" with their jet black curly smoke, a new type of boat had arrived—the gasoline towboat, long and sleek, with a pair of tow knees draped over her square bow and an exhaust like a fire cracker. She was neither beautiful nor dignified, but in her there was latent power never dreamed of. Steamboat men hardly knew whether to laugh or cry at this new baby. Yet, there she was, the forerunner of the modern diesel towboat, which would revolutionize river-borne traffic. In another quarter of a century one of these youngsters would be towing 3,000 tons of freight by barges up the middle of the Mississippi at four miles per hour,—something seven or eight typical packets, "flattened out," could not do with a "full head of steam."

By another one of those strange quirks of fate, when the packets left the lower river, the planned development of the Cumberland as a transportation artery was nearing its climax. The long anticipated erection of locks and dams on the river, which had been urged in 1889, was at last nearing completion. On the river below Nashville, Locks A, B, C, D and Lock I had been placed in operation. Locks E and F were completed in 1922 and 1923, respectively, and these extended pool water at a projected minimum depth of six feet to the mouth of the river. On the upper river, Locks 2, 3, 4, 5, 6, and 7 had all been completed by 1911. These had given pool water at a projected minimum depth of six feet to a distance of nine miles beyond Carthage. Lock 8 was completed in 1924, which extended pool water to Granville, a distance of 141 miles above Nashville. Lock 21, placed in operation in 1911, had afforded similar pool water to a point twenty-nine miles below Burnside, and was of great assistance to the trade area covered by the Burnside packets.

The most regrettable feature in the lock and dam system, looking at the situation as it appeared during this period, was the failure of the government to complete the proposed locks covering the exceedingly treacherous water between

Granville and the shoals at Thomas' Branch just below Lock 21. This failure left the Cumberland minus a reasonably good channel for a long stretch and where it was needed desperately.

Some students of the Cumberland place the blame entirely on Congress for the failure of the locks to be erected at an earlier date and when, no doubt, they would have been of greater help to the packets. Congress was at fault and is subject to criticism, but it is unfair to place all the blame on the doorstep of the legislators. For some reason, which is most difficult to explain, the people of Nashville during this period and even in more recent times have never been properly aroused on matters affecting the Cumberland. The same condition prevails at other towns and cities along its course. Colonel M. T. Bryan, President of the Cumberland River Improvement Association, which strongly urged the locks in 1889, on more than one occasion needed popular support and could not obtain it. John Wesley Gaines and Benton McMillin, members of Congress, who worked incessantly for the locks and dams, complained of public indifference to the river and frequently carried the whole burden of presenting the case for the river before congressional committees entrusted with river appropriations.

There were many landowners in the Cumberland basin who were vitally opposed to the proposed locks. They did not like the idea of trading water for rich bottom land, some of which was inundated for the construction of the dams. A few recalcitrant steamboat men even declared there was no need for locks. The railroads also fought the construction of any more improvements. They insisted traffic on the river did not justify the expenditures, that what traffic existed was no longer diversified but purely local and for the benefit of a small group. It was contended that river improvements in general were a new style subterfuge for a subsidy, encouraging and aiding private enterprise using the river to compete against the railroads, which, in turn, were taxed to defray such expenditures for the benefit of its competitors.

The astonishing feature is that the locks and dams and other later improvements were ever completed in the face of such opposition and the "red tape" which was thrown around the appropriations. The USED which supervised the construction, did all it could to speed the work once it had been authorized and appropriations granted. The locks and dams, conceived primarily to increase steamboat traffic on the river, however, were not finally completed and could not afford maximum service until that type of traffic was definitely on the wane.

It is extremely gratifying, however, to all lovers of the river to know that the delays incident to the completion of the locks and dams did not prove altogether fatal. While it is getting ahead of the story, it should be said that with the advent of gas and diesel towboats and steel barges, all the locks on the Cumberland, small as they were, became of incalculable value and earned every dollar spent on them. They were particularly valuable in the intervening period between steam and modern diesel towboats.

The total cost of the fifteen locks and dams on the Cumberland above referred to was $8,151,472.26. Since the establishment of the office of District Engineer in Nashville in 1873, the total of all governmental expenditures through 1944, including the locks and dams and channel clearance, did not exceed $12,000,000.00. In 1944 there began a new era of multiple purpose dams on the river which will be treated later. Prior to 1873, State and Federal aid combined was less than $500,000.00. It can be truthfully said, therefore, that from 1819 through 1944 no other comparable blessing has cost the people less than the Cumberland River.

While the old locks and dams were being constructed, a very large towboat business on the lower river sprang up. In fact, the stretch below Nashville received a momentary shot in the arm due to such activities. Vast quantities of rough and finished materials were needed and it was necessary to haul it to the lock sites by barges and towboats. Most, if not all, of the locks were faraway from the railroads and the rock, sand, gravel and heavy timbers were

l. to r. *Electra* (1897), *H. W. Buttorff* (1896), *Henry Harley* (1898) and *R. Dunbar* (1895). Nashville Wharf around 1907.

The Nashville Wharf—August 1919. An oil barge has been launched. The *Rowena* of Burnside, Kentucky, one of the last upper river packets, looks on.

obtained from the river and along its banks. This materially reduced the cost of the projects, a fact frequently overlooked. Many towboats were also employed in the actual construction work. Large cargoes of cement as well as iron and steel were towed to the various projects. This construction coming as it did when the river, especially the lower end, was hard pressed for any traffic, had a most beneficent effect on the depressing situation. It was nothing more, however, than a slight breather and had no effect on the picture as a whole.

Private concerns began to realize the advantage of owning their own towboats and barges or chartering them for exclusive use. Sycamore Mills was one of the larger concerns to first adopt such a course. Several large timber and cross-tie companies followed suit and began operations on the river. The cross-tie business was extremely lucrative in the late twenties. Every year there were one or two towboats chartered by private concerns to handle their business. Each year, however, there was a decline in typical commercial common carrier freight.

The scope of service rendered by the lower Cumberland after packets left this part of the river was severely limited. During the remainder of this period, and for a long time thereafter, tonnage on the lower river compared favorably with past years, but the bulk of it was sand, gravel, rock, cross-ties, staves and heavy timber, all for the most part being transported by private concerns or under contract. Moreover, all of these commodities were "children" of the river and were not subject to competition from a transportation standpoint. Such a limited traffic, therefore, was soon dubbed "localized" and critics of the river fought every government expenditure looking to the further improvement of the river.

World War I intervened during this period, but unlike World War II did not help the distressing situation. It did partially divert public attention from the deplorable condition into which the lower river had lapsed.

The sand and gravel business on the Cumberland started

in a big way as early as 1900. Both the quantity and quality of these building materials could hardly be improved upon. They were readily accessible, on both the lower and upper river. This not only saved transportation charges in the early development of the business, but also brought about reasonable consumer prices. There has been a steady increase in volume and a very large distribution with Nashville as the principal concentration point.

From 1905 until the present time some of the leaders in this business have been the Cumberland Valley Sand Company owned and operated by Daniel Lindsey until 1912 when it left the river; W. T. Hardison & Company, one of the oldest concerns on the river and operators of a fleet of towboats, dredges and barges under the management of Humphrey Hardison and his son, Tom; H. E. Richardson, T. L. Herbert, C. M. Hughes and Charles Kempkau, all of whom have been identified with the river for many years. Richardson owned and operated a fleet of towboats and barges and his yards were across from the wharf at Nashville. T. L. Herbert & Company have engaged in the business, both on the Cumberland and Tennessee. This company and its successors have operated a very large fleet of diesel boats and barges and have an extensive trade area. It has also engaged in some private towing. John Herbert, now the head of this company, is one of the ablest river men in this area.

When Richardson decided to leave the river in 1929, his location was taken over by the Cumberland River Sand and Gravel Company ably headed by R. N. Coolidge, another outstanding executive who has an abiding interest in all river activities. This concern now maintains a fleet of modern diesel towboats, dredges and barges, which are familiar sights on the river. It has been very successful and from time to time has engaged in private towing, hauling large cargoes of river-borne freight by barges up the Cumberland from points on the Ohio, Mississippi and its tributaries. It has an arrangement with the leading barge lines on the Western rivers. Coolidge, the Herberts and the Hardisons have done much toward the revival of river transportation, which is an engaging subject belonging to the next period.

The nature and extent of the sand and gravel business on the Cumberland is not generally known outside the trade. For many years it has been one of the largest industries in Nashville. Almost every building, road, bridge or public improvement in Middle Tennessee and contiguous territory has been benefited by the proximity of the Cumberland River and its perpetual sand and gravel beds.

Thus, again the river has rendered a very great service which has been both beneficial to business and the public generally. Those who are wont to minimize the importance of sand and gravel as an item of freight on the assumption that it is purely "localized" and not strictly commercial cargo, should bear in mind that the business is far from being local in the benefits it bestows.

Having covered the affairs of the Cumberland below Nashville with some particularity during this period, let us now direct our attention to those on the upper river, which by 1900 started out with such optimism.

Shortly before Captain Ryman's death he had good reason to believe he would win his fight for control of the upper Cumberland packet trade. It had been a long drawn-out affair and one which had cost him much worry and money. The fight was still not over by any means but it was showing signs of tapering off in favor of Ryman.

A Ryman victory would not shape up, however, as he anticipated. While he was able to regulate traffic and rates, he was still confronted with competition. Even though greatly diminished, if he made the wrong move, it might break out in greater force, especially from the Burnside angle. Also, Colonel Jere Baxter had finally completed the construction of the Tennessee Central Railroad, the first railroad to enter the upper Cumberland territory and connect with Nashville. This was an event which Baxter boasted would change the entire picture. Ryman, who was a shrewd judge of men and events, also knew that the patience of many shippers throughout the upper Cumberland had

Patrol (1905). At Burnside, Ky.

Water Queen Showboat towed by *Grace Devers*. Familiar sight on the
Cumberland during the waning days of the packets.

been exhausted by the long warfare between the steam-boat men and they were itching to get away from the packets and enjoy the benefits of more modern transportation.

Strangely enough the packets were not forced to retire from the upper Cumberland because of any factors in existence during Ryman's lifetime, but by motor trucks and good roads, of which he never dreamed. As previously mentioned, the last of the old time Nashville packets did not leave the upper Cumberland until 1926 or '27. But, for seven or eight years previously there were very few steamboats moving about on the river, thanks to the newly found competition by motor trucks. When one did appear, it was referred to as a "museum piece." Facts also fix 1920 as the fatal year when the packets left the upper Cumberland. The total reported tonnage on the upper river for that year, to be absolutely accurate, was only 137,517 tons, of which less than 30,000 tons was typical packet freight and the rest sand, gravel, rock, cross-ties, staves and handles, transported by privately owned towboats and barges.

By way of comparison, the total reported tonnage above Nashville in 1900 was 289,218 tons, valued at $8,395,-055.00; in 1901, nearly 275,000 tons; in 1902, 200,000 tons; in 1903, 325,000 tons, valued at an even $10,000,-000.00; and in 1904, the year Ryman died, 250,000 tons. From 1904 to 1910 the average annual reported tonnage remained very near the 250,000 ton mark and it is of great significance that practically all of it was of the commercial common carrier packet type freight. Sand, gravel, rock and cross-ties and the gas towboats and barges had not entered the traffic on the upper river. The packets, in other words, until 1910, had a job to do.

But, from 1910 to 1915 there was a gradual reduction in commercial freight. By 1920, improved highways and motor trucks were beginning to eat the very heart out of the packet business. Fate was playing a peculiar part in the scheme of things. The end of the upper river packet business came with cruel suddenness, whereas that on the lower river was a slow cancerous death. Even the Burnside packets operating in the most remote section of the river felt the impact of this motor vehicle competition. Shortly the little traffic that still existed on the upper Cumberland would be of the towboat and barge variety, quite similar to the pattern already in vogue below Nashville.

The Tennessee Central Railroad entered Nashville on May 27, 1902, but, curiously enough, had very little if anything to do with the departure of the packet business. Any fears of the steamboat owners over this enterprise were soon dispelled. They had originated chiefly on account of their inability to put their fingers on the real intentions of its chief sponsor, Colonel Jere Baxter. This persuasive and imaginative Nashvillian had so often indulged in prophecy concerning the aims of the "infant" railroad and the goals it would attain, that his own backers scarcely knew where it would wind up.

On some occasions Baxter would depict his railroad as an octopus stretching all over the Cumberland plateau and down through its hollows to the rich bottom lands of the river. On others, he would describe his "child" as a great trunk line extending from St. Louis to the west, to Knoxville in the east, there to connect with other lines leading to the north and south and the Atlantic Seaboard. Baxter, of course, never failed to mention that the L. & N., through its control of the N. C. & St. L., had "bottled up" Nashville, and the Tennessee Central would unlock the doors behind which was concealed a new era of prosperity.

According to Baxter, Nashville merchants would have a reduced freight rate based on real competition. His road would yield an abundance of coal, iron, grain, livestock, lumber and tobacco from hitherto untouched sections above and below Nashville. On the west, at Hopkinsville, there would be a connection with the Illinois Central, and at Harriman on the east, with the C. N. O. & T. P. (Southern) Railroad.

Colonel Baxter obtained control of the first link in his railroad from the Crawford interests, of which Colonel

Alexander L. Crawford of New Castle, Pennsylvania was the founder. Crawford had completed a line from Monterey to Lebanon, which was named the Nashville and Knoxville Railroad. It was planned and constructed primarily to transport coal from the extensive mines in Overton, Fentress, Cumberland, DeKalb and White Counties, Tennessee to such cities as Knoxville and Nashville, where there was a ready market. From such points the coal could also be transhipped to various other industrial centers. At Lebanon it connected with a branch of the Nashville, Chattanooga and St. Louis. The roadway, however, ran a winding, tortuous course and had many steep grades. Between Nashville and Knoxville there were very few large towns. All of these obstacles were waved aside by Baxter who refused to permit anything or anybody to dampen his enthusiasm.

Colonel Baxter, in building the Tennessee Central, proved he was an expert promoter. He at last obtained sufficient funds, a large part being derived from counties and towns along the proposed line, to extend the N. and K. R. R. to Rockwood, then to Harriman, and from Lebanon to Nashville, and finally to Clarksville and Hopkinsville. This made in all a total distance of 251 miles of main track. There were branches from Monterey to Wilder, a distance of twenty-one miles, and from Carthage Junction, a few miles, on the other side of the Cumberland across from the historic town of Carthage. During World War I another extension was made to Old Hickory, site of the duPont Powder Mills, a short distance from the main line between Lebanon and Nashville. This latter extension proved very profitable.

This story is not concerned with the Tennessee Central any further than to point out the effect it had upon traffic on the Cumberland. Discussion, therefore, of its problems will be limited to that extent. Baxter and his chief backers greatly misjudged the amount of freight the road would receive, both from Nashville and through the Illinois Central and C. N. O. & T. Railroads. Adequate terminal facilities at Nashville could not be obtained. This was a terrific blow.

Robert Rhea (1908). Nashville Wharf

Gracey Childers (1909)

Coal did not flow over the lines as expected. Operational costs were high because of steep grades and poor ballast, especially in the section around Cookeville.

Baxter was caught in a vise. Unlike the powerful L. & N. which was deeply entrenched, after more than fifty years of operation, and, therefore, had a back log of both money and friends, the Tennessee Central from the beginning was at the mercy of the Illinois Central and the C. N. O. & T. P. These roads were called upon to preserve their own competitive status with other roads, including the L. & N. and many of its friends. On this account it was not always possible to throw freight to the Tennessee Central despite the appeals of Colonel Baxter.

The Tennessee Central for a number of reasons was never a competitor against the river in the real sense of the word. It had only one branch or spur above Nashville touching the river, and that was at Carthage. The upper Cumberland steamboats obtained their largest and best paying up-river cargoes from Nashville where it was loaded for delivery to points above Carthage and all the way to Burnside. This territory (Carthage-Burnside) was still untouched by the Tennessee Central or any other railroad. It was impossible for shippers in Nashville, therefore, to forward freight by "all" rail to such points as Granville, Gainesboro, Celina, Rowena, Burkesville, Creelsboro and the many other isolated landings beyond Carthage. Likewise, shippers in Nashville would not send their freight by the Tennessee Central to Carthage and then have it transshipped from there to up-river landings because the river rate to Carthage was lower than that of the railroad. Such freight would also bear handling charges en route. Exactly the same was true on freight from points above Carthage destined to Nashville; namely, the all-river rate was lower than the combined river-rail freight rate. The Tennessee Central thus had the distinction of being hemmed in by the steamboats—a truly novel situation.

In at least one respect the Tennessee Central was a benefactor. It gave the steamboats another railroad connection in Nashville at which freight could be unloaded direct to box cars. It was nothing more than a spur track or incline running to the river's edge along the bluff below the present City Hospital. Nevertheless, it served the excellent purpose of challenging the supremacy of the L. & N.– Ryman dynasty. This connection or spur, however, came too late. The Tennessee Central due to a lack of reciprocity in terminal facilities found it difficult to deliver freight it received from the river, to Nashville merchants located on the tracks of the L. & N. and N. C. & St. L. Railroads.

In 1900 the L. & N. and N. C. & St. L. organized the Nashville Terminal Company, and thereafter erected the Union Depot, issued traffic regulations and published tariff rates on interchanged freight. Baxter found it necessary to almost circle the City in order to join his Knoxville and Hopkinsville main lines. This increased costs of operation and severely limited his terminal connections. He was prevented from building a track between the T. C. Depot at the foot of Broad Street up to and across the Public Square and thence north to connecting lines ultimately leading to Hopkinsville. This blow robbed his railroad of a short and less expensive competing trackage in the nearby North Nashville area, which contained many industries. The wholesale jobbers along the river on Front Street and on lower Broad Street continued to be good customers. But the Tennessee Central soon found that both interstate and intrastate freight, as well as steamboat freight was not being transported as expected.

Death removed Colonel Baxter from this tragic picture in 1904. His loss to the Tennessee Central was irreparable and in eight years the railroad, which he had so courageously sponsored, tasted the bitter dregs of a prolonged receivership.

There is one other matter to be noted in connection with the Tennessee Central and its relationship to traffic on the Cumberland. In 1905 C. M. Pate, President of the Cumberland and Tennessee Transportation Company, an-

Rowena (1904). At Burnside, Ky.

Celina (1913). At Burnside, Ky.

nounced that two packets, the *C. M. Pate,* named for him, and the *Dick Clyde,* an old steamboat newly repaired and decorated, would enter the Nashville and Burnside trade, working in conjunction with the Tennessee Central Railroad at both Nashville and Carthage. The railroad by this time had built tracks down to the river at the latter point. Captains J. S. Walker, W. H. Carroll, John L. Young, W. K. Savage and Robert E. Cranch were all active in this company. It was the first one to seriously compete against the new Ryman Lines, Incorporated, and to have the benefit of the T. C. tracks down to the river's edge at Nashville. The C. & T. T. boats were soon destined to meet with strong opposition from the Ryman Lines and also the other Burnside packets, which after 1910 made a determined effort on their own part to control the upper Cumberland trade area and were working in close conjunction with the C. N. O. & T. P. Railroad.

After a stiff fight lasting about four years, the C. & T. T. sold the *C. M. Pate* to New Orleans interests. The company continued in a meager way for another five years but could not make the grade. The *Dick Clyde,* according to the records, was sold in 1914 to Chess Wyman and Company and thenceforth entered the towing and tie business.

The Burnside & Burkesville Transportation Company, known throughout Cumberland River circles as the B. & B. Line had been organized near the turn of the century. It first built and owned the *City of Burkesville* and then the *Albany.* This company was backed by Captain A. B. Massey and his son, Kenneth. At an early date terminal facilities were erected, which had a double incline track to the C. N. O. & T. P. Railroad. A wharf boat was also maintained. By arrangement with the C. N. O. & T. P. through bills of lading and passenger tickets were issued to any point in the United States. The company did a good business, kept to its own "knitting," built up a strong friendship and prospered. After the *Albany,* the B. & B. Lines owned the *Creelsboro, Rowena* and *Celina,* all excellent packets, infrequently seen at the Nashville wharf.

The Burnside packets extended their field of endeavor and frequently overlapped the territory of Nashville boats between Carthage and Celina. They came less frequently, however, to Nashville. Nashville packets frequently ran up to Burkesville and sometimes to Burnside. Serious difficulties were overcome because the Burnside packets as a rule stayed in their territory and the Nashville packets did the same, although neither admitted any territorial limitations. Nashville packets and those from Burnside exchanged up-river and down-river freight as a matter of courtesy.

Burnside during this period was also blessed with a competing packet line, known as the Cumberland Transportation Company, with W. J. Davidson as president. Norman I. Taylor and his son, George P. Taylor, owners of the Cumberland Grocery Company, a very large and successful enterprise, were among the principal owners of this line and Tom Lewis managed the packets. This company started with gasoline boats, then built the *W. G. Nixon*, a steam towboat and packet. The *Patrol* and the *City of Burnside* were the next C. T. C. line boats. They vied with the B. & B. packets for a number of years. The C. T. C. line also operated terminal facilities to the C. N. O. & T. P. tracks at Burnside and a wharf boat.

In 1917, the B. & B. Lines sold out to the C. T. C. for a reported price of $40,000.00. The *Albany* had been sold to interests on the Ohio River. In its latter days this fine packet had towed cross-ties to Brookport, Illinois. The *Creelsboro* had sunk below Lock 21. The *Patrol* caught out and later sank at Harmon's Creek. The *Celina, Rowena* and *City of Burnside* ran spasmodically until 1928, but not in the packet trade. They, too, felt the sting of highways and trucks. The *City of Burnside* sank at Burnside. The *Celina* and *Rowena* were sold in 1932–3. Shortly thereafter and while being towed down the river, the *Celina* sank at Indian Creek and the *Rowena* at Greasy Creek. Finis could be written for the Burnside packets.

The Burnside packets were manned by men of extraordinary ability. B. &. B. pilots and captains included Dave

Heath and his three sons, Clate, John and Otho. The C. T. C. employed among others Captains B. L. Ham, Frank Campbell, Gordon Thurston, Frank Bedford and Bridges Montgomery. They were all friendly and courageous, knew every crook and bend in the treacherous river and frequently risked their lives in line of duty.

Taking everything into consideration, Burnside contributed more than its share towards river transportation. For a city, quite set apart and never very large, it fought and earned its title of metropolis of the upper Cumberland. Situated at the head of navigation on the river, it served a very large trade area. In the early days of the river, such towns as Waitesboro, Creelsboro and Burkesville were very prominent. These towns, for one thing, were more accessible to the big packets. Burnside came into its own as a river point during 1870–1880, when it appeared coal might be successfully barged down to Nashville and the railroad entered to shape its future destiny.

Some coal had been barged to Nashville from the mines above and below Burnside prior to the War Between the States. Most of the coal along the upper reaches of the Cumberland is found in mines 17 to 30 miles above Burnside. Some coal was mined fifty-one miles below the city around Indian Creek near Rowena.

Before the C. N. O. & T. P. entered Burnside, all coal from above had to be barged over what is known as Smith's Shoals, one of the worst spots in the Cumberland. This impediment, just above Burnside and eight miles long, consists of four separate shoals, which, coming down stream, are named in order of appearance, Shadowen, White Cliff, Long and Mill. Old timers who were successful in navigating Smith's Shoals admitted they received the thrill of a lifetime. Smith's Shoals are truly astounding and dangerous. It is remarkable that over this winding, swift, rocky, shoaly, narrow, picturesque and historical stretch of the Cumberland men had actually barged out coal. By comparison Harpeth Shoals, on the lower river, was nothing more than a ripple.

Some students of history interested in the river seem to think that the coal trade was directly connected with the steamboat business. This is not the case. Packets on the Cumberland had very little, if anything, to do with coal except to use it when available. Prior to the War of 1861–65, a large portion of the coal brought up the Cumberland came in barges from the Pittsburgh area. Steam towboats pushed these barges, then called lighters, lashed together in two tiers of two or three barges each. Some barges in early times floated down the Ohio, waited for a rise to get them over the falls at Louisville and then made their way down to Smithland where they were towed up to Nashville. This procedure saved considerable money.

Coal from the Burnside area started coming to Nashville in some volume by 1855. It was all floated down in barges. Traffic was often hindered by the sudden fall of the river after a "tide" or by no "tide" at all. Frequently bargemen sold their load before they reached Nashville. Despite diligent efforts of the United States Engineers and small appropriations from Congress, the hazards of Smith's Shoals, previously mentioned, were never overcome, and many barges were lost before they reached Burnside.

As late as 1878, one bargeman and no less than eighteen barges carrying 100,000 bushels of coal were lost at the shoals, although the government had spent more than $95,000.00 in that year to make them navigable. The barges used were small. Each carried an average of 6,000 bushels of coal. They carried a crew of three or four men who managed very well after they reached Burnside. From there on the river was by no means gentle, but certainly not a death trap. On arriving at Nashville, the barges on a fair market would "pay out" about $500.00 net from coal and the barges would be sold for what they would bring.

Altogether there were twelve mines in the Burnside area varying from one to four and a half miles from the river. The Poplar Mt. Coal Company mine was the largest in the area, having an annual capacity of 1,200,000 bushels. The average vein of coal was four feet. In 1860 35,174 bushels were brought to Nashville from the upper Cumberland and in 1870 more than 150,000 bushels. By 1880 this had increased to 250,000 bushels. Figures on the coal brought up the Cumberland from Pittsburgh and Kanawha River for similar periods are not available, but it was very much greater than that supplied by the mines in the Burnside area. After the railroads entered the coal fields this trade left the river and never returned.

At a very early date Burnside was a distribution point for wholesale groceries, hardware, farm implements, tobacco, poultry, eggs, timber and lumber. The Kentucky Lumber Company was one of the largest concerns in that part of the State. It rafted and sawed virgin timber for many years. For several miles logs lined the river waiting to be hauled up to the mills at Burnside. In later years, the Chicago Veneering Company was a big operator. The poultry and egg business at Burnside during this period reached its peak. C. N. O. & T. P. freight trains met the packets, and these commodities were delivered in less than twenty-four hours to dealers along that line, especially Cincinnati and Chattanooga.

The Carthage Packet Company, with J. W. Williams, President; W. K. Savage, Vice President, and W. E. Myer, Secretary-Treasurer, opened for business in 1908–09. It operated the *Ed Myer* a fast and snappy steamboat, built by Myers and Williams. The *Ed Myer* was a familiar sight along the river, and did a fair business, but was sold to the Ryman Lines, Incorporated, and for several years operated under W. T. Hunter, her Captain, and J. B. Cook, Clerk.

Captain Hunter, incidentally, on November 19, 1906, became the first Captain on the Cumberland to deliberately "jump" a dam with a steamboat in high water. He accomplished this escapade without mishap at Lock "A," 40 miles below Nashville on the *H. W. Buttorff*. He was also the first to "jump" a dam above Nashville. This feat took place at Lock No. 2, on February 15, 1908, with the *R. Dunbar*. As Captain Hunter often explained, these feats were not particularly dangerous and it avoided any waiting

Burnside (1916)

Jo Horton Fall (1913). One of the last Cumberland River packets.

to lock through. If a pilot knows he has sufficient clearance for his boat to go over a dam without too much "pitch" he may do so with safety. The art is in knowing the depth of the water over the dam. Much publicity, however, was given to Captain Hunter's feat.

In 1910 the packet business on the upper Cumberland narrowed down to the Burnside packets and the Ryman Lines as the principal competitors. After the Ryman Lines, Incorporated, went out of business, as previously indicated, the *Jo Horton Fall* became the only Nashville packet operating on the Cumberland. She was soon joined by the *H. G. Hill*, built in 1919, and the *M. T. Bryan*, all three boats being owned at the time by the Nashville Navigation Company, which operated them on both ends of the river.

This company was chartered on January 19, 1919 with a capital stock of $100,000.00, with Sigmund Mark, W. D. Trabue, H. G. Hill, John A. Tyner and Hunter Perry as incorporators. It was the last company organized in Nashville to operate packets, and while it had high ambitions, it soon found that regular schedules could not be maintained. It made a real effort to revive the steamboat business, but it could not be done. After a short time, its boats engaged in transporting or towing freight under private charter. The company also had some hard luck with its boats. The *H. G. Hill* sank in the mid-twenties at Wooddale Beach above Nashville, and the *M. T. Bryan* burned in 1922 near Paducah. The *Jo Horton Fall* left unceremoniously and I last saw her in Mobile around 1931.

Thanks to the advent of motor trucks and good roads throughout the Cumberland Plateau, the departure of packets on the upper river had been speeded up. The death knell for packets on both the lower and upper river had thereby sounded almost simultaneously. Somehow or other that was appropriate. Neither had anything to live for.

Thus we come to the close of another interesting period in the life of the river, but certainly the most melancholic in the long career of steamboatin' on the Cumberland.

CHAPTER TEN

Epilogue

Period—1930–1960

Competition from motor trucks and good highways which had made substantial inroads against Cumberland River traffic above Nashville shortly before 1920, reached its peak by 1930.

Tennessee in that year had nearly completed its network of main highways and bridges. Other connecting roads, like fingers, extended into remote areas of the Cumberland plateau and throughout the entire river basin. Many localities, which in the old days relied exclusively upon steamboats for transportation, were brought within easy reach of our larger cities. Through the medium of trucks, peculiarly adapted to rolling hills and rural roads, farmers could now haul their products to market and sell them all in one day. Splendid highway bridges across the upper Cumberland, at Hunter's Point, Hartsville, Carthage, Gainesboro and Celina soon were to make it possible for traffic in this section to move without inconvenience North and South across the river and opened up markets in neighboring states which had never before been accessible. Thus, Nashville and Burnside, which had previously received the bulk of up-river freight because of exclusive steamboat transportation and connecting railroads, were now forced to compete on this type of freight with Louisville, Knoxville, Chattanooga and even Cincinnati and Atlanta. The steamboat paradise above Nashville was wiped out.

If the situation respecting traffic on the upper river from 1920 to 1930 was pathetic as compared to the past, that on the lower river was nothing less than tragic. Between railroad competition and that of motor trucks and highways, the river had temporarily succumbed as an artery of transportation for commercial or common carrier freight.

It is generally conceded that from 1920 to 1935 there was less commercial and diversified freight moved on the Cumberland than in any comparable period since the days of old-time barges and keelboats. Statistics issued by the United States Engineers for the period 1920 to 1925 show that the average annual tonnage on the entire Cumberland amounted to 418,311 tons, with an average annual value of $3,029,472.00, and an average ton value of only $7.31 per ton. Any student of the river knows that freight of such small value could not be diversified or commercial freight. Fully 70% of it was sand, gravel and rock, handled by dredges and towboats, owned by Nashville interests.

From 1925 to 1930 conditions grew worse. In 1930 annual tonnage had increased to 690,666 tons, but its value had gone down to $2,537,783.00, or $3.70 per ton. Sand, gravel and rock constituted 84% of the total tonnage, and the balance was mostly cross-ties, handles and staves. Only 169 tons of grain were transported on the river in 1930.

What was now occurring on the Cumberland River, after a fashion had already taken place on practically all of the Western Rivers. Near the close of 1920 certain Nashvillians, with the hope of breathing new life into the river, sponsored the movement for a municipal terminal. At an expense of some $250,000.00 the present Nashville River and Rail Terminal was opened in 1921.

Colonel M. T. Bryan, heretofore mentioned, assisted in establishing the terminal. Mayor William Gupton, George Tompkins, J. O. Tankard, E. T. Lewis and Paul Treanor were the Board of Public Works for the City, and A. E. Potter was President of the Transportation Trustees. The building committee was composed of A. J. Dyer, Chairman; Humphrey Hardison, M. E. Derryberry, Paul Roberts and the ever faithful Bryan. The Tennessee Central Railroad was the only rail connection to the terminal and still is. This is both unfortunate and unsatisfactory to say the least.

Only a very few steamboats were seen on the river between 1920 and 1930. The *Grace Devers, John Heckman,* a very large Missouri River freighter; the *Tom Powell* from the Tennessee trade, the *Alabama* and one or two others appeared to take a final fling at Cumberland River business for a season or two, and then hied back to their home ports. These boats did contract hauling. John A. Tyner and S. S. Kerr, two of Nashville's older grain men, chartered the *John Heckman* and hauled some grain, but they soon gave up.

A few gasoline towboats appeared on the river, but even these left in increasing numbers due to lack of business. What few remained were the familiar sand, gravel and cross-tie boats. Some of these were the *Marjorie,* a Diesel towboat operated by the Cumberland River Sand Company; the *Tom,* operated by Hardison & Co.; the *Harvey,* another diesel boat, owned by T. L. Herbert & Sons; the *Maxwell* and *Old Hickory,* small towboats engaged in handling crossties on the upper river. There was also a gasoline towboat engaged in the poultry and produce business between Carthage and Burkesville, and my own small towboat, the *J. S. Hopkins.* Will Maynard piloted the *Maxwell.*

Menke Brothers, during this interval, brought the *Winona,* a steamboat, to Nashville towing the Showboat *Hollywood.* The river was dying a natural death, but not the colorful Showboat. It did a huge business for two seasons. People heard the familiar calliope and flocked down to see the melodramas of bygone days.

During this same interval the U. S. Department of Engineers operated the steamboat *Warioto* and a diesel towboat *John Irwin.* Henry Richardson, who operated a sand and gravel company, had a small towboat named the *Margaret R* and a steam dredge, the *W. P. Fiske,* which later sank. These were the only boats to break the dead silence which seemed to pervade the Cumberland.

The Nashville city wharf, with its comparatively new river-rail terminal, was practically bereft of boats and traffic.

Tennesseeans, like most citizens in the United States, were not thinking of their faithful rivers as arteries of transportation. They were obsessed with only one traffic idea—speed—which, of course, neither the Cumberland nor any other river could furnish. It was an era of trans-oceanic air flights and stock market manipulations. The radio had arrived to take its part in the life of a nation which was riding for a fall. The great financial depression of the early thirties struck business of all kinds with paralyzing effect.

In all of the confusion, only a very small and often criticised group of citizens focused attention on our inland water-ways. Still fewer clearly saw during this period any future for river-borne transportation. Only a handful were willing to work on the three things which meant success, namely: channel improvements, powerful diesel towboats and standard type barges and modern terminal facilities.

On many a balmy summer afternoon during these dismal times I frequently left my office and journeyed down to the wharf. There I met some old-timer gazing down upon the river, wondering and watching, hoping and praying that somehow or other traffic would come back. It had been only a short time since, standing at the same spot, I had seen the *James N. White, R. Dunbar, J. B. Richardson, H. W. Buttorff, Robert Rhea, Henry Harley, Albany, Electra, Ed Myer, Chancey Lamb, Jo Horton Fall* and a score of others going or coming all heavily laden with freight, or the palatial three-decked excursion boat, *"J. S."*

No longer was the laughter of the roustabouts and the loud commands of the clerks to be heard. The picturesque cobblestones that lined the wharf and the countless horse-drawn drays and vans had all disappeared. Gone were the jingle of the pilot's signal bells, the black, curly smoke from the familiar smokestacks, the raucous noise of steam from exhaust pipes, the swish of the paddle wheels and the prolonged, sonorous blast of the whistle.

It was good to recall the many happy hours spent with the old steamboat masters, mates, pilots, engineers and clerks along the wharf during earlier days. These men who were so kind and considerate toward a boy who professed a love for the river will never be forgotten. While rough and ready in many respects, they had never spoken a mean or hasty word to their young admirer, but on the other hand had always taken time to stop and chat with him. They may have had their faults, but these were not visible.

I wonder how many Nashvillians can recall the life around the wharf on a hot Sunday afternoon during the period 1912 to 1930, when the "soapbox" orators and religious fanatics held forth on both sides of lower Broad Street. How many can now remember the old-time river baptizings conducted by both white and colored churches that took place some 100 feet above the south end of the present terminal?

During these years, in particular, there would be anywhere from five to ten such "orators" standing in the street near the curbing, generally with a Bible in hand, exhorting groups of inquisitive onlookers to accept their theories on religion, politics and economics. As long as I can remember, this odd custom had prevailed on Sunday afternoons. It was particularly prevalent in the years mentioned above. Where it started or how or why, no one seems to know.

Every known subject was discussed by various "orators" and they were "heckled" and criticized, but there was rarely any public disorder. As the summer wore on, those who withstood such a withering fire, always had the biggest crowd. The most popular of the "orators," by unwritten law, was generally given the right to conduct his discussions at the north corner of First Avenue and Broad, where the old watering trough for horses and mules stood.

One of the most picturesque of the many "orators" whom I recall, was dressed as a cowboy. Another traveled by bicycle and advertised he was descended from "royalty." One of the most remarkable events I can now remember was listening to a bearded gentleman who played the biggest harmonica I ever saw and then held his audience spellbound by repeating in full from memory any book in The New Testament and doing it with a very dramatic touch. This "artist" lasted two or three successive seasons and the coins he obtained from passing the hat, I feel sure, provided him a comfortable living.

There was hardly a Sunday afternoon at the wharf during the summer months, that was not enlivened by an old-fashioned negro river baptizing or one conducted by white people on a more sophisticated and less impressive basis. There were far more such baptizings by the negro congregations than by those of the white ones. While both followed the same general pattern, those of the white people could not be compared with the truly great religious fervor of the opposite race. These latter highly demonstrative affairs made a deep and abiding impression on me as a boy. Most of all, I shall never, as long as I live, forget the appealing and rich harmonious singing of these deeply religious folk. Usually there would be two hundred or more in the group whose singing could be heard several blocks away, first faintly, and then rising to great heights, as they descended to the steep bank of the river.

Arriving in mid-afternoon this beautiful singing of old spirituals would continue until all those who were to be baptized had been attired in "sainted white garments." Then the preacher would start his sermon and for thirty minutes he would exhort his congregation until many began to "shout" and repeat with rhythmic cadence "amens" or "Yes, My Lord!." Then the time having arrived, the elders who were to assist in the ceremony would appear with long walking sticks at the water's edge and proceed into the river, probing as they went. The right depth being found (generally waist deep), a circular area was set aside and then the preacher, still intoning a prayer, would walk without hesitation into the middle of the group.

By this time the singing had increased to feverish pitch, but then upon the preacher raising his hand would descend to a beautiful softness and continue. And then from among

The Clarksville Wharf—1935. It was at this historic landing that Commodore A. H. Foote landed on a gunboat on February 19, 1862, to receive the surrender of the City.

The Clarksville Wharf—1935. A big cargo of tobacco is once more being loaded and the *Pharr* is bound downstream with oil barges. In old days Clarksville was one of the largest tobacco distribution points in the United States.

the crowd nearest the river's edge would emerge the first to be baptized—led by an elder into the water and over to the preacher, who slowly and deliberately asked, "Do you believe in Jesus and in His power to wash away your sins?" and receiving an affirmative answer, then said, "I baptize you in the name of The Father, The Son and The Holy Ghost," thereupon, quickly submerging the convert backwards into the water and lifting him up again.

At this point, the convert, whether man, woman or child, would be seized with a volcanic and irrepressible force, compelling instantaneous shouting. He would then run out of the river to the bank where friends would literally grab in and ultimately restore peace. This would be repeated until all the converts had been baptized.

During such events a crowd of several hundred on-lookers would gather, but in all the many years I observed such things I never saw any semblance of disorder and never heard any slurs or frivolous criticisms made. On the contrary, the seriousness and simplicity of these formali-ties was highly impressive and the religious zeal was conta-gious. Somehow, when I now hear the popular version of the old hymn, "When The Saints Go Marching In," which was a favorite at the baptizings, I wonder if it is even the same song.

When I owned the *J. S. Hopkins* we frequently made trips up and down the Cumberland. As we pulled around bend after bend all of us in our imagination hoped to meet one of the old-time packets. Ending the day's run we would tie up to the bank, and after eating our evening meal adjourn to the bow of the boat to finish our coffee. It was agreed by all that while the change in events had affected transporta-tion, nothing could destroy the peace and quiet of the river. While there might be longer rivers, wider rivers, and even more traveled rivers, none surpassed the Cumberland for sheer beauty, particularly that section from Carthage to Burnside where the river like a ribbon winds and twists between beautiful bluffs several hundred feet high. Such reflections remained with us as we turned in for a night's rest hoping that John Henry, our cook, would catch some fish for breakfast on the many hand poles which adorned the fan-tail.

Mention of fishing brings up a subject which should be briefly noted in any story of the Cumberland, even though it is a diversion from the main subject. In the old days it was a common sight to see several fish mongers peddling live fish on the wharf, the nearby streets and the Public Square, especially on Friday and Saturday. The Cumberland and its tributaries were always rated among the best fishing territories in the country. This is especially true since the erection of high dams across its course and that of its tributaries.

When the railroads and modern refrigeration made it possible to procure and import fresh sea foods to Nashville and other points, it hurt commercial fishing along the Cumberland, but it by no means destroyed it. There are still a few commercial fishermen left on the river who have made it their exclusive business. In bygone days they shifted from one place to another along the river, according to the season. A great many raised families in houseboats and shanties along the river, and the fishing skills were handed down from generation to generation. In addition to trot-line fishing, nets and baskets were used.

Not only commercially, but for sport, the river affords some of the finest fresh-water fishing to be found anywhere in the United States. Sportsmen constantly fish the river and its many tributaries and lakes with excellent results.

Around the locks and dams, the chutes, slips and slides along the banks and the mouths of the small tributaries during various seasons of the year many species of fish can be caught with rod and reel. Some of these are—the bass, both large and small mouth; blue channel, white and yellow cat; bream, crappie, jacks (wall-eyed pike), red horse, black horse, shad, drum and sturgeon. Fish which are caught on trot-lines and in nets and baskets generally include catfish, drum, carp, buffalo, and sturgeon. It is not uncommon for commerical fishermen to catch drum weighing between fifteen and twenty pounds, catfish weighing fifty to sixty pounds, carp and buffalo twenty to thirty pounds; and I have known of one sturgeon caught in the river that weighed better than eighty pounds. The world's record wall-eye was caught near Hartsville in 1960 by Mabry Harper. It weighed 25.4 pounds.

The completion of the dams which are being erected throughout the Cumberland area are providing even greater fishing pleasure. Tennessee has become an outstanding recreational center between the Great Lakes and Florida, adding millions of dollars annually to the wealth of Tennessee. Thousands of small boats have made the Cumberland a paradise for lovers of outdoor sports.

Somewhat connected with fishing is the mussel shell business on the Cumberland. Just how long this industry has been in existence is doubtful, but it probably goes back to prehistoric times. It came into its own with the development of mother-of-pearl buttons and has continued spasmodically on the river until the present age.

Prior to the cold, deep water caused by the multi-purpose dams, referred to later on, the bi-valve marine creature called a "mussel" was especially prolific in the Cumberland, thanks to the sand and gravel beds. The mussel is larger than the oyster and is not now considered edible. There is every indication that the Indians ate them. They are now used principally as fish bait on trot-lines and in baskets. The shell is often large and resplendent with colors. They make some of the finest buttons which adorn wearing apparel. Those found in the Cumberland are particularly suited for the manufacture of better class buttons. In years gone by, button manufacturers each year hired many mussel fishermen to get the shells, and then in the late fall, boats came up the river, picked up the shells and paid for them on the spot.

In 1910 one concern at Paducah had 300 small mussel boats employed on the Cumberland and Tennessee Rivers. Other concerns operating between Nashville and Burnside had half again as many boats engaged in this trade.

Paducah boats in one year alone obtained around 2,000 tons of mussel shells from fishermen on the Cumberland.

There are some seventy-eight different species of mussels. The favorite ones found in the Cumberland are the "hard-heads," "pocket-books," "pig-toes," "elephant ears," "warty backs," "muskets" and "sand shells," to mention only a few. I personally knew one mussel fisherman on the upper Cumberland who sold $2,500.00 worth of shells in one year. Mussel pearls are formed like those in oysters but are not as valuable. They are, however, merchantable and of good quality.

But we must discontinue these diversions and return to events on the river during this period.

"Every cloud has a silver lining," according to an old saying. It was to be that way with the Cumberland.

The depressing picture which I have painted in respect to traffic on the Cumberland from 1920 to 1930 was to last for another five years. But by 1930 there were very definite indications that the veil of gloom would lift. It really lifted much sooner than river men thought possible, due to several contributing factors. Let us look at these.

Beginning around 1930, despite strong resistance from various parties, Congress did its part by appropriating sufficient funds to carry out many vital river improvements. While this period, therefore, was the most depressing in actual river transportation, it early became one of the best from the standpoint of preparation for the future. This was particularly gratifying to all river men because the improvements which were made were carefully sifted and painstakingly examined and some degree of permanency established in the overall policy of the government in respect to inland waterways. The very fact that river-borne transportation was at a low ebb and faced strong competition, guaranteed that only deserving projects would be undertaken. Politics and propaganda, for at least once in the history of the United States, played but a small part in these basic matters. Dollar for dollar, no finer or better internal improvements have ever been made and certainly none more vital to the rejuvenation of commerce on our inland waterways. The American people received their money's worth.

During the early thirties the two major rivers of the nation, the Ohio and the Mississippi, and many of their larger tributaries obtained a minimum channel depth of nine feet. In some instances the actual work had not been completed by 1930, but the projects were under way. This one single improvement on the Ohio and Mississippi transformed them into powerful weapons in the fight to preserve river-borne transportation throughout the rest of the country. It acted as a tonic at exactly the right time. The Allegheny, Monongahela and the Kanawha, great coal-bearing rivers, and the Illinois Waterway, connecting the Mississippi with the Great Lakes, received a similar face-lifting. Slowly but surely, the government was building the improvements long overdue which all river men knew were the first links in the chain of success for river-borne transportation.

Many of the very large projects undertaken by the Government during this period had been sponsored for a number of years, but for various reasons they had never been approved by Congress. Most of them had received favorable consideration at the hands of the United States Engineering Department. This agency had not been thrown off balance by the incessant cry for speed in transportation, but on the contrary saw the great value of the slower but voluminous water-borne transportation. It had sifted various recommendations, facts and figures, submitted by an increasing number of river and marine organizations, such as the National Rivers and Harbors Congress, founded in 1901, the Propellor Club, founded in 1922, and still others whose names and activities identified them with particular rivers. These organizations acted as a clearing house and "voice" for all river interests. All of this sifting pointed to the same fact—namely, that the chief function of river transportation was to transport in one movement great volumes of freight rather than lesser quantities at greater speed.

In 1927 one of the worst floods in the history of the United States descended on the states touched by the Ohio,

The Cumberland 300 miles above its mouth. Showing Lock and Dam 7, 8 miles below Carthage. Army maneuvers were held in this area for World War II.

A modern Cumberland River tow—1940. The *Virginia* bound upstream near Clarksville with a cargo of oil, gasoline, grain, sugar and miscellaneous freight.

the Mississippi, the Tennessee, the Cumberland and their tributaries. The suffering and damage caused by this catastrophe had much to do with the crystallization of public opinion in favor of harnessing such destructive power. In the Far West, where soil conservation and irrigation had been a pressing problem for years, the time was also ripe for action.

For many years there had been discussion regarding the vast and unharnessed resources of the Tennessee River and its many swift-moving tributaries. This fine river was recognized as the outstanding potential hydro-electric power facility in the eastern United States. It had been booted around for more than fifty years. Private enterprise had sought to take it over and use it for private gain and Congress had frequently pigeonholed efforts to bring it under complete governmental control. No other single project in the early thirties did more to arouse public interest in the vast natural water resources of the country than the Tennessee Valley Authority, better known as TVA.

The Hoover Administration which came into office in 1928, was exceedingly liberal toward all internal improvements. When the great financial depression struck the United States in the early days of that administration, unemployment also became a pressing problem. Internal improvements were one means of taking up the slack. By 1930 navigation on the inland waterways and other kindred projects such as flood control, soil conservation, irrigation and hydro-electric power were receiving every consideration. Many projects were launched and some were promptly completed.

If the Hoover Administration was liberal toward internal improvements, the Roosevelt Administration, elected in 1932, may be termed exceedingly generous. One of the first acts of President Franklin D. Roosevelt was to urge the creation of the Tennessee Valley Authority. This Act became law in 1933. The record of this governmental agency is too well known to need any discussion. It has received both praise and condemnation. In less than ten years it completely throttled the Tennessee River and was the first in the South to combine all of the multiple purpose benefits derived from navigation, flood control, soil conservation and hydro-electric power.

While the Government was doing its part to make the rivers serviceable, men engaged in river transportation also were busy and found new devices to attract freight back to the inland waterways. During the short span of 1920–1930 marine engineers designed and produced the forerunners of the modern diesel towboats. They were as maneuverable as steamboats and could be propelled by either the familiar paddle wheel or propellors. Cost of operation was considerably lower and their cruising speed was even faster. By 1930 the larger boats of this type were driven by engines varying from 500 to 1,000 H.P. In 1960, they had climbed to 2,000 and 3,000 H.P. and the end is not in sight.

During the decade 1920 to 1930 marine engineers and architects gave river-borne transportation another successful fighting weapon. This was the standard all-welded steel type barge with its many variations. From rather small affairs, with a capacity of 300 to 400 tons, the steel barges now in use on the inland waterways are much more streamlined and are capable of accommodating 1,000 tons and more. In the present era of river-borne transportation the owner selects and orders the particular type or size barge he desires in his business in much the same manner as shippers by rail select and order their boxcars. There is a barge suitable for almost any kind of freight. Protection against rain and other hazards can be afforded the shipper as never before in the history of river transportation. Such "dry" commodities as sugar, coffee, grain, flour and salt, to mention but a few, are transported with ease and safety.

Modern river terminals, the third link in the advancement of transportation on the rivers, have not been fully achieved as yet. The erection of these facilities, however, is only a matter of time. In such cities as Pittsburgh, Cincinnati, Louisville, Cairo, St. Louis, Memphis and New Orleans, barge lines have already been supplied with commodious and serviceable terminals.

Gradually familiar slow-moving cargo has found its way back to the rivers.

With a standard gauge nine foot channel on many of the western rivers, trunk line transportation, somewhat similar to that of the railroads, is now employed. Heavy, slow-moving cargoes now proceed up and down the rivers by accepted and standard methods. Freight in great volume is moved from Pittsburgh to New Orleans, from New Orleans to the Great Lakes, from Minneapolis to the Gulf and from St. Louis to Chicago. It does not go as fast but it goes at a much cheaper rate. In a single trip a towboat and barges now handle freight ordinarily requiring three or four average freight trains. In this manner shippers have found it possible to create reservoirs of supplies. Speed has been circumvented by modern storage facilities.

How much the nine foot channel on the larger rivers and other improvements which have been mentioned helped river-borne transportation may be shown by a few figures.

In 1920 the total domestic water-borne transportation in continental United States amounted to only 124,400,000 tons. In 1930 this total had jumped to 226,700,000 tons. In 1940 it had increased to 366,800,000 tons and in 1947 the total had leaped to 595,509,888 tons. Ten years later in 1957 it had risen to 772,861,135 tons.

Traffic on the Cumberland between Nashville and Paducah was seriously handicapped in the absence of a standard nine foot channel and numerous manually operated locks. It was almost impossible to interest the larger barge lines in doing business on the Cumberland. This is readily explained when it is pointed out that such lines would be confronted with long delays in locking through. The locks were so small that the usual tows for Ohio and Mississippi boats could not lock through without splitting up at least once, but more frequently two or three times. In addition to these troubles, there was but one terminal facility at Nashville.

Nevertheless, very large towboats with big tows did come

up to Nashville in increasing numbers from 1935 to 1945 and once more "old timers" realized that a boom was taking place.

Despite some serious obstacles, traffic on the river in 1948 went to a new high of 1,590,884 tons, the highest in sixty-two years, valued at better than $20,000,000.

In 1950 this had increased to 2,029,729 tons; in 1952 to 2,176,175 tons and in 1954 to 2,320,895 tons. In 1957 with Cheatham Dam giving the river below Nashville a nine foot channel for approximately forty miles and free of the old manually operated locks, the tonnage rose to 3,028,976 tons and in 1960 it was 2,950,100 tons with all the records not in. With the completion of the Barkley Dam and a nine foot channel all the way to Paducah from Nashville it is safe to say the annual traffic will probably average 3,500,000 tons. One can readily understand from these figures what a tremendous revival has taken place in Cumberland River traffic.

It was inevitable that the larger rivers such as the Ohio and Mississippi would first receive the improvements so necessary to river-borne transportation. The development of the Cumberland, however, while somewhat delayed, progressed very rapidly when once it got under way.

From 1832, when Congress made its first appropriation, until 1935, the only improvements on the Cumberland were in behalf of navigation, i.e., channel clearance, locks and dams etc. Since 1935, all of the appropriations have been granted to carry out a comprehensive program for the control of floods, development of electric power and improvement of navigation. From 1935 to 1960, a total of approximately $277,400,000 has been made available for the overall program and when it is completed the total cost will amount to an estimated $577,833,000.

Twelve separate and distinct projects under the above plan have been approved for construction. Out of this twelve, the Wolf Creek, Dale Hollow, Center Hill, Old Hickory and Cheatham projects are completed. The Wolf Creek Dam which forms Cumberland Lake on the upper reaches of the river and Old Hickory Dam a relative short distance above Nashville, together with Cheatham Dam below Nashville are the only dams erected across the Cumberland. The Dale Hollow Dam is across the Obey River and the Center Hill Dam is across the Caney Fork River. Primary benefits from Old Hickory and Cheatham Dams are navigation and power. Cheatham Dam has given the river a nine foot channel from that dam to Old Hickory Dam and has done away with two obsolete locks. Old Hickory has given the river a nine foot channel all the way up to Lock 8, which is some eight miles above Carthage.

The Barkley Dam project is for flood control, navigation and power development and is now nearing ultimate completion. The dam is erected thirty miles above the mouth of the Cumberland and is one of the most needed and ambitious projects on the river. It will assure the Cumberland, at long last, of a nine foot channel from the Ohio to Lock 8, a total distance of approximately 308 miles.

The potentials of Barkley Dam are tremendous. In addition to a nine foot channel it will afford a canal between the Cumberland and Tennessee which in effect means that traffic between these two great rivers can by-pass the long trip down one and over the Ohio to the other. The time saved by such a by-pass can not be estimated. It should be one of the finest improvements ever to take place on our inland waterways.

The Barkley Dam project is also expected to aid in flood control not only in the lower Cumberland basin but on the lower Ohio and even the Mississippi. It should be particularly helpful because of its close proximity to these two rivers and the flow of water can be cut off in the Cumberland when danger is first observed.

This project, when completed, will be one of the largest hydro-electric power units in this part of the United States. It will be seen, therefore, that it would be pure speculation to give any opinion as to what will be the total benefits from the Barkley Dam project or for that matter the already completed Cheatham Dam project.

From the standpoint of navigation these facts will serve to verify the conclusion that a nine foot channel up to Nashville will mean an unprecedented advance in traffic on the Cumberland, and the revival of such traffic which started on the upswing in 1935 will continue unabated. It further seems a self-evident fact that Nashville will remain the metropolis of the Cumberland, which lofty position is an honor of increasing significance. In fact, the river is getting to look like itself once again. In March of 1961 I counted a total of eleven barges and five diesel towboats tied up at the wharf.

I regret to state, however, that traffic on the upper Cumberland has not been revived to any appreciable extent. The reason for this is due entirely to the absence of any large industrial city in that section of the river. There simply is not enough freight to haul.

The present increase in river-borne traffic up to Nashville is difficult to understand unless all the facts are brought out. The difference between traffic on the river now and traffic during the old steamboat days is traceable to a change in the conception of what is the basic function of such traffic. In the old days, the packet operators butted their brains out trying to compete with the railroads on all types of freight as well as cheaper rates.

With the advent of the new and powerful diesel towboats and the modern barges, this has all been changed. The idea of competing with either the railroads or motor vehicles on all types of freight has been abandoned, it being obvious that the river as a transportation artery is not suited to handle certain types of freight, even if cheaper rates might be obtained. This same reasoning applies with equal force to both railroads and motor vehicles.

Now, the operators engaged in river transportation are making every effort to transport what is frequently referred to as typical stock-pile or reservoir type freight whose movement does not depend necessarily upon the element of speed. An example of this type of freight would be petroleum products, cement, fertilizer, salt, grain, scrap iron, sulphur, new automobiles, lumber, fencing, wire, nails, metal and many other articles. All of these items can be stored in warehouses controlled by distributors and delivered to dealers or customers when desired. By anticipating needs the distributors can save considerable money by shipping via river and barge lines.

In order to handle this new traffic several well-known barge lines are now operating into Nashville. The equipment is standard and uniform and can be interchanged without any great delay.

The first big customers of the towboats over the Cumberland were the large national petroleum companies, Standard, Gulf, Shell, Pure, etc. The first shipments of petroleum products amounting to a total of 10,458 tons came up to Nashville in 1932 even before any improvements were made in the channel depth. But it came in specially designed barges and towed by a powerfully-built modern diesel towboat. In 1948, still without channel improvements, these shipments had increased to the almost unbelievable total of 681,547 tons.

Petroleum products were by no means the only freight being hauled up to Nashville. In 1940 the total tonnage on the river was 849,439 tons valued at $12,000,000. Some of the items included steel, grain, fertilizer, sulphur, ties, handles etc. It was good to note that commercial freight exceeded the familiar sand, gravel and rock.

In 1960 some of the river freight brought up to Nashville originated in such far away places as Houston, New Orleans, Baton Rouge, Chicago, Kansas City, Cincinnati and Pittsburgh.

Only one fair conclusion can be drawn from these figures and that is that the Cumberland has once more come into its own as a great artery of transportation and one which is bringing many millions of dollars into Nashville and its trade area.

The other projects which have been authorized as part of the twelve heretofore mentioned are the Percy Priest, Cordell Hull, Celina, Three Islands, Rossview and Laurel

River Dam projects, but with the exception of the Cordell Hull and Celina Dams, they are not in any way connected with navigation on the Cumberland and I see no reason to do more than mention them briefly.

I have already made mention of the destruction caused by floods in the Cumberland basin. A survey shows that Nashville has had a flood of some character almost every year. The overall plan of development as authorized, especially the Percy Priest Dam on Stones River, is calculated to decrease, if not completely do away with, flood hazards at Nashville. The idea seems to be that all of the dams will be synchronized in such a way that water can be trapped at will and the flow of water regulated in perfect harmony, thereby avoiding floods by preventing the danger before it arises.

The high dams already completed on the upper Cumberland and its tributaries have inundated approximately 135,-000 acres of land. Of this area 72,000 acres are in Tennessee. This is a sizeable slice of land to erase by water, but it is slight in comparison to the 800,000 acres already inundated by the TVA. Of this total, approximately 500,000 acres are in Tennessee.

One of the effects of this development has been to lift the State of Tennessee from its former rank of forty-third to thirty-first among states with inland water area. Prior to 1940 Tennessee boasted 385 square miles of inland water area. Now, with state and federal projects combined, it has a grand total of 1,339,099 acres under water and this will be further increased as other projects on the Cumberland are completed and operating at maximum levels.

The government, for various reasons but principally because of insufficient traffic at present, has not erected locks in the Wolf Creek Dam and none are contemplated at either Cordell Hull or Celina Dams, which are power projects. The public must realize the great importance of these decisions which in effect will cut off through traffic from Carthage to Burnside, a distance of approximately 200 miles. From 1920 to 1930 it was thought the river from Paducah to Nashville was "dead," but look what happened! No one can prophesy what the future needs of transportation on the Upper Cumberland might require. Posterity may righteously resent such a momentous decision.

It is noteworthy that while the TVA dams cover "more acreage" individually as a rule than those erected in the upper Cumberland basin, they have "less capacity gallons." This is because the dams in the Cumberland system create reservoirs of tremendous depths, while those in the Tennessee basin are fairly shallow and spread out over the low lands. Few Tennesseeans realize that these deep valleys in the Cumberland plateau are natural gems in the science of dam building.

The Wolf Creek Dam across the Cumberland is 242 feet high but the reservoir covers only 99 square miles. Yet this project has a capacity of 1,984 billion gallons and a capacity of 6,089,000 acre feet at maximum. On the other hand, Kentucky Lake on the Tennessee, formed by a dam 202 feet high, covers 408 square miles, but its capacity is only 1,956 billion gallons and 6,003,000 acre feet at maximum. Believe it or not, therefore, the Cumberland, which has received very little national publicity as compared to TVA can boast of a reservoir which covers only one-fourth as much land as the biggest TVA lake, but has a greater capacity in billions of gallons and in acre feet. The Wolf Creek Dam is seventh among the nation's reservoirs measured in such terms, while Kentucky Lake ranks eighth.

Capacity measured in billion of gallons means the maximum amount of water it takes to fill the reservoir. Capacity in acre feet means the number of acres which would be covered by one foot of water if the maximum water in the reservoir was used.

When the Japanese struck at Pearl Harbor, bringing our country into another World conflagration, the Cumberland River also went to war.

It was clearly evident that World War II would tax all transportation facilities to the limit. No other commodities were of such vast importance to our War effort and National defense as gasoline and oil.

The Cumberland goes to war. Minesweeper built by Nashville Bridge
Co.—launched February 28, 1942.

An immediate demand was created for more modern diesel tow boats and barges to handle various types of slow moving freight on the inland water-ways, including all-important oil and gas. Both the Army and Navy urgently needed specially designed water craft of every character. Many of the ship-building yards on the inland water-ways were awarded contracts for the construction of such vessels. One of these was the Nashville Bridge Company which enlarged its facilities and immediately started war work.

This Company was originally chartered in 1901. Its destiny has been guided largely by its founder, A. J. Dyer and his son Harry Dyer, who is a gifted marine architect. Another son, Wesley Dyer, took an active part in its war efforts. The achievement of the Nashville Bridge Company during World War II was remarkable, and it earned the Navy "E" for this service. Among the craft it built and delivered by May 1, 1944, were five U. S. Navy barracks vessels; six U. S. Navy covered lighters; thirty-seven U. S. QMC deck barges; eleven U. S. QMC oil barges; four U. S. QMC water barges; ten U. S. QMC cargo barges; fourteen U. S. Navy subchasers; two U. S. Mine sweepers. Before hostilities ended several more craft had been completed. Many of the vessels were so large that they had little clearance through the locks on the Cumberland, but all reached salt water without serious injury.

Since the War, the Nashville Bridge Company has continued to grow and prosper. It is now one of Nashville's largest and best known concerns. Its modern diesel towboats and barges reflect great credit upon the talented men who have designed them.

Almost immediately after Pearl Harbor, one small Coast Guard Reserve boat arrived in Nashville, manned by a crew of three or four enlisted personnel, to patrol the river near the Nashville Bridge Company and the wharf. For a short time it was under the supervision of the Captain of the Port at Chattanooga.

During the Spring of 1942, Flotilla 2, Division VI of the Coast Guard Auxiliary was organized with a total membership of ten active small boat operators and a corresponding number of small craft. This was a voluntary, non-military organization. There were ten other such Flotillas in Division VI, and during the early days of the War, they assisted Coast Guard Reservists in protecting both the Cumberland and Tennessee Rivers against possible sabotage. For more than two months the Flotilla in Nashville was assigned active guard duty on the river.

In March, 1942, by Executive Order, the Bureau of Marine Inspection and Navigation, Department of Commerce, (Steamboat Inspection Service) was transferred to the supervision of the Coast Guard. The Nashville Office of the Bureau was under the direct supervision of the District Coast Guard Officer for the St. Louis Ninth Naval District. In this manner, and to afford further military protection, J. W. Schmoker, who was Local Inspector of Hulls with the Steamboat Inspection Service was commissioned Commander in the U.S.C.G.R., and became Captain of the Port at Nashville, and W. P. Fiske, who was Local Inspector of Boilers, was commissioned Lieutenant Commander in the same Service. The personnel in Nashville was enlarged to meet the emergency.

In November, 1942, the small Coast Guard Reserve Unit then in Nashville was increased. An extensive shore and river patrol was established. Three new Reserve boats, including a "picket" boat, were sent to Nashville and a quarter boat was obtained to house the enlisted personnel.

In January, 1943, a sub-Captain of the Port was designated and a complement of fifty-odd Coast Guard Reservists firmly maintained a round-the-clock patrol on the shore and on the river. Ensign J. E. Ivins, U.S.C.G.R., was the first sub-Captain of the Port in charge of operations. He remained about six months and was succeeded by Ensign Roger E. Hammer, U.S.C.G.R., who in turn was succeeded by Lt. (jg) C. G. Bowen, U.S.C.G.

In March of 1943, a Temporary Reserve Unit of the Coast Guard composed exclusively of Nashvillians was organized to take over the patrol duties of the regular C. G. R. unit.

This was similar to other such units throughout the rest of the country. It was a military organization but the members received no pay for their services. They were enlisted to enable Reserve personnel to engage in sea duty. It was this patriotic unit, unknown to most Nashvillians, that kept constant patrol of the river and its facilities during the remainder of the War.

L. E. McKeand, a charter member of the Auxiliary in Nashville was commissioned an Ensign in the Temporary Reserve and in less than ninety days he enlisted a personnel of some seventy-five men, and in July, 1944 they took over patrol duties completely. McKeand later resigned to enter vital defense work in another field. The personnel of the unit was inexperienced and the Nashville Flotilla of the Coast Guard Auxiliary was given the responsibility of conducting a training program. The author headed up this program as commander of the Nashville Auxiliary, ably assisted by Emmons Woolwine, Walter M. Parrish, Dwight H. Woods and Herbert F. Leek, all of whom were experienced small boat operators.

After the resignation of McKeand, the Reserve Unit in Nashville continued to function smoothly with Lt. (jg) Dwight H. Woods, C. G. R. (T) as executive officer, and a quota of 125 men. Lt. Woods was a charter member of the Auxiliary. The Temporary Reserve members served approximately twelve hours each week, and were all uniformed and otherwise organized as a military outfit while on duty.

The Cumberland River, after Pearl Harbor, went to War in still another and most unexpected way. It was announced in 1942 that the Second Army would engage in maneuvers in Middle Tennessee. Army officials agreed that the terrain of Middle Tennessee was ideally suited for training troops for European service. Many of the smaller tributaries of the Cumberland, but particularly the Cumberland itself, served as a splendid training ground for amphibious warfare. No official figures have been released, but it was estimated that in the two years maneuvers were held in Middle Tennessee, around 500,000 troops trained in this area. The

Idlewild. Modern Cumberland River excursion boat.

Golden Eagle. Modern tourist boat seen on the Cumberland.

Cumberland River almost daily was used for the erection of pontoon bridges and for other amphibuous tactics necessary to carry on the training.

The Municipal Terminal at the foot of Broad Street is now leased to the well-known firm of Ozburn-Hessey Storage Co., with Frank P. Ozburn as president; Kenneth Hessey, secretary-treasurer; Walter W. Wells and Stewart Bachmann, vice-presidents. It is indeed gratifying to all lovers of the river to observe the great increase in activity at this facility. One of the difficulties at this terminal has been the absence of a suitable crane capable of lifting such cargo as steel, iron, machinery and other heavy items. A plan is now under way to obtain a crane-derrick capable of lifting twenty-two tons at one clip and if this is done and other minor improvements made, it will lead to even greater increase in traffic. Ozburn-Hessey are connected with the Western Waterways Barge Lines and its barges are now unloaded at their terminal.

The Cumberland Storage and Warehouse Terminal, which is owned and operated by the three Minton brothers, Ollie, Pete and Doug and their brother-in-law, Sam Davidson, was opened for business in the fall of 1958 on the river near the foot of Wharf Avenue. The operators of this modern facility are well-known in river circles and formerly operated the Municipal Terminal. Their terminal is doing an excellent business. In their first year they unloaded 67,-404.26 tons of freight. Four commercial barge lines, the Union, the American Commercial, the Ohio River and the Mississippi Valley, as well as those of Laughlin Steel Company regularly unload at this terminal.

The Cumberland River Sand and Gravel Co., T. L. Herbert & Co., and the Nashville Bridge Company are also prepared to load and unload freight on the river. However, their facilities are used generally in connection with their own business needs and not as public terminals. The United States Engineers had a limited loading and unloading facility on the river below Nashville. This was disposed of sometime ago and is not presently in operation.

There are now 27 different companies operating barges on the Cumberland up to Nashville, some common carriers, others under contract and still others for private use. In addition to those I have already mentioned, it is only fitting that I should at this time mention Louis Igert Towing Company and the Houghland Towing Company, both of Paducah. They are among the oldest and best known. It would be next to impossible to name all of the boats they have operated on the river and their contribution to it.

Thus ends the glorious story of the service rendered by the Cumberland River and the men and boats that have plied its waters. As a faithful servant of the people the river from time to time has contributed to the success of Nashville as a leading cotton market, an outstanding tobacco center, the largest grain distribution point in the South, the second largest hardwood timber market in the United States, and one of the top ranking hog, cattle and meat packing centers south of the Ohio. It has fought side by side with our people in war and peace. It has brought us iron for our foundries, coal for our homes, powder for our guns and water for our daily needs. Its sand, gravel and rock have built our homes, bridges and highways. Its steamboats have given us a glorious tradition, and the men who manned them have left us a rich heritage of faith and fortitude.

It is a far cry back to 1814 and the days of Zadok Cramer, author of the "Pittsburgh Navigator and Almanac," whom I mentioned at the beginning of this story. This keen observer knew what he was talking about when he prophesied a bright future for Steamboatin' on the Cumberland. In his most vivid imagination, however, he could not have foreseen what a truly glorious future it was to be.

From a meager beginning more than 1200 named steamboats and other commercial craft have plied the river and docked at Nashville and other towns and landings along its course. Such a record should stand, not only as a symbol of past achievement, but of future hopes.

The future success of the Cumberland depends upon a

number of factors, but largely upon leadership, just as it did in 1814, when Zadok Cramer was doing the writing. Unlike that celebrity, I am no prophet—the most I can do is to express the hope that what ought to be done, will be done, in order that the Cumberland may continue its maximum service to our people.

F I N I S

Acknowledgements

During the past thirty-five years the author has been gathering information and statistics concerning the Cumberland River and its steamboats. The idea of a book came about because many of the old records were rapidly being destroyed and it appeared that unless someone undertook the job there would be no way of preserving them.

It has been my privilege and pleasure to have known personally many old time river men. The careers of these men in some instances overlapped those of other old timers whom they knew intimately and who came to the Cumberland before the War Between the States. Among such men particular mention should be made of the late Captain James S. Tyner, partner of Captain Thomas G. Ryman. Captain Tyner knew many of the steamboat owners and licensed officers who plied the Cumberland River from 1865 through 1935 when he died. This career overlapped those of men who came on the river as far back as 1835. He spoke with authority on all matters pertaining to the river, but I am particularly grateful for the information he gave me about Ryman and the railroad competition. I am also indebted to the late Captains Tom Gallagher and "Shep" Green who gave me much helpful information. Among the old guard the late Captain W. T. Hunter was of the greatest benefit. He permitted access to his notes on the river and to some of the photographs which are reproduced in the book. His vast knowledge of the Cumberland combined more than fifty years as a licensed officer and as an Inspector with the Steamboat Inspection Service. He took the time and trouble to read the text and to make many helpful suggestions. I have also received valuable information from the late "old time" Captains James L. Gann, W. E. Lovell and W. P. Fiske, the latter connected with the Steamboat Inspection Service for many years. Through Captain Lovell and his wife and the late John Lovell, who served on steamboats as an engineer, I obtained many side-lights on the life of the Lovell family.

I gratefully acknowledge the assistance of the following: the late M. J. Kyle of Celina, who was engaged in the timber and rafting business on the upper Cumberland during his entire lifetime; the late Judge John J. Gore of Gainesboro; the late Mrs. Georgia Ryman Jackson, daughter of Captain Ryman for giving me many facts about her father; John A. Tyner and J. P. Tyner, both now deceased, and Mrs. Martha Tyner Carney, all of Nashville, children of the late Captain James S. Tyner, for much interesting information about their father; Captain Bridges Montgomery, experienced pilot on the upper Cumberland and who knows that end of the river from A to Z and who was also a pilot for the U. S. Engineers; T. A. Clarkson, formerly secretary of the Nashville, Chattanooga and St. Louis Railroad and the Nashville and Decatur Railroad, who made available Annual Reports of the N. C. & St. L. and L. & N. and also gave me other valuable data and in addition read a large portion of the manuscript; Colonel F. S. Besson, Colonel Bernard L. Smith, Colonel O. E. Walsh and Colonel Reading Wilkinson, District Engineers, War Department, and their former able administrative assistants, S. A. Weakley, W. F. Harbison; G. R. Bethurum, Jr., present Chief Technical Liaison Branch, and Statistician Ralph W. Lambert, and the late Captain W. J. Ellison, all in the USED; R. M. Williamson and E. M. Barto, former observers and meterologists with the United States Weather Bureau at Nashville; James E. Brock, A. P. Hill, and Harvey C. Douglas, former Deputy Collectors of Customs at Nashville and Commander J. W. Schmoker, U.S.C.G.R., formerly Officer-in-charge of the Coast Guard

Marine Inspection, until lately the Steamboat Inspection Service at Nashville.

The librarians of the Tennessee State Library and the Nashville Public Library extended every courtesy during my examination of old newspapers and other records on file at these institutions.

Thanks are extended to my friends Harry Dyer of the Nashville Bridge Company, Emmons Woolwine, who drew the sketch of the boat for the frontispiece, and to Walter M. Parrish, J. Louis Adams and John Henderson for their patience and kindness in reading the manuscript and Miss Lily J. Clemons for its early preparation.

During the past thirty-five years the preparation behind the book has not been confined to research. Frequent contact has been maintained with the river by various trips from the head of navigation to its mouth. I have found many interesting characters who have given me various slants on the river. At least one of these must be mentioned—the late Tom McQuiston, who piloted towboats on the Cumberland for many years and served as co-pilot with me on the *J. S. Hopkins* for nearly a decade. There never will be another river man just like him. Some of the others were inveterate "shanty boat" owners, some "cliff dwellers" who fished and hunted for a living, some just plain "river rats" and others who for no particular reason sought a roving life on the river.

A constant perusal of the Waterways Journal has paid rich dividends.

Before concluding, I wish to thank my wife, Mary Stahlman Douglas, Literary Editor of the Nashville Banner, for her assistance during all the years this book has been in preparation. She has given me continuous encouragement and much timely advice. We have enjoyed many trips up and down the Cumberland, in every type of boat. For five summers we had a camp under the willows and sycamores on the banks of the river. For another decade we spent most of our idle hours on our towboat, the *J. S. Hopkins,* which sank in 1938. In 1935 we built a home at Hunter's Point on the Cumberland and from that vantage point we have continued to enjoy the river and have observed the many changes in its life and character.

"Fiddler's Peak"
May 31st, 1961.

Byrd Douglas

Bibliography

Albright, Edward. *Early History of Middle Tennessee.* Brandon Printing Co., 1909.

Anderson. *The Mississippi and Tributaries.* National Republican House, Washington, 1881.

Annual Reports of the Louisville & Nashville Railroad, 1866–1944.

Annual Reports of the Nashville & Chattanooga, and Nashville, Chattanooga & St. Louis Railway, 1848–1944.

Annual Reports of the United States Engineer. 71 vols. Nashville, 1873–1944.

Bond, Octavia Zollicoffer. *Old Tales Retold.* Nashville, 1905. Reprinted by Vanderbilt University Press, 1941.

Brandon, Edgar Ewing. *A Pilgrimage of Liberty.* Lawhead Press, Cincinnati, 1944.

Butler, Mann. *History of the Commonwealth of Kentucky.* Wilcox, Dickerman & Co., 1834.

Chambers, Julius. *Mississippi River.* G. P. Putnam & Sons, New York, 1910.

Cisco, J. G. *Historic Sumner County.* Folk-Keelin Printing Co., Nashville, 1909.

Clayton, W. W. *History of Davidson County.* J. W. Lewis, Publisher, Philadelphia, 1880.

Crew, H. W. *History of Nashville.* Methodist Publishing House, Nashville, 1890.

Davis, Jefferson. *The Rise and Fall of the Confederate Government.* 2 vols. D. Appleton Co., New York, 1881.

Dorrance, Ward. *Where the Rivers Meet.* Scribners, New York, 1939.

Duffus, R. L. *The Valley and Its People.* Knopf, New York, 1944.

Dunbar, Seymour. *A History of Travel and Transportation in America.* Bobbs-Merrill, Indianapolis, 1915.

Dyer, John P. *Gallant Hood.* Bobbs-Merrill Co., 1950.

Geological Survey in Kentucky (Third Report) 1856–57. David Dale Owen, principal geologist. A. G. Hodges, Press, 1857.

Goodspeed, Weston A. *History of Tennessee from the Earliest Times.* Goodspeed Publishing Co., Nashville, 1886.

Gordon, Caroline. *None Shall Look Back.* Scribners, New York, 1937.

Gosnell, H. Allen. *Guns on the Western Waters.* Louisiana State University Press, 1949.

Grant, U. S. *Personal Memoirs.* 2 vols. C. L. Webster Co., New York, 1885–86.

Guild, Jo C. *Old Times in Tennessee.* Tavel, Eastman & Howell, Nashville, 1878.

Hall, James. *Sketches of the West.* J. A. James & Co., Cincinnati, 1837.

Hamer, Philip May, editor. *Tennessee: A History.* 4 vols. American Historical Society, 1933.

Henry, Robert Selph. *"First with the Most" Forrest.* Bobbs-Merrill, Indianapolis, 1944.

Heiskell, S. G. *Andrew Jackson and Early Tennesse History.* Ambrose Printing Co., Nashville, 1918.

Herr, Kincaid. *The Louisville & Nashville Railroad, 1850–1942.* L. & N. Magazine Publisher, 1944.

Hillman, H. W. *Genealogy of the Hillman Family.* Smith Brothers, Pittsburgh, 1905.

Hines, Edward W. *Corporate History of the Louisville & Nashville Railroad Company.* John Martin, Company, Louisville, 1905.

Horn, Stanley F. *The Army of Tennessee.* Bobbs-Merrill, Indianapolis, 1941.

———. *The Decisive Battle of Nashville.* Louisiana State University Press, 1956.

Holland, Cecil F. *John Hunt Morgan*. Macmillan, New York, 1942.

Johnston, William Preston. *The Life of General Albert Sidney Johnston* by his son. D. Appleton, New York, 1878.

Kerr, John Leeds. *The Louisville & Nashville: An Outline History*. Young & Otley, New York, 1933.

Killebrew, J. B. *Resources of Tennessee*. Tavel, Eastman & Howell, Nashville, 1874.

———. *Tennessee, Tobacco, Minerals and Livestock*. Tavel, Eastman & Howell, 1877.

Leahy, Ethel C. *Who's Who on the Ohio River*. E. C. Leahy Publishing Co., Cincinnati, 1931.

Long, A. L. *Memoirs of Robert E. Lee*. J. M. Stoddart & Co., New York, 1886.

Lytle, Andrew. *Bedford Forrest and His Critter Company*. Minton, Balch, New York, 1931.

Morris, Eastin. *Tennessee Gazateer*. W. Haskel Hunt, Publisher, Nashville, 1834.

Official Records of the Union and Confederate Armies. 128 vols. Government Printing Office, Washington, 1881–1901.

Official Records of the Union and Confederate Navies in the War of the Rebellion. Series L, vols. 22–28, inclusive. Government Printing Office, Washington, 1894–1922.

O'Connor, Richard. *Cavalier General Hood*. Prentice-Hall, 1949.

O'Connor, Richard. *Thomas—Rock of Chickamauga*. Prentice-Hall, 1948.

Proceedings of the Annual Meeting of the Board of Supervising Inspectors. 72 Vols. Bureau of Marine Inspection and Navigation, Washington, 1870–1942.

Putnam, A. W. *History of Middle Tennessee*. Southern Methodist Publishing House, Nashville, 1859.

Quick, Herbert and Edward. *Mississippi Steamboatin'*. Henry Holt, New York, 1926.

Ramsey, J. G. M. *The Annals of Tennessee to the End of the Eighteenth Century*. 1853. Reprinted by Kingsport Press, Inc., 1926.

Records of Enrollments and Licenses of Vessels. 29 vols. Deputy Collector of Customs, Nashville, 1837–1944.

Records of Licenses Issued to Masters, Mates, Pilots and Engineers. Steamboat Inspection Service, Nashville, 1870–1944.

Records of the United States Weather Bureau. Nashville, 1870–1944.

Robert, Henry M. *Nashville and Her Trade for 1870.* Roberts & Purvis, Nashville, 1870.

Rothrock, Mary U. *Discovering Tennessee.* University of North Carolina Press, 1936.

Scharf, J. T. *History of Confederate States Navy.* Albany, 1894.

Sherman, W. T. *Memoirs.* 2 vols. D. Appleton Co., 1875.

Tennessee Old and New. 2 vols. Tennessee Historical Commission, Kingsport Press, Inc., 1946.

Tennessee, The American Guide Series. Viking, New York, 1939.

Titus, W. P. *Picturesque Clarksville, Past and Present.* W. P. Titus, 1887.

Twain, Mark. *Life on the Mississippi.* Harper, New York, 1901.

Way, Frederick, Jr. *Pilotin' Comes Natural.* Farrar & Rinehart, New York, 1943.

——. *Directory of Western River Packets* (1950).

White, Robert H. *Tennessee, Its Growth and Progress.* Kingsport Press, Inc., Kingsport, Tenn., 1936.

Wheeler, Mary. *Steamboatin' Days: Folk Songs of the River Packet Era.* Louisiana State University Press, Baton Rouge, 1944.

Whitman, Willson. *God's Valley: People and Power Along the Tennessee River.* Viking, New York, 1939.

Williams, Samuel Cole. *Dawn of Tennessee Valley and Tennessee History.* Watauga Press, Johnson City, Tenn., 1937.

——. *Early Travels in the Tennessee Country.* Watauga Press, Johnson City, 1928.

————. *Tennessee During the Revolutionary War.* Tennessee Historical Commission, Nashville, 1944.

Williams. *Sketch of Clarksville.* Williams Clarksville Directory, 1859.

Newspapers, Periodicals, Pamphlets

Anderson, Douglas. *Old Times on the Upper Cumberland.* Series of articles appearing from time to time in the Nashville Banner, 1925–26.

Beard, William E. *Red Letter Days in Nashville.* Nashville Banner, 1925 and 1936.

————. *Nashville—The Home of History Makers.* Published by Civitan Club of Nashville, 1929.

Born and Burwell. *Geology and Petroleum Resources of Clay County, Tennessee.* Bulletin No. 47, Division of Geology, 1939.

Brooks, Addie Lou. *The Building of Trunk Line Railroads in West Tennessee, 1852–1862.* Tennessee Historical Quarterly, June, 1942.

Burchard. *The Brown Iron Ore of the Western Highland Rim, Tennessee.* Bulletin No. 39, Tennessee, Division of Geology, 1934.

Chappell, Gordon T. *The Life and Activities of General John Coffee.* Tennessee Historical Quarterly, June, 1942.

Clarkson, T. A. *History of the Nashville, Chattanooga & St. Louis Railway and the Western & Atlantic Railroad.* Nashville, 1939.

————. *Brief History of the Nashville, Chattanooga & St. Louis Railway.* Nashville, 1944.

Golden, G. H. *William Carroll and His Administration.* Tennessee Historical Magazine, February, 1902.

Horn, Stanley F. *Nashville During the Civil War.* Tennessee Historical Quarterly, March, 1945.

Hunter, W. T. *Original Biographical Notes and Comments on the River.*

Inventory of the County Archives of Tennessee, No. 11, Cheatham County (1938) and No. 95, Wilson County (1941). Historical Records Survey, W. P. A.

Newspapers. All newspapers published in Nashville from 1819 to the present which are available in Nashville libraries. Old files of newspapers published in towns along the Cumberland. These are few and for the most part badly preserved.

The Cumberland River: A Memorial to Congress. Proceedings of the Cumberland River Improvement Association in Annual Convention. Pamphlet, Nashville, 1891.

Weakley, S. A. *Cumberland River Floods.* Nashville, 1935.

Wilson & Clark. *Mussels of the Cumberland River and its Tributaries.* Bureau of Fisheries Document No. 781, Government Printing Office, Washington, 1914.

APPENDIXES

APPENDIXES

Appendix "A"

An original listing of Regular and Transient Packets, towboats, and other boats appearing at Nashville on the Cumberland River from 1819 to 1944, and other historical data pertaining to them, their owners and operators. Compiled from the records on file at the Office of the Deputy Collector of Customs, from the Annual Reports of the Bureau of Marine Inspection and Navigation (Steamboat Inspection Service), the Annual Reports of the District Engineers, United States Engineering Department, in Nashville, and from old newspapers published in Nashville and other cities and towns in Tennessee. Other sources of information are credited in the comments included as part of the list.

A list of United States Naval vessels—1861–65—known as the Western Flotilla or Mississippi Squadron which saw service on the Cumberland, Tennessee, Ohio and Mississippi Rivers.

A list of Confederate States of America Naval vessels—1861–1865—that saw service in the defense of the Mississippi River.

Regular Packets Plying the Cumberland River during the Period 1819–1830 * —Their Known Captains, and the Date of Launching

Andrew Jackson (Barner, 1823); *Belle Creole* (1823); *Caledonia* (1824); *Car of Commerce* (1827); *Citizen* (Davis); *Clinton, Columbia* (Anderson Miller, 1825); *Columbus* (Dehart); *Commerce* (Scroder, 1826); *Congress, Courier* (Ed Vaught, 1820); *Criterion, Crusader, Cumberland No. 1* (Crawford, 1819); *Cumberland No. 2* (Sterling M. Barner, Lawless,

1827); *DeWitt Clinton* (T. T. Minor, 1826); *Eclipse* (DeForrest, 1823); *Emerald* (James Lake, Wray, Wm. Bodfish, 1824); *Emigrant* (1829); *Fairy* (Henry Harrison, 1827); *Favorite* (W. F. Horne, 1822); *Franklin* (Joe Irwin, 1817); *Friendship* (1826); *General Carroll* (Gordon, 1826); *General Clark, General Coffee* (Snodgrass, 1826); *General Greene* (T. T. Minor, 1820); *General Jackson* (B. Hoskins, Joseph Smith, John Young, S. K. Green and T. T. Minor, 1818); *General Neville* (1822); *General Robertson* (Joseph Smith, 1819); *General Wayne* (Holbert, 1825); *Henry Clay* (Shalmoss, 1819); *Herald* (1824); *Hercules* (T. S. Peterson, 1826); *Home, Indiana* (1822); *James O'Hara* (Ed Vaught, 1828); *Lady Washington* (Athy, McClain, 1826); *Lafayette* (Ed Young, 1825); *Louisville* (Lawless, 1823); *Mechanic* (John Hall, 1823); *Mexico* (Clarke, 1823); *Mississippi* (1819); *Montgomery* (T. Gilbert, 1828); *Nashville No. 1* (Thos. Yeatman, John Hall, Thos. Bellsnyder, 1822); *Nashville No. 2* (Jesse Johnson, 1827); *Nashville No. 3* (T. T. Minor, Jacob Hunter, 1828); *Natchez* (1822); *New Orleans, New York* (1815); *North America* (Scott); *Pacific* (Wood, Joseph Smith, 1829); *Paragon* (Noble, 1819), *Patrick Henry* (Bartlett, 1824(?)); *Paul Jones* (1825); *Pennsylvania* (Hart, Stone, 1822); *Philadelphia* (Tyson, 1826); *Phoenix* (1828); *Pittsburgh* (Walker, 1823); *Planet, President* (Joe Miller, 1824); *Providence* (Lansdale, 1818); *Rambler* (Frank Stratton, 1823); *Red Rover No. 1* (Joseph Miller, 1828); *Riego, Rifleman* (Sterling M. Barner, T. Gilbert, 1818); *Rocket* (1820); *Rome* (H. P. Horne, Paddleford, 1828(?)); *Smithland No. 1, Spartan, St. Louis* (1818); *Talisman* (1828); *Talma* (William Dickey, 1829); *Tallyho* (Hunter, Dortch, Bellsnyder, 1829); *Telegraph* (1821); *Tennessee No. 1* (1822(?)); *Traveler* (1828); *United States* (1819); *Wasp, William Penn* (Sterling M. Barner, 1825).

TOTAL 79

---

* Many of these boats continued to ply the river during the next succeeding period. Boats are listed in the above and each succeeding schedule for the period in which they are known to have first plied the river.

Regular Cumberland River Packets during the Period 1830–1840, Their Known Captains and Date of Launching

American (M. D. F. Brooks, 1836); *Bolivar* (Robert Graham, E. S. Burge, 1831); *Bonnets O Blue* ** (Ed Vaught, 1832); *Brandywine* (Hamilton, 1828); *Burksville* ** (1834); *Cora* (James Woods, 1829); *City of Clarksville* (Joseph M. Irwin, 1839); *Cumberland No. 3* (Joseph M. Irwin, 1839); *Daniel Webster* (T. B. Eastland, 1839); *Dover No. 1* (Garrison, 1832); *Ellen Kirkman* (John Wilson, Sterling M. Barner, 1837); *Emigrant No. 2* (1832); *Erie* (Turner, 1826); *Erin* (Jacob Hunter, White, 1833); *Excell* (David Dashiel, 1839); *Forrester* (Earhart, 1827); *Favorite* * (W. F. Horne, 1831); *Gallatin* (Jacob Hunter, 1839); *General Jackson No. 2* (1833); *Gondolier* (became the Rambler, 1831); *Harry Hill* ** (A. L. Davis, Thos. H. Newell, 1832); *Hawk-Eye* (Jacob Hunter, Joseph Miller, Merritt S. Pilcher, C. M. Bradford, 1829); *Hermitage* ** (Ashbel Savage, 1838), *Hugh L. White* (John Wilson, 1839); *Huntress* (H. H. Harrison, 1834); *Jefferson* * (E. S. Burge, 1832); *Jim Brown* * (Chas. P. Jones, 1838); *John Randolph* (Joseph Miller, 1836); *Josiah Nichol* ** (Daniel Dashiel, 1838); *Lady Jackson* * (Will Hales, Ament, 1832); *Madison* (1835); *Metamora* (Thrashly, 1832); *Memphis* * (C. M. Bradford, Smith, 1831); *Mount Vernon* (A. Erwin, Jr., Lenox, Donnelly, 1832); *Nashville No. 4* (A. L. Davis, 1837); *Native* (H. H. Harrison, 1834); *Passenger* ** (Davis Embree, 1835); *President* * (Thos. Gilbert, 1831); *Rambler No. 2* * (W. H. Horne, 1831); *Randolph* (Joseph Miller, 1833); *Red Rover No. 2* (Pilcher, 1838(?)); *Reserve* (A. L. Davis); *Rocky Mountain* (Joseph F. Gibson); *Shoal Water* (C. T. Reeder, Davis Embree); *Shylock* ** (A. L. Davis, 1837); *Signal* (John Wilson, 1831); *Smithland No. 2* ** (James Lee, 1839); *Statesman* (Forsythe, 1831); *T. Gilbert* (Garrison, 1839(?)); *Tennessean* (S. M. Barner, 1829); *Tobacco Plant* * (Barton, 1831); *Toledo* (John S. Petty, 1837); *Tom Yeatman* (A. L. Davis, James Irwin, 1830); *Tuscumbia* (Jacob Hunter,

1832); *Wanderer* (Norvell, 1830); *Water Witch** (E. S. Burge, 1831); *Water Witch No. 2* (E. S. Burge, 1835).

TOTAL 57

* Built at Nashville
** Built at Smithland (except *Dover* built at Dover and *Burksville* built at Burksville, Kentucky).
All other boats were built at either Pittsburgh, Brownsville, Wheeling, Cincinnati, Louisville or Jeffersonville.

Transient *** Packets and Steamboats Plying the Cumberland during Period 1830–1840

Aid, Amulet (Harrison, 1829); *Argus* (Crooks, 1831); *Arabian* (Forsythe, 1835); *B. I. Gilman* (J. G. Anderson); *Boston* (Cadwalader, 1831); *Buffalo, Calavar, Charleston* (Thomas, 1830); *Coquette, Compromise* (Norton, 1832); *Constellation* (A. S. Robeson, 1837); *Conveyance* (Earhart); *Cygnet* (Welch); *David Crockett, Delaware* (Price, 1828); *Dispatch, Detroit* (John Carlisle, 1835); *Duquesne, Eagle* (1830); *Envoy* (Rodgers, 1831); *Express* (Reid, 1831); *Facility* (Fuller, 1827); *Fame* (Frompton, 1832); *Free Trader* (Boggs, 1832); *Fulton, Gallipolis* (1832); *Gladiator* (1834); *Helen Mar* (Fuller, 1832); *Hero* (Page); *Hunter* (Dean, 1834); *Illinois* (Ferguson, 1831); *Isora, Juanita* (1832); *Junius* (Ferguson, 1832); *Kentucky* (Clarkson); *Lady Byron* (1830); *Lady Franklin* (1829); *LaGrange* (1825); *Lily* (Manners); *Logansport* (Scantlan); *London* (Patterson); *Loyal Hanna* (Stone); *Miami* (Farmer, 1831); *Miner* (Hamet, 1833); *Monroe* (1835); *Newark,* (Read); *New York No. 2* (I. D. Spargo, 1835); *Nile* (Farrow, 1829); *Olive Branch* (Holcombe, 1833); *Osceola, Pekin* (Lee); *Pioneer* (Dawson, 1835); *Reindeer* (T. Sloan, 1834); *Rio* (F. F. Stamson, 1838); *Roanoke* (Cook, 1835); *Salem* (Ford); *Saline, Smelter* (Alex Badger, 1837); *Star of the West, Sylph* (Armstrong, 1829); *Tide, Tremont, Troy, Uncas* (Deer, 1830); *Utica, Virginia* (1826); *Virginian* (U. S. Govt. First government boat to work on channel of the river, Petty, 1829); *Visitor, Warren* (Enders, 1836); *Waterloo* (Fond, 1833); *Wheeling, William*

Hulbert (Blackston W. Martin, 1836), *W. L. Robeson* (Isiah Sellers, 1835).

TOTAL 74
TOTAL REGULAR PACKETS AND TRANSIENTS . . 131

*** A "Transient" boat is distinguished from a regular packet in that a transient boat's home port was not on the Cumberland, or it did not ply the river regularly during this period, and followed no set schedule.

Regular Cumberland River Packets during the Period 1840–1850, Their Known Captains and Date of Launching

America (Jesse Johnson, M. D. F. Brooks, 1849); *Alps* (James M. Scantlan, 1842); *Allegheny Mail* (Davis, 1844); *A. W. Vanleer* (Jacob Hunter); *Belle of Clarksville* ** (W. Gerard, 1842); *Belle of Nashville* (Newcomb, 1841); *Brooklyn* (S. J. Fowler, 1848(?)); *Brownsville, Burksville No. 2* * (Thos. J. Harmon, 1843); *Caney Fork No. 1* * (A. L. Davis, 1845); *C. E. Watkins* (E. D. Farnsworth); *Charles Carroll* (E. D. Farnsworth, 1846); *China, Clarksville No. 1* (Jacob Hunter, 1845); *Clipper* (Jacob Hunter, 1849); *Coaster* (Joiner, 1841); *Colorado* (C. T. Reeder, 1846); *Commerce* (Calvin G. Cabler, 1846(?)); *Conductor* ** (John W. Want, 1849); *Consignee* (J. A. Crouch, 1848); *Countess* ** (J. V. Throop, 1847); *Courson* (Thos. H. Newell, 1845); *Cumberland No. 4* (Jos. C. Leake, 1848); *Cumberland Valley* ** (David Duvall, 1842); *Dan Hillman* ** (1846); *Dime* * (A. L. Davis, 1847); *Doctor Watson* ** (J. V. Throop, 1845); *Dover No. 2* (Will J. Harmon, 1835); *Dover No. 3* (Gustavus Hodge, 1847); *Embassy* (C. W. Anderson, 1848); *Felix Grundy* (Sam J. Fowler, 1845); *General Taylor* (H. D. Newcomb); *Gondola* ** (J. V. Throop, 1840); *Governor Jones* (M. D. F. Brooks, 1844); *Harry Hill No. 2* (Thos. Newell, 1847); *Isaac Garrett* * (Chas. Ramos, 1845); *Jamestown* (J. D. Leake, A. D. Jenkins, 1845); *James Dick* (Thos. Bellsnyder, A. J. Jenkins, 1845); *James Woods No. 1* (James Lee, 1841); *John Marshall* (Thomas Gilbert, 1841); *Josephine, Julia Gratiot* (F. S. Thacker, 1837); *Kate Kearney, Lady Madison, Lilly of the West* (H. H. Harrison,

1844); *Lucy Long* * (Thos. Newell, 1844); *Lynwood* (Wm. Phillips, 1843); *Magyar* (J. V. Throop, 1849); *Manhattan, Marshall Ney* (John Carlisle); *May Duke* (Wm. Strong, 1845); *Melodeon* (Jacob Hunter); *Milwaukee* (S. J. Fowler); *Mingo Chief, Minstrel* (H. B. McComas, 1842); *Monedo* (Joseph Miller, 1846); *Nashville No. 5* ** (P. K. Barclay, Joseph Miller, 1841); *North Carolina* (C. W. Anderson, 1845); *Old Hickory* (R. Y. Northern, 1845); *Odd Fellow* ** (Opum Field, 1845); *Paducah* (J. M. Terrass, 1847); *Paragon* (James Lee, 1839); *Pinto* (Samuel Milliken, 1842); *Pontiac* (S. J. Folwer); *Radnow* (C. T. Reeder, 1843); *Red Rover No. 3* (Merritt S. Pilcher, C. T. Reeder, 1840); *Rose of Sharon* (F. Norment, 1843); *Sam Seay, Senate* (Warren Willard, 1844); *Shelby* (C. T. Reeder, 1850); *Sligo No. 1* (Calvin G. Cabler, 1844); *Sligo No. 2* * (Calvin G. Cabler, 1849); *Smithland No. 3, Star of the West* ** (Chas. Simpson, 1842); *St. Louis Oak* (John S. Petty, 1842); *Susquehanna* (Joseph Miller, 1845); *Suwanee* (T. Gilbert, J. C. Leake, 1846); *Swiss Boy* (O. H. Hughes, 1847); *Talleyrand No. 1* (Jacob Hunter, Drew, 1842); *Talleyrand No. 2* (Jacob Hunter, 1847); *Tennessee* (T. Yeatman, 1846); *Thames* (Calvin G. Cabler, 1843(?)); *Trident* (J. V. Throop, 1838); *Umpire* (O. H. Hughes, 1846(?)); *Uncle Ben, Wasp No. 2, Westwood* (S. Bradford, 1843); *W. Newton* (Joseph Miller, 1849); *W. Tennessee* (T. Brooks, 1840).

TOTAL 89

* Indicates boat built at Nashville
** Indicates boat built at Smithland

Transient *** Packets and Steamboats Plying the Cumberland during Period 1840–1850

Agatha, Agnes, American Eagle, Argo, Ark, Atlas, Auburn, Balloon, Belle of Pittsburgh, Blue Ridge, Bridgewater, Cashier, C. Connor, Cicero, Cinderella, Columbian, Confidence, Daniel Boone, DeKalb, Dolphin, Domain, Edwin Shippen, Enterprise, Euphrates, E. W. Stephens, Exchange, Fashion, Fort Pitt, Fortune, Fulton, Gallant, Geneva, Genesee, Gladiator, Guide, Hail

Columbia, Hard Times, Harry Tompkins, Harry of the West, Hatchey Planter, Hibernia, Highlander, Huntsville, Iola, Iris, J. B. Porter, James Ross, John Go Long, John Drennon, Kentucky, Kittaning, Lancaster, L. Collins, Louisville, Magic, Manchester, Maria, Mary Ann, Mayflower, May Queen, Melrose, Mermaid, Missouri Mail, Neck of the Woods, North Bend, Ohio Mail, Oneta, Oneida, New Orleans, Orpheus, Oswego, Penelope, Pensacola, Phoenix, Pilot, Planet, Potomac, Prairie Bird, Princeton, Richard Clayton, Rhine, Rhode Island, Ringold, Saladin, Samuel Dale, Santa Fe, Scioto Belle, Seventy-Six, Spartan, St. Charles, Tioga, Tributary, Triumph, Tuscarora, Valley Forge, Wave, Western, William Penn, Yucatan, Zanesville.

TOTAL 101
TOTAL REGULAR PACKETS AND TRANSIENTS . . 190

*** Names of captains and dates of launching have been omitted with this and succeeding periods. To include such facts would extend this study of the Cumberland beyond its scope and purpose. The author felt it necessary to list all boats, however, in order to verify certain statistics in the context.

Regular Cumberland River Packets during the Period 1850–1860, Their Known Captains, and Date of Launching

Acacia College (P. M. McGuire, 1857); *Alconia* (Joseph Miller, 1851); *A. L. Davis* * (Wm. Strong, 1853); *Ambassador* (James Wyatt, A. L. Davis, 1851); *Atlantic* (E. D. Farnsworth); *Beauty* (Jesse Joiner, 1849); *Bedford* (J. N. Corbitt); *Belle Key* (Peyton A. Key); *Blanche Lewis* (James Lee, 1855); *B. M. Runyan* (James Miller, 1858); *Cape May* (R. L. Dismukes, 1850); *Castle Garden, C. E. Hillman* (J. N. Corbitt, 1860); *Charter* (Elijah Carroll, 1856); *Chattanooga* (Baugh); *City of Huntsville* (Calvin G. Cabler, 1852); *Colonel Dickinson* (B. J. Caffery); *Cumberland No. 5* (1854(?)); *Cumberland Valley No. 2* (H. G. McComas, 1853); *Cumberland Valley No. 3* (1856(?)); *Doctor Robertson* (Calvin G. Cabler, 1854); *E. A. Ogden* (James Lee, 1855); *Eastport* (Samuel Milliken, 1852); *E. Howard* (R. Y. Northern, 1852); *Ella* (James Loring, 1854); *Embassy* *, *Emma*

Brown (R. B. Baugh, 1854); *Emma Watts* (S. Brown, 1851); *Fairfield* (John A. Couch, 1854); *Friendship, General Anderson* (1860); *Glenco, Globe* (T. Gilbert, 1849); *Grand Turk* (1857(?)); *Hartsville* * (David Hughes, 1853); *H. H. Harrison, Hazel Dell, H. D. Bacon, H. R. W. Hill* (Thos. Newell, 1852); *H. T. Yeatman* (Jacob Hunter, 1851); *Humboldt* (Wm. Strong, 1855); *Iroquois* (C. S. Patterson, 1847); *Jacob Hunter, James Johnson* (Jesse Johnson, 1856); *James Woods No. 2* (William Boyd, 1860); *John Galtor Gault, John A. Fisher* (Thos. J. Harmon, 1859); *John P. Tweed* (J. W. Lovell, 1851); *John Simpson* (1850); *Joseph Savage* (O. W. Davis, 1857); *Julian* (Jesse Erwin, 1851); *Justice* (R. B. Baugh, 1851); *Lizzie Lake* ** (P. H. Stephens, Allen Duncan, 1855); *Lookout* (Wiley Sims, 1852); *Louella* * (Chas. Ryneman, 1851); *Louisa* (A. L. Davis, 1851); *Loyal Hanna* (Wm. Henig, 1847); *Melrose, Minnetonka* (Ed. Dashiel, 1857); *Mohican* (James F. Irwin, 1848); *Monticello* (R. L. Dismukes, 1854); *Nashville No. 6* (Thos. Bellsnyder, 1849); *Navigator* (John B. Davis, 1850); *Nettie Miller* ** (J. B. Scyster, 1854); *Newsboy, Noble Ellis* * (William Dix, 1860); *Odd Fellow No. 2* (J. C. Leake, 1852); *Planter, Red Rover No. 4* (Wm. Strong, John Dashiel, 1857); *Republic* (O. W. Davis, Armstrong, C. G. Cabler, 1850); *Rescue* (R. L. Dismukes); *Rock City* * (Jesse L. Dortch, 1854); *Rough and Ready* (Towboat—named for iron furnace on lower river); *Sallie West* (J. V. Throop, 1853); *Sam Cloon, Sam Kirkman, Scotland* (R. L. Dismukes, 1855); *Senator* (W. J. Harmon, 1850); *Shipper* (J. V. Scyster, 1849); *Shylock No. 2* (O. W. Davis, 1852); *Sligo No. 3* (Chas. Ryman, 1856); *St. Cloud* (Wiley Sims); *Statesman* (J. Slidell); *Stella Blanche, Summit* (Robert Hodge, 1850); *Tempest, Tennessee* (W. C. Henegar, 1853); *Tennessee Belle* (Dean); *Toledo* (T. M. Manning, 1851); *V. K. Stevenson* (J. V. Scyster, 1856); *Warren* (J. W. Robinson, 1851); *W. H. Day* (A. L. Davis, 1852); *William Gavin* (C. T. Reeder); *William Henry* (Joseph Ambrose, 1853); *W. Newton, William Phillips, Winefred* (M. Daniels, 1854).

TOTAL 97

* Indicates boat built at Nashville
** Indicates boat built at Smithland

Transient Packets and Steamboats Plying the Cumberland during Period 1850–1860

Albertine, Alida, Altoona, American Star, Americus, Ann Lennington, Arkansas Traveller, Armada, Ashland, Asia, Atlanta, Aunt Letty, Baltimore, Banjo, Bay City, Bay State, Beatty, Bee, Belfast, Belle Creole, Belmont, Ben Coursin, Ben Golding, Black Diamond, Caddo, Caledonia, California, Caroline, City of Cairo, Chas. Belcher, Chicago, Choctaw, Clara Dean, Clara Poe, Clifton, C. Marshall, Conewago, Converse, Cremona, Crescent, Cuba, D. A. Given, David Gibson, Decotah, Defender, Delaware, Delegate, Denmark, Diamond, Dunlieth, Eclipse, Editor, Edmonia, Edward Walsh, Effie Afton, Equator, Emma Dean, Excell, Express, Fairy Queen, Fannie Farrar, Fannie Sparhawk, Fawn, Flora, Fleetwood, Forest City, Forest Rose, Fusilier, Gazelle, General Gaines, Glenwood, Golden Age, Gossamer, Greek Slave, Harmonia, Hartford, Hastings, H. Bridges, H. D. Newcomb, Hermon, Hickman, Highland Mary, Hudson, Huron, Ida May, Ionian, Irene, Ironton, Isaac Shelby, James Raymond, J. B. Corson, Jeanette, Jenny Gray, Jenny Lind (circus boat), *J. G. Cline, J. H. Conn, J. H. Lucas, J. Morrissett, John Bell, John Tompkins, Julia Ann, Kate French, Kate Larchet, Kentucky, Knoxville, LaCrosse, Lake of the Woods, Last Chance, Latrobe, Lebanon, L. F. Linn, Lightfoot, Logan, Louis Whiteman, Lucy May, Lucy Robinson, Ludelle, Lunettc, Lydia Collins, Madonna, Magnolia, Mattie Wayne, Olive, Malta, Mansfield, May Queen, Midas, Minerva, Minnehaha, Mohawk, Moses, Greenwood, Neptune, Newton Waggoner, New York, North America, Northern Light, North River, N. W. Graham, Ophelia, Pennsylvania, Peru, Portsmouth, Princess, Progress, Quaker City, Rapidan, R. B. Hamilton, Reliance, Reserve, Return, Richard H. Lee, Robert Campbell, Robert Rogers, Rochester, Rosalie, Sacramento, Sam Snowden, Schuylkill, S. F. J. Trabue, Shelby, Shenango, Sir William Wallace, S. P. Hubbard, St. Clair, St. Frances, St. Louis, St. Nicholas, Submarine, Swallow, T. C. Twichell, Tiber, Tigress, Tom Scott, Twin City, Uncle Tom, U. S. Mail, U. S. Aid, Vermont,*

Washington, Wenona, White Bluff, William A. Eaves, William T. Nelson, Yorktown.

TOTAL 184
TOTAL REGULAR PACKETS AND TRANSIENTS . . 281

Regular Cumberland River Packets during the Period 1860–1870, Their Known Captains, and Date of Launching

A. Baker (J. H. Trover, W. H. Lovell, 1864); *Abe McDonald* (William Dix (?)); *Ad Hine, A. H. Kilgour* (John Kilgour); *Aid* (Issac T. Leake); *Alert* (H. C. Henegar); *Alpha* (Thos. G. Ryman, 1864); *Anna White* (Joseph F. Miller); *Belle of Peoria, Bermuda* (Thos. G. Ryman, John A. Couch, 1864); *Bertha* (U. B. Peirsell); *B. H. Cook* (1869); *Burksville No. 3* (J. W. Lovell, Wiley Sims, 1869); *Camelia* (Thos. Poe, T. H. Golding, R. C. Mason); *Clipper* (J. T. Boone, 1865); *Ella* (1867); *Ella Hughes* (William Dix, 1867); *Emma* (Jones, 1869); *Emma Floyd* (James Shenowith, 1863); *Fannie Brandees* (1864); *General Seigel, George S. Kinney* (William Kiber, 1863 (?)); *George H. Kiber* (John T. Kiber); *Havana* (E. Pearce); *Hugh Martin* (J. C. Feelty); *Ida* (L. C. Spiller); *Imperial* (H. G. McComas); *I. N. Phillips* (John Clark, 1866); *Irene, James Fiske, Jr.* (1870); *Jesse Dortch* (1863); *J. H. Baldwin, John Lumsden* (O. H. Davis, 1868); *J. L. Graham* (Ben Goad); *J. R. Gilmore* (R. W. Harmon); *J. T. McCombs* (Wilkes); *Kate Putnam* (George Reid, 1864); *Kingfisher* (Will Harmon); *Lewellin* (1869); *Lizzie Martin, Louella* (B. K. Hazlepp); *Marmora, May Duke* (A. L. Davis); *Mercury, Mollie Able *** (1864); *Mollie Gratz* (W. H. Lovell, 1866); *M. S. Mephan* (Harry E. McComas) *Nashville No. 7* (Beatty, 1860); *Noble Ellis, Onward* (J. S. Melton); *Palestine, Pink Varble* (1865); *Pioneer* (H. King); *Rebecca* (Sam Hildreth); *Revenue, Rob Roy, Robert Moore* (John Farrell); *Rose Hite,* (G. W. Evans, 1864); *Rowena* (Alex Frazier); *Sam Orr* (Wm. McClury, 1861); *Talisman* (William Strong, Wiley Sims, 1863); *Tennessee No. 2* (J. W. Peterson);

Tyrone (Tom Harmon, 1864); *Umpire* (John S. Bateman, 1868).

TOTAL 64

* Built in Nashville

The small number of regular packets plying the Cumberland during this period was the direct result of the War Between the States. On the other hand, the transient steamboats bringing supplies and troops to Nashville greatly increased as shown by the following list.

Transient Packets and Steamboats Plying the Cumberland During Period 1860–1870

Abeono, Adda Lyon, Adelaide, Alex Speirs, Alice, Amelia, Amelia Poe, Americ, Anna, Annie Laurie, Anglo-Saxon, Appleton Belle, Arcola, Argonant, Argos, Arizona, Armadilla, Armenia, Attalata, Bateman, Belle, Ben Franklin, Bon Accord, Bill Henderson, Brilliant, Bravo, Brown, Buckeye State, Burd Levi, Capitola, Caroline, Carrie, Carrie Jackson, Carter, Champion, Charleston, Charmer, Chas. Brown, Chateau, City Belle, City of Mobile, City of Pekin, City of Savannah, Clara Belle, Clara Denning, Cleona, Colona, Colossus, Commercial, Commodore Perry, Convoy No. 2, Cora S., Cordelia Ann, Cornelia, Crescent City, C. T. Dumont, Curlew, Damsel, Dan Rice, Des Moines, Dispatch, D. H. Blunk, Diana, Doctor Kane, Done No. 2, Dora, Duke, Duke of Argyle, Echo No. 2, Effie Deans, E. H. Fairchild, Ella Faber, Emperor, Farragut, Fort Wayne, General Grant, General Halleck, Glenwood, Goldfinch, G. P. Webb, G. R. Gelman, Guibon, Hard Times, Hambleton Belle, Hartupee, Helen, Henry Fitzhugh, Hercules, Huntress, Huntsman, Ida Handy, Idaho, Iowa, Island City, Jacob Poe, James Montgomery, Jason, J. B. Ford, J. D. Hine, Jennie Hopkins, Jennie Hubbs, J. H. Dicken, J. H. Doane, J. H. Johnson, J. Means, J. H. Trover, J. H. Webb, Jim Watson, J. L. Hyatt, Kate Capell, Kate Howard, Kate Kearney, Kate Morrison, Kellogg, Kenton, Kentucky, Keystone, Laclede, Ladonia, Lady Pike, Lake Erie, Lancaster No. 4, Lawrence, Lavinia, Logan, Leni Leoti, Leona, Leonora No. 2, Liberty, Lilly, Lina Drown, Linden, Linton, Little Condor, Little Giant, Live Oak, L. M. Kennett, Lorena, Louise, Lucy Bertram, Luna, Majestic, Mariner, Mary

Cook, Mary Miller, Masonic Gem, Melnotte, Milbrey, Monsoon, Montana, M. V. Baird, Nannie, Nannie Byers, Nangetuck, Navigator, Nettie Rogers, New Golden State, Nightingale, Nora, Norman, Nymph, Ohio Valley, Ollie Sullivan, Omaha, Paragon, Phantom, Piketon, Pilgrim, Pine Grove, Pine Hill, Pocahontas, Prairie Rose, Prima Donna, Princess, J. S. Pringle, Raven, Richmond, R. K. Dunkerson, R. L. Woodward, R. M. Patton, Robert Fulton, Romeo, Rose Hambledon, Sallie List, Sam B. Young, Satan, Savannah, Schuyler, Science No. 2, Shamrock, Sherman, Shreveport, Silver Cloud, Silver Lake, Silver Moon, Silver Spray, Sioux City, Sonora, Spray, Star, Star Gray Eagle, Starlight, Stephen Bayard, Stephen Decatur, Superior, Tacony, Telegraph, Thistle, T. J. Emory, Trio, Try Us, Tycoon, Undine, Venango, Venus, Victor, Volunteer, War Eagle, Western Virginia, Westmoreland, W. F. Curtis, Whale, W. J. McClay, W. T. Carter, W. W. Crawford, Yorktown No. 2. Also, the J. P. Webb, J. R. Hoyle, J. S. Hall, Judge McClure, Judge McGowan, Julia, Juliet, J. W. Cheeseman.

TOTAL 233
TOTAL REGULAR PACKETS AND TRANSIENTS . . 297

Regular Cumberland River Packets during the Period 1870–1880, Their Known Owners, Date of Launching, and Other Historical Information

Ada Heilman (Arthur & Massengale, owners, Captain John L. Bateman 1871—Burned at Paducah 6–27–1874). *A. G. Henry* (Referred to as Cumberland and Ohio packet—1880). *Alex Kendall* (A. T. Armstrong, 1874—named for Nashville tobacco merchant). *Andes* (operated by the Nashville, Louisville and Cincinnati St. L. Line—Chas. Mubleman, Captain). *Arch P. Green* (J. W. Lovell, owner. W. H. Lovell—1873—sold to John B. Anderson in 1878). *Armada* (a side wheel packet—first on Cumberland in 1870—owned by Ben F. Egan of Paducah—R. Y. Northern, Captain. Ran from Nashville to Paducah.) *Bart E. Linehan* (owned by Tom Gallagher—1880. Later sold to New Ryman Line. Had a colorful career on both ends of the Cumberland and also the Ohio. Burned at Nashville 3–30–1905). *B. G. Wood* (M. M. Leake, A. T. Armstrong, R. F. Fergus—1875. A well known Nashville packet—named for Nashville merchant). *Bolivar H. Cooke* (James W. Lovell, owner and Captain—1873.

Named for Nashville dry goods merchant. Sold to Thos. G. Ryman and when Peoples Line was liquidated in 1878 she was purchased by George S. Throop of Evansville). *B. S. Rhea No. 1* (Owned by Thos. G. Ryman, built at Paducah in 1878 and captained by James S. Tyner. The forerunner of the *B. S. Rhea No. 2,* which became the flagship of the Ryman Line packets and on which Tyner served for 16 straight years. Named for one of Nashville's most prosperous grain merchants). *Caney Fork No. 2* (Built at Paducah—1880. W. H. Lovell, Captain. Operated only short time as packet, then entered towing.) *Celina No. 1* (James W. Lovell, owner—Wiley Sims, Captain—1876. Later sold to Kendall Line—W. H. Carroll, Master). *Clyde* (Built at Jeffersonville—1880). *C. N. Davis* (T. A. Lovell. An upper Cumberland packet in the Good Intent Line. W. S. Bowman had an interest in this boat). *C. W. Anderson* (Thos. G. Ryman owner. J. A. Couch, Captain—1876. Regular packet Nashville to Cairo). *Dora Cabler* (James W. Lovell and one of the best packets owned by him. Built in 1877—Thomas Lovell, master. Ran between Nashville and Evansville in 1878 and later switched to Nashville and Burnside). *E. B. Stahlman* (James W. Lovell—1876. Another fine Lovell boat. Operated in the Peoples Line—Nashville to Burnside and was sold in 1878 to John H. Throop, Jr. of Evansville. Employed on lower river as regular packet. Destroyed by ice on January 11, 1879. Named for Major E. B. Stahlman, outstanding railroad executive and later publisher of the "Nashville Banner"). *Eddyville* (Thomas G. Ryman, William Strong, James S. Tyner—1871. Operated on both ends of Cumberland and a very fine packet. There is a tradition that James W. Lovell owned this boat prior to Ryman but this has not been verified. William Dix at one time operated her in the Nashville-Burnside trade). *Emma Graham* (a regular packet between Nashville and Evansville—Hod Knowles, Captain). *Frank P. Gracey* (Registered owners, Capt. Wiley Sims of Nashville, G. J. Gammer and John Goff of Evansville. Named for outstanding citizen of Clarksville. A very fine packet. Built in 1872. Destroyed by fire February 15, 1873 at Dutch Bend on Ohio River). *Gus Fowler* (A Fowler boat of Paducah. Built 1880 and named for Captain Gustavus Fowler of that city. One of the largest and most palatial packets of this era. Seen frequently at Nashville). *Henrietta* (owned by Shep Green of Nashville, who was her captain. A small but keen packet built in 1879 and had a long and colorful career on the lower Cumberland). *Hettie Bliss* (Built at Nashville in 1875. Owned and operated on the upper river by W. H. Lovell, who did a fine business with a small boat. Her gross tonnage was 31.20 tons. She went up Obey and Caney Fork rivers and where the larger boats could not go. Even now, residents in the upper river section speak of this boat). *John S. Bransford* (owned by James W. Lovell and one of the better known Nashville–Burnside packets. Built in 1872. Named for a Nashville financier. W. E. Byers, Captain. After collapse of Peoples Line in 1878, she was purchased by Alex Kendall). *John S. Hopkins* (referred to as an Ohio and Cumberland packet, but there is no record of her at Nashville, except in Spring of 1881. She was built at Pittsburgh in 1880 and burned December 20, 1881 at Evansville. Owned by the Fowlers of Paducah). *Julian Gracey* (A well known, shallow draft packet built at Clarksville in 1880 and owned by Clarksville interests. Frank Gracey, A. J. Cowleshaw, James Lee and James M. Grasty served as her masters. Named for the son of Captain Frank Gracey. Ran up Red River and also on both the lower and upper Cumberland). *Katie Vertrees* (A small boat of 22.19 gross tons. Owned and captained by F. W. Youree). *Laura L. Davis* (A Nashville–St. Louis packet. O. W. Davis, owner and captain. A large and handsome packet of 510.61 gross tons built in 1873). *Matt Gracey* (another Clarksville packet. Named for the brother and partner of Captain Frank Gracey of Clarksville. W. D. Cowleshaw, Master. Well known on the Cumberland and a popular boat). *Mollie Ragon* (operated by Ben F. Egan of Paducah. Built at Evansville, 1870. R. Y. Northern, captain. A large packet which ran from Nashville to Paducah. The *Armada* was sister ship to this boat). *Nashville No. 8* (built Cincinnati, 1871—396 gross tons. Captain, P. K. Barclay. Ran as regular packet between Nashville and Cincinnati, then switched or sold to interests on Ohio River in 1873 under Captain Kern. Came back to Cumberland around 1874 or 1875 and J. W. Lovell had an interest in her. W. S. Bowman was her last master on Cumberland). *R. M. Bishop* (H. M. Allison). *Sam Fowler* (W. H. Lovell—formerly the Caney Fork. An up-river packet and did a lot of business). *Shannon* (A large Ohio River packet. Built at Cincinnati in 1870—546.48 gross tons. Seen frequently on the Cumberland). *Shipper's Own* (Said to be one of the finest packets owned by Capt. Thomas G. Ryman, who was her master. Built at Pittsburgh in 1873—354.02 gross tons. Ran as regular packet—Nashville to Cairo. Also plied the upper Cumberland). *Silverthorne* (Josh V. Throop, owner and master. Built in Evansville—1872. 209 gross tons. A fine packet and a popular one. Nashville to Evansville was her regular run). *Thomas D. Fite* (James W. Lovell, owner and master. Built at Jeffersonville in 1880—314.56 gross tons. This was the flagship of the Lovell Line for several years. She was as "elegant" as any packet to run in the Nashville-Burnside trade). *T. T. Hillman* (Built at Paducah in 1875—196.45 gross tons—named for Thomas Tennessee Hillman, iron magnate, son of Dan Hillman, one of the pioneers of that industry. Owned by Capt. Thomas G. Ryman. Joe L. Ambrose, master—burned at Miami Bend on Missouri River August 29, 1882). *West Wind* (Captain William Strong. A regular Nashville to Evansville packet. Also ran one or two seasons in a combine with the *Ella Hughes* and *Burksville* between Nashville and Burnside in the upper Cumberland Packet Company Line. William Dix was superintendent of this Company). *W. L. Buckham* (William Nelson was captain of this packet which ran between Nashville and Cincinnati for two seasons).

TOTAL 40

NOTE—The names of Captains in the above and succeeding schedules are not always given. Most of the packets had several different captains or masters during their careers. For the sake of brevity, it was deemed the better policy to list the names of these captains and other licensed officers beginning with the year 1870 under a different schedule in the Appendix, followed by the names of the packets on which they were employed. By this cross reference, both the names of the packets and the names of the officers serving on them may be readily ascertained.

Transient Packets and Other Steamboats on the Cumberland River during the Period 1870–1880

Ajax No. 2 (a towboat—W. D. Cowleshaw). *B. D. Wood* (1873 —listed in Nashville in 1874–1875). *B. H. Hunt* (Vansickle—a towboat). *Brill* (M. A. Cox—a towboat). *Charles Brown* (Ben F. Hall). *Exchange* (1866). *George Spangler* (1873). *Gray Eagle* (John Cartwright). *Glasgow* (Andy Robinson—towboat). *Grafton. G. W. Thomas. Hornet* (1880). *Hot Spur* (In Nashville 1878). *J. E. Rankin. John A. Gilmore* (1871—a towboat between points on the Ohio River and Nashville. A large boat 503.09

gross tons). *John Harper. Josh V. Throop* (An Evansville-Nashville packet built in the former city in 1880. Owned by the Throop family and named for its best known member. Captain "Josh" was beloved by all rivermen and captained many of the finest packets on the river). *J. S. Neal* (listed as a towboat). *Kanawha* (listed as a towboat). *Kate Robinson* (listed in Nashville in 1872). *Laura Knight* (F. W. Youree, owner and master). *Liberty No. 4* (listed as a towboat). *Lida Norvell* (listed as a towboat). *Lucille Nowlin. Mary Clees* (An upper river boat engaged in towing. Joseph Clees and Stamford Breedlove, masters. Sunk March 25, 1881 above Nashville, exact location not verified). *Messenger* (Built at Pittsburgh in 1865—437 gross tons). *Penguin* (1877—listed as a towboat). *Petrel No. 2* (a towboat). *Rover* (Greenelee—a towboat). *R. W. Skillinger. Sallie Carney* (W. T. Woollard, owner, J. T. Green, master). *Sam Brown* (a towboat). *Silver Springs* (William Searcy of Clarksville, master. A small boat—28 gross tons). *S. K. Hale* (a towboat owned by St. Bernard Coal Company. Thomas Pierson, Master. 30.45 gross tons). *Spray* (Advertised in winter of 1870 as regular Nashville packet to operate between Nashville and Evansville. Arrived in February, made several trips under Captain Gus Brown, but did not return in subsequent years). *Storm* (a rather large towboat from Pittsburgh—engaged in hauling coal). *Sylvan City* (A towboat—operated by Southern Pump Company on upper Cumberland—W. H. Lovell, Master). *Tom Jasper* (listed as a towboat). *Tom Reece* (a towboat). *Varmint* (A towboat, W. H. Lovell, Master). *Wild Cat* (Towboat).

TOTAL   41
TOTAL REGULAR PACKETS AND TRANSIENTS . .   81

Regular Cumberland River Packets during the Period 1880–1890, Their Known Owners, Date of Launching, and Other Historical Information

Benton McMillin (James W. Lovell—1883. Later became the *Pike*—See illustration. Plied the upper Cumberland for many years and a favorite packet. Named for Governor Benton McMillin). *B. S. Rhea No. 2* (Ryman and Tyner. Built Jeffersonville—1886—203.77 gross tons. A regular Nashville and Puducah packet. Beautifully equipped and one of the best managed packets on the Cumberland. Tyner her Captain.). *Burnside No. 1* (There is no record of this boat registered in Nashville. The newspapers carry her name, on several occasions. Tradition is that she plied between Burnside and Celina—seldom venturing to Nashville). *City of Clarksville* (Official records show she was built at Jeffersonville in 1886—194.6 tons. No record of ownership, but "old timers" state she was owned by Clarksville interests. Ran on the Cumberland-Nashville-Clarksville-Paducah for 5 years. Later entered Ohio trade, then on the Ouachita River. Sunk in 1908 on Red River). *Crusader* (Formerly the *Sam Fowler*—rebuilt at Nashville in 1884—302.07 gross tons. Later used as a sand digger—Fountain Spillers, Master). *Dover* (Thos. G. Ryman owned this boat and put her in the Nashville-Dover trade to compete with the *Henrietta* and other independent packets). *E. G. Ragon* (Thomas G. Ryman—Built Jeffersonville in 1887—309 tons. This was one of Ryman's finest packets. She ran regularly from Nashville to Cairo and other points on the Ohio). *Ella* (A Lovell Line boat and a good money-maker between Nashville-Burkesville-Burnside). *H. K. Bedford* (owned by Armstrong and Parmenter. Built Jeffersonville—1885—A well known Nashville-Burnside packet for several years). *I. T. Rhea* (Thomas G. Ryman, built at Jeffersonville—1888—199.54 gross tons. Named for I. T. Rhea, Nashville grain man and for years associated with the Cumberland and Tennessee steamboat trade. This boat was formerly the Sam P. Jones. Sunk April 6, 1895, head of Brook's Island—Cumberland River. A splendid boat and one of the most popular). *J. H. Hillman* (Thomas G. Ryman. Built at Jeffersonville—1882—281.68 tons. Regular packet—Nashville to Paducah—Cairo-Evansville for about 7 years. Sold to J. R. Handly who converted her to the *J. J. Odil*). *J. J. Odil* (J. R. Handly—1889. The former *J. H. Hillman*. Named for one of Nashville's leading merchants. W. B. Harris, Master. Ran the Nashville-Burnside trade for several years). *Joe Fowler* (A Fowler packet—built at Jeffersonville, 1888—356 tons, and a superb boat. Identified in the Paducah-Evansville trade but ran regularly up to Nashville). *John Fowler* (Owned by Alex Kendall and Arch P. Green. Built at Jeffersonville 1886—237 gross tons. Used in Nashville-Burnside trade. Since this was typical packet in that trade, her measurements might be interesting—149 long—30 feet breadth, 3½ feet draft. W. A. Crawford, A. T. Armstrong, Masters). *John W.*

Hart (A Lovell Line packet—built at Jeffersonville—1890—99.20 gross tons. Ran in Nashville-Burnside trade for five years. Sunk at lower Holliman Island above Granville on the Cumberland April 5, 1895). *J. P. Drouillard* (Thomas G. Ryman. A typical Nashville-Paducah-Cairo-Evansville packet. Originally the *Bolivar H. Cook*. Named for an iron industrialist of Nashville. A very popular boat. Length, 165 feet—breadth 31—draft 5. Dismantled in 1892 after a lengthy career). *L. P. Ewald* (Jeffersonville—1881—359 tons. Owned by Major L. T. Armstrong and Wiley Parmenter. Sold to Thos. G. Ryman and renamed the *Sam P. Jones*). *L. T. Armstrong* (built at Jeffersonville—1888—197 tons. Owned by Major L. T. Armstrong and Thomas H. Armstrong. Regular packet—Nashville to Burnside. Sold around 1890 to Capt. Thomas G. Ryman, who operated her for two seasons. Burned on Alabama River 1892). *Matt F. Allen*—(Lovell Line packet—Nashville-Burnside. Built at Jeffersonville—1887—245.12 tons. Another of the fine Lovell boats and one which did a tremendous business). *Nashville No. 9* (Also refererd to as the *City of Nashville*—built at Jeffersonville in 1881—319.46 tons. A Lovell Line packet—employed on both ends of the Cumberland. She was sold around 1891 to interests on lower river. Renamed the *Allen J. Duncan,* then operated on the Ohio for several years). *Nat F. Dortch* (A Lovell Line packet. Operated in Nashville-Burnside trade. Named for prominent tobacco merchant and broker in Nashville). *Pearl* (A Lovell Line packet. Built at Paducah—1882—A very small boat. Later sold to J. R. Handly who put her in towing business for Handly, Dismukes, Shaffer Lumber Company. H. S. Robinson, Master). *Sam J. Keith* (Owned by T. H. Armstrong. Built at Jeffersonville—1882—358.31 tons. Ran Nashville to Burnside trade. Named for Nashville financier and did a large business for several seasons. Dimensions—162 feet long, 32 feet in breadth, 5-foot draft). *Sam P. Jones* (Thomas G. Ryman—the former *L. P. Ewald* of this period. Named for the famous Evangelist who converted Captain Ryman. A popular Nashville-Burnside packet for several seasons. Referred to by river people as *Samp Jones*). *W. H. Cherry* (A Ryman Line packet, and a large one. Built at Jeffersonville—1882—396.07 tons. Highly advertised as the "most refined" packet owned by that line. She ran the Nashville-Paducah-Cairo trade and became a popular boat). *William Porter* (Owned by T. H. Armstrong. Was advertised as an upper river packet in 1888. She was an Independent Line boat).

TOTAL 26

Transient Packets and Other Steamboats on the Cumberland River during the Period 1880–1890

Charles A. Blackman (Built at Evansville—1884—25.29 gross tons. Thomas Nolan, Master). *Clayton H. Webb* (Cincinnati—1888—98 gross tons—a towboat on upper Cumberland). *Crescent* (Built at Burnside—1888—34.82 tons. Owned by Burnside interests. Operated in that section). *Dora Mae* (Nashville—1885—a top-water towboat. Harvey Carroll, pilot). *E. T. Holman* (registry shows her to be a towboat—built at Nashville—1887—71.59 gross tons). *Galatea* (A small steam tug—Carroll, Master). *Hibernia* (Built at Rock Castle—1881—152.88 tons. Ayer & Lord Tie Company—towboat). *Ida* (A top-water towboat—22.82 tons—W. P. Jones, Master). *James R. Skiles* (Built at Bowling Green—1884—82.86 tons—a busy towboat during this period). *J. D. Carter* (Built at Nashville in 1886—82.21 tons. Owned by J. R. Handly and employed principally in the lumber trade. This boat had a belt drive). *J. H. Hickman* (A towboat). *John Orm* (A towboat—1881—15.55 tons. John Orm Lumber Company). *Kenton* (A towboat. Owned or chartered by the Nashville Coal Company—H. S. Robinson, Master). *Louise* (Another top-water towboat). *Lucy Robertson* (A towboat). *Paducah* (A small towboat—said to have blown up at Nashville or vicinity). *Sycamore* (Built at Evansville in 1889. The former *O. E. Stockell*. Later became the *Dan Lindsey*. Employed by Sycamore Powder Mills to haul its products to Nashville. Major E. C. Lewis frequently rode this boat to the mills while he owned them). *T. L. Herbert* (A towboat used by The Herbert Sand Company, built at Cincinnati—1883—316.83 tons). *T. Shiver* (listed as a towboat). *W. B. Cole* (listed as a towboat).

TOTAL 20
TOTAL REGULAR PACKETS AND TRANSIENTS . . 46

Regular Cumberland River Packets during the Period
1890–1900, Their Known Owners, Date of Launching,
and Other Historical Information

Alex Perry (A Ryman Line packet—built at Jeffersonville, 1891
—172.96 tons. Named for Nashvillian who helped found the
stockyard business. James S. Tyner was her first master. She
ran the Nashville-Paducah-Cairo trade. Burned in 1896). *Ashland City* (A Ryman Line packet. Built at Jeffersonville, 1892—
94.55 tons. John A. Roundtree, Master. Captain Ryman operated
this packet between Nashville and Clarksville to ward off competition and to give daily service to shippers between such
points). *Bob Dudley* (A Ryman Line packet. Built at Jeffersonville, 1897—159.73 tons. Length 160, breadth 29, draft 3. Ran
in the Nashville-Burnside trade. Named for one of founders of
Gray-Dudley Hardware & Foundry Co., T. H. Armstrong, Master. A fine packet which ran until December 20, 1916, when she
sank at the Nashville wharf, later broke loose and was completely destroyed when she hit the Jefferson Street Bridge. She
was sold in 1905 to the New Ryman Line, Inc.). *Burnside No. 2*
(Another Burnside packet and owned by interests at that place.
Ran mostly between Burnside and Celina). *Chancey Lamb* (A
Ryman Line packet and towboat. Built Dubuque, Iowa, 1892—
194 tons. Sunk near Clarksville February 14, 1911. She was
purchased by the new Ryman Line in 1905 and sold in 1907 to
John B. Ransom & Company of Nashville. Operated from 1894
to 1900 as packet in Nashville-Burnside trade, and thereafter
as a towboat on both ends of the Cumberland). *City of Burkesville* (owned by the Burnside & Burksville Transportation Company. Regular packet between Burnside and Celina. A small
boat but did a good business). *Crescent* (*New Crescent*—owned
by Burnside interests. This boat was listed as a packet and may
have been the *Crescent* of 1880–1890 built over in 1891—88.88
tons. There is no record of her ownership. Old timers say
she entered the towing business around 1896 and was later dismantled). *D. A. Goodwin* (Built at Evansville, 1889—69 tons.
This was a packet which was seen on the river for only a season
or two. She became the *O. E. Stockell* which in turn became the

Sycamore. Her trade was between Nashville and Evansville. There is reason to believe she was built in 1887 and not in 1889 as shown by the records). *Dick Clyde* (Built Rock Island in 1881—76 tons. First a packet and later a towboat. On the Cumberland she ran in the Nashville-Burnside trade almost exclusively. Sister ship to the *C. M. Pate*—Nashville to Carthage. Sunk at Dover Straits below Nashville May 9, 1900. Raised). *Dick Fowler* (Owned by the Fowlers of Paducah. Built Evansville, 1892—367 tons. A very large and handsome packet. Regular trade, Evansville-Cairo. Seen at Nashville frequently and a popular boat). *Henry Harley* (Owned by J. R. Handly, of Nashville and other members of his family. Built at Jeffersonville 1898—162 tons. Length 160, beam 29, draft 3⁹⁄₁₀ feet. Regular trade Nashville to Burnside. Named for Nashville merchant. Ran without interruption until January 13, 1917 when she was blown on to the bank at Nashville and was dismantled. She was purchased by the New Ryman Lines. One of the last Cumberland River packets). *H. W. Buttorff* (A Ryman Line packet. Built at Jeffersonville, 1896—254 tons. James S. Tyner owned an interest in this fine packet and was her first master. Regular trade Nashville to Paducah. Length 160, beam 30, draft 4. Named for one of founders of Phillips & Buttorff Company, Nashville, and prominently identified with river affairs for more than 40 years). *James N. White* (owned by J. R. Handly, H. J. Shaffer, W. M. Farriss and W. D. Cowleshaw, who was her first master. Built at Nashville in 1893—77.19 tons. Not a large or handsome packet but under skillful management did as much business as the best. Regular run Nashville to Burnside. The machinery for this boat came from the *Pearl.* She was also captained by S. B. Walker, J. J. Linder and by W. T. Hunter who ran her for years with his father W. A. Hunter as mate). *J. B. Richardson* (A Ryman Line packet. Built at Jeffersonville 1898—191 tons. One of the last packets built by Captain Ryman. Regular run Nashville-Paducah-Evansville or Cairo. W. S. Bowman first master. Burned at Paducah Nov. 18, 1913. She then belonged to the Cumberland River Steamboat Company headed by W. W. Parmenter and Thomas G. Ryman, Jr., who had purchased her in 1910 from the New Ryman Line. Named for prominent shoe merchant of Nashville). *John W. Thomas* (A Lovell Line boat, built at Jeffersonville 1897—158.42 gross tons. J. W. Lovell, master. Named for president of N. C. & St. L. Railroad. Regular run Nashville-Burnside. Sunk at Butler's Landing, upper Cumberland, 1901 (?) Raised and sold to Louisville & Evansville Packet Company. One of the last packets operated personally by Captain Lovell). *O. E. Stockell* (Built in Evansville 1889 (?), became the *Sycamore*. Named for a prominent Nashvillian. Ran for a short time between Nashville and Paducah. She was converted to a towboat. Owned by W. W. Parmenter, A. T. Armstrong, Alex Kendall and S. B. Walker. W. E. Dodd, Master. Due to a question regarding date of change to *Sycamore* she is listed in this period). *P. D. Staggs* (Owned by Alex Kendall and A. T. Armstrong. Built at Jeffersonville 1893—261.88 gross tons. A. T. Armstrong, Master, killed on board by drunken raftsman near Nashville Feb. 2, 1895. A good packet, regular run Nashville-Burnside). *R. Dunbar* (A Ryman Line packet. Built Jeffersonville 1895—252 gross tons. Length 160, beam 29.4, draft 6.4. T. G. Ryman, Jr. her first master. J. S. Tyner and Tom Gallagher owned an interest in this packet. Regular run Nashville-Burnside trade. She was sunk at Matlock's Bar above Nashville on July 21, 1904. Raised and ran for years. After Captain Ryman's death, was sold to New Ryman Line which sold her in 1913 to Ralph E. Gaches, Point Pleasant, W. Virginia. Became the *General Crowder*. A very popular and money-making packet). *R. T. Coles* (made her maiden trip from Nashville up river January 9, 1897. She had a short career. Sunk at Kings Eddy below Hunters Point on the Cumberland April 3, 1897. Said to be a very nice but small packet). *Tennessee* (Built at Jeffersonville 1897—248 tons. S. K. Hill, master. Built for Tennessee River trade, and owned by St. Louis and Tennessee River Packet Company. Captain W. T. Hunter is authority for statement this boat ran in Nashville-Paducah trade for several seasons between 1897 and 1905). *Thomas Parker* (a packet and a towboat. Built in St. Louis 1894—57.83 tons. Registered owners, W. T. Carroll, Alex Kendall and W. W. Parmenter. After several seasons in Nashville-Burnside trade became a towboat—Carroll, Master). *Will J. Cummins* (owned by Cumberland River Packet Company—W. S. Bowman, master. Built at Jeffersonville 1895—177.25 gross tons. Named for prominent Nashville industrialist. Sunk April 19, 1901 near Bear Creek Island on lower Cumberland. This packet was exceptionally well proportioned and very fast. She ran a race with the *R. Dunbar* [see text]. Regular runs—both the upper and lower Cumberland). *W. K. Phillips* (Ryman Line Packet—

built Jeffersonville 1892—195.06 tons. Shep Green owned an interest in her and was her first master. She ran regularly in Nashville-Paducah-Cairo trade, but also was frequently seen in the trade above Nashville. One of Ryman's best packets. Sunk at Dover Island lower Cumberland, 1897. John A. Couch also captained this boat).

Total 23

Transient Packets and Other Steamboats on the Cumberland River during the Period 1890–1900

A. Frank (towboat). *A. L. Goldberg* (towboat, built at Nashville 1895—58.20 tons. Registered owners, W. T. and Humphrey Hardison, Harvey Parrish, M. M. Leek, master. Used in sand and gravel business of Hardison & Company). *Al Martin* (towboat). *Bessie* (towboat). *City of Paducah. Eclipse* (a small light draft towboat. W. S. Bowman is said to have been her master). *Eileen* (towboat). *Emma Cooper* (towboat). *Eureka* (a towboat). *Fred Hartwig* (towboat). *Fritz* (towboat). *Gasconade* (a towboat. Built at Loutrie Island, Missouri 1891—74 tons. Operated in St. Louis and on the Missouri River). *G. M. Sively* (towboat). *Grace Smith* (towboat). *Jacob Heatherington* (towboat). *Jacob Richtman* (towboat). *Jack Frost* (towboat). *J. F. Buckham* (towboat). *J. M. Powell* (towboat). *John Orm No. 3* (towboat. Built at Paducah 1888—95.33 tons. Dodge Lumber Company, registered owners). *John T. Carson* (built at Nashville—1892— 47.60 tons. Official registry silent as to ownership. No renewal of her papers after 1894). *Josie* (towboat). *Key City* (towboat). *Lora* (towboat). *Lyda* (towboat). *Maggie Bell* (towboat). *Neomie Bauer* (towboat). *Olivette* (towboat). *Pattie* (towboat). *Pavonia* (towboat—built at Metropolis 1892—132 tons. Registered owner—Illinois Tie Company). *Peter Hontz* (towboat). *Polar Wave* (towboat). *R. A. Speed* (towboat). *Raymond* (a towboat. Built at Nashville 1893—45.16 tons. Joseph Irwin registered owner. A. J. Cowleshaw, master). *Rock City* (towboat. Built at Nashville 1897—54.22 tons. Benedict Bros. registered owner. James Leek, Master). *Russell Lord* (towboat). *Ten Broeck* (towboat). *T. H. Davis* (C. and E. I. Railroad, owner). *T. L. Herbert No. 2* (towboat. Built at Nashville 1900 —80 tons. Nashville Towboat Company, registered owner. M. M. Leek, master). *Three Brothers* (towboat—built at South Carrollton, Kentucky—1895—59 tons. G. H., C. E. and J. F. Walcott, owners). *Victor* (towboat). *Wash Hansell* (towboat). *Woolfolk* (towboat). *W. T. Harwell* (towboat. Built Nashville 1891—24.48 tons. J. J. Smith, owner and George R. Smith, master).

TOTAL   44
TOTAL REGULAR PACKETS AND TRANSIENTS . .   67

Regular Cumberland River Packets during the Period 1900–1920, Their Known Owners, Date of Launching, and Other Historical Information

Albany (A Burnside packet and later a towboat. Built at Burnside 1901—98 tons. One of the best known boats to ply the Burnside trade. Wound up her career on the Ohio). *Celina No. 2* (A. "B. & B. Line" packet. Owned and operated by the Burnside and Burksville Transportation Company. A well known packet in the Nashville-Burnside trade. See text). *City of Burnside* (A Burnside packet owned by Burnside & Burksville Transportation Company, operators of the "B & B Line." Built at Burnside 1916—161 tons. An excellent packet and one of the last). *C. M. Pate* (Built Marietta 1904—82 tons. Came on Cumberland in 1905 from Pittsburgh. Operated Nashville-Burnside under Cumberland and Tennessee Transportation Co. C. M. Pate, Master. Her papers surrendered at New Orleans April 21, 1909. Sister ship of the *Dick Clyde*). *Creelsboro* (A Burnside packet. See text. Sunk near Falkenberg Landing, 4 miles below Lock No. 21 on Cumberland River. Exact date unknown). *Ed Myer* (A packet and later a towboat. Built at Carthage in 1909—66 tons. West Williams and Ed Myer. Purchased in 1910 by New Ryman Line. Regular run—Nashville to Clarksville). *Electra* (New Ryman Line packet, purchased in 1905. Operated until 1910 and then sold to Cumberland River Steamboat Company and then sold to interests in Mobile. See text). *Fountain City* (A Burnside Packet—built at Burnside and owned by B. & B. Transportation

Company of that city. Sunk near Bart in upper Cumberland—pool of Lock No. 21, exact date unknown). *Gracey Childers* (Rebuilt at Nashville—formerly the *Rose Hite* out of Pittsburgh. Enrolled in Nashville 1909—215 tons. Owned by Capt. J. S. Tyner who was her master. Operated for a short time as a regular packet—Nashville-Paducah. Destroyed by fire Sept. 3, 1909). *Grace Devers* (A packet and towboat—operated on the Cumberland for several seasons). *H. G. Hill* (A regular Cumberland River packet. Owned by Nashville Navigation Company—R. D. Crider, master. Built at Paducah 1919—203 tons. Split in two and sunk near Wooddale Beach above Nashville in 1922(?). W. L. Berry was Superintendent of Nashville Navigation Company at the time. One of the last Nashville packets). *Jo Horton Fall* (Regular Cumberland River packet. Owned by Nashville Packet Company, built at Jeffersonville 1913—156 tons. F. B. White, master, also Thos. G. Ryman, Jr. and T. H. Armstrong. Sold in 1919 to Nashville Navigation Company. J. S. Tyner, master. Left Cumberland in 1928. The last Nashville packet). *M. T. Bryan* (A small packet and towboat. Owned by Nashville Navigation Company—built in Chamberlain, S. D. 1903—97 tons. Formerly the *Grosventre*. W. H. Brown, master. Destroyed by fire in 1922 near Paducah. Named for Col. M. T. Bryan, President of the Cumberland River Improvement Association). *Nashville No. 10* (a regular Cumberland River packet. Built in 1910 at Jeffersonville—251 tons. Owned by Cumberland River Steamboat Company—J. S. Tyner, master. Financial difficulties beseiged the owner and she was sold in 1919. See text). *Patrol* (A Burnside packet—operated for several years. A small boat but a good one. See text). *Robert Rhea* (A fine regular Cumberland River packet. Built at Marietta 1908—182 tons. Owned by the Cumberland River Steamboat Company of Nashville. Thos. G. Ryman, Jr., W. W. Parmenter, principal stockholders. Always known as "Little Tom" Ryman's boat. Sold to New Ryman Line 1910 and sold by it on Nov. 2, 1916 to I. T. Rhea. License surrendered at St. Louis on April 19, 1919). *Rowena* (A regular Cumberland River packet. Built Burnside 1904—184 tons. Owned by Burnside and Burksville Transportation Company, Burnside. Named for town of Rowena—one of the last Burnside packets. Sunk Greasy Creek 1934(?)).

TOTAL 17

Transient Packets and Other Steamboats on the Cumberland River, during the Period 1900–1920

Alabama (A Tennessee river boat. Appeared on the Cumberland from time to time). *Belle of Calhoun. Bertha H.* (A towboat. Built at Nashville 1912—49.67 tons. Owned by Herbert & Company, Nashville. Wm. Leek, master). *Blue Spot* (towboat). *Cal J, Neare* (towboat—built Jeffersonville 1884—39 tons. Operated by N. C. Lyon, Carthage and Cumberland Hickory Company). *Castalia* (towboat). *Charles Turner* (towboat). *Charon* (formerly the *J. T. Davis*. Operated in 1918 as ferry for war workers at Old Hickory Powder Mills). *Claiborne* (towboat). *Comet* (towboat—owned by Arrow Transportation Company. Built at Paducah 1910—42 tons. Emory Vaught—master). *Daniel Lindsey* (formerly the *Sycamore*. Enrolled 1909. Daniel Lindsey of Nashville and Cumberland Valley Sand Company, owners. W. G. Powell, master. Operated as a towboat for the above company. License surrendered at Louisville in 1916). *Eclipse* (towboat. W. F. Hunt, owner; J. F. Leek, master. Enrolled 1907). *E. Douglas* (towboat). *Eileen* (towboat). *Fannie Wallace* (towboat). *Fritz* (towboat. W. E. Lovell, master. Owned by Monongohela Coal Co., Pittsburgh). *Golden Fleece* (a small towboat and packet. Nashville–Tobacco Port). *Harth* (towboat). *Illinois* (towboat). *India Givens* (formerly the *P. D. Staggs*. A towboat). *I. N. Hook* (towboat). *Inverness* (towboat). *John B. Heckman* (A large Missouri river towboat. Operated by charter to S. S. Kerr and John A. Tyner of Nashville). *John S. Summers* (towboat). *John W. Love* (Formerly the *George W. Cowling*. Built at Metropolis 1896—88 tons. Ran as a packet between Paducah-Joppa-Metropolis on Ohio River. The *Love* was a towboat on the Cumberland. The New Ryman Line purchased her on Sept. 30, 1907. She sank at Lock No. 1, Cumberland River October 2, 1907. Raised and sold to interests on Ohio River). *J. S.* (An excursion boat). *J. T. Duffy, Jr.* (towboat). *Kentucky* (A Tennessee River packet often seen on the Cumberland). *L. H. Burhman* (towboat). *Little Clyde* (formerly the *Wenona* owned by Arrow Transportation Company—J. F. Beatty, master. A towboat built at Rumsey, Kentucky 1907—55 tons). *Lora* (towboat). *Lotus Sims* (sidewheel packet from St. Louis. Operated on Cumberland season of 1903). *Lula E. Warren* (towboat). *Mackie* (a sand and gravel towboat or dredge owned by W. T. Hardison & Company. Built at Nashville 1905—77 tons. Pink L. Dews, master). *Mary A. Anderson* (towboat). *Mary F. Golden* (towboat). *Mary Hill* (towboat). *Mary M. Michael* (towboat). *Mary N.* (a towboat). *Margaret* (towboat). *Martha H. Hennen* (towboat). *Maud Kilgore* (towboat). *Morning Star* (towboat). *Nellie* (towboat). *Ohana* (towboat). *Old Reliable* (towboat—Enrolled in name of W. T. Hardison with R. A. Goad, master. Probably a chartered vessel). *R. A. Speed* (towboat). *Red River* (New Ryman Line packet. Built at Jeffersonville 1899—97 tons. A cotton boat which was to be converted into packet on the Cumberland. She was never converted and was sold in 1906 by the Ryman Lines to Wm. Lucas and William Maikel of New Orleans). *Red Spot* (A Tennessee River towboat. Appeared in Nashville several seasons). *Robert Gordon* (towboat). *Sam A. Connor* (towboat). *Sterling* (towboat). Owned by Cumberland and Tennessee Transportation Company, C. M. Pate, President). *Ten Broeck* (towboat). *Thomas A. Nevins* (towboat). *Tommyhawk* (towboat—Arrow Transportation Company; built Rumsey, Kentucky 1910—70 tons. J. F. Beatty, master). *T. R. Taggart* (towboat. Built at Nashville 1909—42 tons. Operated by T. R. Taggart who was her master. Later sold to Foster-Creighton Company, Nashville, who operated her through 1916. Tom Westbrook of Nashville also owned an interest in her). *Victor* (towboat). *Victoria* (towboat). *Vincennes* (towboat). *Wilford* (towboat). *W. L. Berry* (towboat). *Woodruff* (towboat). *W. P. Fiske* (a steam sand dredge owned by Henry Richardson. Sunk above Lock No. 2. Capt. Ed Bell lost his life in the accident. Named for W. P. Fiske, Steamboat Inspector, Nashville). *W. T. Hardison* (a towboat, owned by W. T. Hardison & Company; R. A. Goad, master). *W. T. Scovell* (bought by New Ryman Lines in 1905. Sold in 1906 by that Line to interests in Vicksburg—headed by Frank Hirsch and John A. Quackenboss. Never operated on Cumberland). *W. T. Hunt* (towboat). *"W. W."* (steam excursion boat. Arrived from Owensboro in 1918). *John Ross* (towboat—Nashville Navigation Company).

TOTAL 68
TOTAL REGULAR PACKETS AND TRANSIENTS . . 85

Regular Cumberland River Packets during the Period 1920–1944, Their Known Owners, Date of Launching, and Other Historical Information

There were no additional or new packets on the River during this period

TOTAL   0

Transient Towboats and Other Steamboats on the Cumberland River, during the Period 1920–1944

A. I. Baker. Yocona. Ellen Richardson. J. N. Pharp. Fairplay. City of Helena. McBridge. Slack Barrett. Arthur Hider. J. J. Mc-Vicar. Captain Alphin. Destrahan. Patricia Barrett. Marie Richardson. Joseph Chotin. City of Pittsburgh. Tallulah. Golden Eagle (Tourist). *Idlewild* (Excursion). *Percy Swain. Winona* (towed Menke Showboat. *Hollywood*). *Joe Cook.*

TOTAL   22
TOTAL REGULAR PACKETS AND TRANSIENTS . .   22

United States Engineering Department Steam Towboats from 1871–1944

Colbert. Cumberland. Henry. Hiwassee. John. John Phoenix. Kentucky. Tennessee. Warioto. Weitzel. White Oak.

TOTAL   11

Some of the Showboats Appearing on the Cumberland at Nashville

Jenny Lind.   Water Queen.   Hollywood.   Golden Rod.

RECAPITULATION
OF
STEAMBOATS PLYING THE CUMBERLAND RIVER
1819–1944

Period	Regular Packets	Transient Packets, Towboats, etc.	Total
1819–1830	79	0	79
1830–1840	57	74	131
1840–1850	89	101	190
1850–1860	97	184	281
1860–1870	64	233	297
1870–1880	40	41	81
1880–1890	26	20	46
1890–1900	23	44	67
1900–1920	17	68	85
1920–1944	0	22	22

TOTAL NUMBER	493	TOTAL NUMBER 787	1,279
ADD U. S. E. D. STEAMBOATS			11
TOTAL OF ALL STEAMBOATS LISTED			1,290

List of United States Naval Vessels—1861–1865, Known as the Western Flotilla or the Mississippi Squadron, Broken Down as to Years Commissioned. (This List Includes Only Vessels Serving on the Cumberland, Tennessee, Ohio, Mississippi Rivers)

1861: *Benton, Cairo,* Carondelet,* Cincinnati,* Conestago,* Essex, Lafayette, Lexington,* Louisville,* Mound City, Peosta,* Pittsburgh,* St. Louis,* Tyler **

1862: *Black Hawk, Brilliant,* Chillicothe, Choctaw, Cricket, Curlew,* Eastport, Fairplay,* Fern, Forest Rose,* General Bragg, Indianola, Judge Torrence, Juliet, Little Rebel, Marmora, Mingo, New Era, Petrel, Prairie Bird, Queen of the West, Rattler, Alfred Robb,* Romeo, St. Clair,* Samson, Sallie Woods, Signal, Silver Lake,* Springfield, Switzerland, Tennessee, Thistle, W. H. Brown*

1863: *Argosy, Avenger, Champion, Covington, Elk, Exchange, Ft. Hindman, Gazelle, General Burnside, General Grant, Gen-*

eral *Lyon, General Pillow,* General Price, Glide No. 1, Glide
No.* 2, *Hastings, Kenwood, Key West,* Kinsman, Kosciusko,
Moose,* Naumkeag,* Neosho,* Nyanza, Osage, Ouachita,
Paw Paw,* Queen City, Reindeer,* Rodolph, Silver Cloud,*
Stockdale, Tawah,* Tensas, Tuscumbia, Victory,* Wave*
1864:   *Abeona,* Colossus, Elfin, Fairy, Fawn, Gamage, General
Sherman, General Thomas, Grossbeak, Huntress, Ibex, Kate,
Kickapoo, Lavinia Logan, Meteor, Milwaukee, Naiad, Nymph,
Oriole, Ozark, Sibyl, Siren, Tallahatchie, Undine*
1865:   *Benefit, Chickasaw, Collier, Marietta, Mist, Tempest,
Tennessee, Volunteer*

* Vessel saw service on the Cumberland River.

Confederate States of America Naval Vessels 1861–1865, and Their Disposition, That Saw Service in the Defense of the Mississippi River

Arkansas (destroyed to avoid capture Baton Rouge Aug. 5, 1862), *Bienville* (destroyed to avoid capture Lake Pontchartrain, April, 1862), *Calhoun* (burned by Confederates at Battle of New Orleans April, 1862), *Carondelet* (destroyed by Confederates Lake Pontchartrain April, 1862), *Cotton* (burned in Bayou Teche, La., to avoid capture January, 1863), *Diana* (captured by U. S. Navy, recaptured by Confederates, burned in Bayou Teche, La., April 12, 1863), *Eastport* (never completed; captured on Tennessee River in 1862 by Federals and later completed and used), *Governor Moore* (destroyed at New Orleans, April 24, 1862), *Jackson* (sunk at New Orleans by Confederate crew in April, 1862), *Livingston* (destroyed up Yazoo River June 26, 1862), *Louisiana* (destroyed to avoid capture at New Orleans April 28, 1862), *Manassas* (sunk at the Battle of New Orleans April 24, 1862), *McRae* (formerly the Marquis de La Habana—sunk in Mississippi River on April 29, 1862), *Maurepas* (Sunk in White River, Arkansas, June, 1862, to obstruct navigation), *Mississippi* (Burned at the Battle of New Orleans April 19, 1862 to avoid capture), *New Orleans* (floating battery —burned at Island No. 10 in 1862), *Pamlico* (Burned on Lake Pontchartrain in April, 1862), *General Polk* (Burned to avoid capture in Yazoo River June 26, 1862), *Pontchartrain* (burned to avoid capture in Arkansas River in 1863), *Queen of the West* (captured by Confederate Navy, later sunk in Atchalafaya River, April, 1863), *Resolute* (burned to avoid capture on Mississippi River April 24, 1862), *St. Mary* (Burned to avoid capture on Yazoo River June, 1862), *Savannah, Sumter* (Sold December 19, 1862), *Tennessee* (burned to avoid capture at Memphis in 1862), *Tuscarora* (Burned accidentally at New Orleans in 1862), *V. H. Ivy* (Burned to avoid capture on Yazoo River in 1863).

Mississippi River Defense Fleet

General Sumpter (captured at Memphis June 6, 1862), *Little Rebel* (Captured at Memphis June 6, 1862), *General Sterling Price* (Sunk by Federal Navy at Memphis June 6, 1862), *General Quitman* (Destroyed at New Orleans April 24, 1862), *General M. Jeff Thompson* (sunk at Memphis June 6, 1862), *General Earl Van Dorn* (burned to avoid capture in Yazoo River in 1862), *General Bragg* (captured at Memphis June 6, 1862, and later used by Federal Navy), *General Beauregard* (blew up and sunk at Memphis June 6, 1862), *Defiance* (destroyed to avoid capture at New Orleans April 28, 1862), *Colonel Lovell* (sunk at Memphis June 6, 1862).

Appendix "B"

Partial list of the old-time masters, mates, pilots, and engineers on the Cumberland River who received their licenses at Nashville, 1870 through 1908, and some of the boats on which they served, together with a partial list of some of the old-time clerks and latter-day licensed officers. Taken from the records on file at the Bureau of Marine Inspection and Navigation (Steamboat Inspection Service) in Nashville, and from information supplied by old-time steamboat owners and operators, and contemporary newspapers.

NOTE—Names of all known masters and pilots prior to 1870 are listed with the boats on which they served. Such names were obtained directly from contemporary newspapers for the most part, and in many instances from the Collector of Customs Office. Names of mates and engineers prior to 1870 could not be ascertained. The Bureau of Marine Inspection records at Nashville prior to 1870 are not available and contemporary newspapers did not list them.

List of Old-Time Masters, Mates, Pilots and Engineers on the Cumberland River Licensed at Nashville, 1870 through 1908, and Some of the Boats on Which They Served

Legend

| M—Master | P—Pilot |
| MT—Mate | E—Engineer |

A

George D. Aaron (E-1870—*Ryman Line Boats* and many others). John T. Abston (MT-1873—*Burkesville, John Fowler*). William Agnew (P-1885—). G. W. Alexander (E-1879—*Sam Fowler*). Thomas M. Allen (P-1887—*J. J. Odil, Henry Harley*).

U. S. Allison (E-1868, M-1873—*Fisk, Hugh Martin*). Joe Ambrose (M-1873—*Burkesville, T. T. Hillman*). John B. Anderson (M-1873—*Arch P. Green*). A. T. Armstrong (M-1874—*J. S. Bransford, L. P. Ewald, John Fowler, O. E. Stockell, Alex Kendall, H. K. Bradford, P. D. Staggs,* among others). George W. Armstrong (E-1873, P-1874—*Silver Spring, Matt Gracey*). John A. Armstrong (P-1905, M-1907). Luke T. Armstrong (MT-1883, P-1873—*Arch P. Green, Benton McMillin, P. D. Staggs, L. P. Ewald, L. T. Armstrong, Sam J. Keith,* many others, especially above Nashville). Thomas H. Armstrong (M-1878—*Dora Cabler, Sam J. Keith, William Porter, John Fowler, L. T. Armstrong, Henry Harley, Bob Dudley, L. P. Ewald*). A. E. Arterburn (E-1903). George W. Ashcraft (M-1879—*Celina, Thomas D. Fite, Matt F. Allen*). Benjamin Atkinson (E-1865—*Julia No. 2, Dora Cabler, C. N. Davis*). Ephriam Aumiller (E-1858—*Nashville, Little Condor No. 2*). John D. Austin (MT-1888). William Austin (M-1871—*B. H. Cooke, Eddyville, J. S. Bransford*).

B

Hu L. Ballou (E-1862—*Converse, Last Chance, J. S. Bransford, Arch P. Green, B. G. Wood, George S. Kinney, T. T. Hillman, Dora Cabler, Julian Gracey, John D. Carter*). John Barnes (MT-1887—*City of Clarksville*). Frank Baugh (MT-1889—*B. S. Rhea*). Eph H. Bean (E-1859—*Kate Morrison, Aid, George I. Kinney, Eddyville, Mary Clees, Sam Fowler, Charles A. Blackman, Pearl, L. T. Armstrong, George W. Kiber*). Eph. H. Bean, Jr. (E-1875—*George I. Kinney, George W. Kiber, Sam Fowler, Thomas D. Fite, J. J. Odil, Josh V. Throop, Pearl, J. R. Skiles, Bob Dudley*). Joe A. Belk (M-1901, P-1897—*R. Dunbar, Bob Dudley, Harvey* (USED), *Cumberland, Henry* (USED). John L. Belk (MT-1890, M-1894—*H. K. Bedford, Georgia Lee, Henry Harley, Peters Lee*). Ed Bell (P. 1905—*W. P. Fiske*). W. L. Berry (M, P,—Boats on the Tennessee). Wm. E. Bowles (MT-1873—*Arch P. Green, John S. Bransford, Eddyville, T. T. Hillman, B. H. Cooke, J. H. Hillman*). William S. Bowman (M-1875 —*B. H. Cooke, Nashville, Sam P. Jones, I. T. Rhea*). Nelson Broadfoot (M-1884—*John Orm, A. I. Baker*). N. T. Broadfoot (M-1881—*John Orm*). Robert Broadfoot (M-1881, E-1875, MT-1891—*John Orm*). W. S. Broadfoot (E-1884). G. T. Bronager (E-1899—*John A. Hart*). John Bryant (MT-1890). William

Bryant (MT-1873). William R. Burton (P-1867—*John Lums-den, James Gilmore, Little Condon, Silverthorne, Graften*). William E. Byers (M-1871—*J. S. Bransford, B. H. Cooke, Dora Cabler*).

C

A. N. Cabler (P-1871—*I. N. Phillips, Abe McDonald, John A. Hart*). Calvin G. Cabler (M, P, before 1860). Leroy Cage (E-1870—*Burkesville, J. S. Bransford, Dora Cabler, Thos. D. Fite, Ella, Matt F. Dortch*). Americus Carroll (E-1880, *Caney Fork*). Columbus Carroll (E-1872—*Kendall, Celina, Josh V. Throop, Odil*). Ed F. Carroll (P-1888—*P. D. Staggs*). Harvey Carroll (MT—Handly boats—Lovell Line and Ryman Line). James B. Carroll (P-1885—*Dora May*). James H. Carroll (MT-1871—*Burkesville, Arch P. Green, T. T. Hillman, Julia No. 2, Dora Cabler, Thos. D. Fite, L. P. Ewald, Josh V. Throop, W. H. Cherry*). John B. Carroll (M-1873, P-1870—*Jim Watson, Florence Lee, B. H. Cooke, Celina, Caney Fork, J. P. Drouillard, H. K. Bedford, City of Nashville*). William H. Carroll, Sr. (M-1879, P-1854—*Jim Watson, Little Condon, Celina, Dora Cabler, Porter, P. D. Staff, Henry Harley*). William H. Carroll, Jr. (M-1871, P-1857, MT-1881—*Burkesville, F. P. Gracey, Eddy-ville, B. H. Cooke, Celina, Dora Cabler, Josh V. Throop, Benton McMillin, Fowler*). John T. Cartwright (P-1858, M-1872—*Alpha, Umpire, Ella Hughes, B. H. Cooke, E. B. Stahlman, T. T. Hillman, Eddyville, George W. Kiber, J. S. Bransford, L. P. Ewald, Pearl, Clayton H. Webb*). Bowen Carter (M-1890). John Chenault (E-1870—*Newsboy, George I. Kinney, B. G. Wood, Mary Clees, Caney Fork, G. H. Kiber, Crusader, John Orm No. 3*). James H. Christley (E-1879—MT-1888—*Sam Fowler, W. H. Cherry, I. T. Rhea, Bob Dudley*). John F. Clees (E-1876—*Mary Clees*). Charles J. Clements (E-1862—*Umpire, B. H. Cooke*). Reddick Cobb (E-1873, *Ajax No. 2, Matt Gracey*). Dan Colyer (E-1878—*Matt Gracey*). James M. Couser (MT-1870—*Eddy-ville, G. W. Fowler*). James Courtney (E-1868—*Lucy Coker, R. N. Phillips*). Albert J. Cowleshaw (P-1861, P-1880, M-1895—*Julian Gracey, J. H. Hillman, City of Nashville, J. B. Richard-son, H. W. Buttorff, B. S. Rhea, Dover, W. H. Cherry, E. G. Ragon*). W. D. Cowleshaw (M-1872—*Ajax No. 2, Matt Gracey, E. T. Holman, Wietzel (U. S.), Sycamore, H. W. Buttorff*). W. D. Cowleshaw, Jr. (E-1883—*Julian Gracey, City of Nash-*

ville, E. T. Holman, Pearl, many others). William Craddock (MT-1870—*Rapidan No. 2*). Robert E. Crank (P-1900, M-1906, E-1892—*E. T. Myer, C. M. Pate, Dick Clyde* (USED) *Colbert, Chancey Lamb,* others). William B. Crank (P-1887, MT-1872— *B. H. Cooke, Ella, Julian Gracey*). William A. Crawford (M-1885, P-1883—*Benton McMillin*). Ed P. Crider, Jr. (MT-1883—*B. S. Rhea, Alex Perry*). Robert D. Crider (P-1898, M-1908—*J. B. Richardson, Clyde*). William L. Crowl (M-1874—*Jim Fiske, Jr.*).

D

William Dale (E-1876—*Eddyville*). Aaron Davis (E-1883— *B. S. Rhea, E. T. Holman*). W. W. Davis (M-1885—*Crusader*). James E. Dean (P-1856—*John Lumsden*). Lewis Dennis (MT-1886—*City of Nashville*). Logan Dennis (MT-1882—*Ella, L. P. Ewald*). Lewis Denny (Lovell boats). Pink L. Dews (M-1873— *Aid No. 2, Aida Heilman, Arch P. Green, B. G. Wood, Ella, W. H. Cherry, J. H. Hillman, I. T. Rhea, Sycamore* (USED), *Wietzel, Suzette*). John S. Dirickson (P-1895—*James N. White,* others). W. T. Dodd (P-1876, MT-1879, M-1880—*H. L. Hale, Sam J. Keith, Sam Fowler, Henry Harley, T. T. Hillman* (USED), *Wietzel*). Jesse L. Dortch (P-1873). John W. Dozier (E-1893— *Clyde* (USED) *John*). Newton Drennon (E-1886, *I. T. Rhea*). William Duckworth (E-1858—*Lookout, B. H. Cooke, Celina, Dora Cabler*). Wilson F. Dunn (M-1876, P-1858, P-1872— *A. Baker, Eddyville, Mary Clees, Queen City, H. W. Buttorff, J. S. Bransford*). Jesse du Souchet (E-1879—*B. S. Rhea*).

E

Joseph Earhart (E-1880—*Sam Fowler, Julian Gracey, J. R. Skiles, J. D. Carter, J. J. Odil*). William H. Edwards (M-1890, P-1870, *Talisman, Uncle Tom, Jim Fiske, T. T. Hillman, C. W. Anderson*). George Eleazer (M-1875—*Joseph Ambrose*). Andrew Evetts (MT-1871—*Eddyville*). Henry D. Evetts (M-1871, MT-1870—*Rapidan, John S. Bransford, Jim Fiske, Jr.*). William Evetts (MT-1872, *Rapidan, C. W. Anderson*).

F

George W. Farnsworth (M-1874—*John Gilmore*). Joe Farrell (MT-1884—*Celina, Benton McMillin, Eddyville, Bob Dudley,*

J. H. Hillman, Sam P. Jones, Electra, practically on every boat that ran upper Cumberland). John Farrell (P-1881, MT-1874— *E. B. Stahlman, John S. Bransford, Dora Cabler, Celina, J. B. Richardson*). Sam W. Felts (P-1906—*Nashville, J. B. Richardson, H. G. Hill*). Robert F. Ferguson (M-1880, MT-1879—*B. G. Wood*). Peleg Fiske (E-1875—*Rainbow, James Guthrie, Henry Harley,* all boats Louisville & Evansville Packet Co.). William P. Fiske (E-1899, E-1902—*James Guthrie, City of Owensboro,* Lee Line at Memphis, *Natchez, Henry Harley, Jo Horton Fall, Dunbar, Herbert*). David G. Fowler (M-1872—*James Fiske, Jr.*). Joseph H. Fowler (M-1871—*James Fiske, Jr., Gus Fowler*). Myer S. Frank (M-1877—*Mary Clees, George W. Kiber*).

G

Charles Gallagher (*Harvey*). Thomas M. Gallagher (M-1881— *B. S. Rhea, J. H. Hillman,* most Ryman Line boats). Glenn L. Gann. James L. Gann (P-1904—*Henry Harley, Jo Horton Fall, Bob Dudley,* many others). John E. Gann (P-1895, M-1900— *George W. Cowling, R. Dunbar, Henry Harley, Bob Dudley, Jo Horton Fall,* many others). Robert P. Gann (MT-1907—*Jo Horton Fall*). J. V. Garvey (MT-1888—*B. S. Rhea*). John Gavin (E-1867—*George I. Kinney, Mary Clees, Eddyville, L. P. Ewald, Thomas D. Fite, Hettie Bliss, Sam Fowler, Sam P. Jones*). Ben L. Goad (M-1872, P-1859—*Ella Hughes, Eddyville, Burkesville, J. S. Bransford, Abe McDonald, Ella, City of Nashville, H. K. Bedford, Matt F. Allen, John W. Hart, Ashland City*). Robert A. Goad (M-1880—*Eddyville, Little Anna, H. K. Bedford, Matt F. Allen, Henry Harley, James N. White*). Frank P. Gracey (M-1876, P-1876—*Matt Gracey, Julian Gracey*). Julian Gracey (E-1891). William Gracey (M-1873—*Eddyville, Celina, B. H. Cooke, C. N. Davis, J. P. Drouillard*). James M. Grasty (P-1883 —*Julian Gracey, Electra, W. T. Scovell, Red River, B. S. Rhea, L. P. Ewald, E. G. Ragon, Dover*). George M. Green (M-1882, P-1881—*J. P. Drouillard, Sam J. Keith, L. P. Ewald, Sam P. Jones, Olivette, Fowler, I. T. Rhea, L. T. Armstrong*). John T. Green (M-1874, P-1857—*Ada Heilman, Burkesville, Eddyville, B. S. Rhea, B. G. Wood, George W. Kiber, L. P. Ewald, J. P. Drouillard*). Shep Green (M-1884, P-1883—*J. T. Hillman, Henrietta* (USED), *Pilot, J. P. Drouillard, E. G. Ragon, W. K. Phillips, Julian Gracey, Nashville, J. B. Heckman, Tennessee*). Thomas Green (P-1878—*Nashville*). "Cab" Green (pilot). Robert H. Grissom (MT-1880—*C. N. Davis, J. P. Drouillard, Sam P. Jones, H. K. Bedford, John Fowler*). William R. Grubbs (P-1858, M-1874—*Umpire, A. P. Green, J. S. Bransford, Julia B, C. N. Davis, Thomas D. Fite, N. K. Bedford, Matt F. Allen, J. J. Odil, James N. White*). Alex Guthrie (E-1859—*Burkesville*).

H

Cannon Harmon (MT-1880—*B. G. Wood*). Richard Harmon (P-1864, E-1868—*Newsboy, Tyrone, Shippers Own, B. H. Cooke, T. T. Hillman, Katie Vertrees, Eddyville, C. W. Anderson*). Thomas M. Harmon (M-1872, P-1861—*Tyrone, T. T. Hillman, E. B. Stahlman, John S. Bransford, Celina, Caney Fork, Julian Gracey, Josh V. Throop, J. H. Hillman, C. A. Blackman*). Will T. Harmon (E-1866, *Umpire, Ella Hughes, B. H. Cooke, T. T. Hillman, Eddyville, Abe McDonald, Mary Clees, Dora Cabler, Hettie Bliss*). William J. Harmon (M-1872—*Tyrone, Eddyville, Sam Fowler, Celina, Silverthorne, Dover*). Bedford Harris (E). Thomas Harris (P—*Dick Clyde*). William J. Harris (P—*Henry Harley*). Winton B. Harris (M-1874—*J. S. Bransford, Crusader, J. J. Odil, James N. White*). William J. Havens (E-1880—*L. P. Ewald*). Henry J. Hite (M-1878—*Eddyville, Mary Clees*). J. W. Hovious (E-1879—*W. H. Cherry, J. H. Hillman, J. P. Drouillard*). Fountain E. Hughes (M-1872, P-1864—*Ella Hughes, B. H. Cooke, Eddyville*). Rich Humphrey (P-1870). William A. Hunter (MT-1870—*Shippers Own, A. Baker, Nashville, Dora Cabler, C. W. Anderson, City of Nashville, Sam P. Jones, Pearl, Clyde, James N. White, Henry Harley, J. B. Richardson* and others). William T. Hunter (P-1893, M-1894, MT-1891—*Pearl, J. J. Odil, Reuben Dunbar, James N. White, Henry Harley, Bob Dudley, J. B. Richardson, H. W. Buttorff, John W. Thomas, P. D. Staggs, Belle of Calhoun, Clyde, Tennessee* (USED), *Warioto, Lora, J. C. Irvin, Ed Myer* (USED), *Cumberland* (USED), *Henry* (USED), *John*).

J

Andrew Joyce (E-1880—*George W. Kiber, L. P. Ewald, T. D. Fite*). John Joiner (M-1873—*Wasp*). George W. Jones (MT-1883—*Eddyville*). Joseph M. Jones (E-1863—*Alpha, John S. Bransford, B. H. Cooke, B. S. Rhea, J. H. Hillman*). W. T. Jordan (E-1870—*Talisman, Ella Hughes*). A. W. Joyce (MT-1886—*John Fowler*).

K

Alex Kendall (M-1880—*John S. Bransford, Sam J. Keith*). John H. Kennedy (E-1875—*Matt Gracey*, Ryman line packets). Robert C. Kennedy (MT-1878—*J. H. Hillman*, Ryman Line packets). James F. Kiber (M-1871—*George S. Kinney*). James P. Kilgore (P-1886—*E. G. Ragon*, Ryman Line). John W. Kinney (E-1860—*John Lumsden, Burkesville*). J. W. Kirkpatrick (E-1882—*John S. Bransford, Sam J. Keith, Julian Gracey, John Fowler*). John Kirkpatrick (E—Cumberland (USED) Boats). Robert M. Kirkpatrick (E-1861—*Umpire, Eddyville, Sam J. Keith, J. H. Hillman*). Nick Klippert (MT-1872, *B. S. Rhea*). James M. Knapp (E-1874—*John S. Bransford*, Lovell line packets).

L

John Lawson (E-1868—*T. T. Hillman*). James Lee (P-1875—*Matt Gracey, Julian Gracey*). Henry Leech (E-1856—*Umpire*). Isaac T. Leek (P-1866, M-1872—*Aid No. 2*, many other earlier boats). James A. Leek (MT-1875—*Aid No. 2, B. G. Wood*). James F. Leek (P-1887—*John Orm No. 3* (USED), Engineer). Joe F. Leek (M-1890). Madison M. Leek (MT-1876, M-1877—*Aid No. 2, B. G. Wood, James R. Skiles, E. T. Holman*). Tom Leek (P-1871—*Aid No. 2*). James J. Linder (P-1894—*James N. White*, other upper Cumberland packets). Ben F. Lovell (P-1859, M-1873—*Burkesville, Arch P. Green, John S. Bransford, Julia No. 2, E. B. Stahlman, Eddyville, C. N. Davis, Thomas D. Fite, H. K. Bedford, J. J. Odil*). Charles H. Lovell (E-1880—*Caney Fork, Hettie Bliss*). Frank Lovell (M—*Odil*, other upper river packets). James P. Lovell (M-1877, P-prior to 1870—*Julia No. 2, Ella, Pearl*). James W. Lovell (P-1859, M-1872—*Burkesville, John S. Bransford, Arch P. Green, Julia No. 2, Dora Cabler, Ella, City of Nashville, Benton McMillin, Nat F. Dortch*). John Lovell (E-1889—All Lovell Line boats, USED boats, others). Thomas A. Lovell (M-1874, E-1865—*Burkesville, Dora Cabler, Thomas D. Fite, John S. Bransford, Matt F. Allen, John W. Hart*). Thomas Lee Lovell (E-1887—*Matt F. Allen*, other Lovell Line packets). Tom J. Lovell (MT-1876, M-1883—*City of Nashville, J. T. Hillman, Skiles, Reuben Dunbar* (USED) *Cumberland, Ed Myer, Pearl*). William E. Lovell (P-1890, M-1898—*Henry Harley, Reuben Dunbar, Bob Dudley*). William H. Lovell (P-1866, M-1872—

Burkesville, Eddyville, Arch P. Green, Alex Kendall, Hettie Bliss,
Dora Cabler, Sam Fowler, B. H. Cooke, W. H. Cherry, City of
Nashville).

M

Edward J. Marshall (M-1882—*J. P. Drouillard,* lower river
packets). Charles Martin (MT-1895—*Bob Dudley*). Dave Mar-
tin (MT-1888—*I. T. Rhea, W. K. Phillips, Gracie Childers,*
Lucile Nowlin, H. W. Buttorff, Henry Harley). Edward J. Martin
(MT-1906—*Dunbar, H. W. Buttorff*). John Martin (MT-1894—
Clyde, Lucile, Nowlin). Lonnie Martin (Big Lonnie) (MT—
H. W. Buttorff, other Ryman Line boats). Lonnie Martin (Little
Lonnie) (MT—*Dunbar,* other Ryman Line boats). John E.
Massengale (M-1873—*Ada Heilman, Nashville*). A. C. Matheney
(P-1856, M-1871—*Ada Heilman, B. H. Cooke, A. I. Baker, Dora*
Cabler, B. S. Rhea). James S. Matheney (P-1861, M-1873—
Armada, many other earlier packets). William C. Matheney
(MT-1875—*Alex Kendall, L. P. Ewald, I. T. Rhea*). Robert L.
Meadors (P-1909—*Ed Myers, Bob Dudley, Henry Harley*).
Thomas J. Meadors (P-1902, M-1904—*Henry Harley, Bob Dud-*
ley (USED) Pilot). Gustavus Mellow (P-1894—Lovell Line,
Handly packets, Armstrong boats). Fred Mitchell (P-1858—
Armada, many other earlier packets). James H. Mix (E-1876—
James Fiske, Jr., Fowler packets, others). James Monroe (E-1863
—*Alpha, Burkesville, George S. Kinney*). Bridges Montgomery
(P-1910—C.T.Co. packets—USED—*Golden Eagle*—and many
others). W. S. Montgomery (P-1909—*Jo Horton Fall,* Cumber-
land, Tennessee and Ohio boats—Cumberland River Sand Co.
boats). Patton Moore (MT-1873, M-1882—*John S. Bransford,*
Ada Heilman, Julian Gracey, Sallie Carney, B. S. Rhea, B. G.
Wood, Sam Fowler, J. H. Hillman). Talt Moore (MT—Ryman
Line boats). William Moore (MT—New Ryman boats). John R.
Morris (M-1878—*B. S. Rhea, B. H. Cooke, Bob Dudley*). Joseph
Morrissey (E-1876—*Matt Gracey,* Ryman Line packets, Lovell
Line and Independent packets). Ralph Moss (P-1856, M-1879—
Talisman, John Lumsden, Eddyville, C. W. Anderson).

Mc

William McCartney (MT-1873—*Celina, T. T. Hillman, Mary*
Clees, George S. Kinney, C. W. Anderson). John P. McElhaney

(MT-1873—*Burkesville, T. T. Hillman, Mary Clees, G. W. Fowler, B. S. Rhea*). Dan B. McKinley (P-1859—*Umpire*, early packets). Sylvester McMahon (M-1871, P-1864—*Armada, James Fiske, Jr.*). James McWhirter (E-1873—*Ella Hughes, Burkesville, B. H. Cooke, T. T. Hillman, Ella, City of Nashville*).

N

Thomas Nave (E-1855—*Rapidan No. 2*). Jacob P. Newman (E-1866, *Eddyville*, early Ryman boats). John H. Newman (P-1871, M-1882—*Armada, John S. Hopkins, City of Nashville, B. S. Rhea*).

O

Patrick O'Brien (MT-1876—*James Fiske, Jr.*).

P

Franklin J. Parker (E-1876—*E. B. Stahlman, Hettie Bliss, G. W. Kiber, Sam Fowler, Silverthorne, Benton McMillin*). Stephen Parker (MT-1877—*T. T. Hillman*, Ryman Line boats). Wiley Parmenter (M-1878—*Celina, Sam Fowler*, other boats). Wm. H. Parrish (P-1863, M-1875—*Tyrone, George I. Kinney, T. T. Hillman*). Jesse Pittman (P-1877—*E. B. Stahlman, Dora Cabler, Josh V. Throop*). David G. Powell (MT-1872—*Umpire, Eddyville*, many others). William G. Powell (P-1900—*Sycamore*, many others). Charles Pullias (MT-1871—*Ella Hughes, I. T. Rhea*). Mitchell A. Pullias (MT-1873—*T. T. Hillman, J. S. Bransford, C. N. Davis, B. S. Rhea, Thomas D. Fite, Matt F. Allen*). William B. Pullias (P-1905, M-1907—*Henry Harley*, later packets).

R

James M. Ramsey (M-1893—Ryman and Lovell boats). George Rhea (E—*James N. White*, other Ryman Line boats). James Rhea (E-1877—*B. G. Woods, Thomas D. Fite, Ella, H. K. Bedford, J. J. Odil*). Thomas I. Rhea (E-1878—*John S. Bransford, Matt F. Allen, Skiles, L. T. Armstrong*). William Rhea (E—*Henry Harley*, Ryman Line boats). Joseph C. Russell (M-1879, P-1875 —*E. B. Stahlman, Dora Cabler, L. P. Ewald*). John C. Ryman

(P-1889, E-1883—*M. V. Moore, J. P. Drouillard, Bob Dudley, T. T. Hillman*). Milton F. Ryman (M-1881, MT-1880—*Sam Fowler, W. H. Cherry*). Thomas G. Ryman (M-1876—4th renewal—*Alpha, E. G. Ragon, L. P. Ewald, Ashland City, Dover, Ed Myer, C. W. Anderson, W. H. Cherry, J. B. Richardson, Henry W. Buttorff, Bob Dudley, Electra, Chancey Lamb, Henry Harley, R. Dunbar, Julian Gracey,* Ryman Line boats). Thomas G. Ryman, Jr. (M-1894, MT-1899—*J. B. Richardson, R. Dunbar, H. W. Buttorff, Jo Horton Fall,* others).

S

James M. St. John (E-1878—*B. S. Rhea*). Joe M. St. John (E— U. S. Boiler Inspector). Pleasant St. John (E-1863—*Alpha, Eddyville*). William St. John (M-1880, E-1866—*Celina, Sam Fowler, John S. Bransford*). Thomas Sargent (E-1866—*Eddyville*). Wiley Simms (M-1871, P-prior 1870—*Talisman, Frank P. Gracey, Celina, John S. Bransford*). William Slinkerd (E-1870—*E. B. Stahlman, B. S. Rhea*). C. C. Spillers (M-1874— *Ida*). Fountain E. Spillers (P-1861—*George S. Kinney, E. B. Stahlman, Katie Vertrees, Eddyville, Caney Fork, Ella, L. P. Ewald*). Lafayette Spillers (M-1873, P-1859—*Tyrone, Abe McDonald, T. T. Hillman, Eddyville, B. S. Rhea*). William Spillers (M-1873—*Ida*). Charles U. Stockham (E-1872—*Harley,* St. Louis and Tennessee Packet Company, U. S. Boiler Inspector). William Strong (M-1876, P-prior 1870—*E. B. Stahlman, West Wind, May Duke, Red Rover No. 2, Humboldt*).

T

W. B. Taylor (E-1854—*Rapidan*). Harvey H. Thompson (M-1877, P-1868—*T. T. Hillman, Nashville*). Wm. W. Tucker (E-1879—*B. S. Rhea, Thomas D. Fite, Benton McMillin,* upper and lower river packets). James S. Tyner (P-1865–1870, M-1878 —*B. S. Rhea, Alex Perry, H. W. Buttorff, Gracie Childers, Henry Harley, J. B. Richardson, Nashville*).

W

Rufus M. Westbrook (MT-1874—*Burkesville, Alex Kendall, Eddyville*). James Weston (E-1874—*James Fiske, Jr.*). James M. White (E-1870—*Ella Hughes, T. T. Hillman, C. N. Davis*).

Thomas D. Wilkey (E-1882—*J. C. Warner*). Jim Wilkinson (P—*Albany, H. W. Buttorff*). Harry Wills (P—*Celina, H. W. Buttorff*). James Wolfe (E-1862—*Burkesville, Ella Hughes, B. G. Wood, C. W. Anderson, Kiber*). Fred D. Wyatt (E-1854—*C. W. Anderson*). Thomas L. Wyatt (E-1861—*Ella Hughes*).

Y

C. P. Yarbrough (M-1871—*J. N. Phillips, Ella Hughes, Abe McDonald, C. W. Anderson, Celina, Sam Fowler, B. S. Rhea, J. H. Hillman, H. W. Buttorff*). John L. Young (P-1900—*Upriver boats, Harley, James N. White*). F. W. Youree (M-1876—*Katie Vertrees, Caney Fork*). Joseph Zanone (E-1872—*Ella Hughes*).

Some of the Old Time and More Recent Clerks on Steamboats Plying the Cumberland River

1860–1880: Alex Hard, William Spillers, John Harper, William Gracey, G. W. Bradley, B. F. Egan, George W. Splane, W. E. Kuhn, John Harper, Robert W. Wise, Joseph Paul, Wash Weaver, D. B. Davis, J. W. Patton, Jolly Hard, William Harrison, W. E. Byers, T. M. Gallagher, George W. Ashcraft, Wiley W. Parmenter, W. H. McBride, J. S. Massengale, R. B. Parker, Thomas Gibson, E. M. Marshall, T. H. Paine, C. H. Arthur, W. T. Davis, H. H. Holland.

1880–1890: W. B. Pullias, P. W. Wakefield, J. R. Pipes, Frank Eakin, W. S. Carroll, R. E. Morton, J. L. Campbell, D. D. Atchison, Scott Daniels, Alvin Williams, W. W. Houston, Al Bishop, Frank Baugh, T. F. Edmondson, Tiff Strider, Charles Fuhrer, W. M. Pennington, Cannon Harmon, Harry Sullivan, J. E. Schvenlaub, Samuel Harrison, Thomas H. Turner, James Rucker, J. C. Ralls, George Jobes, A. R. Dalton, Jim Grubbs, John A. Tyner, Alex C. Read, R. E. Goad, Luther Allen, George Semor, John J. Gore, John Garner, Ben Read.

1890–1920: Frank White, James P. Tyner, Felix Grasty, Bob Scott, Jim Read, Ben L. Goad, Lonnie Martin, George H. Brickley, Robert Parker, Frank Aiken, Fred Smith, Lee Barney, Ed Cowleshaw, Lige Matthews, Raymond Turner, John Freedle, Jim Cook, William Cardwell, Herbert Worland, Louis

Connor, Robert Turner, Roman Gooslee, Newt Holland, Elijah Gregory, Tom Stoval, James Rucks, John Montgomery, Howard Maddox, "Rabbit" Maddox, Pat Farrell, Herbert Harris, W. B. Harris, Jr., Marvin Akin, Jakie McCauley, William Geiger.

Names of Some of the Present-Day Masters, Pilots, and Engineers, Holding Licenses on the Cumberland River

Hubert Donaldson (Celina, Tennessee). Eugene Horner (USED). Herschel J. Horner (USED). Homsey Mitchell (USED). L. D. Plumlee (Nashville, Tenn.). Avery Powell (USED) Ernest Petty (USED). Lester Petty (USED). Pete Meadors (Gainesboro, Tennessee).

Appendix "C"

1. A complete list of the District Engineers, United States Engineering Department, assigned to the Nashville District, and a list of the Locks and Dams on the Cumberland (prior to 1950), the dates placed in operation and their costs; navigable mileage of the river, its elevation and data on Cumberland Falls.
2. A complete list of the Deputy Collectors of Customs at Nashville as shown by the records of that office and other historical information concerning such office and its records.
3. A complete list of the officers in charge of the Weather Bureau in Nashville and other historical information concerning floods and freezes on the Cumberland River.
4. A complete list of the Inspectors of Hulls and Boilers (Steamboat Inspectors) at Nashville from 1852 through 1944 as furnished by the National Archives at Washington.
5. A summary of packets arriving and departing from Nashville in 1833 and 1838 as referred to in Chapter II.

United States District Engineers
1873–1944

Godfrey Weitzel	1873 *	Walter S. Winn ⎱ Civil-	1917
Walter McFarland	1873	A. B. McGrew ⎰ ians	1918
W. R. King	1876	J. B. Cavanaugh	1919
J. W. Barlow	1887	Lytle Brown	1919
Henry M. Robert	1891 **	Robert R. Ralston	1919
John Biddle	1893	Harold C. Fiske	1920
Dan C. Kingman	1898	J. L. Schley	1920
M. B. Adams	1899	J. R. Slattery	1921
Dan C. Kingman	1900	Harold C. Fiske	1923
M. B. Adams	1900	E. G. Dent	1924
John S. D. Knight	1901	Harold Fiske	1925
M. B. Adams	1901	Lewis H. Wilkins	1926
W. J. Borden	1903	John F. Conklin	1929
Clinton B. Sears	1903	Frank S. Besson	1929
H. C. Newcomer	1904	R. R. Neyland, Jr.	1933
W. G. Caples	1907	C. E. Perry	1934
Wm. W. Harts	1907	Bernard Smith	1938
CAF. Flagler	1910	O. E. Walsh	1940
Wm. W. Harts	1910	Wm. A. Davis	1943
CAF. Flagler	1911	Reading Wilkinson	1943
Edgar Jadwin	1911	Howard V. Canan	1946
H. Burgess	1911	Arthur W. Pence	1949–
Jarvis J. Bain	1916	Henry Walsh	1950
Lytle Brown	1916	G. M. Dorland	1952
Jarvis J. Bain	1917	Eugene J. Stann	1956
		Vincent F. Carlson	1959

* U. S. District Engineer first assigned to regular duties at Nashville in 1873. The Nashville District was officially established on August 18, 1888 by Special Order #191.

All reports of the District Engineers—1873–1944—are to be found among the archives at the Nashville Office.

** This is the same Henry M. Robert who became famous as the originator and author of Robert's—"Rules of Order" published in 1873 and revised in 1915. Robert was born in 1837 and died in 1923. He graduated from West Point and was assigned to the engineers. During the Civil War he worked on defenses for Washington, Philadelphia and the New England Coast. From 1867 to 1895 he was in charge of various river and harbors work. See Columbia Encyclopedia.

LOCKS (Dimensions, Date and Cost) CUMBERLAND RIVER
(Prior to 1950)

	Placed in Operation	*Cost*
LOCK A	November 26, 1904	$ 490,010.77
LOCK B	November 9, 1916	679,681.93
LOCK C	September 2, 1918	721,381.33
LOCK D	December 21, 1916	629,254.94
LOCK E	November 20, 1922	1,075,810.00
LOCK F	November 1, 1923	1,110,743.30
LOCK 1	November 26, 1904	395,634.45
LOCK 2	October 9, 1907	340,241.65
LOCK 3	October 15, 1908	348,354.46
LOCK 4	November 17, 1909	346,429.99
LOCK 5	October 18, 1909	373,590.40
LOCK 6	October 21, 1910	369,357.48
LOCK 7	October 18, 1910	378,568.15
LOCK 8	September 15, 1924	680,915.21
LOCK 21	October 20, 1911	361,498.20
	TOTAL	$8,301,472.26

ALL LOCKS WHEN BUILT WERE 52 FEET WIDE, AND
280 FEET LONG

NOTE—The elevation of the Cumberland River at its mouth—
Smithland, Kentucky—is 302 feet. Its elevation at the head of navigation—Burnside, Kentucky—is 587 feet. The total navigable mileage of the river is 516 miles.

Cumberland Falls are 46 miles above Burnside and have a vertical
fall of 55½ feet.

A List of Deputy Collectors of Customs (Surveyors), in Charge of the Nashville Office

Joel M. Smith	1837–1854
Jesse Thomas	1854–1861
Adam Woolf	1870–
H. A. Hasslock	1891–1894
W. E. Morton, Deputy Surveyor	1894–
J. H. Collins	1894–1899
J. W. Dillon	1899–1907
John J. Gore	1907–1910
(United States District Judge for the Middle District of Tennessee, 1923–1939)	
Wm. E. Morton, Deputy Surveyor	1910–
Wm. B. Turman	1910–1912
James E. Brock, Deputy Collector	1912–1917
J. N. Dunivin	1917–1919
James E. Brock	1919–1920
A. P. Hill	1920–1935
Harvey C. Douglas	1935–1960
F. L. Crowe	1960–

The Available Records at the Deputy Collector of Customs' Office in Nashville Are as Follows:

Enrollment of Vessels from 1837 through 1861
Licenses of Vessels from 1870 through 1878
Enrollment of Vessels from 1891 through 1905
Licenses of Vessels from 1905 through 1910
Enrollment of Vessels from 1912 through 1922
Permanent Enrollment Records 1922 to present date

The Deputy Collector of Customs at Nashville, prior to June 27, 1923, operated under the New Orleans Office of the Treasury Department, but on that date, by Executive Order, it was placed under Headquarters, District of Tennessee, District No. 43, Memphis, which comprises the States of Arkansas and Tennessee.

Until June 27, 1923, the Deputy Collector of Customs' Office at Nashville only enrolled vessels on the rivers within the limits of the State of Tennessee. This accounts for the fact that many of the old boats that operated on the Cumberland River from points in Kentucky are not included in the records of the Nashville Office.

United States Weather Bureau, Nashville, Tennessee

Prior to 1895, all official weather reports were kept by the War Department, Signal Service, United States Army, Division of Telegrams and Reports for the Benefit of Commerce. The first volume of these reports on file at the U. S. Weather Bureau in Nashville begins November, 1870 and are signed by Thomas L. Watson, Sergeant USS—Observer. The reports were made weekly. Sergeant Watson was succeeded by Sergeant L. N. Jesunofsky and he in turn by Sergeant J. B. Marbury, and in April, 1895, H. C. Bate became the first Inspector of the present U. S. Weather Bureau in Nashville. He served until 1909. Roscoe Nunn then became Observer and was succeeded by Edward A. Jones in 1925, who served until 1932. Jones was succeeded by

R. M. Williamson who served until September, 1943, when E. M. Barto took over the office. He served until October 31, 1956. B. L. Henry was temporarily in charge from November 1, 1956 through November 26, 1956. Ernest M. Ramey was Observer from November 27, 1956 through January 26, 1957 when Henry was again temporarily in charge until Harold J. Smith became Observer on March 4, 1957.

FLOOD STAGES OF MORE THAN 50 FEET ON THE
CUMBERLAND RIVER
1808–1944
Flood Stage at Nashville, 40 feet

	Feet		*Feet*
1808 *	54	1865	52.1
1815 *	51.5	1867	51.2
1826	52.1	1882	55.3
1847	54.9	1890	50.7
1850	53.1	1927	56.2
1862	52.2	1937	53.8

* Based on tradition, no proof.

From 1875 to 1960, the Cumberland River has been frozen over four times, namely, December 31, 1876; January 13, 1893; February 3, 1905 and January 26, 1940. Taken from the official U. S. Weather Bureau Annual Meteorological Summary of 1939, as compiled by R. M. Williamson, Local Observer.

* * * * * * *

From 1875 to 1944, the total number of floods (40 feet or higher) is 58. The greatest number of successive years with floods was the period from 1915 to 1920, inclusive, and the longest period without a flood is five years from 1904 to 1908, inclusive.

There have been seven flood stages on the Cumberland River after March in any year—April 28, 1850; April 10, 1886; April 4, 1902; April 7, 1912; November 20, 1915; July 5, 1928; April 10, 1935.

The Cumberland River has had three floods in one season. This was from December, 1911 to May, 1912.

* * * * * * *

"The Cumberland River drains an area of 17,750 square miles, which is equal to 42% of the area of the State of Tennessee. The relative importance of the various tributaties is indicated by the following data showing the area of each in square miles beginning at the headwaters:

	Square Miles Drained
Poor Fork	149
Clover Fork	232
Martin Fork	123
Laurel River	281
Rockcastle River	770
Buck Creek	304
South Fork	1,382
Obey River	922
Roaring River	285
Caney Fork River	3,294
Stone River	918
Harpeth River	895
Red River	1,416
Little River	515

NOTE—The Nashville Union and American of February 1, 1872, carried this statement concerning the River:—"River frozen over first time since 1856, worst freeze 1832, when wagons and teams crossed ice for a week."

List of Local Inspectors of Hulls and of Boilers at Nashville

Hulls	*Date of Authorization*
Edward D. Farnsworth	December 6, 1852
Henry H. Harrison	November 2, 1855
Edward P. Farnsworth	April 8, 1864
Edward S. Jones	October 7, 1869
James A. Gardenhire	January 19, 1886
George W. Ashcraft	April 1, 1890
George M. Green	September 11, 1894
Joseph H. Mathews	March 9, 1914
Wm. T. Hunter	July 1, 1915
John W. Schmoker	December 1, 1939

Boilers	*Date of Authorization*
John Wilson	December 6, 1852
Samuel Harrison	January 21, 1870
Joe H. Allison	June 27, 1881
Fred D. Wyatt	February 18, 1888
Collin C. Dugger	August 2, 1890
Fred D. Wyatt	December 26, 1894
Charles A. Stockham	June 25, 1900
John B. Harris	August 26, 1903
Wm. J. MacDonald	February 29, 1904
Joe M. St. John	August 13, 1906
Wm. P. Fiske	June 14, 1918

Officer in Charge—Marine Inspection *
Commander Clay Clifton—June 1, 1947
Commander Alton E. Fowler—Dec. 7, 1959

* "The Officer in Charge" under U. S. Coast Guard combines the duties formerly held by the Inspector of Hulls and the Inspector of Boilers under the Bureau of Marine Inspection and Navigation.

The "Proceedings of the Annual Meetings of the Board of Supervising Inspectors" for the years 1871–1944 inclusive, containing reports of the Nashville Office, are on file in Nashville.

Summary of packets arriving and departing from Nashville March 18, 1833 through April 29th, 1833 and referred to in Chapter Two.

March 18, 1833: *Rambler* arrived from St. Louis; *Erie* arrived from Kanawha.

March 20, 1833: *Memphis* arrived from New Orleans; the following departed on same date—*Rambler* to St. Louis; *Burkesville* to upper territory; *Jefferson* to Cairo; *Erie* to Louisville; *T. Yeatman* to Smithland; *Tallyho* to Cairo.

March 22, 1833: *Red Rover* (first boat by this name) arrived from New Orleans; *Lady Jackson* arrived from Cincinnati; *Free Trader* departed to Louisville.

March 25, 1833: *Charleston* arrived.

March 27, 1833: *Juanita* arrived.

March 29, 1833: *Pacific* arrived from New Orleans; *T. Yeatman* arrived from Florence.

March 30, 1833: *Tennesseean* arrived from New Orleans; *Metamora* arrived from Louisville and the *Compromise* arrived from Smithland.

April 1, 1833: Arrivals—*Nashville* from New Orleans; *Rambler* from Creelsboro; *Tallyho* from Florence; *Jefferson* from Smithland; departures—*Pacific* to New Orleans; *Tennesseean* to New Orleans.

April 8, 1833: *Hawk Eye* arrived from Pittsburgh; *President* from New Orleans; *Rambler* from Paducah; *Red Rover* from New Orleans.

April 11, 1833: *Bonnets O'Blue* arrived from Pittsburgh.

April 13, 1833: *Free Trader* arrived from Pittsburgh.

April 15, 1833: *Jefferson* arrived from the junction of north and south forks of Cumberland River.

April 20, 1833: Arrivals—*Tobacco Plant* from New Orleans; *Lady Jackson* from Pittsburgh; *Tallyho* from Gallatin Landing. Departures—*Harry Hill* to Smithland.

April 29, 1833: Arrivals—*Lady Washington* from Pittsburgh; departures—*Lady Jackson* to Smithland; *Harry Hill* to Smithland; *T. Yeatman* to Smithland.

Summary of packets arriving and departing from Nashville March 5, 1838 through April 3, 1838, and referred to in Chapter Two.

March 5, 1838: *Toledo* departed to St. Louis.

March 6, 1838: *Bolivar* arrived from Smithland; *Rocky Mountain* departed to New Orleans.

March 7, 1838: *Passenger* arrived from Smithland; *Bolivar* departed to Burkesville; *Passenger* departed to Hartsville.

March 9, 1838: Arrivals—*Salem* from Louisville; *Tuscumbia* from Smithland; *Ellen Kirkman* from New Orleans; departures—*Salem* to Louisville; *Tuscumbia* to Rome.

March 10, 1838: *American* departed to St. Louis.

March 11, 1838: Arrivals—*Passenger* from Hartsville; *Tuscum-*

bia from Rome; *Signal* from Smithland; *Lady Jackson* from St. Louis.

March 12, 1838: *Fairy* arrived from Smithland; *Signal* departed to Gallatin; *Native* departed to Smithland.

March 13, 1838: D. *Webster* arrived from New Orleans; departures—*Tuscumbia* to Carthage; *Fairy* to Smithland; *Ellen Kirkman* to New Orleans.

March 14, 1838: Arrivals—*Bolivar* from Smithland; *Signal* from Gallatin; departures—*Passenger* to St. Louis; *Lady Jackson* to Smithland.

March 15, 1838: Arrivals—*Tuscumbia* from Carthage; *Fairy* from Smithland; D. *Webster* departed to New Orleans.

March 16, 1838: *Signal* departed to Smithland; *Bolivar* departed to Smithland.

March 17, 1838: *Tuscumbia* departed to Smithland.

March 18, 1838: *Bolivar* and *Lady Jackson* arrived from Smithland.

March 19, 1838: Arrivals—*Arabian* from Pittsburgh; *Toledo* from St. Louis; Departures—*Fairy* to Smithland; *Bolivar* to Smithland; *Toledo* to St. Louis.

March 20, 1838: Arrivals—*Delaware* from Pittsburgh; *Newark* from Pittsburgh;—Departures—*Arabian* to Pittsburgh.

March 21, 1838: Arrivals—*Signal* from Smithland; *Roanoke* from Pitsburgh; *Deleware* departed to Pittsburgh.

March 22, 1838: *Newark* departed to Louisville.

March 23, 1838: *John Randolph* arrived from New Orleans; *Signal* departed to Smithland.

March 24, 1838: Arrivals—*Constellation* from New Orleans; *Bolivar* from Smithland; *Tuscumbia* from Smithland;—Departures—*Roanoke* to Pittsburgh; *Tuscumbia* to Smithland.

March 25, 1838: Arrivals—*Lady Jackson* from Smithland; *B. I. Gilman* from Smithland; Departures—*B. I. Gilman* to Smithland.

March 26, 1838: Arrivals—*Signal* from Smithland; *Bolivar* departed to Gallatin; *John Randolph* departed to New Orleans.

March 27, 1838: Arrivals—*Tuscumbia* and *T. Gilbert* from Smithland; Departures—*Constellation* to New Orleans; *Signal* to Smithland.

March 28, 1838: Arrivals—*Bolivar* from Gallatin; Departures—*Lady Jackson* to Smithland; *Tuscumbia* to Smithland; *Bolviar* and *T. Gilbert* to Smithland.

March 30, 1838: *Lily* arrived from Pittsburgh.

March 31, 1838: Arrivals—*Nashville, Signal* and *Passenger* from Smithland; *Lily* from Pittsburgh; Departures—*Bolivar* to Smithland.

April 1, 1838: *Lady Jackson* and *Tuscumbia* arrived from Smithland.

April 2, 1838: Arrivals—*T. Gilbert* from Smithland; Departures —*Tuscumbia* and *T. Gilbert* to Smithland.

April 3, 1838: Arrivals—*Huntress* from Pittsburgh; *B. I. Gilman* from Alton; Departures—*Passenger* and *Huntress* to Smithland; *B. I. Gilman* to Alton.

Appendix "D"

Various signals used from the Pilot House to the Engine Room on steamboats operating on the Cumberland River; a glossary of certain expressions used by rivermen on the Cumberland; description of the Cumberland River and its tributaries, and other miscellany.

Steamboats and Packets, Inland Waterways, Using 2 Bells and Gong Signals between the Pilot House and Engine Room on Boats Using Bell System

(Furnished through courtesy of Mr. Eugene Horner)

Ahead or Stop	Astern or Slow	Gong
#1 Bell	#2 Bell	

(When at rest 3 strokes of gong get ready. From pilot house.)
(When ready 3 strokes of gong or 3 short blasts [negro whistle] by engineer.)

WHEN AT REST OR STOPPED

1 jingle of No. 1 head full speed
1 jingle of No. 1 and 1 jingle of No. 2 head slow speed
1 jingle of No. 1 and 1 stroke of gong head half speed
1 jingle of No. 1 and 1 jingle of No. 2 and 2 strokes of gong head dead slow
1 jingle of No. 1 and 2 strokes of gong full stroke speed ahead
1 jingle of No. 1 STOP when going ahead at any speed
1 stroke of gong to reverse engine when stopped

WHEN AT REST OR STOPPED

1 jingle of No. 2 astern full speed
2 jingles of No. 2 astern slow speed
2 jingles of No. 2 and 1 stroke of gong astern half speed
2 jingles of No. 2 and 2 strokes of gong astern dead slow speed
1 jingle of No. 2 and 2 strokes of gong astern full stroke speed
1 jingle of No. 1 STOP going astern at any speed

When going ahead or astern dead slow speed 1 jingle No. 2 full
  speed
When going ahead or astern dead slow speed 1 gong half speed
When going ahead or astern full speed 1 gong half speed
When going ahead or astern full stroke speed 1 jingle No. 2 slow
  speed

Four strokes of gong after anchoring all at rest

Steamboat Pilots to Engineer Signals Used on Steamboats and Packets and Other Boats Using Two Bells and Gong

(Furnished by Capt. Bridges Montgomery, U. S. E. D.
"WARIOTO")

No. 1 Bell	No. 2 Bell	Gong
Ahead or Stop	Astern or Slow	

WHEN STOPPED TO GO AHEAD

At dead slow speed—1 on 1, followed by 1 on 2 followed by 2
  gongs
At slow speed—1 on 1, followed by 1 on 2
At half speed—1 on 1 followed by 1 gong
At full speed—1 on 1
At full stroke speed 1 on 1 followed by 2 gongs
To stop 1 on 1

WHEN GOING AHEAD—(*To increase speed*)

To go ahead from dead speed to slow speed—2 more gongs
To go ahead from slow speed to half speed—1 more gong
To go ahead from half speed to full speed—1 gong more
To go ahead from full speed to full stroke—2 gongs more

WHILE GOING AHEAD (*to reduce speed*)

To come from full stroke to full speed—2 gongs
To come from full speed to half speed—1 gong
To come from half speed to slow speed—1 on 1 bell
To come from slow speed to dead speed—2 gongs

To come to stop while going ahead or stern at any speed—1 on 1
Bell

EXAMPLE: 1 on 1 followed by 1 on 2 followed by 2 gongs—
spoken would be as follows:

"1 jingle on number 1 bell followed by 1 jingle on
number 2 bell, followed by 2 strokes of the gong."

Steamboat Pilots to Engineer Signals Used on Steamboats and Packets and Other Boats Using Two Bells and Gong

(Furnished by Capt. Bridges Montgomery, U. S. E. D.
"WARIOTO")

No. 1 Bell	No. 2 Bell	Gong
Ahead or Stop	Astern or Slow	

WHEN STOPPED TO GO ASTERN

At dead slow speed—2 on 2 followed by 2 gongs
At slow speed—2 on 2
At half speed—2 on 2 followed by 1 gong
At full speed—1 on 2
At full stroke speed—1 on 2 followed by 2 gongs
To stop—1 on 1
To reverse engine when stopped—1 gong

WHILE GOING ASTERN—(To increase speed)

To go astern from dead speed to slow speed—2 more gongs
To go astern from slow speed to half speed—1 more gong
To go astern from half speed to full speed—1 more gong
To go astern from full speed to full stroke—2 more gongs

WHILE GOING ASTERN (To reduce speed)

To come from full stroke to full speed—2 gongs
To come from full speed to half speed—1 gong
To come from half speed to slow speed—1 on 2
To come from slow speed to dead speed—2 gongs

To come to stop while going ahead or astern at any speed—1 on 1 Bell

EXAMPLE: 2 on 2 followed by 2 gongs—spoken would be as follows:

"2 jingles on number 2 bell followed by 2 strokes of gong."

Glossary

Various Expressions Used by Masters, Pilots and Other
Members of Crew, in Operation of River Steamboats

Pool water: Water between one lock and another lock

Give 'er time: Very often in narrow channels a boat will "find
her way" and it is best not to aggravate the situation by pressing her too hard, but give the boat time

Fast or racy water: Denoting swift water in a narrow channel
or at high tide

Open channel: That part of the river above pool water

Wing dam: A dam so constructed as to throw all available water into one groove and thereby making a channel

Coffer dam: A dam built around an object and when pumped
out will leave it dry

Rip-rap: Heavy stone thrown along the banks to keep the water
from washing it

Furrow: A wave behind a paddle-wheel

Slip or slide in the bank: Frequently when the river falls rapidly, it leaves a bank wet and the pull of the current will
cause the bank to cave in and slide or slip into the river

All gone: An expression used after all lines are out and the boat
made secure

Now we're boating: An expression designating everything is
moving along nicely and the boat is running on schedule time

Skinning the nigger: An expression used when the stem exhaust is let out on top of the roof of a boat, creating a terrific
noise and scaring the cook and others, especially new hands

High and dry: When a boat is beached or docked

Lazy wheel: When the paddle wheel is moving very slowly and
without any exertion on the engines

Slough: A small formation of water backed up a creek from the
river or the back side of an island

Chute: Between the mainland and an island in the river or a channel not often used

Wharf: Where the boats tie up

Swell: When a boat has been dry-docked and put back in the water, the hull swells and becomes watertight. Also an expression used to denote the water in a river during a rise

Tide: River men invariably refer to a rise of the river as a tide

Ways: Where boats are pulled out of the water

Watch: When an officer or member of the crew is on duty

Bump: When a boat strikes some under-water obstacle or the bank

Squall: A sudden wind or rain storm

Dead ahead: When a boat is running in the middle of the channel straight ahead

Dead astern: Just the opposite

Cast away: Untie lines; ready to leave

Spar her out: A heavy timber or spar from the bank to the boat so as to hold the head or stern away from the bank

She'll find her way: In a narrow place, when the channel is unknown, by the Pilot taking his time, the boat will help him to find the deep water

Drawbridge: A bridge that lifts or moves so as to let a boat through

Cut her loose: Untie all lines

Nose 'er in: A method of landing by putting the bow of the boat into the bank

Tow head: Found at the upper or lower end of an island or the beginning of an island

Snag: A sunken tree or other object in the water

Piling: A timber that has been driven in the bottom of the river

Drift: As the tide rises, it floats many trees and other debris down the river

Sawyer: A tree or log, one minute under the water and the next showing. The motion is a sawing effect, hence the name. Sometimes headed up the current, sometimes down

Planter: A tree or log firmly fixed to the bottom of the river bed

Ship-up: An expression used in operation of steamboats— meaning "reverse"

Ship-shape: Boat neat and properly kept

Snow ball: The effect obtained by the water and spray going up and over the paddle wheel while the boat is underway

Laboring: An expression used when a boat is passing over shallow water

Drive her through: Full speed ahead—the Pilot by so doing might get around or through a hard place on the river without flanking

Come aboard: The welcome or greeting when guests or passengers come on the boat

Mess: Meal

Mess bell: On all boats

Water haul: When a boat makes a trip and comes back without a pay load

Purring like a kitten: Engine running smoothly

Flood tide: A very high river

Crest of the tide: It has reached its peak

On a stand (tide): River stationary

Narrow channel: Very little room to spare

Shallow channel: Very little depth

There she is: When another boat is sighted

Here she comes: When another boat appears around a bend

There she goes: Another boat has passed

Short cut: A pilot takes a course or a channel different from the customary one

Wallow: A boat that is overloaded will often have the effect of being unsteady and this is referred to as "wallow"

Scraping through or over: When the hull is going over a sand or gravel bottom

Off the channel: Pilot is out of position at a given location

White cappers: Wind raises these on the river like waves. Also referred to the caps of the waves in wake of paddle wheel

She's a stranger: A new boat on the river unknown to a pilot or captain seeing her the first time

Knee mechanics: Crap shooters

"Old man": The Master or Captain of the boat

Dry rot: A disease affecting the timbers of a boat. Sometimes not visible to the eye and which softens the inside of the timber but leaves the outside apparently good

Swamped: A boat is swamped just about the time it is ready to sink

Scuttle: A boat purposely sunk

Home port: The port where the boat received her registry or was documented

Head of steam: Steam is raised—the boat is ready to move

Warped: When a boat is out of true alignment

Fancy stuff: Decorations—something new—innovation

Its like a hog wallow: When the river is very muddy

Lower anchor: Heave it overboard

Raise anchor: Pull it up

Take or get a purchase on it: Put a knot or bend around the object so as to enable it to be moved, stopped, or not to slip

Eat your fill: To eat a big meal and completely satisfy your appetite

Up for his rating: When a man is to take an examination for a higher license

All clear: The boat is ready to leave

All fast: Lines are secured as directed

Blow him (or her) down: If the pilot on another boat refuses to obey signals, this is the usual expression to give the danger signal or four rapid blasts of the whistle

The bottom dropped out: An expression denoting a very sudden fall in the river

John boat: A boat used by raftsmen, similar to a skiff or flat bottom paddle boat, but with higher sides and pulled by oars in oarlocks cut in the gunnels

Good boy: Denoting a member of the crew has done a good job

Man overboard: Some person has fallen off the boat into the river

All ashore that's going ashore: A loud announcement made by the Mate that the boat is about ready to leave and all who are not going must leave

Head-on landing: The bow of the boat only is made fast

Hot town: A town or city where a good time may be had

Line through: Frequently in very swift water, or where the depth is both swift and shallow, the Captain would send a part of the crew up the bank for quite a distance where they would make a line fast to a tree. The other end of the line would be placed around the capstan and the main engines started. By taking up slack on the capstan, and also by driving the boat hard, it would gradually pass over the "hump" and on to deep water

Hogging a boat: If a boat was beached in shallow water or stuck on a sand bar, the crew sometimes would get in the water and with pick and shovels dig the sand and gravel away from the hull. In old days before the capstan a "shin crack" (a device made by a good size sapling with another strong sapling running waist high horizontally through it) would then be put in a hole dug in the ground on the bank. A line made fast to the boat would then be run to and around the "shin crack." Several members of the crew would turn the "shin crack," thus taking up slack in the line, and if the boat was not too badly stuck, it would be pulled off. In this procedure, the current of the river was always brought to bear in the direction of the line, and was also used to take away the loose gravel. This was called "hogging a boat"—because the sand and gravel were "rooted up." A "shin crack" was a very dangerous device and if the pressure was suddenly released, the horizontal sapling used as the turning handle would swing around in the opposite direction and kill or knock down everybody in its path.

Loose headed: Traveling without a tow

She's in her sins: Roustabouts' way of saying a boat is entering the "open channel" or that part of the river above lock (or pool) water

Fanning the willows: Running so close that the boat strikes overhanging boughs of the willow trees

Packet: In river parlance, a registered steamboat licensed to carry passengers and cargo on regular runs and schedules. The designation originally applied only to a vessel which also carried mail and government dispatches.

The Cumberland River

The Cumberland River rises on the western slope of the Cumberland Mountains, which are a part of the Appalachian System, and constitute the dividing ridge between southwestern Virginia and southeastern Kentucky. The source is near the 37th parallel, and from thence to Burnside, Kentucky, a distance of 168 miles, it flows through a very broken, hilly, and for the most part, densely wooded region, partaking of the nature of a mountain stream. In its course through this region it is fed by the waters of Laurel and Rockcastle Rivers, Buck Creek, and numerous smaller mountain streams, all of which, with the mainstream, cover a drainage area of from 2,500 to 3,000 square miles. At Burnside, 518 miles from its mouth, it receives its first important tributary, South Fork, which rises in Tennessee and flows northward, receiving the drainage of from 1,200 to 1,500 square miles of territory. From Burnside, Kentucky, to Celina, Tennessee, a distance of 135 miles, several tributaries flow into the main stream, from both the north and south, but mostly from the south. The principal one of these is the Obey River, which receives the drainage of several hundred square miles on the western slope of the Cumberland Plateau, and enters the main stream just above Celina.

From near the State line, the river debouches into the northeast corner of the Great Central Basin of Tennessee, which in the remote past extended far inland as an arm or estuary, of the then inland sea. Trending southwestward in its first course, it flowed along the southern border of what is now known as the Highland Rim, but which was at the geological period referred to the northern shore of this great lake, and it is a notable fact that from Celina to where the river again cuts through the Highland Rim, 35 miles below Nashville, a total distance of 225 miles, the tributaries on the north side are short and not of any great importance, heading in the southern slopes of the Highlands and flowing out rapidly to the parent stream, sometimes causing sudden rises in the river at Nashville and below.

From Celina to Carthage, a distance of about 75 miles, there is no tributary of any importance until Caney Fork is reached, entering from the south, and draining an area of 2,000 square miles. This tributary is perhaps the most important one of the Cumberland System, its individual drainage area being the greatest of any of the tributaries of the main stream, and it forms a very important factor in the stages of the river from Carthage down. Its sources are on the western slopes of the Cumberland Plateau, and almost to the western edge of the eastern Highland Rim. Its course and that of its numerous tributaries lie mostly in the Highland Rim, but for at least 50 miles of its course, it flows through another one of those estuaries of the great lake of the past geological age referred to; then it debouches properly into the Basin, through which it reaches the parent stream. This stream for the greater part of its course, is rapid-flowing, with falls in that part which flows through the Highland Rim, and it drains rapidly. The next important tributary below Carthage is Stone's River, which rises in the foothills of the eastern Highland Rim. Its course lies entirely in the Central Basin, and it enters the parent stream fourteen miles above Nashville. This tributary drains an area of from 1,200 to 1,500 square miles and forms a very important factor in the sudden local rises in the main stream when the local rains are heavy.

Below Nashville, there are two principal tributaries, Harpeth River on the south, and Red River on the north. The former runs through the western portion of the Central Basin and enters the parent stream just below where it cuts its way into the Highlands and where the Harpeth shoals are situated; the latter stream, rising in southern Kentucky, almost parallels the main stream, its course being entirely through the Highlands, and unites with it just below Clarksville. Below this, there are numerous small tributaries, but none of any importance.

From Burnside, Kentucky, which is considered the head of navigation, to its mouth, a distance of 518 miles, the Cumberland, at ordinary stages of water, has more navigable miles in proportion to its actual length, than any other stream in the United States, with perhaps one or two exceptions; for more than 300 miles above Nashville it runs through a country depending almost entirely on river transportation, and for 250 miles through some of the most fertile regions of the State of Tennessee.

* * * * * * *

This Excellent Description of the Cumberland River is from an Article by Mr. H. C. Bate, Local Forecaster, United States Weather Bureau, Nashville, Tennessee. Mr. Bate Was the First Inspector Assigned to Nashville When the Bureau Was Detached from the War Department and Officially Designated as "United States Weather Bureau."

Index

THE CUMBE

Its principal tow